COLBERT'S WEST INDIA POLICY

By
STEWART L. MIMS

OCTAGON BOOKS
A division of Farrar, Straus and Giroux
New York   1977

Copyright 1912 by Yale University Press

*Reprinted 1977
by special arrangement with Yale University Press*

OCTAGON BOOKS
A DIVISION OF FARRAR, STRAUS & GIROUX, INC.
19 Union Square West
New York, N.Y. 10003

Library of Congress Cataloging in Publication Data

Mims, Stewart Lea, 1880-
  Colbert's West India policy.

  Originally presented as the author's thesis, Yale, 1912.

  Reprint of the ed. published by Yale University Press, New Haven, which was issued as v. 1 of Yale historical studies.
  Bibliography: p.
  Includes index.
  1. Colbert, Jean Baptiste, 1619-1683. 2. West Indies, French—Commerce. 3. Compagnie des Indes Occidentales. I. Title. II. Series: Yale historical studies; 1.
HF3558.W5M6   1977   382'.0944'0729   76-56114
ISBN 0-374-95764-9

Manufactured by Braun-Brumfield, Inc.
Ann Arbor, Michigan
Printed in the United States of America

TO THE MEMORY OF

EDWARD GAYLORD BOURNE

WHOSE PROFOUND LEARNING AND MANLY QUALITIES
INSPIRED HIS PUPILS TO TRY TO FOLLOW
IN HIS FOOTSTEPS

YALE
HISTORICAL STUDIES

I

PUBLISHED UNDER THE DIRECTION OF THE
DEPARTMENT OF HISTORY
FROM THE INCOME OF

THE FREDERICK J. KINGSBURY
MEMORIAL FUND

PREFACE

Some five or six years ago in a course offered to graduate students of Yale University by the late Professor Edward Gaylord Bourne, I became much interested in the so-called economic causes of the American Revolution. I found then, and have continued to find, much inspiration in the work of Mr. George L. Beer. All of that author's work shows a thorough and comprehensive grasp of the forces and ideas which directed and gave shape to the commercial-colonial policy of Great Britain. Study convinced me, however, that neither Mr. Beer nor any other writer had worked out or clearly presented a most striking economic fact which was of considerable importance in the commercial history of the British North American colonies, namely, the rapid growth and expansion during the eighteenth century of the French West Indies, the most important of which were Martinique, Guadeloupe, and the western half of St. Domingo.

Mr. Beer and some of his predecessors have pointed out the fact that New England traders obtained from these islands their most important supply of molasses for their rum distilleries, which became of great importance to their economic and commercial life, and that they also found in these same islands a profitable market for large quantities of lumber, of "West India" cod and other salt fish, of live stock and food-stuffs. It is, in fact, writ large in the Molasses Act of 1733 and again in the Sugar Act of 1764 that the trade between these two groups of colonies had become of such great importance as to arouse the opposition of the British West India planters and to cause the British government to take steps to interrupt,

PREFACE

or at least to discourage, this trade so seriously as to render it unprofitable. Many students are already familiar with the violent protests of Massachusetts and of Rhode Island against George Grenville's policy, and have seen in them an indication of the importance of the trade.

The French West Indies, however, have remained but a name. Students have watched New England ships sail with their cargoes of fish, lumber, live stock and foodstuffs and have let them, so to speak, disappear into the unknown, whence they saw them reappear with cargoes of sugar and molasses. None has seen fit to follow them to Martinique or to Guadeloupe or to St. Domingo to catch a glimpse of the great prosperity of these islands and to learn the secret of their extraordinary development which enabled the French to drive the English from the sugar markets of Europe and made of them the most profitable market which New England traders could find.

It was in quest of this secret that I set out some three years ago for France to find, if possible, buried away in unprinted manuscripts the story of the economic and commercial development of the French West Indies which no one had ever tried to tell, but which I believed was, nevertheless, one of both interest and importance.

My immediate interest in the story lay rather in that part of it which had to do with the eighteenth century, when these islands first became of any considerable importance, and to that I first turned my attention. But even at the beginning of my work, I found it quite impossible to deal intelligently with many questions of the eighteenth century without knowing something more accurate than was to be found in any printed work of the commercial policy which had directed and shaped the growth of the islands during the preceding century. The result was that I decided to make a thorough study of the early period for myself as a foundation for my later work.

PREFACE

It was in this way that I came to write the present study for the ministry of Colbert and will offer shortly another of similar character for the period 1683-1715. I hope that these two studies will make it possible to present more intelligently a later study for the reign of Louis XV, in which I shall deal with the story of the trade between the New England colonies and the French West Indies.

It was with much hesitation that I decided to make the bold venture of writing a volume which dealt with any phase of the ministry of Colbert. His name and his work have attracted so many scholars of great ability that I naturally felt some misgiving in exposing myself to such a body of critics. A more serious objection was the fact that I had never made any thorough study of Colbert and had collected material on his ministry merely to aid me in writing an introduction to a volume on the later period which I had in mind. But as I found at the end of my researches that I had amassed enough notes from unpublished, and in some cases, unexplored material which would permit me to state the problem confronting the great minister in the reorganization of the French West India colonies and to give an account of the measures he took to solve it, I was subjected to the temptation of expanding my introduction into a volume. The temptation grew stronger when I realized that no serious student had ever tried to study in detail any single problem which Colbert encountered in his efforts to build up colonial commerce. I yielded to the temptation.

An attempt has been made, therefore, in the present volume to present the results of my study and to offer them for what value they may have for special students of Colbert and for those interested in the history of the West Indies. I have tried to present the essential lines of Colbert's commercial policy toward the French West

PREFACE

Indies, as they are traced in the legislation and correspondence of the period. For the most part, I have done so without comment or criticism, permitting the documents in many cases to tell their own story. I have left to more competent hands the task of stating the larger principles of economy which guided Colbert in framing his more comprehensive plan for the upbuilding of French industries and French commerce. That task can not well be performed until more detailed studies have been made on many subjects which are related to the history of his commercial and industrial policy. I shall feel amply rewarded for my work, if the contents of this volume prove of value to him who undertakes this larger and more important task. I regret very much that I have not been able to treat many questions which would prove both interesting and profitable to students of the West Indies. Thus, such questions as the cost of production of sugar, the fluctuation of its price, the methods employed in its cultivation, the great social transformation wrought by its introduction as a staple product in the islands, or others, such as the cost of slave labour, the system of land grants, colonial currency, the sources of capital invested in the islands, as well as all questions of administration and kindred questions have been either entirely omitted or touched upon only superficially. This has been done, partly because the material found proved inadequate for a satisfactory treatment of these questions, and partly because I have attempted to present here primarily a study in imperial policy and not a study in West India history. The history of the French West Indies did not, in fact, become important until the eighteenth century. Their production and their commerce during the seventeenth century were small and a detailed history of either would be of minor interest. The policy which was pursued by Colbert, however, to stimulate their production and to

PREFACE

increase their commerce with the mother country proved of permanent value, because it laid the base for the marvellous development of Martinique, Guadeloupe, and especially St. Domingo, in the eighteenth century. This is the justification offered for placing the emphasis upon questions of imperial policy and upon conditions within the islands only as they affected or were affected by that policy.

I have yielded, perhaps unwisely, to the temptation of devoting too much space to the history of the West India Company. New material found in the Archives Coloniales at Paris made it possible to state more accurately many old facts and to add many new ones concerning its history.

An examination of the bibliography and footnotes will reveal the sources from which my study has been drawn.

I am under obligations to many who have aided me in my work. I shall always recall with much pleasure the kindness shown me by many librarians and archivists in Paris and in the various ports of France where my work called me. To M. Nicolas and M. Wirth of the Archives Coloniales; to M. Stein and M. Bourgin of the Archives Nationales; to M. Charles de La Roncière, the sympathetic and obliging conservateur of the Bibliothèque Nationale, at Paris; to M. Léon Maitre, late archivist of the Archives Départementales de la Loire Inférieure, whose patience and willingness to aid me in unravelling the tangles in the admiralty records of Nantes were inexhaustible; to M. Cultru, chargé de cours at the Sorbonne, who proved an inspiration to me many times during my stay at Paris; to H. P. Biggar and his assistant, M. Beauchesne, both of whom were ever ready to communicate any information, relating to my subject, which they found in the Canadian correspondence; to one and all I wish to express my gratitude. Of my own countrymen, I am indebted to Mr. Waldo G. Leland of the Carnegie Institution, whose

PREFACE

sojourn at Paris coincided with my own and who was ever willing to aid me; to my colleague, Professor Emerson D. Fite of the faculty of Yale College, for suggestions; to Mr. Andrew Keogh of the Yale University Library, for suggestions and aid in the arrangement of the bibliography. I am under special obligations to Professor George Burton Adams for making possible the publication of this volume in its present form. I am most indebted to Professors Wilbur C. Abbott and Max Farrand for their kindness in reading my manuscript, going over it patiently with me and offering many invaluable criticisms. I am grateful to Mr. E. Byrne Hackett of the Yale University Press for his patience and kindness in aiding me in the many problems which arose in the transformation of my work from manuscript to its present form. Finally I should not fail to express here my everlasting gratitude to him to whose memory this study is dedicated. It was he who first inspired me to begin my work. I only wish that I could offer something worthy of the inspiration which he imparted while still among us and of the hallowed memory which he has left to us his former pupils.

CONTENTS*

	Page
Preface	vii
Introduction	1

CHAPTER I
The Establishment of the French in the West Indies and the Commencement of Trade, 1626-1660 . 14

CHAPTER II
The Awakening and the Period of Preparation . . 52

CHAPTER III
The Establishment of the West India Company. Its Concessions, Privileges and Composition . . 68

CHAPTER IV
The West India Company, 1664-1665 . . . 83

CHAPTER V
The West India Company, 1666-1667 . . . 123

CHAPTER VI
The West India Company, 1668-1670 . . . 150

CHAPTER VII
The West India Company, 1670-1674. Its Trade in Slaves, Salt Beef, Live Stock. Its Downfall . 165

* For detailed reference see Index.

CONTENTS

Chapter VIII
The Exclusion of Foreign Traders 182

Chapter IX
The Fight Against the Dutch 195

Chapter X
Freedom of Trade and the Rise of the Private Trader 225

Chapter XI
Colonial Exports—Tobacco 249

Chapter XII
Colonial Exports—Sugar 260

Chapter XIII
Colonial Imports—Indentured Servants and Slaves . 281

Chapter XIV
Colonial Imports—Food-Stuffs 310

Chapter XV
Colonial Imports—Live Stock, Lumber, Manufactured Goods 326

Chapter XVI
Conclusion 332

Bibliography 341

Index 365

COLBERT'S WEST INDIA POLICY

INTRODUCTION

"AS I cast my glance throughout the length and breadth of France to find out what is the condition of its commerce, I am dumfounded to see into what a low state it has sunk. I am seized with a feeling of disgrace and of sorrow, when I see the greater part of our merchants idle, our sailors without employment, our harbours without vessels, and our ships wrecked and stranded upon the beach. . . . Like Diogenes I might carry a lantern at noontide in our cities and our ports in search of a French merchant."[1]

Thus wrote Jean Eon, a Carmelite, at Nantes, in 1646. It is only one of many striking passages in his interesting book, *Le Commerce honorable*, which describes in mournful numbers the state of France of his day. The pessimism which is breathed into his book was only too well justified by the deplorable condition into which the industrial and commercial life of France had sunk at the eve of Colbert's ministry. The industries, established under the stimulating economic policy of Sully and fostered by Richelieu, were in a state of decadence. The woollen industry had almost ceased to exist in Languedoc, which had been its most thriving center. The Dutch and English, the latter of whom had formerly brought their wool to France to be manufactured, had established manufactories of their own and had largely supplanted the French as furnishers of woollens to the markets of Europe.

The silk mills of Tours and Lyons were declining. The foundries, the forges, the factories of steel, and the tanneries had been almost abandoned.[2] "So that instead of gaining large sums as they did in former times, the French

[1] *Le Commerce honorable*, Nantes, 1646, p. 20.
[2] G. Martin, *La grande industrie en France sous le règne de Louis XIV*, Paris, 1899, Chap. I.

gain nothing, for much specie is leaving the kingdom and none enters."[3]

The navy and merchant marine, too, were in a most deplorable condition. "The power of the king by land is superior to that of all others in Europe, by sea it is inferior. . . . France has not at the present hour 200 vessels in good condition in her ports."[4] The number of vessels even for coasting trade was certainly small.[5] The inquest ordered to be made in 1664 by the *conseil des finances* at the suggestion of Colbert, to find out "the number and quality of vessels which were in the ports of the realm," showed that in all the ports of France there was a total of only 2368 vessels, representing an aggregate tonnage of 129,605 tons.[6] There were only 329 vessels of more than 100 tons. Some of these even were too old or disabled for service.[7] So that Colbert probably knew whereof he spoke, when he remarked that France had not at that time 200 vessels in good condition in her ports.

The Dutch were at the height of their maritime suprem-

[3] P. Clément, *Lettres, instructions et mémoires*, II, 1, cclxvii, Discours sur les manufactures du Roy, a memoir by Colbert in 1664.

[4] Clément, II, 1, cclxxi, Colbert, Mémoire sur le Commerce.

[5] "That is a fact which is very easy to prove by visiting our coasts and our harbours, where one sees so many foreign ships that the small number of French ships is lost from sight. Thus for ten or twelve of our ships one may count fifty or sixty belonging to foreigners." *Le Commerce honorable*, p. 20.

[6] There were: 1063 of 10 to 30 tons; 345 of 30 to 40 tons; 320 of 40 to 60 tons; 178 of 60 to 80 tons; 133 of 80 to 100 tons; 102 of 100 to 120 tons; 72 of 120 to 150 tons; 70 of 150 to 200 tons; 39 of 200 to 250 tons; 27 of 250 to 300 tons; 19 of 300 to 400 tons. Bib. Nat. MSS., 500 Colbert, 199, contains the results of this most interesting inquest. Detailed information is given in the reports made from the different ports. It is a mine of information which has not been thoroughly exploited.

[7] Thus it is recorded in the inquest made at Nantes that *La Pellagye*, a vessel of 140 tons, built at Croisic in 1648, "was fit for nothing except to be torn to pieces."

TOWARD THE FRENCH WEST INDIES

acy. Colbert estimated that out of a total of 20,000 vessels in the merchant marine of Europe, 16,000 belonged to them. They had become the great carriers of Europe. Their cities had become the great entrepôts of international trade. Their ships were upon every sea and in every harbour to take advantage of every opportunity to profit by trade and transport. The ports of France were no exception to the rule. They, too, were frequented by great numbers of Dutch traders. For the item of transport alone in the coastwise and foreign trade, the French paid, according to Colbert's estimate, an annual tribute of 4,000,000 livres. Commerce also was almost entirely in their hands.

"It is certain," remarked Colbert, "that with the exception of a certain number of vessels which go from Marseilles to trade in the Levant, no commerce exists in the kingdom. This is true even to the point that in the islands of America, occupied by the French, there are 150 Dutch ships annually which carry on trade with them, importing food-stuffs produced in Germany and goods manufactured in Holland, and exporting sugar, tobacco and dye-woods. They carry these latter commodities to Holland, which, after manufacturing and paying an import and export duty upon, they bring to France to sell."[8]

Jean Eon estimated, in 1646, that the "balance of trade" was against France in her dealings with all the principal nations of Europe. He justified this statement by the following statistics:

Holland:[9]
    Imports from . . . . 21,445,520 livres.
    Exports to . . . . . 16,701,466 livres.

[8] Clément, II, 1, cclxxi.
[9] *Le Commerce honorable,* pp. 28 ff. The details of the imports from and exports to Holland were as follows:

THE COMMERCIAL POLICY OF COLBERT

Great Britain and Ireland:
- Imports from . . . . 15,372,000 livres.
- Exports to . . . . . 12,904,100 livres.

Portugal:
- Imports from . . . . 4,992,500 livres.
- Exports to . . . . . 5,851,950 livres.

Italy:
- Imports from . . . . 4,124,500 livres.
- Exports to . . . . . 3,020,000 livres.

Holland, Imports from:

Pepper, cinnamon, nutmeg, mace, ginger, etc.	3,193,130 livres.
Sugar	1,885,150 livres.
Medicine, drugs, etc.	842,080 livres.
Precious stones, cottons, woollens, ebony, plumes, etc.	1,835,200 livres.
Indigo, Brazil wood, camphor, gums	1,035,220 livres.
Swedish copper, Polish lead, tin, ironware, etc.	1,500,000 livres.
Cannon, powder, firearms	1,235,000 livres.
Russian leather, furs, etc.	675,300 livres.
Linen, flax, tar, Norwegian timber	1,700,170 livres.
Herring, salt salmon, whale oil	454,300 livres.
Butter, cheese, tallow, etc.	200,000 livres.
Total	21,445,520 livres.

Exports to:

Wine, cognac, brandy	6,192,632 livres.
Wheat, other grains	3,450,450 livres.
Salt	2,488,750 livres.
Cloth, linen from Normandy and Brittany and Guienne	1,583,432 livres.
Olive oil, olives, from Marseilles and Provence	715,177 livres.
Laces, paper, glass, thread	915,525 livres.
Honey, preserved fruits, etc.	355,500 livres.
Total	16,701,466 livres.

The author states that these statistics were compiled from memoirs in the principal ports of France and represent the average for five years and states that "they have been carefully compiled by reliable persons who understood the theory and practice of trade."

TOWARD THE FRENCH WEST INDIES

An explanation of the inferiority of the French in trade was suggested by the same writer:

"The French have long since entertained a very disparaging opinion of commerce, which they consider suited only to debased souls. . . . Every one aspires to gain honour and leisure and believes that neither the one nor the other is to be enjoyed in the pursuit of commerce. This is the opinion which the majority of Frenchmen hold and especially those of the *tiers état,* who have means and desire to elevate their children to the most honourable stations. They cultivate in them no love for trade or give them no instruction in matters of commerce, but send them to colleges where they pass many years in the study of the sciences. To be sure instruction is very good and necessary in the moulding of a virtuous life and in rendering one of service to God, the king and the state. Nevertheless, the energy of our young men is wasted in these colleges and they are fitted only for a life of elegance, of idleness, and of no service to the state. For as soon as they leave college, some give themselves over to the pursuits of love, which Diogenes calls the affair of those who have nothing to do. . . . Others spend their time playing at *jeu-de-paumes* to sweat at their pleasure and thereby gain an appetite to eat up in a short time all their patrimony. Others take to cards and dice, and thus pass their days and nights in foolishly dissipating the fortunes which their fathers have acquired by hard work. Still others pass their time in drink-shops. . . . Our young are thus reared to lead an idle and spendthrift life. . . . The indifference of the French to commerce comes not only from the small esteem and the little inclination which they have for it, but also from the fact that they are strongly diverted by ambition. . . . They have ambition to acquire the offices of justice which the state in its need has created in great numbers, so that the majority of those who are rich and have means to carry on commerce abandon it, in order to acquire such positions for their children. . . . It is for this reason that for the maintenance of trade there remain only those of low estate, who, by reason of their moderate means, are unable to buy offices from the state, and who for the same reason are incapable of carrying on an extensive trade and are forced to confine themselves to retail trade, or at best, to the coasting trade, both of which are of small value to the nation in comparison with foreign commerce which brings us gold and silver and many other things necessary and useful for our life. Whenever, from that small number of Frenchmen who are engaged in foreign commerce, some one amasses a fortune, which is the very moment when he is the most capable of pursuing foreign trade, he abandons it in order to place his children in some office of state."[10]

From this picture the author turns his eyes toward the life of other nations:

"From the age of fifteen and twenty, they [the Dutch] are to be seen upon the quais loading and unloading cargoes, or in the stock-exchanges engaged in business, or in the market-places choosing and buying the best products. . . . Thus from their youth they form habits of trade, become endowed with skill which insures their success. . . . They learn foreign languages and, like the ancients, acquire by conversation a knowledge of those things which are the most beautiful and the most necessary for the enjoyment of life and its spiritual welfare."

There is to be found in these two passages an explanation of the decadence of commerce in France, which gives a profound insight into the very difficult problem that confronted Colbert in his determination to build up national industries and national trade. The life of the nation was centered in the court, in the attainment of rank and places as high as possible in the great social and political hierarchy of the *ancien régime*. A man's worth seemed measured by the amount of success which he had met with in this pursuit. Commerce was considered an occupation below the dignity of the well-bred. A mer-

[10] Ibid., 44 ff.

TOWARD THE FRENCH WEST INDIES

chant who met with success forsook his calling to become another satellite in the mad whirl of office-seekers, courtiers and dilettantes. Ministers, warriors, artists, littérateurs, officials, noblemen, the clergy, were all received with favour at the court and throughout the kingdom, but the merchant was regarded with disfavour or indifference.

The importance of this fact did not escape Colbert. In his memoir on commerce, read in the first session of the *conseil de commerce* presided over by the king on August 3, 1664, he exposed the poor state of commerce in the realm and then proposed the remedies. It was not by mere chance that the following recommendations came first to the great minister's mind:

"Receive with special marks of favour and protection all merchants who come to the court.

"Aid them in everything which concerns their commerce. Permit them to present their cause in person before the council of His Majesty, when they are involved in cases of importance.

"Let there be always some merchants in the suite of His Majesty."[11]

These recommendations are ample proof that commerce was not an honourable calling in France, and that the conditions described by Jean Eon persisted. The fact offers at least a partial explanation of the deplorable state of commerce in the realm. But wherever one may search for the causes and whatever explanation one may offer, it is certain that Mazarin willed to Colbert a France in a state of industrial and commercial decadence.

At Mazarin's death Colbert was at first made intendant of finance (March 16, 1661). He rapidly rose in the king's favour. In January, 1664, he was made *surintendant des bâtiments et manufactures*, in 1665, controller-

[11] Clément, II, 1, cclxxi.

THE COMMERCIAL POLICY OF COLBERT

general, and finally, in 1669, minister of the marine, thus uniting in his hands all the important branches of administration except that of war. But from the first he exerted a large influence upon the direction of affairs. For the first three years of his service to the king his time was largely absorbed by the prosecution of the "affair Fouquet" and by the reorganization of the finances of the kingdom. It was not until 1664 that he had worked out a large plan for the upbuilding of industry and the establishment of commerce. In that year he showed characteristic energy. He organized the *conseil de commerce;* he framed the high protective tariff of 1664; he developed a comprehensive plan to restore industry and create manufactures, to build up a strong navy and merchant marine; and he organized the East and West India Companies. Most of the details of this plan have been made so familiar by the studies of Joubleau, Clément, Neymarck and others, as to make it unnecessary to restate them here. It will be permitted to recall, however, that the development of over-sea commerce occupied the most important place in the great minister's plan for the regeneration of France:

"The happiness of a people consists not only in a considerable diminution of taxes, such as has been made within the last few years, but even more in the maintenance of commerce which alone can bring into the kingdom an abundance that will serve not as a means of luxury to the few, but as a blessing to the many. Commerce stimulates manufactures, by opening markets for their products and gives employment to a large number of people of almost every age and sex. It is thus an agent which harmonizes an abundance of temporal things with the spiritual welfare of a people, for idleness begets wrongdoing, while hard work fortifies one against it. After a careful examination of all the means to bring happiness to our subjects and after much reflection over a subject of such importance, we have been more and more convinced that over-sea

TOWARD THE FRENCH WEST INDIES

commerce is the means. It is certain, both from sound reason and from the experience of our neighbours, that the profit gained much outweighs the toil and pain expended therein."[12]

These words may or may not have been written by Colbert, but they may be taken as representing his ideas, for he remarked later, in speaking of the East India Company, that it was the most difficult enterprise which the king had undertaken since he began to rule, and the success of which would prove the most glorious and the most advantageous for the welfare of the realm.[13] Again in the preamble of the tariff of 1664 it is remarked that although measures had been taken to build up commerce within the realm, yet most attention had been paid to the upbuilding of navigation and foreign commerce which was "the only means of making the kingdom prosperous."[14] It is quite certain from the constant attention which Colbert paid to the establishment of such a commerce that these ideas were his own and that upon them this policy was founded.

The success of the Dutch with their wealth and power upon the sea exerted a large influence upon his mind. He attributed their success to trade, asserting that the Dutch East India Company had assets amounting to no less than 800,000,000 livres; that Holland had become the entrepôt in Europe for the rich trade with the Indies; and furthermore that the Dutch had made themselves masters of the trade with the ports of the Baltic, with the French West Indies, and of the carrying trade of Europe.

Colbert decided to organize two large companies which would at least dispute with them the trade with the two Indies. There is something stupendous in the way in which he projected the East and West India Companies. To the one he assigned, as the field for its activity, the vast

[12] The preamble of the letters-patent of the East India Company.
[13] Clément, III, 2, lxv.
[14] Ibid., II, 2, p. 789.

THE COMMERCIAL POLICY OF COLBERT

expanse from the Cape of Good Hope eastward even to the straits of Magellan, including all the East Indies, China, Japan, and all the oriental seas; to the other, he granted immense territories in the three continents of North America, South America and Africa, and many prosperous islands in the West Indies. Is it not in a sense a new demarcation line by which the world is split in twain and a half given to each company for its exploitation?

Of the two companies, Colbert considered the East India Company of greater importance. Its organization became a matter of great moment. Charpentier, a member of the Academy, was called into service to paint in glowing colours the paradise at Madagascar which offered its hospitable shores to serve the company as a base for trade with the rich Orient.[15] The king, the queen, the queen-mother, the princes of royal blood, noblemen, officials of high rank, subscribed for varying sums. A veritable campaign was pursued by Colbert to persuade or force judges, revenue-farmers, intendants and merchants throughout the kingdom to subscribe to the funds of the company. Everything was done to make the enterprise appear attractive as an investment. National pride was appealed to by pointing out the success and superiority of the Dutch in the oriental trade. Special rights were offered to subscribers of 10,000 and 20,000 livres. In short, the organization of the company was made an affair of state.

The organization of the West India Company was not regarded as a matter of such importance. It had no Charpentier to describe its brilliant prospects, no queen or queen-mothers, no princes and very few noblemen to appear as its sponsors and supporters. This point is of some importance, because it shows clearly that Colbert expended much more effort in the organization of the

[15] Charpentier, *Le Discours d'un fidèle sujet,* Paris, 1664.

TOWARD THE FRENCH WEST INDIES

former company and expected much larger results from it. In this he was destined to be disappointed, for the West India Company yielded much larger results and in the light of these results deserved much more attention and much more financial support than it at first received at the hands of the minister.

The problems of the two companies were quite different. That of the East India Company consisted in the creation of trade with the far-distant Orient. The attempts which had been made already in 1604, 1611, 1615 and 1642 had proved practically fruitless, so that at the commencement of Louis XIV's personal reign all the products of the Orient came by the way of Holland or of England. There were thus no precedents to guide the new company except those of failure and of ill-omen. The seriousness of this is proved by the fact that the company spent the first four years of its existence battling with the problem of establishing an entrepôt at Madagascar as a base of its operations to build up trade with the Orient. All of its preliminary expeditions, representing a large expenditure of money, got no farther than Madagascar, and it was not until 1669 that one of its vessels returned directly from the Indies to France.[16]

The problem of the West India Company was also to prove exceedingly difficult. The long list of companies, organized since the sixteenth century for the exploitation of different parts of the territory of the new company, was a long list of failures and augured ill for the success of the enterprise. But the task before it was not so constructive in character as that of the other company. The route to Canada was well known, for many hardy sailors of the ports of France were engaged in the fisheries of Newfoundland, and Canada was a French colony. The

[16] P. Kaeppelin, *La Compagnie des Indes Orientales et François Martin,* Paris, 1908, Chap. I.

THE COMMERCIAL POLICY OF COLBERT

French Antilles contained in many cases prosperous colonies and a good trade already existed. A French settlement had been recently made at Cayenne. On the west coast of Africa, French trading-posts were already established. So that the new company fell heir to many valuable assets and had as its problem, rather, the union of those separate colonies in its hands and development of their resources. This difference may account, in a measure, for the greater stress which Colbert laid upon the organization of the East India Company, but the principal reason remains that he regarded that company as of much greater importance.

In addition to these two companies, Colbert, during the course of his ministry, organized for various purposes five other commercial companies, namely, the Company of the North, the Company of the Levant, the Company of the Pyrenees, the first and second companies of Senegal.

The Company of the North was organized in 1669 with the purpose of building up a trade with the ports of Northern Europe, especially with those of the Baltic, and thus of making France independent of the Dutch trader. It was granted a monopoly of trade with Holland, the coasts of Germany, Sweden, Norway, Muscovy, and other countries of the North. De Lagny, who was later to become director of commerce, and Colbert de Terron, intendant at Brouage, were especially charged with the direction of the enterprise. Premiums were offered for the exportation and importation of cargoes to and from the North. The king agreed to take on liberal terms, masts, lumber, tar, and other articles necessary for his navy.

It was in this same year that Colbert formed the plan of organizing a new company to re-establish commerce with the Levant. An idea of the importance which he attached to this enterprise may be gained from a letter which he wrote to one of its prospective directors:

TOWARD THE FRENCH WEST INDIES

"I beseech you to consider the affair as one of the greatest importance to the interests of the nation and one in which, consequently, I feel the greatest concern. I feel sure that you will apply yourself with the utmost diligence in order that the enterprise may succeed in accordance with my wishes."[17]

Letters-patent were issued to the Company of the Levant in July, 1670. Its capital was fixed at 3,000,000 livres and the king agreed to furnish one-fourth of it.[18]

The Company of the Pyrenees was organized in 1671, in preparation for the war with the Dutch, in order that the royal marine might not lack masts and lumber, supplied ordinarily by trade with the North, which might be interrupted during the war.

Finally, in 1673, a company was organized for the exploitation of Senegal and another for the same purpose in 1679 and 1681. Their history is recorded below.

All of these companies received the attention of Colbert and were organized to do a very definite work in the fulfillment of his larger plans. Their history is interesting, not so much for what they actually accomplished, as for the insight which they give into what he wished to accomplish and attempted to do. It reveals the vast importance which Colbert attached to foreign and colonial commerce.

[17] Clément, II, 2, p. 507. Letter to Sir Dallier, January 9, 1670.
[18] Bonassieux, *Les Grandes Compagnies de Commerce,* p. 179.

CHAPTER I

THE ESTABLISHMENT OF THE FRENCH IN THE WEST INDIES AND THE COMMENCEMENT OF TRADE, 1626-1660

IN the year 1625 there set sail from Dieppe a small brigantine, armed with four cannon and equipped with a crew of thirty or forty men, "all of whom were good soldiers, well seasoned and well disciplined." It was commanded by Pierre d'Esnambuc and his companion of fortune, Urbain de Roissey. The latter was known among the English as the "pirate of Dieppe" and records exist of some of his piratical exploits.[1] It may be that the two captains sailed as pirates, bent upon finding some prey on the high seas and that their sojourn shortly afterwards at St. Christopher was only an incident in their voyage. Thus the beginning of colonization by the French in the West Indies, which resulted from this sojourn, would seem, as de La Roncière affirms it to be, the result of an adventure. It may be, on the other hand, that the two captains sailed with definite intentions, for it was affirmed in the permission granted them the following year to establish a colony that these two captains had been in search for some fifteen years "of some fertile lands in good clime which could be colonized by the French." As pirates or as founders of colonies, they set sail to the westward. Near Jamaica they encountered a large Spanish galleon from which, after three hours of fighting, they escaped. They sought refuge with their badly damaged vessel at St.

[1] See Du Tertre, *Histoire générale des Antilles françaises*, I, 3 ff.; de La Roncière, *Histoire de la marine française*, IV, 649 ff.; Bréard, *Documents relatifs à la marine normande*, pp. 179, 212, 213; Pierre Margry, *Pierre d'Esnambuc.*

Christopher, where they arrived probably in the summer of 1625.

Much to their surprise, certainly much to their joy, they found a small band of Frenchmen already established there and living in peace with the savages. It was a band composed of those who from time to time had sought refuge in the island. Thus in their number was Chantail, a refugee from an unsuccessful expedition to Cayenne. D'Esnambuc was hailed with joy as "an angel from heaven" and during his sojourn in the island he came to be "loved as a father, honoured as a chief and obeyed as a master."[2] The island proved particularly attractive to him. Its situation impressed him as excellent, its soil as fertile and well adapted to the cultivation of tobacco. The members of the little colony were favourably disposed toward the plan of remaining in the island to form a permanent settlement. D'Esnambuc promised them that he would return to France, seek additional funds and come back to live with them. He straightway loaded his vessel with excellent tobacco and some articles obtained in trade from the Indians and set sail for France. He arrived at Dieppe probably in the summer of 1626.

After selling his cargo at good profit, d'Esnambuc turned his face toward Paris to plead his cause. He appeared clad in such excellent attire and gave such a good account of his voyage that all with whom he talked were convinced of the excellence of the island and of the profit to be gained by its settlement. Thanks to the influence of some friends, he obtained an interview with Richelieu. The great cardinal was so favourably impressed that he decided to aid d'Esnambuc to carry out his plans.

The act of association for the organization of the Company of St. Christopher was drawn up and signed on October 31, 1626. It bore the signature of Richelieu,

[2] Du Tertre, I, 4.

THE COMMERCIAL POLICY OF COLBERT

for the sum of 10,000 livres, of which 8000 livres were to be paid by the gift of a vessel; of Rusé d'Effiat, intendant general of the marine, for 2000 livres; of de Flécelles and Bardin-Royer, *présidents des comptes*, each for 2000 livres; and of four others for a total of 7000 livres. The initial subscriptions amounted to only 22,000 livres, but the associates pledged their credit to the amount of 45,000 livres. It was proposed to expend the capital of the company for the purchase and equipment of three vessels. The purpose was declared to be the settlement of "the islands of St. Christopher, Barbuda, and the others at the entrance of Peru," situated between the 11th and 18th degrees north latitude and not already occupied by Europeans. The establishment of trade and the conversion of the natives to the Holy Catholic faith were the declared motives. A monopoly of trade for forty years was granted to the company.[3]

On the same day, October 31, 1626, a formal permit was issued to the two captains to return to St. Christopher. They straightway left Paris, d'Esnambuc going into Normandy and de Roissey into Brittany, in order to enlist settlers. The former succeeded in enlisting 322 men, whom he embarked in *La Catholique*, a vessel of 250 tons belonging to the company, and the latter, 210 men, whom he embarked in *La Cardinale* and *La Victoire*. D'Esnambuc set sail from Havre near the end of January and rejoined de Roissey in Brittany, whence "this little

[3] The text of the act of association is to be found in Du Tertre, *op. cit.*, I, 8-11, and in Moreau de Saint-Méry, *Loix et Constitutions*, I, 18-19. The clause of the document defining the concessions of the company reads as follows: "Pour faire habiter et peupler les isles de St. Christophe et la Barbade et autres situées à l'entrée du Pérou." The Antilles were very frequently referred to in the seventeenth century as the "isles du Pérou." See Bréard, *op. cit.*, 145. As to the term "la Barbade," it is used somewhat loosely to refer either to Barbuda or to Barbadoes.

TOWARD THE FRENCH WEST INDIES

fleet, composed for the most part of poor people gathered here and there and very little accustomed to the fatigues of the sea, set sail on February 24, 1627."[4]

They had not gone 200 leagues upon the sea, before provisions began to fail. Limited rations of water and food were meted out. Sickness set in and death began to claim many victims. After more than two months the three vessels anchored at Sandy Point, at the western end of St. Christopher. Of the seventy embarked in *La Cardinale*, only sixteen had survived the voyage. More than half of those embarked in the other vessels had died during the passage. Those who remained were more dead than alive. Thus the fleet which had been awaited by the little band at St. Christopher and which, according to their hopes, was to bring them not only strong companions to aid them, but also an abundant supply of food and of other things necessary for their comfort, arrived at last in a deplorable state of poverty. The great joy which they had felt at the appearance of the ships was changed into bitter disappointment, and then bitter disappointment into pity, as they saw the poor wretches totter upon their feeble limbs, as they were set ashore.

D'Esnambuc and de Roissey divided the colony between them, the former going to the western end of the island, and the latter to the eastern. Between the two settlements were the English under the command of Thomas Warner, who had come to the island almost simultaneously with the French. Four hundred of them had lately landed fresh and strong from England. A treaty was made which fixed the boundaries and assured peace between the two nations.

De Roissey was straightway sent back to France with *La Cardinale* to implore aid from the company. He arrived at Roscou in Brittany toward the last of Septem-

[4] Du Tertre, I, 15.

ber, 1627. Instead, however, of hastening his preparations to return and carry aid to the distressed colony, he allowed himself to be persuaded by de Razilly to take part in a secret expedition into the Irish Sea. De Razilly assured him that a vessel had already been sent to carry aid to the colony.[5] In fact, a vessel had been sent, but unfortunately its cargo of provisions was so badly damaged during the voyage, that the colony received very small benefit therefrom. It was not until the following spring that de Roissey returned to St. Christopher in command of *La Cardinale* and another small vessel, both of which had been equipped at the cost of 3500 livres furnished by the company. Of the 150 new settlers carried by the two vessels, many died during the voyage and the colony again received but small aid. Shortly afterwards another vessel was sent out by the company, this time with 120 new settlers. Again the few survivors were more of a tax than an aid to the colony at their arrival.

There was such need that d'Esnambuc decided to go to France himself to plead the cause of the colony. Richelieu seems to have been touched by the account which he gave of the colony's suffering and of the danger which it ran of being crushed by the English. In addition, he was aroused by the report which reached him that the Spanish king was planning to send the powerful fleet under the command of Fadrique of Toledo by way of St. Christopher on its way to Brazil and that orders should be given to crush the new French settlement. He therefore commanded a strong fleet to be equipped and sent to the defense of the king's subjects.

On June 25, 1629, a squadron of ten vessels under the command of Cahuzac sailed from Havre for St. Christopher.[6] Three hundred new settlers were sent out with the

[5] De La Roncière, *op. cit.*, IV, 652-653; Du Tertre, I, 21.
[6] De La Roncière, *op. cit.*, IV, 653-654.

TOWARD THE FRENCH WEST INDIES

fleet at the expense of the company. The fleet arrived in the island at the end of August. Cahuzac quickly forced the English to respect the treaty which they had made with d'Esnambuc, and relieved the colony from the constant fear of being crushed by a stronger neighbour. Unfortunately, however, he grew impatient at waiting for the Spanish fleet and set sail to seek his fortune in the Gulf of Mexico. This proved disastrous, for the Spanish fleet appeared at the end of October, composed of 35 large galleons and 14 merchant vessels armed for war, and attacked the settlement at the eastern end of the island. In spite of the courage shown by some, such as the young du Parquet, the cowardice of de Roissey rendered the task of the Spaniards easy. The French fled in wild disorder to gain the western end of the island. At their arrival they declared that all was lost, that the Spaniards were in pursuit and that all must flee for their lives. De Roissey demanded an immediate convocation of the council of war and threatened to have d'Esnambuc stabbed, if he opposed the plan of flight. In spite of d'Esnambuc's opposition, the whole colony embarked in two vessels which were at Sandy Point and sailed for Antigua. Unfavourable winds and tides drove them to St. Martin. Thence de Roissey, in spite of the protests of d'Esnambuc, set sail with one of the vessels for France. He was imprisoned in the Bastille by the orders of Richelieu. As for d'Esnambuc and those who remained faithful to him, after a brief sojourn at St. Martin and after vain efforts to settle in the islands of Antigua and Montserrat, they decided to return to their former settlement. This proved easy from the fact that the Spaniards had left no troops to maintain their possession of the island and from the fact that d'Esnambuc had the good fortune to find at Antigua a French vessel under the command of Giron, who had deserted the fleet commanded by Cahuzac during its sojourn at St. Christopher. By aid of this vessel the little colony was re-established in its old quarters.[7]

Thus, at the beginning of 1630, the French were recommencing the colonization of St. Christopher. Of the 1100 or 1200 settlers who had been sent out, only 350 remained after four years of toil and struggle. The expenditures had been great, the returns small, the results discouraging. Henceforth, the company made but few efforts to send aid and the settlement was largely left to its fate. In spite of the heroic efforts of the brave leader, it would probably not have survived, had aid not come from another quarter.

In 1628, even while d'Esnambuc was on his way to France to seek aid, there arrived at the coast of St. Christopher, so Du Tertre relates, a ship from Zeeland:

"The Dutch captain, finding the tobacco most excellent, traded with the French, even letting them have some merchandise on credit. He encouraged them to work, consoled them in their misery and urged them to prepare a quantity of tobacco for him, promising them that he would come back in six months with a supply of food-stuffs and of everything of which they had need. Our Frenchmen, seeing themselves thus succoured by foreigners in the midst of their necessity, regained their courage and began straightway to clear their lands, to plant crops which would furnish them food, to cultivate tobacco and to build houses."[8]

It is thus that the historian records the appearance of the first Dutch merchant to trade with the French settled in the West Indies. One naturally pauses before the fact, for it is the beginning of a trade which increased rapidly and became the chief artery of the economic life of the French West Indies for nearly half a century. It was no mere chance that the vessel was Dutch. How many times

[7] This account has been taken from Du Tertre, I, 28-31.
[8] Du Tertre, I, 23.

TOWARD THE FRENCH WEST INDIES

in the colonial history of the seventeenth century one finds the Dutch merchant arriving to bring help and comfort to a colony all but abandoned by the mother country. He seems ubiquitous. He is in the distant Orient, on the coasts of Africa, in South America, in Mexico, in North America, everywhere in the islands, sometimes trading at ports which he himself has established, sometimes and very often with colonies which other nations have founded. He seems omniscient. He knows the way to everywhere and is acquainted with the needs of all. The French, the Spanish and the Portuguese were much superior as explorers, the English as permanent colonizers, but the Dutch were the traders par excellence of the seventeenth century. As such, they rendered just as valuable services to the permanent conquest of the New World as did the others as explorers and colonizers. They nursed many a colony through its years of infancy and nourished many another through a stage of weakness, until its life was assured.

Following the re-establishment of the colony at St. Christopher in 1630, d'Esnambuc became thoroughly discouraged at the failure of the company to send aid. The resolution was taken to abandon the island. Accordingly only a very small amount of food-stuffs was planted in order that the harvest of tobacco might be as large as possible. Six months later, however, the plan of returning was abandoned and naturally enough, the food supply began to fail. Famine set in. All were suffering and "would have perished, had not divine Providence sent back the Dutch captain who had traded with them the year before. He brought them flour, wine, meat, shirts, cloth, and in general, a supply of all things of which they had need and he gave it to them at six months' credit, contenting himself with the amount of tobacco which they had on hand."[9] The merchant sold this tobacco so advantageously at his

[9] Du Tertre, I, 36.

return to Holland that some merchants of Flushing and of other Dutch ports decided to establish a regular trade with St. Christopher. Henceforth they sent so many ships there that all the needs of the colony were satisfied. "It is true to say," Du Tertre remarks, "that without the aid of the Dutch our colonies would never have survived."[10]

The influence of this upon the colonists at St. Christopher was quickly felt. Thoughts of leaving their plantations were abandoned. The attention of all was concentrated upon the cultivation of tobacco, "they thought of nothing else than to produce good merchandise in order to attract the Dutch. They no longer took the trouble to send anything to France."[11]

The directors of the Company of St. Christopher complained bitterly of the fact that the Dutch were absorbing all the trade, saying that they had made considerable advances for the establishment of the colony and that it was not fair that foreigners reap the benefit therefrom. The planters replied that if they were forced to respect all the regulations and obligations which the company wished to impose upon them, and to rely upon it to furnish them with necessary provisions, they would not have a shirt upon their backs; and that it was necessary to trade with the Dutch. In order to silence these complaints, the company decided to equip *La Cardinale*, and sent it to the relief of the colony. It arrived at St. Christopher with a cargo of food-stuffs in 1631, but "in such small quantities that the planters thought that the company was making fun of them."[12] They were more firmly resolved than ever to trade with all who brought them aid.

To protect the company both against the Dutch and the private French trader, a royal declaration was issued

[10] Du Tertre, I, 37.
[11] Ibid.
[12] Ibid., I, 40.

TOWARD THE FRENCH WEST INDIES

on November 25, 1634, which forbade trade in the islands except with a written permit from the directors. The declaration apparently had no effect. Less than three months later the directors confessed that the company was bankrupt and unable to continue its commerce. The company was entirely too small and the field of its activity too limited to command the attention of the stockholders and none of them took any interest in its affairs. A petition was made to the king to permit the formation of a new company with increased capital and larger concessions. It was thus that the Company of St. Christopher came to an end. On the whole, it was a distinct failure, but it must be recorded that with its capital and under its nominal administration, at least, a permanent settlement had been made by the French in the West Indies, from which, in the following period, other settlements developed and the power of the French was definitely established in the Antilles. So far as commerce was concerned, the company proved itself unable to satisfy the needs of the planters and after the first three or four years of its existence, left the field entirely free to the Dutch.

The Company of St. Christopher was reorganized at the beginning of 1635 under the name of the Company of the Isles of America. The most notable additions to its personnel were Berruyer and Nicholas Fouquet. The former was "captain of the sea-ports of Veulette and petite Dalle-en-Caux." The latter, a "conseiller du roy," became one of the directors, not only in his own name but also as representative of the interests of Richelieu. During the first five years the meetings of the directors were held at his apartments.[13] It is impossible to estimate the importance of the rôle which he henceforth played in the colonization of the West Indies.

[13] Arch. Col., F_2, 19, passim.

THE COMMERCIAL POLICY OF COLBERT

The contract for the organization of the company was signed at the hotel of Richelieu, rue St. Honoré, on February 12, 1635, and was confirmed by letters-patent of March 8. Permission was granted to continue the colonization of St. Christopher and to settle any other islands not occupied by European powers between the 10th and 30th parallels north latitude. The company assumed the obligation to transport, or have transported, to the islands of its concession, during the course of twenty years, at least 4000 persons. For the satisfaction of this obligation the number already at St. Christopher was to be counted. Article 10 of the letters-patent accorded a monopoly of trade for twenty years.[14]

It is impossible to state with precision the amount of work which the company accomplished, but it is certain that a notable advance was made during its existence in the occupation of new islands and in the increase of the power of the French in the West Indies. The narratives of Mathias du Puis, of Bouton, and especially of Du Tertre, enable one to say that the company showed considerable activity in the importation of new settlers and indentured servants. From the register, containing the minutes of the meetings of the directors from January 31, 1635, to September 4, 1648, some idea may be gained of the efforts which it made to promote plantation and to establish regular trade.[15]

Even before the formation of the new company, de l'Olive, the lieutenant of d'Esnambuc at St. Christopher, formed the plan of establishing a new settlement in one

[14] "During the space of twenty years no subject of His Majesty other than the said associates shall trade in the ports, harbours and rivers of the said islands except by the permission of the directors, under penalty of confiscation of vessel and cargo to the profit of the company." The text of the letters-patent is to be found in Moreau de Saint-Méry, I, 29-36; and in Du Tertre, I, 46-55.

[15] The register is to be found in Arch. Col., F_2, 19.

TOWARD THE FRENCH WEST INDIES

of the three islands of Guadeloupe, Martinique or Dominica. During the course of the year 1634, he sent the trusted Guillaume d'Orange[16] to make explorations in the three islands. Satisfied by the information thus gained, he set sail for France and arrived at Dieppe at the close of that year. Shortly after his arrival, he made the acquaintance of du Plessis, who had made the voyage to the West Indies with Cahuzac in 1629, and who had recently formed the plan to return to St. Christopher at the head of a band of new settlers. Du Plessis was easily persuaded to join de l'Olive in his larger scheme. They went to Paris together in order to gain the permission of Richelieu and of the new company.

A contract was signed with the company on February 14, 1635, whereby de l'Olive and du Plessis were bound to transport, within three months, to the one of the three islands chosen, 200 men, to construct dwellings and storehouses, to build one fort the first year, and another the following. After the first year and for the five succeeding years, 100 men were to be sent out annually and fifty for the four years thereafter. The company reserved the right to send on its own account whatever number of settlers it chose, and stipulated that the two contractors should grant lands to such settlers and furnish them food during the first year of their residence in the islands. Only Frenchmen of the Catholic faith were to be transported to the proposed colony. During the first six years every male inhabitant was to pay to the company a tax of sixty pounds of tobacco or forty pounds of cotton, according as the one or the other was planted in a given year. For the four succeeding years, the tax was to be 100 pounds of tobacco and fifty pounds of cotton. An

[16] See an interesting study recently made of him by le Vicomte du Motey, *Guillaume d'Orange et les Origines des Antilles Françaises*, Paris, 1908.

additional tax of one-tenth was to be paid on all other products. After the first six years the cultivation of tobacco was to be permitted only on alternate years and the maximum production for a planter in any one year was not to exceed 900 pounds. Commerce with foreigners was to be strictly forbidden. During the space of ten years de l'Olive and du Plessis were to enjoy the command of the colony, conjointly, if only one island was occupied, separately, if two were occupied.[17]

A sub-contract was let by de l'Olive and du Plessis, whereby some merchants of Dieppe agreed to transport to Guadeloupe, in the space of ten years, 2500 men, all of whom were to be French Catholics. In return the merchants were to enjoy, during six years, the right to levy a tax of twenty pounds of tobacco on all those whom they transported. They were also to enjoy a monopoly of trade.[18]

De l'Olive and du Plessis set sail from Dieppe on May 25, 1635, in command of two vessels with 550 men on board. After an unusually good voyage of one month and three days they arrived at Guadeloupe and decided to establish the colony in that island. From the first, suffering was most acute. Famine set in and many died from hunger. It was the same old story of lack of preparation. The merchants of Dieppe had not supplied the vessels with adequate provisions. Even those furnished were of poor quality, for the meat and salt fish were in a state of putrification. No store of beans or peas or cassava plant to serve for planting had been provided. For no less than five years most deplorable conditions reigned at Guadeloupe. The famine became so great at times, according to Du Tertre,[19] that some ate their own excre-

[17] Du Tertre, I, 66-69.
[18] Ibid., I, 70-71.
[19] Ibid., I, 80.

TOWARD THE FRENCH WEST INDIES

ments and it was reported that one poor wretch was found gnawing the arm of a dead comrade. To add to these miseries, the colony was often attacked by the savages. No aid came from France. The merchants of Dieppe became frightened at the prospects of loss and refused to carry out their contract. The young colony was consequently left to suffer from want of supplies. It fell a victim also to misrule and rebellion, so that Mathias du Puis remarked that during the six years of his residence he saw more rebellions, persecution, oppression of the innocent in Guadeloupe than in the whole of a great empire.[20]

In spite, however, of these trying years, the settlement at Guadeloupe proved permanent. By 1642, emigration from the ports of France to the island was noticeable.[21] The development of the colony was very satisfactory in the following period.

The establishment of a French settlement at Martinique dates from this same year, 1635. D'Esnambuc, having decided to take possession of that island, chose about one hundred of the most experienced planters of his colony, men who were thoroughly acclimated to the tropics and hardened to the labour of clearing lands and tilling the soil. He equipped them with good firearms and ammunition and with all sorts of farming utensils. Sprouts of the cassava plant and potatoes, as well as a supply of peas, beans and other grains for planting, were given them. The little colony set sail from St. Christopher at the beginning of July and arrived at Martinique about a week later. A fort was built and du Pont was placed in command. Du Pont was captured a short time afterwards by the Spaniards and was succeeded by du Parquet, one

[20] Mathias du Puis, *Relation de l'établissement d'une Colonie française.*
[21] Du Tertre, I, 208.

THE COMMERCIAL POLICY OF COLBERT

of d'Esnambuc's nephews. He was, according to a contemporary, "a brave gentleman well endowed with all the qualities necessary for the situation," and lived in such good fellowship with the savages that they called him the great captain and their "compère."[22]

With the administration of du Parquet there began an era of steady development of the new colony. The company in France was so contented with what he accomplished that it appointed him, at the close of 1637, lieutenant-general of Martinique. De Poincy, the successor of d'Esnambuc and governor-general of the islands, wrote Fouquet in 1639 that there were 700 men at Martinique capable of bearing arms.[23] Bouton stated in 1640 that there were about 1000 Frenchmen in the island.[24] The history of the early years of this colony furnishes a contrast to that of Guadeloupe. It was a striking proof of the immense advantage of founding new settlements with men who had already been acclimated to work in the tropics.

Following this successful establishment of a colony at Martinique, an expedition was sent out from St. Christopher to take possession of the island of Tortuga, or la Tortue, an island off the northern coast of St. Domingo. The English had already made a settlement there as early as 1631, but were surprised by the Spaniards in 1635 and driven out in 1638. They returned, however, shortly afterwards, together with some of the French from St. Domingo. In 1639 there appeared at St. Christopher a Frenchman from Tortuga to inform de Poincy that the French were being maltreated by the English and implored aid. He gave the assurance that the island could be very

[22] J. Bouton, *Relation de l'Etablissement des Français depuis l'an 1635 en l'Isle de la Martinique*, 39; also Du Tertre, I, 104.

[23] Arch. Col., F_2, 15, Letter from de Poincy to Fouquet, August 16, 1639.

[24] Bouton, *op. cit.*, 41.

TOWARD THE FRENCH WEST INDIES

easily captured and made a French possession. De Poincy promptly seized the opportunity of getting rid of the Protestants at St. Christopher, and at the same time received favourably the idea of establishing a new colony. He proposed the affair to Levasseur, the chief of the Protestants, and offered to bear half of the expenses of the enterprise. His proposal was accepted. A small bark was fitted out and forty or fifty Huguenots, under the command of Levasseur, sailed for Tortuga. They made a landing in that island near the end of August, 1640. The English were easily driven out and the French took possession. From the first Levasseur ruled with an iron hand and evidently tried to make his government entirely independent both of de Poincy and of the company, for the directors in their meeting of March 2, 1644, voted that de Poincy be instructed "to surprise Levasseur in the island of Tortuga."[25] Levasseur seems, however, to have remained in control of the colony until his assassination in 1652.

Some of the French who had been chased from St. Christopher in 1629 by the Spaniards settled on the northern coast of St. Domingo, but not until the ministry of Colbert did their settlement develop into anything more than a small colony of freebooters and buccaneers which maintained a small trade in hides with the Dutch.[26]

A very considerable emigration from the ports of Normandy and Brittany made this expansion and development of new colonies possible. From the port of Honfleur alone more than 600 indentured servants went out to the West Indies between January, 1637, and June, 1639.[27] The

[25] Arch. Col., F$_2$, 19, fol. 466.
[26] Charlevoix, *op. cit.,* II, 6.
[27] Bréard, *op. cit.,* 187 ff. Some contracts by which servants bound themselves to captains of ships and to the Company of the Isles of America have been published by Bréard, and by du Motey, *Guillaume d'Orange et les Origines des Antilles Françaises.*

total population of the French West Indies was estimated in 1642 to be more than 7000.[28] This increase in territory and population was accompanied by a corresponding increase in production and commerce.

It has already been noted that the most important production at St. Christopher was tobacco. Its cultivation was also begun in the other colonies at their occupation and, as in that island, it became the chief production. The increase in production was so great that the price of tobacco fell. The company tried to prevent this by limiting the maximum production by any individual planter to 900 pounds annually and by forbidding its cultivation on alternate years.[29] De Poincy made an agreement in 1639 with the English governor that no tobacco should be planted by the planters of either nation during the period of one and a half years, and he issued an ordinance on May 26, ordering that all tobacco actually planted be uprooted.[30] Another solution attempted was to diversify the crops. Thus, instructions were sent to Sieur Gentilly, general agent at St. Christopher, "to force all the planters in St. Christopher as well as at Martinique, to plant a large quantity of cotton."[31] Similar instructions were sent to the agent at Martinique in the following year.[32] When the orders were given in 1638 to limit the plantation of tobacco to alternate years, instructions were sent to the islands that cotton, roucou, or other things

[28] It was so stated in the preamble of the letters-patent which renewed the privileges in 1642. Du Tertre, I, 209.

[29] Arch. Col., F_2, 19, fols. 335, 339.

[30] Du Tertre, I, 143-144. This order and agreement were also sent to Guadeloupe, but de l'Olive refused to obey it and he was sustained by the directors on the ground that an enforcement of it in that island would be a violation of the contract with the merchants of Dieppe.

[31] Arch. Col., F_2, 19, fol. 109, September 3, 1636.

[32] Ibid., fol. 119.

TOWARD THE FRENCH WEST INDIES

be planted.[33] A proposal to cultivate indigo was favourably received by the company in 1643.[34]

But it was in the cultivation of sugar-cane that the future prosperity of the islands lay and it was to this that the directors devoted much attention about 1640. In their session of October 6, 1638, they discussed the proposal made by a Sieur Turque to undertake the production of sugar and other merchandise. The directors offered free passage for him, his wife and six men, with exemption from ordinary taxes in the island, provided that he plant no tobacco, but only sugar-cane and other products, and provided that he depart during the course of the current year.[35] No record has been found that Sieur Turque ever went to Guadeloupe to carry out any such plan. But in April, 1639, the company accepted the proposal of Trezel, a Dutch merchant of Rouen, to carry out a somewhat similar plan for Martinique.[36]

[33] Ibid., fol. 339.
[34] Ibid., fol. 464.
[35] Ibid., fol. 341.
[36] The entry in the register of the company is as follows: "After having taken note of the proposal made by Sieur Trezel of Rouen for the cultivation of sugar-cane and for the establishment of mills for the manufacture of sugar in the island of Martinique, and after having heard the aforesaid Sieur Trezel regarding his plans therefor, it was ordered that Mess. Martin and Chanut draw up a contract with him with the following stipulations: 2400 arpents of land to be granted by the company for the establishment of necessary building and the plantation of sugar-cane; a monopoly of the cultivation of sugar-cane in the aforesaid island of Martinique for the remainder of the current year and for six years following; the monopoly to be protected by the imposition of the penalty of confiscation and fines on all those who attempt to violate it; . . . the said six years to be prolonged in case of war; . . . the privilege of establishing one or two plantations of sugar-cane in the island of Guadeloupe without, however, a monopoly of its production in that island; . . . a premium of one-tenth of all sugar and other products to be paid directly to the company and one-fortieth to some person designated by the company; the sugar produced to be trans-

THE COMMERCIAL POLICY OF COLBERT

Trezel sailed almost immediately to carry out his plans.[37] He evidently found the task before him much more difficult than he had anticipated, for he demanded more liberal terms before he was willing to carry out his contract. The company made several concessions, the most important of which were: That the double tax of one-tenth and one-fortieth was not to be paid during the first six years; and that at the expiration of the six years, the planters of Martinique who cultivated sugar-cane were to pay a tax of one-tenth to Trezel from 1645 to 1651; that he was permitted to employ fifteen of his men in the plantation of tobacco; and that he was allowed to trade with foreigners in sugar, tobacco and other products in exchange for foodstuffs for the nourishment of his men.[38] In the following year (1641), the company granted him free passage on one of its ships for three men and four tons of merchandise "in consideration of the great expense to which Sieur Trezel has been forced and of the promise which he gives of setting up a sugar-mill in the island of Martinique."[39] In 1642 Trezel complained of bad treatment, stating that "all his utensils had been scattered and that under pre-

ported only to France and its sale to foreigners to be strictly forbidden; no cultivation of tobacco to be permitted; at the expiration of the aforesaid six years only the tax of one-tenth to be imposed by the company and the monopoly to cease and all the planters of the said island of Martinique thereafter to enjoy the liberty to plant sugar-cane at their pleasure." Arch. Col., F₂, 19, fol. 354, April 6, 1639. See also fols. 35 ff.

[37] His presence and the manner of his reception are indicated in a letter written by du Parquet under the date of August 17. "I was delighted at the arrival of Sieur Trezel. I hope that by the aid of God he will succeed in the production of sugar. As to the orders which you have sent that no one else is to be permitted to cultivate sugar-cane, it is not necessary to give them as there is no one here rich enough to do so. If, however, some one makes an attempt, I shall at once forbid him to continue." Du Tertre, I, 109.

[38] Arch. Col., F₂, 19, fol. 388.
[39] Ibid., fol. 416.

TOWARD THE FRENCH WEST INDIES

text of certain debts, his plantation had been sold," that thus all the expenditures which he had made for the manufacture of 50,000 pounds of sugar were lost. The directors instructed the company's agent at Martinique to investigate the statements of Trezel and at the same time to consider the advisability of re-establishing the enterprise on the basis of one-third being owned by the company, one-third by du Parquet, and one-third by Trezel.[40] This plan did not materialize, for only a few months later the following entry was made in the minutes of the company:

"As the contract made with Sieur Trezel has not had the success hoped for, owing to the weakness and bad faith of the contractor, the company, being unwilling that a matter of such great importance be postponed longer, is hereby resolved to furnish the funds for the establishment of the enterprise."[41]

In accordance with this resolution it was decided to purchase sixty negroes, and to obtain forty or fifty workmen of all sorts for the construction of necessary buildings and for the other work necessary for the cultivation of sugar. Guadeloupe was chosen as the island best suited to the enterprise. It was further resolved to find "some person of distinction" to whom the management of the work could be confided.[42] The choice fell upon Charles Houel, one of the stockholders of the company.[43] He had recently returned from a voyage to the West Indies, made under the orders of the company "in order to gain a perfect knowledge of all which was going on in the islands and to render the company a faithful account thereof, and particularly in order to find some island where he might

[40] Ibid., fol. 178.
[41] Ibid., fol. 472.
[42] Ibid., fol. 439.
[43] Du Motey, *Guillaume d'Orange,* 153. "Charles Houel, écuyer, sieur de Petit-Pré . . . fils d'un riche financier Louis Houel, sieur de Petit-Pré, conseiller du Roi, contrôleur général des salines du Brouage et traites de Saintonge."

THE COMMERCIAL POLICY OF COLBERT

establish himself."[44] Houel was made governor of Guadeloupe and entrusted with the entire management of the enterprise. All the clerks, workmen and slaves of the company were placed under his orders. He was granted one-tenth of all the sugar to be produced in the island.[45]

A contract was made with Rozer, a merchant of Rouen, to deliver sixty negroes at Guadeloupe at the rate of 200 livres apiece, one-third of the entire sum to be paid immediately and the other two-thirds after their delivery. In October following, Rozer demanded the payment of the 8000 livres and the payment for two additional slaves which had been sold to de Leumont, the company's agent at St. Christopher.[46]

The cultivation of sugar-cane was definitely begun at Guadeloupe in accordance with these plans.[47] No monopoly was asserted by the company, for all the planters were encouraged to begin the plantation of sugar-cane

[44] Du Tertre, I, 207.

[45] Arch. Col., F₂, 19, fol. 449.

[46] Prompt payment was demanded on the ground that the negroes "had cost more than was expected by reason of the fact that the Dutch were making large demands for them at the coast of Guinea." Ibid., fol. 462. Houel claimed, in 1648, that he had furnished the funds for the purchase of these slaves and demanded the cession of Marie Galante, where he might take the "sixty negroes which the company seemed unwilling to pay for" and establish himself as proprietor. Du Tertre, I, 441.

[47] A contemporary traveller observed that "Mess. of the Company of the Isles of America possessed at Guadeloupe a large plantation of sugar-cane which I saw. They have also a good mill which was being prepared when I was there and which has since been completed according to information which I have received. Eighty negroes have been sent there in addition to the 100 which I saw myself and more land has been acquired, so that M. Houel told me that he hoped to manufacture 150,000 pounds of sugar annually." Bib. Nat. MSS., Franç., 18593, fols. 367-368. The relation cited at this reference was probably written about 1647, see Jacques de Dampierre, *Essai sur les sources de l'histoire des Antilles françaises, 1492-1664*, Paris, 1904.

TOWARD THE FRENCH WEST INDIES

by the offer of exemption from the tax of sixty pounds of tobacco during the first year.[48]

It seems probable that Trezel re-established his plantation and sugar-mill at Martinique, for on June 3, 1644, he was granted free permission to send vessels to the islands during the space of six years, free passage for six tons of merchandise on a ship then being equipped by the company at Dieppe, and finally he was granted an exemption from all taxes on sugar produced by him during the year 1647.[49]

Plans to begin the cultivation of sugar-cane at St. Christopher were contemporaneous. In 1639, de Poincy proposed such a plan and it was promptly accepted by the directors in their meeting of June 1.[50] De Poincy, however, met with obstacles. Thus he wrote to the directors in the following year:

"We haven't enough land to produce roucou and cotton. They are products which occupy too much space. I admit that the soil is suited to the production of both. . . . The planters do not know or wish to know anything except how to produce tobacco, unless some one first shows them the way. What I say about the cultivation of roucou and cotton is also true of sugar-cane. In regard to that there is another difficulty. It is the lack of water which is absolutely necessary and of which we have no supply except that from a small brook. . . . This lack could of course be supplied, so far as power to turn the mills is concerned, by the employment of horses or of oxen, but it would still be necessary to have a supply of water."[51]

[48] Arch. Col., F_2, 19, fol. 452.
[49] Ibid., fol. 472.
[50] Ibid., fol. 357. Two months later the exclusive privilege of manufacturing brandy in the islands of Martinique and St. Christopher was granted to a M. Fagues. It is possible and even almost certain that it is there a question of the manufacture of brandy from sugar-cane. See fol. 362.
[51] Arch. Col., F_2, 15, letter from de Poincy, November 15, 1640.

This difficulty proved only temporary, for only a few years later both Pelleprat and de Rochefort make special mention of the production of sugar at St. Christopher.[52] De Rochefort remarked that de Poincy had three mills for crushing cane on his principal plantation, and three more on another in the quarter of Cayonne, and that all six of these mills were turned by oxen or horses, except one which was turned by water. He added that all the principal planters had followed the example of their governor by planting sugar-cane.[53]

It is not to be supposed for a moment that the plantation of sugar-cane had become general, as yet, in any of the islands. Maurile de St. Michel, who was in Guadeloupe in 1647, remarked that Houel, the governor, raised sugar-cane, but that the average planter raised tobacco.[54] But the fact that the plantation of sugar-cane had been begun in all the islands was most significant and was the most important single fact connected with the administration of the Company of the Isles of America. The broad road to the future had been opened and the economic development of the islands was assured. It remains to trace the development of commerce which accompanied the increase in population and production.

In the beginning, the new company seems to have intended to assert its monopoly and undertake to carry on the commerce with the islands in its own ships. It established agents at Nantes, St. Malo, Dieppe, Havre and La Rochelle, and in the islands at St. Christopher, Guade-

[52] Le Père Pierre Pelleprat, *Relation des missions des PP. de la Compagnie de Jésus dans les Isles et dans la Terre Ferme de l'Amérique*, Paris, 1665, pp. 8-9.

[53] Cesar de Rochefort, *Histoire naturelle et morale des Antilles de l'Amérique*, p. 312.

[54] F. Maurile de St. Michel, *Voyage des Isles Camercanes en l'Amérique et une relation diversifiée*, p. 41.

TOWARD THE FRENCH WEST INDIES

loupe and Martinique.[55] The directors gave instructions that the planters be prevented from buying anything from the English except live stock or cotton, and from selling their tobacco to them, and in general from trading with foreigners, so far as it was possible, and finally from returning to Europe in Dutch and English vessels or from sending their merchandise thither by such vessels.[56] Private French traders were forbidden to trade in the islands except by first obtaining a passport from the company. Passports were granted on condition of returning directly to Dieppe or Havre, and of providing on the outward voyage free passage for three servants belonging to the company and free transport for "a certain number of tons of merchandise," and on the return voyage free transport for ten tons of merchandise for every 100 tons of the vessel's tonnage.[57]

In view of the fact that the company attempted to assert its monopoly, the question is naturally asked what it did to satisfy the needs of the planters through its own efforts. "I have not been able to find out," says Du Tertre,[58] "the details of the succour which this company sent out to St. Christopher, but there is every appearance that it was considerable and that many settlers were enlisted at Dieppe and Havre." But the principal aid which the company sent out to the islands was in the shape of new settlers, for there is some evidence that the com-

[55] Arch. Col., F_2, 19, fols. 155, 257, 109, 119, 159, 167.

[56] Ibid., fols. 109, 119, 159, 167.

[57] Ibid., fol. 89. These conditions were not always enforced, however, for there are several cases where others were substituted. Thus, a permission was granted to a captain of La Rochelle in 1637, on condition of carrying out six muskets and of bringing back a "certain quantity of tobacco for the company." Fols. 293-296. The company insisted on private traders having passports. It ordered prosecution of a captain in 1635 and another in 1637 for infractions of this rule. Ibid., fol. 253.

[58] Du Tertre, I, 58.

pany's activity in matters of trade, properly speaking, was not important. Although mention is made from time to time of vessels belonging to the company going out to the islands,[59] the company came to depend more and more upon private French and foreign traders to supply the needs of the islands. Permits to trade seem to have been granted freely. Thus they were given to merchants at La Rochelle in 1637, 1638, 1642, to some at Nantes in 1637 (2), 1639 (2), 1643, 1644.[60] In a general assembly, held December 2, 1637, the company decided that stockholders could send vessels to the islands on the same conditions as other individuals.[61] But the results of the activ-

[59] Thus it is noted in the minutes of August 25, 1635, that one of its vessels was captured on its way from St. Christopher with a cargo of tobacco (fol. 251). Under the date of July 1, 1637, mention is made of the arrival of a vessel at Nantes from St. Christopher with a cargo of tobacco likewise (fol. 296). On July 28, 1641, free transport of four tons of merchandise and three men on a vessel being equipped at St. Malo or Dieppe. A similar thing was done on June 3, 1644, for a vessel being equipped at St. Malo (fols. 417 and 473). It is not certain but very probable that in both cases it was a question of vessels belonging to the company. On May 14, 1640, the directors ordered that a letter be written to de Poincy to inform him that the vessel lately sent out from St. Malo had been captured. Near the close of 1641 the company made a contract with Rozer, a merchant of Rouen, to send in partnership with him a cargo of merchandise to the islands. For this purpose a vessel of 200 tons was chartered at La Rochelle. In the following year, before the return of the vessel, the company offered to pay Rozer 36,000 livres for his share, which represented only an original investment of 18,000. The vessel was bringing a cargo of tobacco, the price of which had risen recently (fol. 418). Again, at the close of 1642, the directors decided to equip a vessel of 100 tons and send it to the islands (fol. 438). Unless some oversight has been made, these are all the indications which the minutes contain of the expedition of vessels to the islands. Of course, one cannot be certain that the minutes contain a complete list of all the vessels which were sent out. But it is probable that the reason why more indications are not given is that the company sent very few vessels to trade with the planters.

[60] Arch. Col., F_2, 19, fols. 170, 293, 306, 352, 325, 444, 473.

[61] Fol. 315.

TOWARD THE FRENCH WEST INDIES

ity of the private French trader were not great and the planters relied more and more completely upon the Dutch for their supplies.

It will be recalled that the company gave instructions to exclude foreigners. But in actual practice, it either permitted foreign trade, by reason of its inability to assert its monopoly, or tolerated it, by reason of the fact that it was unable to supplant the Dutch in the satisfaction of the planters' needs. It permitted it in the case of Trezel, for on April 4, 1640, the directors permitted him to barter tobacco, sugar, or other products for food-stuffs in trade with foreigners. It tolerated it in the case of trade at St. Christopher. De Poincy made a contract with Mess. de Ruberque, merchants of Middleburg, whereby they agreed to furnish all things of which the island had need. "In order to facilitate this trade de Poincy permitted them to send an agent and construct a store at Sandy Point. This agent, thanks to the profit which he assured to de Poincy, was permitted to monopolize almost the entire trade of the island."[62] The minutes of the company contain a very interesting item of evidence which shows that the foreigner became the mainstay of the planters. On September 13, 1641, the directors took the following action:

"In consideration of the fact that according to the memoirs of M. de Poincy and the letters from the agents in the islands, the planters are entirely without supplies, which are ordinarily brought them by the Dutch and English traders, who have ceased to come of late, by reason of the fact that the plantation of tobacco has temporarily ceased [due to the ordinance of May, 1639], and that the lack of these necessities has caused sickness, it is hereby resolved to send relief to the islands."

This is a most categorical statement that under normal conditions the supplies of the planters were furnished by

[62] Du Tertre, I, 165-167.

foreigners, and it is not without significance that the company took the resolution to send a vessel to the islands more for the sake of relieving suffering than for the purpose of carrying on commerce. The foreigner was not long absent and the company again subsided into inactivity. Near the close of the period of the company's rule in the islands, which came to an end in 1648, the Dutch seem again to have almost completely monopolized trade. They had built up a lucrative commerce and their vessels were going to the islands in ever increasing numbers.

In spite of this development of the islands the Company of the Isles of America proved a failure and was bankrupt in 1648. Du Tertre attributed its downfall to two principal reasons, namely, civil warfare and the triumph of the personal interests of the individual governors at the expense of those of the company. Both of these causes require a moment's explanation.

At the death of d'Esnambuc in 1634, the company appointed Sieur de Longvillier de Poincy, a chevalier in the order of St. John of Jerusalem and chief of the squadron of the king's vessels in Brittany, as lieutenant-general of all the French islands of America. He arrived at St. Christopher in February, 1639, and seems to have begun almost immediately an administration which promoted his own personal interests rather than those of the company. In 1640, as has been noted already, he made a contract with a Dutch firm of Middleburg to furnish all supplies necessary at St. Christopher. He attempted, according to Du Tertre, to monopolize all the trade of the island. For this purpose he forbade the inhabitants to board vessels which came to St. Christopher, in order that he might buy all the merchandise imported into the island and sell it to the planters at a profit. He employed no less than seven clerks for the distribution of goods thus bought.

TOWARD THE FRENCH WEST INDIES

In addition he laid heavy taxes upon the people so that "he and his clerks grew very rich at the expense of the poor planters who groaned under the monopoly."[63]

The company decided to replace him in 1644 and sent out as his successor Sieur de Thoisy. From the moment of de Thoisy's arrival in the islands, in November, 1645, de Poincy refused to acknowledge him and straightway prepared to defend himself by force of arms. A civil war broke out, which spread to all the islands. St. Christopher, Guadeloupe and Martinique suffered most from the conflict. De Poincy was able not only to remain in control of St. Christopher, but forced his rival to embark for France in January, 1647. The authority of the company was thus defied and it was too weak to reply. It was, however, not merely humiliation that the company suffered, but in addition its revenue from taxation in the islands was cut off. No revenue came from St. Christopher during the struggle, for de Poincy held all with an iron hand in that island, and the planters of the other islands, "profiting from the state of affairs, refused to pay taxes to the company."[64]

As to the selfish rule of the several governors, it is certain that de Poincy at St. Christopher, Houel at Guadeloupe, du Parquet at Martinique, and Levasseur at Tortuga had all the power in their hands. It has just been seen that de Poincy was strong enough to defy the company and rule his island in accordance with his own wishes. It has also been noted that efforts to bring Levasseur into obedience proved fruitless. He apparently maintained no relations with the company whatever. Houel's voyage to Guadeloupe in 1646 was made as much in his own interests as in those of the company. He was seeking an island where he might make his fortune. He was a stockholder

[63] Du Tertre, I, 123, 166, 290.
[64] Ibid., I, 439.

and easily succeeded in having himself appointed governor of the island. He furnished a large part of the capital for the establishment of the sugar industry, a fact which gave him an upper hand in his relations with the company. When the complaint was made that the company was receiving no revenue from Guadeloupe, he replied that he had employed his own capital to make the affairs of the company succeed, and that the company was his debtor and not he the company's. When it became a question of disposing of the several islands in 1648, Houel wrote to his brother-in-law, de Boisseret, instructing him to buy the island of Guadeloupe in partnership with him, assuring him that for the year 1650 he would produce at least 100,000 pounds of sugar and a large quantity of tobacco.[65] This statement shows very conclusively that if the company was receiving no revenue from Guadeloupe, it was due, not to the fact that the island was not productive, but rather to the fact that Houel was guarding the proceeds for himself. Du Parquet, at Martinique, seems to have been the only one of the governors who administered affairs in the interest of the company.

The downfall of the company was undoubtedly due in part, and perhaps principally, to these causes. It may have been due also to the fact that its capital was too small and that the directors paid too little attention to its affairs. But whatever may have been the causes, it is certain that the company was in a bankrupt state in 1648. The revenue from the islands had become small, the company had been deeply humiliated from the defeat administered by de Poincy and creditors had become very pressing. A special general assembly of the stockholders was called to deliberate over the crisis. It was held on the first Friday of June, 1648. After having taken into consideration that the several governors had become masters

[65] Du Tertre, I, 443.

of the islands, that the officers of the company were no longer respected, and that in order to lift it out of its embarrassments it would be necessary for the stockholders to subscribe 4000 livres for each share held, it was decided to sell the several islands.

In accordance with this decision, Guadeloupe, together with Marie Galante, Desirade and the Saints, was sold to Houel and de Boisseret (September 4, 1649) for 60,000 livres, Martinique, with St. Lucia, Grenada and the Grenadines, to du Parquet (September 27, 1650) for 50,000 livres, and St. Christopher to the Knights of Malta (May 24, 1651) for 120,000 livres.[66] Thus was inaugurated a period of proprietary rule, which lasted until the establishment of the West India Company in 1664. It is not the purpose here to recount the history of the islands under this régime of proprietary rule, but merely to call attention to the most important facts which bear directly upon the development of trade and industry.

The expansion which has been noted for the period 1635-1648 continued for the period 1648-1664. In March, 1648, de Poincy, on learning that the Spaniards had abandoned the island of St. Martin, sent his nephew with 300 men to take possession of it. The Dutch sent a similar expedition from St. Eustatius about the same time and for the same purpose. By a treaty of March 23, the two nations agreed to divide the island between them, about two-thirds going to the French and one-third to the Dutch. The island of St. Bartholomew was occupied in the same year by a small colony of fifty or sixty men sent out from St. Christopher. It was abandoned in 1656, after a furious attack by the savages, but reoccupied in 1659. In 1650, de Poincy placed one of his lieutenants, de Vaughan, in command of some 160 of the bravest men at St. Christopher and ordered him to attack the Span-

[66] Du Tertre, I, 443 ff.

THE COMMERCIAL POLICY OF COLBERT

iards at St. Croix and take possession of the island. De Vaughan was successful and in the following year 300 more men were sent out to establish a permanent colony.[67]

From Guadeloupe an expedition occupied, in October, 1648, the groups of small islands lying between it and Dominica, known as the Saints, and in the same year Marie Galante was occupied.[68]

At Martinique du Parquet was not idle, but also took part in the movement of expansion. In 1648, a small colony was sent to St. Lucia, but the island was occupied more with the idea of preventing its occupation by another nation than with that of founding a productive colony. In June, 1650, du Parquet himself set sail with a well-equipped colony of 200 men to take possession of Grenada. After a successful occupation he reinforced the colony in the following year by sending 300 additional settlers. The island was sold in 1656 to de Cérillac, in whose hands it remained until its cession to the West India Company in 1664.[69]

This expansion in territory was accompanied by a growth in population. The population of the French West Indies was estimated in 1642 to be more than 7000,[70] and in 1655, Pelleprat, a Jesuit missionary, estimated it to be 15,000 or 16,000 Frenchmen and 12,000 or 13,000 slaves.[71]

There was also a very notable increase in the production of sugar. Biët stated that, according to reports which he had received from the islands, there were planters who produced 10,000 pounds of sugar per week and that the poor planters, which he had seen in 1654, had become

[67] For all of these facts concerning the colonies founded from St. Christopher see Du Tertre, I, 409-413, and II, 32, 33, 37.
[68] Ibid., I, 425 ff. and II, 40-41.
[69] Ibid.
[70] Ibid., I, 209.
[71] Pelleprat, *op. cit.*, 3, 15, 54.

TOWARD THE FRENCH WEST INDIES

"little lords."[72] A memorialist of 1660 noted that a large amount of sugar was being produced in the islands and that it had supplanted tobacco as the most important product.[73] De Tracy wrote to Colbert in 1664 that so much land was being devoted to the plantation of sugar that the islands were suffering from a failure to plant food-stuffs.[74] Colbert himself stated in 1664 that the Dutch carried away with them from the French West Indies annually, 2,000,000 livres worth of sugar and 1,000,000 livres worth of tobacco, cotton, dye-woods, indigo, etc.[75] This increase in production had been made possible by a large importation of indentured servants and still more of slaves. "Traders bring many ships every year laden with slaves. Three arrived at Martinique last year [1654] which disembarked 600 or 700."[76] St. Christopher and Guadeloupe were perhaps no less favoured, for the same writer observes that de Poincy at St. Christopher had no less than 600 or 700 slaves on his plantations.[77]

Trade steadily increased under proprietary rule. French traders seem to have profited very little from it, however. A few vessels went out from Dieppe, Havre, St. Malo, Nantes and La Rochelle.[78] The principal trade of

[72] Antoine Biët, *Voyage de la France Equinoxiale en l'isle de Cayenne entrepris par les François en l'annee MDCLIII,* Paris, 1664, 314-315.

[73] Arch. Nat. Col., C₈, 2nd series, I, Relation des isles de l'Amérique.

[74] Du Tertre, III, 98.

[75] Clément, *op. cit.,* II, 1, cclix, Discours sur les manufactures.

[76] Pelleprat, *op. cit.,* 54-55.

[77] Ibid.

[78] Pelleprat made the voyage to the islands in 1651 in a vessel from La Rochelle. *Op. cit.,* p. 27. Du Tertre notes the presence of a vessel from Nantes at St. Domingo in 1659. Du Tertre, III, 131. *L'Aurore* (200 tons), from Dieppe, was on a voyage to the West Indies in 1664. Bib. Nat. MSS., 500 Colbert, 199, fols. 101-108. In the same year, *Le Phenix* (60 tons), *Le Petit Soleil* (50 tons), and *Le St. Antoine* (140 tons), all from St. Malo, were in the islands. Ibid.,

these vessels, especially those of the northern ports, was in indentured servants.[79] Foreigners, for the most part Dutch, controlled almost all the rest of the trade.

Pelleprat remarked that foreigners brought wine, beer, brandy, oil, butter, salt-meat, biscuit, cloth and everything else necessary for the planters, and took in exchange tobacco, sugar, indigo, ginger, tortoise shell, and other articles.[80] Biët, during his short sojourn in the islands in 1654, remarked that the ships of all nations were trading in the harbours of Guadeloupe.[81] Maurile de St. Michel, in a chapter on the establishment of the Carmelites at Guadeloupe, states that during the voyage of Fathers Cosme and Innocent in 1648, from France, no less than thirty passengers died, and during that of Father Athanase, in 1650, forty-five died. He stated that the deaths in each case were due to the "filth and infection of our vessels," and added that the safest thing to do was to go to Holland to embark in a Dutch vessel, because the Dutch cleaned their ships often, fed passengers well and did not take such a large number aboard.[82] Du Tertre made the outward voyage in 1654 in a Dutch ship from Texel and returned the following year in another to Flushing. Father Feuillet came from St. Christopher to Flushing by a Dutch vessel in 1658. Houel returned to France by another in 1664.[83]

It was the Dutch who saved Martinique from disaster in 1654. In that year the attacks of the savages were so persistent that "the island was on the point of succumbing to the ferocious brutality of the barbarians and the rebel-

fols. 237-260. Three vessels from Nantes, one of 140 tons, another of 200, another of 250, were there the same year. Ibid., fols. 221-234.

[79] Du Tertre, II, 464.
[80] Pelleprat, *op. cit.*, 8.
[81] Biët, *op. cit.*, 315.
[82] De St. Michel, *op. cit.*, 328.
[83] Du Tertre, I, 508, 528, and III, 79.

TOWARD THE FRENCH WEST INDIES

lion of the slaves, when God sent four large Dutch vessels armed for war to their aid." The Dutch landed 300 soldiers, drove off the savages and saved the colony from calamity.[84] A memorialist of 1660 remarked that the French trader was subjected to such heavy duties that it was no longer possible for him to compete with his Dutch rival in the trade with the island. He stated that the Dutch were importing all sorts of merchandise and offered them much cheaper than the French and that they offered much lower rates for the transportation of freight from the islands to Europe.[85] Formont, a Parisian banker, who had interests in the islands and who had engaged in trade there, remarked in a memoir, written in 1662, that the trade with the French West Indies had become so important that they sent no less than 100 or 120 large vessels there annually.[86] Colbert himself estimated that out of a total of 150 vessels which traded in the French Antilles in 1662, three or four at most sailed from the ports of France.[87]

De Rochefort asserts that the trade with St. Christopher and the other islands had led to the establishment of "rich and powerful firms at Middleburg and Flushing," and that the trade of these islands had become, for the traders of these towns, what the mines of Peru were for the Spaniards. The merchants of Flushing called the French planters "our planters."[88] The relation between them became intimate. "The planters a few years ago having expressed the fear that in case of rupture between France and Holland they would suffer heavy losses, the Dutch straightway offered them the right of *bourgeois* and

[84] Du Tertre, I, 469.
[85] Arch. Nat. Col., C$_8$, 2nd series, I, Relation des isles de l'Amérique.
[86] Ibid., Mémoire du Sieur Formont pour montrer l'utilité du commerce des isles et les moyens de le bien établir.
[87] Lavisse, *Histoire de France*, VII, 1, 235, note 1.
[88] De Rochefort, *op. cit.*, 311.

granted them insurance policies in firms of Amsterdam, Middleburg and Flushing."[89] The most important planters of Martinique accepted the offer, and by paying twelve livres a year received insurance for all of their property. In 1657, when a rupture between the two nations seemed imminent, the Dutch sent post haste a frigate to the islands to assure the merchants and planters that no matter what happened, their property would be as safe as if it were in Dutch possessions.

Du Tertre recounts an incident which occurred in 1663 at St. Christopher, which gives a very good idea of the immense importance of Dutch commerce in the islands at that date:

"In the year 1663 there occurred something most remarkable in this island [St. Christopher]. It was the conflagration of all the storehouses belonging to the Dutch merchants. More than sixty were consumed with all the merchandise which they contained. The loss was estimated at more than 2,000,000 livres. . . . The island suffered very much during four or five months, because all the salt beef and bacon, wine, oil, brandy, flour, cloth, and other goods were entirely burned, so that the planters were deprived of all these things in a single day and were forced to await aid from Holland, which had always proved their refuge in time of necessity. The Dutch did not fail them, in spite of their own losses, for they had no sooner received news of the disaster than they freighted a large number of vessels with all sorts of merchandise. . . . Such a large quantity of supplies was imported that some poor Dutch merchants, who had brought a quantity of meat, wine and brandy, which could not be preserved a long time, were forced to sell them at a loss of one-third."[90]

Du Tertre does not fail to explain the superiority of the Dutch and the reason why the French planters regarded

[89] Du Tertre, II, 464.
[90] Ibid., I, 586.

TOWARD THE FRENCH WEST INDIES

them with favour. At the close of his second volume he devotes a most interesting chapter to the subject of trade. The chapter has all the greater significance, when it is recalled that the author spent some years of his life as a sailor and had made many voyages to and from the islands, a fact which gave him ample opportunity to observe and to know whereof he spoke in discussing matters of navigation and trade.[91] A passage from it is as follows:

"There is to be found in the storehouse of the islands everything of which the planters have need. Merchants take pains to have such an assortment of merchandise that the planter is not obliged to go from store to store in order to find all that he desires. Everything is much dearer than in France, for a pair of slippers sometimes costs 100 pounds of tobacco, that is to say fifteen livres in money. I have had merchants in France tell me that those who understand well the needs of the planters can make a profit of 100 per cent on the merchandise which they import into the islands.

"It is undoubtedly for that reason that the Dutch offer goods much cheaper, for they are contented with much less profit and offer goods brought from France even at less cost than the French merchants. Notwithstanding the great losses which they have suffered, amounting in some cases to the shipwreck of thirty to forty ships in a single year, they have never permitted themselves to be rebuffed, but have always furnished the islands abundantly with all things of which they had need. That is the principal reason wherefore our planters abandoned trade with the ports of France and placed all of their affairs in the hands of the Dutch. To this reason must be added the excess of duties which must be paid in France on goods imported from and exported to the colonies. In some cases such duties exceed the cost of the goods. . . . I have seen poor planters indebted for more than 100 écus after paying duties on shipments to France on which they had hoped to realize a profit of 5,000 livres.

[91] See Dampierre, *op. cit.*, 108, for a very interesting sketch of his life.

THE COMMERCIAL POLICY OF COLBERT

"Besides all of these reasons, the greater part of all the French vessels which went to the islands before the formation of the West India Company, were in such a bad state that there was no security for their cargoes. The Dutch, on the other hand, had a goodly number of large, beautiful vessels and were often satisfied with half of that which the French demanded for the transportation of freight. There is no occasion for surprise, therefore, if all the products of our islands were laden in their ships.

"So that if we consider the matter closely, we will understand that not only our planters are justified in placing their affairs in the hands of the Dutch, but also that the Dutch, who are the best informed traders in the world, have persistently sought to maintain this trade by reason of the profit which they found therein. The freedom of the ports of Holland has also attracted our planters, and besides, the Dutch merchants have shown such affection and such fidelity in their relations with our planters that they have become masters of all the affairs of the islands."[92]

Thus at the eve of Colbert's ministry, the French were in possession of no less than fourteen islands in the West Indies, the most important of which, St. Christopher, Guadeloupe, and Martinique, were already well cultivated and productive, and another, St. Domingo, was capable of wonderful development and was destined to become the most productive colony of all. The importation of servants from France and of slaves from the coast of Africa had made possible a notable development in the productivity of the colonies. Sugar had become an important product and had already begun to serve as a solid base for the prosperity of the islands. The poor little planter of the small tobacco patch, with his few servants about him, had been replaced by the "little lord" of the large plantations of waving sugar-cane who had many slaves to do his bidding. The small number of vessels which came in

[92] Du Tertre, II, 460.

TOWARD THE FRENCH WEST INDIES

former times only at the tobacco harvest, came now in great numbers and at all seasons.

The profit of all this development, however, had passed into the hands of the Dutch. Most of the capital which had made possible the development of the sugar industry had been furnished by them. Dutch ships brought slaves from the coast of Africa in abundance and thus made possible increased production. Dutch traders and Dutch ships were everywhere, to import and export all the merchandise of the French West Indies. For a whole generation they had been knitting, one by one, the ties which bound the planters closer and closer to them. Now by gratitude, now by affection, now by personal interest, the French planter had become attached to Holland. Politically these fourteen islands were under the rule of French proprietors and were theoretically in the possession of the French king, but industrially and commercially they were in the possession of the Dutch.

It remained for Colbert to bring them under the veritable rule of the French king and lay hold of their riches for the profit of the nation.

CHAPTER II

THE AWAKENING AND THE PERIOD OF PREPARATION

THE fact that the commerce of the French West Indies had become relatively important and was in the hands of the Dutch did not fail to attract attention in France before the beginning of Colbert's ministry. The important part which Fouquet played in the affairs of Company of the Isles of America has already been noted. It was at his apartment that the meetings of the directors of the company were most frequently held and it was to him that colonial governors addressed their correspondence. Thanks to the favour of the queen-mother, he received in 1652 the very important appointment of *surintendant des finances* and came to play a capital rôle in the affairs of the kingdom. His interest in the affairs of the West Indies continued, for he maintained a plantation at St. Lucia and another at Martinique. He sent two vessels from Belle Isle with cargoes of workmen and supplies and implements for the cultivation of his plantation in the latter island in 1661.[1] At the moment of his disgrace, as he recounts in his *Défenses*, he had formed a large plan:

"I was thinking of nothing else [he is speaking of his establishment at Belle Isle] than of the establishment of a commercial company and of building up the colonies. I had already talked with the king in regard to my plans. I had orders from the late Cardinal Mazarin, as well as from Cardinal Richelieu, to occupy myself with the matter of the American colonies.

[1] Gabriel Marcel, *Le Surintendant Fouquet, Vice-Roi d'Amérique*, p. 15.

TOWARD THE FRENCH WEST INDIES

De Feuquières, d'Andilly, Lavocat, Clément, Chanut, some merchants and I were on the point of forming a company. That is why I lent money to de Feuquières for the office of Viceroy of America. . . . . I hoped to render a great service to His Majesty by taking away from foreigners the commerce of the islands which they had usurped and at the same time to find a good investment for the revenue derived from Belle Isle."[2]

This passage shows very clearly that Fouquet was a predecessor of Colbert in his plans to drive out the Dutch and to reserve the trade of the islands for Frenchmen.

Others called attention to the importance of taking some steps to accomplish the same thing. A memorialist of 1660 presented the matter as follows:

"As for that which regards trade, it is to be remarked that the heavy duties which French captains and merchants are obliged to pay to the king make it impossible for them to continue to trade with the Antilles, because the Dutch not only import there all sorts of merchandise and offer them for sale at much lower prices than the French, but they also demand much less for the transportation of freight from the islands to Europe."

The remedy suggested by the writer was the creation of one or two free ports in France, where all the merchandise, either exported to or imported from the islands, might be free from duties.[3]

Formont, a Parisian banker, wrote a memoir in 1662 which is of unusual interest in giving the point of view of a man of affairs:

"The commerce of the islands of St. Christopher, Martinique, Guadeloupe and others under the king's dominion is so profitable and so considerable that if it were once established

[2] *Recueil des défenses de M. Fouquet,* Amsterdam, 1665-1667, tome III, 360.
[3] Arch. Nat. Col., C_8, 2nd series, I, Relation des Isles de l'Amérique.

THE COMMERCIAL POLICY OF COLBERT

in France and carried on by Frenchmen, as could easily be done, the king, as well as all his subjects, would derive great profit therefrom not only by gaining a market for a large quantity of merchandise produced in France, but also by the importation of colonial products which would serve as a means of exchange with the ports of the Baltic.

"The great number of vessels which Dutch merchants constantly send to the French islands is proof that trade with these islands is very profitable, for otherwise they would not send 100 or 120 large ships there every year. . . . . In order that the French may profit from this commerce it is necessary to exclude all foreigners from the privileges of trade there, as the Dutch, Spanish and English have done in regard to their colonies. . . . . In this way the French could enter into the possession of all this trade and the other nations would have no right to make objections because they were excluded. . . . . Inasmuch, however, as France is not in condition to undertake all of the trade of the islands immediately, it seems wise to permit the Dutch to continue to trade for a season. To establish this trade upon a solid basis in France, His Majesty, if it so pleases him, should first issue a declaration exempting from all import duties all products brought from the islands in French bottoms."

Formont explains the importance of this latter suggestion by pointing out the fact that the import duties were most unreasonable and prohibitive of trade. Thus sugar, which sold for 30 livres the cwt., paid a duty of almost 12 livres; tobacco, selling for 20 livres the cwt., paid 10 livres, and ginger, which sold for 5 livres, paid a duty of about 12 livres. In Holland, on the other hand, these same products paid only a uniform duty of 5 sous the cwt. This was why the Dutch had been able to increase their navigation, to establish a large number of refineries where they refined the raw sugar imported from the French West Indies, and to manufacture the tobacco from the same islands, and to re-export this tobacco and

TOWARD THE FRENCH WEST INDIES

this sugar into the ports of the Baltic, into Flanders and even, in great quantities, into France. Without some such measure to take the burden off the French trader and thus place him on a fairer basis of competition with his Dutch rival, Formont asserted that "it was impossible to draw the trade of the islands to France and to take it out of the hands of the Dutch, who had become absolute masters of it." Formont closed his memoir with a warning: "If one continues to abandon this commerce to the Dutch, these colonies, which have cost the lives of so many Frenchmen to establish, will, to the disgrace of the nation, be lost forever."[4]

The author of another memoir, bearing the date of 1663, wished to accord two years of grace for the Dutch to settle up all their affairs in the islands, and to organize a French company, composed of very rich persons, to carry on this trade. He proposed that this company should equip, annually, four ships at Dieppe with cargoes of cloth, hats, shoes, stockings, tinware, etc., and a certain number of other vessels in the same port to fetch slaves from the coast of Angola and Guinea; three more at Havre and one at Honfleur with the same cargoes as at Dieppe; two at St. Malo with cargoes of cloth, bacon and brandy; four at Nantes with wine, brandy, bacon and cloth; three at La Rochelle with the same articles; and finally one at Bordeaux or Bayonne with wine, dried fruit, olive oil and fuel oil. One is incidentally impressed with the distinctly national character which the writer wished to give to the proposed commerce.[5]

A proposal was made in 1663 by Sir Nacquart, an admiralty officer at Dunkerque, "to form a new company for trade with the French islands of America." It is so

[4] Arch. Nat. Col., C$_8$, 2nd series, I, Mémoire du Sr. Formont.

[5] Ibid., series F (Com. des Col.), I, Mémoire des moyens qu'il faudrait tenir pour empescher aux estrangers le négoce des Isles de l'Amérique et de l'utilité à la France.

out of harmony with what Colbert attempted to do, when he turned his attention to the problem, and at the same time throws such an interesting light on the strong hold that the Dutch had upon the trade with the islands that it deserves a moment's notice. Nacquart proposed to form a company which would equip its vessels at Amsterdam, "where ships and cargoes of goods suitable for the trade are to be had much better and much cheaper than at any port in France." The company should make it a rule, while its vessels were being loaded at Amsterdam, to post the news when they would call at Havre, "in order that those who are accustomed to send servants to the islands may have them in readiness." It should also make an agreement with the Dutch West India Company, whereby permission would be granted to send its vessels to Curaçao and Bonaire to get live stock for the planters.[6] It is not difficult to understand why the plan was not seriously considered.

All of the memoirs just cited may have been written spontaneously by their authors as an attempt to awaken the interest of the government in establishing trade with the richest colonies which France possessed, and to arouse it to the danger of losing them forever, if action were not taken promptly to save them. They may have been written, on the other hand, in response to requests by Colbert for information or advice which he desired to have to aid him in the solution of the difficult problem before him. There is an item of evidence to support the latter view. A memoir entitled "Mémoire instructif de l'estat présent du gouvernement de la Martinique," and bearing the date of 1663 is endorsed, "En response à une demande de M. Colbert."[7] It was written by Count d'Estrades, viceroy

[6] Arch. Nat. Col., C$_8$, 2nd series, I, Proposition au Roy d'une nouvelle compagnie à establir pour le commerce des isles françaises de l'Amérique.

[7] Arch. Nat. Col., C$_8$, 2nd series, I.

of America, in response to a letter written to him by Colbert on September 21, 1662.[8] This fact certainly proves that Colbert was seeking information and advice in regard to the islands at least as early as the date of his letter. The supposition is very natural that the other memoirs, which date from almost the same time and are preserved in the same carton as the d'Estrades memoir, were also written in response to his requests. It is also possible that these memoirs represent only a part of the total number written. In any case Colbert's attention was being called to the fact that France was in possession of some rich colonies from which she was deriving no benefit and near the close of 1662 he began to make definite plans in regard to the islands.

During the course of the year 1662, the report reached France that the administration of Martinique had become corrupt, that the island was in a state of anarchy, and that more than 1000 planters had left it.[9] Colbert wrote to d'Estrades for definite information in regard to the matter. D'Estrades confirmed the report and at the same time took occasion to recount the history of the state of the island. At the death of du Parquet in 1658 the government of the island had fallen into the hands of Sieur de Vaudroque, the uncle and guardian of his children. After four years of his administration, justice had become corrupted by his constant interference in order to protect his own personal interests and those of his friends; police regulations were no longer observed; taxes were imposed arbitrarily and unequally.

"All of these disorders not only prevent the growth of the island, which is capable of a development ten times greater than it has yet received, but also will probably work its total ruin from the fact that it will so weaken it as to subject it

[8] Arch. Nat. Mar., B_2, I, fol. 109 verso.
[9] Ibid.

THE COMMERCIAL POLICY OF COLBERT

to foreign attack, or to cause the decrease of its commerce, which can thrive only under a régime that guarantees law and order, or to subject it to rebellions and internal strife."

In regard to the cessation of trade, d'Estrades stated that both the Dutch and French traders were already abandoning the island in great numbers, "some of whom are so determined under the present conditions to leave that they have withdrawn their affairs with losses estimated at eight, ten and twelve thousand livres."[10]

The matter was all the more serious in Colbert's mind, because he regarded Martinique by reason of its location, the conveniency of its harbours and the fertility of its soil, as the most important of the French Antilles, and the one which could best be utilized as the military base from which the king's power could be maintained and as the *entrepôt* for trade with the others. Colbert said to d'Estrades that it was of the utmost importance "to form a prompt and wise plan of doing something which would insure the authority of the king and prevent the deterioration of the island."[11]

The forming of the plan, or at least its execution, was not prompt because the season was "too far advanced," when Colbert wrote his letter to d'Estrades in September, 1662, to send anyone to Martinique before the following spring. As a matter of fact, more than a year elapsed before anything was actually done. In the mean time Colbert had formed the plan of sending "a man of ability and of authority" to visit not only Martinique, but also all the other French possessions in America in order to assert that king's authority and to bring them into closer relations with the realm.[12]

[10] Arch. Nat. Col., C_8, 2nd series, I.
[11] Arch. Nat. Mar., B_2, I, fol. 109.
[12] Arch. Nat. Mar., B_2, 2, fol. 132. "Je connois bien à la verité qu'il seroit du service du Roy d'apporter un remède à la trop grande

TOWARD THE FRENCH WEST INDIES

The logical choice of such a man would have fallen upon Count d'Estrades, viceroy of all the French possessions in America, but he had recently been sent as ambassador to Holland and was not available. Alexandre Prouville de Tracy was chosen in his place. De Tracy was at this time about sixty years old, having been promoted in 1651 to the rank of lieutenant-general,[13] and had "grown grey in the most glorious campaigns of His Majesty's army."[14] He was a seasoned soldier, a man of exceptional character, of a most remarkable sense of honour for the period, a loyal subject and a most conscientious official. Colbert never made throughout his career a more happy choice of a man for the performance of an important task.

De Tracy's commission bore the date of November 19, 1663. He was made "lieutenant-general in all the lands of our obedience situated in North and South America and in the islands of America." As such, he was given supreme command by land and sea of all the forces of His Majesty in America, as well as supreme judicial power in all cases whatsoever. He was instructed to administer the oath of allegiance to all the governors, members of the *conseils souverains* and the three estates, and "to establish the power of the king," and "to make all the people obedient unto him."[15]

auctorité que les gouverneurs des Isles de l'Amérique ont usurpée, mais comme l'on ne peut pas le tenter sans avoir en main des forces suffisantes pour se faire obéir et ne pas mettre en compromise l'auctorité de Sa Majesté, je vous diray en secret que je prends des à présent des mesures pour cela et que l'année prochaine ou la suivante j'espère que nous pourrons armer une escadre de vaisseaux afin de l'envoyer dans les Isles non seulement pour fortifier nos colonies, mais même pour y establir un bon ordre dans l'administration de la justice de la police et de tout ce qui pourra procurer aux habitants de ces quartiers-là une liberté entière dans leur commerce."

[13] Clément, I, 5, note 3.
[14] Du Tertre, III, 17.
[15] The text of de Tracy's commission is to be found in Du Tertre, III, 17-19.

THE COMMERCIAL POLICY OF COLBERT

De Tracy set sail from La Rochelle on February 26, 1664. He accompanied de La Barre, who was just leaving France with a colony to establish a French settlement at Cayenne. After remaining with de La Barre a short time to see that all went well with the new colony, he set sail for Martinique, where he arrived the first of June. He remained in the West Indies, for the most part in Guadeloupe and Martinique, until the close of the following spring. He then proceeded to Quebec, arriving there on June 30, 1665, and remaining in Canada until August 26, 1667, when he set sail for France. Colbert was so pleased with the way that he acquitted himself of his work that some two years later in a letter to a governor in the East Indies he cited him as a model. He there spoke of him as having given a "new life to Canada and the West Indies."[16]

The task before de Tracy in the West Indies was gigantic. He had not cast anchor at St. Pierre (Martinique) before certain planters and officers came aboard to ask redress against the injustice of the governor and they were so favourably impressed with his personality and the way in which they were received that they declared, on returning ashore, that he was an "incomparable man who would make the islands flourish under his administration."[17] The planters were so deeply in debt to the Dutch and to one another that there were many lawsuits to be settled. The courts were in such a state of corruption and confusion that de Tracy was forced to undertake the arduous task

[16] Clément, III, 2, p. 434, Letter to M. de Mondevergue, Mar. 30, 1669. For an account of de Tracy's work in Canada, see Th. Chapais, *Jean Talon, Intendant de la Nouvelle France (1665-1672)*, 64 ff.

[17] The facts related here, unless otherwise stated, are taken from Du Tertre, III, passim. Du Tertre was perhaps acquainted with de Tracy and certainly had access to the journal which he kept during his sojourn in the islands, for he says in one place, "tout ceci est tiré mot par mot du register de M. de Tracy," p. 77.

of judging cases personally. He showed such diligence and such impartiality in his decisions that "even those who were condemned went away content and praised him." His rectitude as a judge was maintained by the scrupulous way in which he refused all manner of favours. He refused both at Martinique and at Guadeloupe to lodge at the chateau of the governor. He refused to accept any presents, even those of fresh meat, confining himself to a diet of salt meat and leading a most frugal life. His conduct in this respect was so extraordinary that Colbert wrote to him in the following terms:

"If it is true that it would have been an error on your part to have failed to render an exact account of the disorders which reign in the islands, it is equally true that it would have been wrong for you to conceal the fact that you are leading such a frugal life and observing such rigid discipline. Although the sacrifices which you are making by refusing to accept the presents of refreshments, which are being offered you, and by confining yourself to a diet of salt meat, might prove prejudicial to your health and hence detrimental to the advancement of His Majesty's service, yet I am compelled to tell you that it has proved entirely agreeable to him to see that one of his commanders knows how to adjust himself to an austere life, which so few know how to do. His Majesty has not been able to praise enough to his satisfaction the good discipline which has characterized the conduct of your soldiers, who have not even turned aside from their line of march to take an orange from the premises of a farmer. If this proof of their self-restraint and of their obedience to their commanders has won the admiration of the planters in the islands, it is certain that it has not failed to call forth here praise for their chief. The great number of suits, which you have settled by forcing payments to poor servants and artisans at the hands of the little tyrants who have grown rich by the sweat of those poor wretches, has also given us cause to praise your zeal and your charity."[18]

[18] Arch. Nat. Col., C$_8$, 2nd series, I, letter from Colbert to de Tracy, September 22, 1664. This letter is of unusual interest in giving

THE COMMERCIAL POLICY OF COLBERT

De Tracy published an ordinance on June 19, 1665, which put an end to the chaos that had been reigning in Martinique under the arbitrary rule of Vaudroque. Creditors were protected by being empowered to lay claim upon the movables and even the slaves of their debtors. Uniformity in weights, measures and currency was re-established. Servants and slaves were protected against the tyranny of their masters. As a protection against the abuse of power by governors, permission was granted to emigrate to any other French colony. Arbitrary taxes were abolished and all officers were forbidden to levy other taxes than those which were wont to be levied during the administration of the late du Parquet.[19]

From Martinique de Tracy passed to Guadeloupe, where in a remarkably short time he put an end to the unrest and discontent caused by the strife between Houel and his nephews. Houel was put aboard a vessel and sent to France to answer for his conduct to the king. Arbitrary taxes were abolished and du Lion was placed in command of the island. Order and peace were completely restored. De Tracy accomplished similar work in the other islands.

Contemporaneous with the mission of de Tracy was Colbert's approval of the plan to organize the Company of Cayenne. Only very superficial facts of the formation of that company seem to be known, for it has almost escaped notice that it was connected with a much larger plan.

Lefebvre de La Barre presented to Colbert, probably at the close of 1662, a plan for the "formation of a company for the establishment of the colony at *Cap du Nord et Cayenne*," to be composed of some twenty members and

an insight into what de Tracy was doing in the islands and at the same time in disclosing what Colbert wished to have accomplished.

[19] The text of this ordinance is to be found in Du Tertre, III, 71-76.

TOWARD THE FRENCH WEST INDIES

capitalized at 200,000 livres. He said that it would be more prudent to organize only a small company, because the success of the enterprise depended upon keeping it secret from the Dutch, who would become jealous at once and try to thwart its plans. Besides it would be difficult to enlist a large number of subscribers for the enterprise, as two attempts of the French to establish colonies at Cayenne had already proved failures.[20] De La Barre proposed two chief ends for the company to realize, (1) the establishment of a strong colony at Cayenne and the occupation of the coast between the Amazon and the Orinoco, (2) the establishment of a trade with the French Antilles. In regard to the latter he was very explicit:

"As soon as a good post has been established and a colony of 500 or 600 men has been founded, the company intends to strengthen itself by enlarging the number of its members and increasing its capital. It will then equip 10 or 12 ships for an over-sea trade. I mean by that, trade with the Antilles and the mainland, which has become important. It will be very easy to do this for, inasmuch as the risk is very small to undertake a trade which merchants of every nation of Europe carry on every day, new members will not be difficult to find. . . . . The small company in this way, together with the support of the king and that of his ministers, will become large and powerful. Its ships will find not only a good port of refuge at the coast for its vessels, but also a supply of provisions. . . . . One will be able in less than two years to take possession of the trade of the islands and drive out the Dutch who will have no right to complain. This trade amounts to more than

[20] In regard to the jealousy of the Dutch, there is a very interesting passage in an anonymous letter dated at Amsterdam, January 24, 1664, "Mess. d'Amsterdam apprenans le dessein que l'on a en France de faire une descente dans l'isle de Cayenne où ils ont une colonie de 2000 en prennent de l'ombrage et y envoyent à ce qu'on dit plus de vaisseaux et de gens de guerre." Bib. Nat. MSS., 500 Colbert, 203, fol. 405.

THE COMMERCIAL POLICY OF COLBERT

6,000,000 livres annually. These two plans are so closely united that the one cannot succeed without the other."[21]

It seems very clear from this passage that de La Barre in the proposal for the establishment of a colony at Cayenne was at the same time proposing the commercial conquest of the French Antilles. His suggestion of the utilization of Cayenne as a basis for the establishment of trade with the Antilles was not a good one, for experience proved that Cayenne was far too much to the leeward to make such a thing practicable. In regard to his other suggestion, however, that the smaller company serve as a basis for the formation of a larger one, it was actually adopted by Colbert.

One naturally asks what sources of information de La Barre had at his command in the formation of such a plan. Du Tertre remarked that he "derived nearly all of his information in regard to the enterprise from Sir Bouchardeau, a man of honour and intelligence, who in the voyages which he had made to the mainland of South America and to the islands had acquired a certain knowledge which gave him a reputation as being very well informed in regard to the affairs of America."[22] Bouchardeau became a member of the company and undoubtedly aided de La Barre in carrying out his plans, for he went with him to Cayenne on the initial voyage in 1664. A memoir of 1662, found among the documents relating to the history of Cayenne, proves, however, that information was sought elsewhere and probably utilized. The memoir is anonymous and it is impossible to say to whom it was addressed, but it is improbable that it was not communicated both to de La Barre and Colbert. The author states that he had just returned from a voyage to Havre

[21] Arch. Col., C_{14}, I, fols. 85 ff.
[22] Du Tertre, III, 13. See also a note on Bouchardeau in Arch. Col., C_{14}, I, fol. 84, "B. a esté deux fois sur les lieux."

TOWARD THE FRENCH WEST INDIES

and Dieppe and that at the former place he had conferred with a captain, Paul Languillet by name, and at the latter with "a friend," in regard to Cayenne. Captain Languillet had made a voyage to Cayenne in 1660-1661 in the employment of the Dutch. He reported that at that time there were about thirty or forty men and women at Cayenne, and that one hundred and twenty slaves had recently been imported to cultivate the soil. In addition there were about fifteen or twenty families of Jews who were planters. The fort which had been built by the French (in 1652) was now under the command of Languedek, a Dutchman, and had been named Nassau. Large quantities of cane had been planted and some land had been cleared for the cultivation of tobacco, which surpassed in quality that of Brazil. Cotton and roucou grew naturally there and the cassava-plant could be easily made to grow, as could indigo. This settlement had been made by individuals and not by the Dutch West India Company. In addition to this information, given by the captain, the memorialist volunteered the following reflections:

"You will not take it amiss, if I repeat to you what I have already said in regard to enterprises of the French in establishing colonies. Captain Languillet has confirmed my opinion by saying that those who have previously tried to make a settlement at Cayenne failed, because its leaders conducted themselves with too little gentleness and with too much ostentation and pretentions and paid too little attention to production. He is of the opinion that failure awaits other attempts unless these faults are eliminated. Most of those who formed part of the last expedition were lazy and knew not how to work, a fact which caused disorders in the colony. To insure success, there is more need of a good fatherly leader who will know how to direct workmen than of a captain, all decorated with plumes and accompanied by blasts of trumpets, who knows how to command soldiers. . . . Experience teaches that the enter-

THE COMMERCIAL POLICY OF COLBERT

prises of the French have served merely for blazing the trail for other nations."[23]

Colbert straightway approved the plan presented by de La Barre, pledged his support and gained the favour of the king for the enterprise.[24] Inspired by this encouragement, de La Barre communicated his design to Pélissary, one of the treasurers of the marine, who in turn communicated it to Bibaud, one of his friends. These three, after conferences with Bouchardeau, decided to form a company. They succeeded in enlisting some fifteen others and raising a subscription of 200,000 livres.[25] Letters-patent were issued in October, which granted to the company the mainland of South America between the Amazon and the Orinoco, together with the island of Cayenne, and also a monopoly of commerce.[26]

The company sent out its first expedition from La Rochelle on February 26, 1664. It was composed of two vessels belonging to the king, *Le Brézé* (800 tons) and *Le Terron*, and of four belonging to the company, two flutes of 300 tons each, a fly-boat of 120 tons and a frigate of 150 tons.[27] There were aboard, according to a contemporary English writer, "near 1500 passengers and soldiers to recover and assert the French title as to these islands [Antilles], as to Canada and Cayenne,"[28] but there were aboard, according to Du Tertre, who perhaps was more accurately informed, only "1200 healthy strong men."[29] A food supply for one year was taken in the

[23] Arch. Col., C$_{14}$, I, fols. 190-194.
[24] Du Tertre, III, 13.
[25] A list of the stockholders is to be found in Arch. Aff. Etr., Mém. et Doc., Amérique, V, fols. 41-42.
[26] The text of the letters-patent is to be found in ibid., fols. 46-50.
[27] Bib. Nat. MSS., Mél. Col., 119 *bis*, fol. 917, letter from Colbert de Terron, Mar. 16, 1664.
[28] *Cal. St. Pa., Am. & W. I., 1661-1668*, 898.
[29] Du Tertre, III, 23.

TOWARD THE FRENCH WEST INDIES

cargo. The fleet arrived at Cayenne in May. The Dutch offered no opposition, but accepted a peaceful settlement by which they were paid something for their plantations and left the French in possession of the islands.[30] Possession was taken of the mainland on May 22. The news was published in France in July that de La Barre had met with success, that there were already three villages inhabited by three hundred families and that there "were large plantations of sugar-cane, so that according to appearances a profitable commerce could be built up in a short time."[31]

With the establishment of the colony at Cayenne and the mission of de Tracy to all the French Colonies of America, came to an end the period of preparation. The ships which bore de La Barre and de Tracy had hardly disappeared beneath the horizon before Colbert began to put in operation his larger plans for the upbuilding of commerce with the colonies across the seas.

[30] The treaty is to be found in Arch. Col., C_{14}, I, fols. 74, 90. The contract made with the Dutch governor granted him 21,850 florins for his plantation. The following items were given: A very beautiful and excellent plantation, situated at Matoury, together with ten houses, a quantity of sugar-cane ready for the mill and other planted some 10 months ago and a large crop of cassava-plant, 8000 florins; a tract of land with cane, 6000 florins; 26 trained negroes, 6850 florins; 1 dwelling-house and kitchen, 1000 florins.

[31] *Gazette,* 1664, p. 761.

CHAPTER III

THE ESTABLISHMENT OF THE WEST INDIA COMPANY. ITS CONCESSIONS, PRIVILEGES AND COMPOSITION

EXACTLY at what date the project to establish the West India Company took form in the mind of Colbert, it is impossible to say with absolute precision. Unfortunately a letter written to Colbert by Berthelot, who was soon to become one of the general directors, was not dated by the author. It is endorsed in another hand, however, "Mars, 1664," and very probably is of that date. A passage of that letter is as follows: "You may count definitely upon me for the enterprise of establishing trade with Cayenne and the acquisition of the islands of St. Christopher, Martinique and Guadeloupe and other things which will be done to sustain and extend this trade."[1] If the date of this letter is really March, it is possible to say that the plan to form a company for trade with the American colonies was made not later than that time. The plan was certainly formed before April 17, for on that day the members of the old Company of the Isles of America were commanded to bring before a specially appointed commission all papers bearing upon the sale of the several islands to proprietors. The preamble of the *arrêt* which gave this order stated very clearly that the king had decided to have the islands transferred "into the hands of a strong company, which would be able to equip a number of vessels in order to colonize and furnish them with all the merchandise of which they had need."[2]

[1] Bib. Nat. MSS., Mél. Colbert, 119, fol. 794.
[2] Moreau de Saint-Méry, I, 98-99.

TOWARD THE FRENCH WEST INDIES

Letters-patent were issued in May, 1664. To the company were granted the mainland of South America from the Amazon to the Orinoco, together with the island of Cayenne, all the French West Indies, Canada, Acadia, Newfoundland, and "other islands and the mainland of North America, from the north of Canada to Virginia and Florida," and finally, the western coast of Africa from Cape Verde to the Cape of Good Hope.

All lands within this concession, conquered and colonized by the company during the space of forty years, as well as the Antilles, already inhabited by the French, were granted with full and perpetual property rights. For the West India islands sums were to be paid to the several proprietors which would represent the original purchase price plus a certain amount for improvements and increased value, to be determined by commissioners appointed by the king. No other claims based on concessions made to former companies were to be considered valid. The company became full suzerain of all the aforesaid lands with no other obligation than that of acknowledging the king as its lord. At each change of king "a crown of gold of the weight of thirty marks" was to be presented to the new king. At the end of the forty years, it was empowered to dispose freely of all the aforesaid lands together with all forts, vessels, merchandise, etc., on the condition, however, that no sale thereof be made to foreigners without the special permission of the king. It was empowered to build forts, to manufacture ammunition, to levy troops, to build and equip whatever number of ships it chose, with the privilege of flying the royal pennant at their masts. It was further given the power to appoint governors, judges, all sorts of officials for the administration of the lands in its concession, and to make all sorts of regulations, as well as the power to declare war and make treaties with non-European kings and princes. The king pledged the support of his arms and of his vessels to defend the company against the attacks of foreigners.

A monopoly of trade was granted for the space of forty years. A single exception was made to this in the case of the fisheries of Newfoundland to which all the subjects of His Majesty were to be admitted without exception.[3] A premium of thirty livres was offered by His Majesty for every ton of merchandise exported to the colonies from France and forty livres for every ton imported into France from the colonies. This was changed almost immediately afterwards to an exemption from half the import and export duties usually paid on such cargoes.[4] A right of entrepôt was granted, whereby colonial products might be re-exported into foreign countries free from all export duties. Exemption was accorded from all import and export duties on ammunition, food supplies and other things necessary for the building and equipment of the company's vessels. Sugar, refined in any refineries established by the company, might be exported to foreign markets free of duty, if shipped in French bottoms.

The company was to be composed of the stockholders of the Company of Cayenne, of all French subjects of whatever quality and estate, and finally of all foreigners who chose to subscribe. Subscriptions could be made for 3000 livres or more. A subscription of 10,000 livres gave the right to attend the general assemblies of the company and of exercising deliberative power therein, and one of 20,000 made one eligible as general director and conferred the right of *bourgeois*. Officials subscribing 20,000 livres were freed from the obligation, imposed by the royal

[3] This exception is easily explained by the fact that too many interests of all the principal ports were centered in this industry. A study of the inquest of 1664, referred to above, reveals the fact that a great majority of the vessels suited to ocean voyages were engaged in the fisheries. Bib. Nat. MSS., 500 Colbert, 199.

[4] Moreau de Saint-Méry, I, 114.

TOWARD THE FRENCH WEST INDIES

declaration of December, 1663, of residing in the localities where the duties of their offices were to be discharged. Foreigners, contributing the sum of 20,000 livres, acquired and enjoyed the rights of native-born Frenchmen during the time that such a sum remained to their credit in the company. If this time were prolonged to twenty years, the enjoyment of these rights would become permanent.[5]

The administration of the company's affairs was vested in a central bureau at Paris and in subsidiary bureaux in the provinces wherever interests demanded their establishment. The former was to be composed of nine general

[5] Colbert made one serious attempt to interest foreigners in the company and thus to enlarge the narrow limits of its personnel. On being informed that an effort had been made by the Spanish king to attract the German princes to trade with the Indies, he drew up a memoir on the subject, in which he attempted to show that the French could offer much greater advantages. The most interesting passages of the memoir are the following: "If the kings of the North and the princes of the Empire are of a mind to consider seriously the establishment of trade with the two Indies, the king is able to make them propositions which are safe, solid and much more advantageous than all those which the Spaniards can propose. His Majesty has recently formed two large companies, one for trade with the West Indies, which already has a capital of 4,000,000 livres and fifty vessels employed in its commerce, the other for trade with the East Indies, which has a capital of 10,000,000 livres and employs more than thirty vessels. . . . The former is at present in possession of the islands of St. Christopher, Martinique, Guadeloupe, Marie Galante, the Saints, St. Croix, Grenada, Tortuga, and other islands, in which there are at present 20,000 Frenchmen; of a considerable settlement in the island of Cayenne of 1000; of Canada, where there are more than 5000 Frenchmen; of Newfoundland, with 200, and finally of a settlement on the coast of Africa [Senegal]. The kings and princes who wish to enter into this company may do so for considerable sums. In order to give a proof of the king's good will, His Majesty will furnish double the amounts furnished by them. His Majesty will also grant them the privilege of being represented by a director in the central bureau of the company's administration at Paris." Clément, II, 2, p. 429.

The plan of making a settlement on the coast of South America seems to have been seriously considered at one time by the electors of Mayence and of Bavaria. Du Fresne, who was in Germany at

directors who were to be elected in a general assembly of stockholders, three each year for a term of three years in such a way that at the end of each election six old and three new ones remained. The latter were to be composed "of merchants and of none others." The capital of the company was not fixed. Subscriptions were to be received during the period of three months, counting from the first of June.

The letters-patent thus provided for the organization of a gigantic commercial company with an immense field for exploitation, with complete and extensive powers, and with enticing inducements to attract subscribers.

the beginning of 1665 in quest of iron-workers for the establishment of foundries in France, was charged by Colbert with the task of interesting the German princes in his proposal. He wrote from Würtzburg on January 29, 1665, exposing at length the Elector of Mayence's ideas in regard to the matter and his willingness to undertake in the following spring a settlement under the protection of the West India Company. In August the two electors of Bavaria and of Mayence made the following proposals:
1. Concession of one degree of territory on the coast of Guiana. 2. The said land to be held as a fief from the king of France. 3. Shipments to be made from France. 4. Full liberty within the said concession. 5. The right to sub-feoff. 6. Privilege of making a contract with the West India Company for the transportation of settlers and of provisions. 7. Privilege of buying slaves, either at the coast of Africa directly or from those to whom the company granted the privilege of that trade. 8. Privilege of trading with all French colonies in America and with the French in Europe. Arch. Col., C_{14}, II, fols. 197-199. All of these proposals were granted. To Article 6, however, a condition was made that the ships of the West India Company alone could be used for commerce with the proposed settlement; and one also to Article 7, that slaves should be bought only from the company. No record has been found that there was a sequel to these negotiations with the Electors. Attention has been called to them because they show that Colbert made one serious attempt, at least, to give a larger development to the narrow personnel of the West India Company. His efforts proved fruitless, however, and it remained an enterprise directed for the most part by officials who had never had the necessary experience to manage its affairs wisely.

TOWARD THE FRENCH WEST INDIES

Their official registration met with opposition at the hands of the proprietors of the several West Indies. First of all, they paid no attention to the *arrêt* of April 17, which ordered them to bring all papers concerning the purchase of the islands before a designated commission, or yet to a similar *arrêt* of May 8. Their opposition continued throughout the months of May and June. Béchameil, who had been especially charged by Colbert with the organization of the company, wrote on July 1:

"I thought that I should be able to notify you today of the ratification of the letters-patent which had been agreed upon Saturday evening by the presidents [of *Parlement*]. The commissioners and M. Ferrand, reporter, in a meeting held this morning agreed to abide by the decision of the presidents, but at the moment of their adjournment they found themselves surrounded by Mesdames Champigny, Houel and de Cérillac with their families, who said that they had filed protest against the registration of the letters-patent. They cried out loudly against the concession which the king had made of their possessions in control of which one wished to place the company, even before it paid anything or guaranteed them against loss."

Béchameil added that it was of the utmost importance to prevent *Parlement* from forcing the company to make satisfactory settlements with the proprietors before entering into the possession of the islands.[6] Another letter from the same person on July 10 states that a satisfactory contract had been made with M. and Mme. de Champigny for the cession of their share of Guadeloupe and of the islands of Marie Galante and Desirade. The opposition of Houel for the cession of his share of Guadeloupe, and that of de Cérillac for the cession of Grenada continued. No agree-

---

[6] Bib. Nat. MSS., Mél. Colbert, 122, fol. 13, and also fol. 127, for a letter of July 3, in regard to the same matter.

ment was yet made with the Knights of Malta for the cession of St. Christopher.[7]

In spite, however, of this opposition of the proprietors, the letters-patent were officially registered in the *Parlement* of Paris on July 11, and on the 27th of the same month at the *Chambre des Comptes*. The company was thus empowered to enter into the possession of the lands of its concession, before contracts had been made for their transfer, for such contracts were not made until several months later.[8]

No contract was made with Houel for his possessions at Guadeloupe. He refused to sell and remained theoretically in control of them until the edict of revocation of the West India Company in 1674, when they were declared annexed to the royal domain.[9]

Before attempting to follow the history of the company in the exploitation of its grant, some questions of capital importance may be asked. Of whom was the company composed? Who were its directors to guide it in the conquest of the commerce of such a vast field? Whence came the funds placed at its disposal?

[7] Ibid., fol. 353.

[8] They were as follows: One on November 28, 1664, with the Company of Rouen, whereby the possessions of that company on the west coast of Africa (Senegal), together with its ships and merchandise, were ceded for the sum of 150,000 livres (Chemin Dupontès, *Les Compagnies de colonisation en Afrique occidentale*, p. 32); one in July, 1665, whereby the Knights of Malta agreed to cede the islands of St. Christopher, St. Martin, St. Bartholomew and St. Croix for the sum of 500,000 livres tournois; one on August 25, with M. and Mme. de Champigny for the cession of their share of Guadeloupe and of Marie Galante and Desirade, for 120,000 livres; another on August 27, with de Cérillac for Grenada in payment of 100,000; one with the Sir Dyel d'Enneval on August 14, whereby Martinique was ceded for 240,000 livres. For the statements regarding the contracts with the Knights of Malta, with the de Champignys, de Cérillac, see Du Tertre, III, 250, 266-267; for that with d'Enneval, see Arch. Col., F_2, 17, Contract d'acquisition de la Martinique.

[9] Du Tertre, III, 267, and Moreau de Saint-Méry, I, 283.

TOWARD THE FRENCH WEST INDIES

Fortunately a list of all the subscriptions, made from the beginning, June 2, 1664, until December 27, 1669, the date of the last subscription, has been preserved in the national archives at Paris. Under the date of June 2, appear the names of no less than twenty-three persons whose subscriptions, varying from sums of 10,000 to 30,-000 livres, amount to the formidable total of 520,000 livres.[10] It is upon this fact that a recent French writer, M. Chemin-Dupontès, has asserted that the West India Company met with success at the hands of public subscribers.[11] We are forced, however, to disagree with the assertion.

In the letters-patent, issued on October 12, 1663, for the formation of the Company of Cayenne, the names of its members are given. There are sixteen and all of them appear on the list of June 2. Thus sixteen out of a total of the twenty-three names are accounted for. Did the remaining seven also belong to the Company of Cayenne? Evidence points to that conclusion. In the first place, the names of the sixteen stockholders appear three times in the letters-patent, and in each case a blank space is left at the end of their enumeration, as though the list were not yet complete and more names were to be added later. Berthelot, a revenue farmer, wrote to Colbert some time before the formation of the West India Company that he could count upon his support in the affair of the maintenance of trade with Cayenne and of the acquisition of the French West Indies and added: "I shall pass the rest of the day with M. de Rambouillet ———— [not legible], my associates, and I shall let you know the results of my interview."[12] The names of both Berthelot and de Rambouillet

---

[10] This list is to be found in Arch. Nat., G_7, 1312, Estat général de toutes les actions de la Compagnie des Indes Occidentales.

[11] Chemin-Dupontès, *op. cit.*, 36.

[12] Bib. Nat. MSS., Mél. Colbert, 119 *bis,* fol. 794.

appear on the list of June 2, for the sums of 30,000 livres each. It is impossible to say for certain that these subscriptions were not made with a view to the establishment of the West India Company, but Berthelot's letter rather implies that the subscriptions were made to the Company of Cayenne. If that is true, it means that at least eighteen out of the twenty-three subscribers of June 2 to the West India Company were stockholders in the earlier company. As to the remaining five no information has been found.[13] Thus, although it is impossible to say that all the twenty-three subscriptions of the list of June 2 represent subscriptions made to the Company of Cayenne, there is a strong probability that such was the case. This means that the so-called favourable reception at the hands of the public, noted by M. Chemin-Dupontès, was nothing more than a simple transfer to the books of the new company of the capital stock of the Company of Cayenne. Such a transfer had been ordered by an *arrêt* of May 30: "The company, which has been formed for the colonization of the island of Cayenne and of the mainland of South America, is hereby dissolved, and the funds subscribed to that company hereby become the property of the West India Company."[14]

It remains to be asked whether the members of the earlier company increased their original subscriptions at the formation of the Company of the West Indies. Du Tertre states that each of the twenty stockholders of the Company of Cayenne subscribed originally 10,000 livres, or a total of 200,000 livres, but pledged their credit for an additional 10,000 livres, or for a total of 400,000 livres. De La Barre, who certainly had more opportunity

[13] Du Tertre asserts that the Company of Cayenne was composed of twenty, but that may be a rough statement which means eighteen as well as twenty-three. Du Tertre, III, 13-14.

[14] Arch. Nat., E, 1717, fol. 163.

to know the facts, states, however, in a memoir, written probably on the eve of the formation of the company, that all the associates were "resolved to furnish to the amount of 30,000 livres each, according to needs and circumstances."[15] Whether such "needs and circumstances" arose before the formation of the West India Company, we do not know. The initial expedition which the company sent to Cayenne was a large one and must have cost a considerable sum to fit out. It was composed of no less than four vessels belonging to the company, two of which were of 300 tons, and of over 1200 soldiers and settlers. It was much larger than the first fleet sent out by the West India Company at the end of the year. How great an expenditure of funds this required it is not possible to say, but it may well be that the stockholders were called upon to increase their original subscriptions in order to insure the strength and success of the establishment of the colony. Of the twenty-three subscriptions of June 2, there are eleven of 30,000 livres, five of 20,000 livres, four of 15,000 livres, and three of 10,000 livres. This might mean that all but three of the stockholders found it necessary to increase their original subscriptions to finance the enterprise. In that case, the somewhat formidable sum of 520,000 livres for one day's subscription represented nothing in the way of capital for the new company except the value of the new settlement at Cayenne and did not furnish the ready cash which is so necessary in launching a commercial enterprise.

This explains why the West India Company did not send out its initial expedition before December, some seven months after its letters-patent were granted. It would likewise explain the letter of distress which Bibaud, one of the directors, wrote to Colbert on June 10:

[15] Arch. Col., C_{14}, I, fol. 85.

THE COMMERCIAL POLICY OF COLBERT

"I feel obliged to say to you, Monseigneur, that the small fund which the company has at present and the poor prospects which it has of obtaining more, unless it is aided by the king, will ruin its reputation. It is certainly an excellent affair and one of the best that has ever been proposed in France. There are very few merchants of the seaports who would not subscribe to the enterprise, if they saw that our force was in proportion to the grandeur of the design. They know as well as we that four or five millions are necessary to make the company strong enough for that and to prevent it from failing. That is why those merchants instead of uniting with us are talking publicly of our weakness."

Bibaud added that a delay on the part of the king to come to the aid of the company meant ruin.[16] In spite of the urgent appeal of Bibaud, the royal treasury remained closed throughout the year 1664, and public subscriptions came in exceedingly slowly. Thus, for June 3, there was one of 10,000 livres, another on August 18 for 15,000 livres, and that was all until September 7. That is to say, if we except the sum of 520,000 livres entered on the subscription list of June 2, which has been under discussion, the total subscriptions for the three months of June, July and August amounted to only 25,000 livres. If the books of the company had been closed on the first of September, as was provided by the letters-patent, the company, whose task was the commercial conquest of a hemisphere, would have had at its disposal about enough money to pay a first-class clerk.

The months of September, October, November and December were more productive. During the month of September, there were four subscriptions of 20,000 livres, four of 10,000 livres and one of 3000 livres, making a total of 123,000 livres; during the month of October, there were ten subscriptions for a total of 123,000 livres;

[16] Bib. Nat. MSS., Mél. Colbert, 121, fol. 365.

TOWARD THE FRENCH WEST INDIES

in November, eight for a total of 71,000 livres; in December, ten for a total of 121,000 livres. This made a grand total of 438,000 livres for the four months.

Although the fact that the subscriptions of these four months showed a marked increase over those of the three preceding months might be taken as indicating that public interest had at last been aroused in the enterprise, it is much more probable that the difference is to be accounted for by the fact that Colbert had created, in the meantime, the East India Company and had begun to wage a veritable campaign for subscriptions to that enterprise. The story is too old to be repeated here of how Colbert brought pressure to bear upon revenue-farmers, judges, courtiers and officials to make them contribute funds. The long list of names of these classes among the stockholders of that company proves the success of his efforts. Colbert recommended to the king, in his famous *Mémoire sur commerce*, of August, 1664, that both the East and West India Company receive the hearty support of His Majesty and that everything be done to encourage them. A comparison of the lists of stockholders of the two companies will show that out of a total of thirty-six who subscribed to the West India Company during the months of September to December, seven also subscribed to the East India Company. This is a very strong indication that the new subscriptions to the West India Company were a result of Colbert's campaign of browbeating and intimidation, and that they were made out of a spirit of complacency to the king and to his powerful minister, rather than from any great interest in the company.

At the close of the year 1664, the nominal capital of the West India Company was 983,000 livres. For reasons already assigned, it is probable that not more than half of this amount represented ready capital for the company's use. This was quite insufficient to insure success.

THE COMMERCIAL POLICY OF COLBERT

Before continuing the inquiry as to the subscriptions which were made to the company in the following years, it may be asked who were the subscribers and from what classes they came.

Of the first twenty-three names on the subscription list, representing, as we have seen, the stockholders of the Company of Cayenne, information has been gleaned from various sources in regard to twenty. Of the twenty, only two were merchants and all the rest occupied various positions in the administrative hierarchy of the realm. Thus there were Béchameil, a secretary of the *conseil d'état*, Matharel, a secretary in the department of the marine, Menjot, one of the secretaries to the king, Colbert de Terron, intendant at Brouage, de La Sablière and Berthelot, revenue-farmers, etc. Very little information has been found in regard to the thirty-six new names which appear on the list from June 3 to December 31. The occupations of only nineteen are known. But of these, only four were merchants and the remaining fifteen were officials of various rank.

The point is of capital importance not only for the company under consideration, but also for all commercial companies organized during the reign of Louis XIV. Failing to gain support of merchants, either because they were too poor, or because they were not willing to risk their money in such enterprises, Colbert and his successors resorted very often to the expedient of launching such commercial enterprises by employing government officials and employees, men for the most part without experience in such matters and ignorant of the conditions of the trade which they attempted to carry on. That fact accounts for the failure of many a company and has received as yet too small attention at the hands of historians.

In 1665, the total subscriptions amounted to 1,604,360 livres. Of this sum, the king subscribed 187,000 livres on March 26; 100,000 livres on April 22; 100,000 livres on May 16, June 22, July 31; 300,000 livres on September 4, and 500,000 livres on December 4, making a total for the year of 1,387,000 livres; Colbert himself subscribed 30,000 livres; the President of the *Parlement* of Paris 8000 livres; des Forges, a revenue-farmer, 8000 livres; three members of the company increased their holdings by subscriptions amounting to a total of 22,000 livres. This leaves only 149,360 livres subscribed during the year by individuals of whom no information has been found.

The total subscriptions for the two years, 1666-1667, amounted to 1,846,440 livres. Of this sum the king contributed 1,135,000 livres; the *fermiers des aides*, 200,000 livres; the *fermiers des gabelles*, 150,000 livres; 278,940 livres were paid to the company by various farmers of the department of justice. All these sums made a total of 1,773,940 livres, leaving only a remainder of 72,500 livres for the two years, subscribed by individuals of whom no information has been obtained.

The total subscriptions for the year 1668 amounted to only 144,000 livres, of which the king subscribed 100,000 livres; the salt-farmers at Paris, 10,000 livres; the farmers of fines imposed by the Chambre de Justice at Paris, 6500 livres; making a total of 116,500 livres and leaving only 27,000 livres for subscriptions by individuals.

For 1669, the total was 944,545 liv. 8s. 6d. Of this the king contributed 404,545 liv. 8s. 6d. The remaining sum was all subscribed by members of the company, evidently as the result of corporate action which may have been dictated by Colbert.

Thus of the grand total of 5,522,345 liv. 8s. 6d., the king furnished no less than 3,026,545 liv. 8s. 6d. Almost all of the remainder was furnished by revenue-farmers, tax-collectors and officials, acting in the great majority of cases under the orders of Colbert. Only very insignificant sums were furnished by merchants or others capable of directing such an important enterprise. The West India Company was thus, from the first and remained throughout its history, a commercial enterprise created by the government, supported by it and directed by the king's greatest minister. The almost unlimited powers which had been bestowed upon it by its letters-patent were powers only in name. It was subjected at every moment to the orders of Colbert and became the puppet of his will. In a word, the company was maintained and controlled by the state to perform a national service and to make possible the success of a national policy.

CHAPTER IV

THE WEST INDIA COMPANY, 1664-1665

COLBERT imposed a difficult task upon the West India Company. He wished by a stroke of the pen to exclude the Dutch from the islands and to have the company satisfy at once the needs of the trade which they had been accustomed to carry on. He chose the somewhat plausible excuse of the danger of admitting Dutch vessels to the islands while the pest raged at Amsterdam. Accordingly an *arrêt* of September 30, 1664, forbade the governors of the islands to receive Dutch vessels, and "the trade with the Dutch began to stop, . . . and the inhabitants to suffer."[1]

Preparations to trade were made by the company immediately after the granting of its letters-patent. Béchameil, Matharel, Bibaud, Bouchet, Berthelot, Dalibert and Jacquier, all members of the Company of Cayenne, became the first directors of the new company. Béchameil was especially charged by Colbert with the direction of affairs and seems to have kept him constantly informed of what was being done. On June 5, he reported in person the details of the company's preparations. On June 28, he wrote: "In obedience to your orders I shall tell you that the West India Company is busy buying merchandise for the cargoes of the two vessels which are being equipped for the islands."[2] Two days later in another letter he complained that his colleagues were showing indifference to the company's affairs, but added that progress was being made

[1] Arch. Nat., E, 1717, fol. 209; Du Tertre, III, 92.
[2] Bib. Nat. MSS., Mél. Colbert, 119, Berthelot to Colbert, June, 1664.

and that he personally was working persistently at the task.³ Another letter of July 21 informs us that an expedition to the islands was being prepared at La Rochelle, and one on July 24 declared that within three or four days the cargoes for this expedition would be complete, but added: "We are expecting every day the arrival of our three vessels which are to come from Holland and Bayonne. If they arrive at the time which we expect them, they will be ready to sail for the islands on August 1."⁴

Either the "three vessels from Holland and Bayonne" did not arrive or other obstacles arose which prevented them sailing, for, as a matter of fact, the first expedition of the company did not sail from La Rochelle until more than four months later. This delay may have been due to the fact that the company, as has been shown, did not have adequate funds at its command to equip an expedition at such an early date. In the meantime, something had to be done to supply the pressing needs of the islands. The situation was all the more exacting, because news which Béchameil received was rather disconcerting:

"I have received intelligence from Holland that no vessel has sailed for the islands for a long time, and that none will be sent because it is feared that our company will prevent them from discharging their cargoes."⁵

There seems very little doubt that the Dutch had considerably diminished the number of vessels which they sent ordinarily to the islands, for Du Tertre tells us that suffering was great there.⁶ One might explain this diminu-

³ Ibid., 121 *bis,* fol. 1010.
⁴ Ibid., fol. 809.
⁵ Bib. Nat. MSS., Mél. Colbert, 122, fol. 699.
⁶ Du Tertre notes the arrival of two Dutch vessels at Martinique two months later. One of these vessels had a cargo of 300 slaves, the other a cargo of horses from Curaçao. "This aid, brought by the Dutch at a time when need was so great, reopened the wound which had been made by the rupture of commerce with them." Du Tertre, III, 101.

TOWARD THE FRENCH WEST INDIES

tion by saying that it was due to the approaching struggle with England, or yet, as has been suggested, by the fear that the West India Company would assert its monopoly and prevent Dutch vessels from discharging their cargoes. A letter from Matharel, one of the directors of the company, written on July 22 to Colbert, suggested another explanation of more than passing interest:

"There is reason to believe that the Dutch have delayed sending several vessels which had already been partly freighted for the islands, because they feared to find an opposition on the part of our company to the sale of their merchandise and to the freighting of their vessels for the return voyage. I am of the opinion that with these motives there is mixed a bit of malice aforethought with the desire to cause by this means a dearth of supplies in the islands and to make the planters cry out against our company, if it cannot supply promptly the aid and refreshments which they need. M. Béchameil, who is of the same opinion, will inform the other members of the fact and they will not fail to take measures to meet the situation."[7]

Béchameil was of the opinion that to meet the crisis the merchants of La Rochelle, Dieppe and Havre, who were accustomed to send vessels to the islands, should be compelled either to send some on their own account, or to charter them to the company.[8] No records have been found, however, which show that this suggestion ever bore fruit. The first fleet of the company was not ready to sail before the middle of December. On December 13, de Chambré, the general agent of the company for the islands, wrote that four vessels were ready to sail and that for "the most part they were new, mounted by one hundred pieces of artillery, well equipped in every respect, well laden with

[7] Bib. Nat. MSS., Mél. Colbert, 122, fol. 793.
[8] Ibid., fol. 699.

THE COMMERCIAL POLICY OF COLBERT

cargoes of food supplies and merchandise for the islands."[9] Aboard the flag-ship, *L'Armonye,* was de Chambré, on the vice-admiral, the *St. Sebastien,* were de Clodoré, the new governor of Martinique, his wife, priests and curates, and clerks who were to be charged with the distribution and sale of the company's merchandise.

The fleet sailed from La Rochelle on December 14, with favourable winds. The third day out a storm arose which separated all the vessels, but they were all reunited except *Le Mercier,* which was seen no more by the others, until their arrival at Martinique. On reaching the Canaries, *La Suzanne* left the other two in order to pursue her way to Cayenne, for which her cargo was intended. *L'Armonye* and the *St. Sebastien* called at the Cape Verde Islands to pay their compliments to the Portuguese governor and thus prepare the way for good relations between him and the company. This done, they continued their route to Martinique, where they arrived in February, 1665.[10] There they found *Le Mercier,* which had sailed with them from La Rochelle, *Le Terron,* a vessel of the king, which had sailed also from La Rochelle a short time before them with a cargo of provisions for the troops of de Tracy, and *La Fortune,* a vessel belonging to the company which had sailed from Nantes about the middle of December.[11]

[9] Ibid., 134 *bis,* fols. 454-455. The fleet was composed as follows:

	Tons	Passengers Can- non	Crew Soldiers
L'Armonye (flying the Admiral's pennant)	300	24	160
St. Sebastien (Vice-Admiral's)	250	16	153
Le Mercier	400	16	120
La Suzanne	300	16	160

The fleet had thus a total of 1250 tons, was armed with 72 cannon and had on board 593 persons. Du Tertre, III, 160.

[10] *Relation de l'Amérique,* I, 14.

[11] Arch. Nat. Col., C₇, I, letter from du Lion, April 8, 1665; *Gazette,* 1665, No. 156.

TOWARD THE FRENCH WEST INDIES

The arrival of these five large vessels, with cargoes of food supplies and of merchandise, was hailed with joy. For a moment the bitterness, which had been felt at the news that the islands had been placed in the hands of a company, was forgotten. When the sale of merchandise began, the planters gathered in great numbers from all parts of the island. Everyone sought to have a supply of wine, of salt meat, of powder, of lead, of cloth, of shoes, of hats, and of everything of which they had need. The willingness of the company to grant credit seemed unbounded. Consequently nothing seemed too dear to buy. The worst knaves and the most insolvent planters were the loudest in their demands and bought the most. Many persons who would not have been given a pound of salt meat on credit by the Dutch, received a whole barrel from the company. The distribution of merchandise was made with such confusion, that to those who had demanded salt meat was bailed out brandy.[12]

The extravagance which the company displayed on this occasion was due to lack of judgment and to failure to protect its interests. It had chosen a corps of employees who were unprepared for their duties. De La Barre insists that for this fact the directors were not to be blamed, as they were forced "to take those who offered to go into a land so little known as yet and the directors believed that they had accomplished much in being able to find persons who were willing to make a voyage which appeared, even to the most hardy, a great undertaking."[13] The agents who were chosen believed that the company was under obligations to them for their willingness to go to the islands, and they conducted themselves as though all were owed to them and they owed nothing to the company. Whatever may be the explanation of the choice which was

[12] Du Tertre, III, 166-167.
[13] *Relation de l'Amérique,* I, 15-16.

made of inexperienced and, as events proved, of rather insolent agents, two very deplorable facts resulted from it. In the first place, the affairs of the company were very poorly administered and serious financial losses were inevitable from such a scene as the début at Martinique; in the second place, the haughty character and the domineering spirit of these agents alienated the planters, for de La Barre remarked "that their severity, presumption and foolish pride destroyed in the planters all the respect which they might have had for the company."[14]

The relatively small amount of supplies furnished by the company caused dissatisfaction. "It seemed like a drop of water upon the tongue of a man with a fever."[15] The planters began to murmur and cry out against the company, saying that it could not satisfy their needs itself and yet prevented the Dutch from doing so. Still greater was the disappointment and still greater the discontent, when the *St. Sebastien* and *L'Armonye* sailed from Martinique without discharging their cargoes. It was then that the planters began to consider more closely the West India Company and began to fear the renewal of suffering which the islands had experienced under the earlier companies. They cursed it and expressed openly their sorrow at the exclusion of Dutch traders. If there had been some means of escape, many would have left the island. Efforts to silence these complaints and to calm this spirit of discontent proved ineffective. A rebellion was threatened and would probably have broken out at once had not de Tracy been at Martinique and exerted his influence for the company.[16]

It was indeed fortunate that de Tracy was still in the islands and that the inauguration of the company could

[14] Ibid., pp. 17-18.
[15] Du Tertre, III, 167.
[16] Ibid.

take place under his high authority. The dignity of the high commission which he held from the king, and the sterling qualities which he possessed as a brave soldier and an honest man, inspired both fear and love for him among the planters of the islands.

February 19, 1665, was chosen as the day for the formal ceremony of the company's inauguration at Martinique. On that day, in obedience to official summons by de Tracy, the *conseil souverain*, the clergy, the nobility, representatives of the *tiers état* assembled in the marketplace before the Chamber of Justice. They were surrounded by a great crowd of the common people. De Tracy appeared and, accompanied by de Chambré and de Clodoré, entered the Chamber, followed by the different estates. Only a small part of the common people could gain admission to the hall.

After the assembly was called to order, de Chambré arose and declared that he was bearer of the king's proclamation which made the West India Company lord of the islands. In presenting it to de Tracy, he demanded in the name of this company that it be read and officially registered and that the company be placed in possession of the island of Martinique. The registration of the proclamation was forthwith made. The acquiescence of the whole assembly was obtained on the condition that the interests of the children of du Parquet, the former proprietor of the island, be safeguarded. De Tracy thereupon declared the company in possession of the island. De Clodoré then presented his credentials and was declared governor. Oaths of fidelity to the king, to the company and to de Clodoré were straightway taken by the *conseil souverain* and the three estates. Whereupon, de Tracy expressed his high esteem for de Clodoré and exhorted all to accord him their obedience and their support. A reply by de Clodoré formally ended the ceremony.

THE COMMERCIAL POLICY OF COLBERT

The assembly quit the hall and gathered in the square, where several barrels of wine furnished by the company had been tapped. The health of the king was drunk amid the shouts of the people, "Vive le Roi!" and the booming of the cannon of Fort St. Pierre. "The health of the company was drunk even by the planters, for wine makes all the world akin." Feasting followed, and the same toasts were drunk with joy. Thus the day passed, and the West India Company had entered, apparently under good auspices, into the possession of Martinique.[17]

On the morrow, February 20, de Tracy, with de Chambré, sailed for Guadeloupe. Here on March 3, before an assembly composed of the three estates, he declared the company in possession of the island and renewed in its name the powers of du Lion as governor.[18] In the months following, the company took formal possession of St. Christopher, St. Martin, St. Croix, St. Bartholomew, St. Domingo, Marie Galante and Grenada.

Nowhere does the inauguration of the company seem to have been received with joy or without murmur. At St. Christopher, so we learn from a letter written by de Sales, the governor, the oath of allegiance to the company was taken with a pronounced lack of enthusiasm, some of the important planters absenting themselves from the

[17] Du Tertre, III, 168.

[18] Arch. Nat. Col., C_7, I, Prise de pos. de l'isle de la Guad. We learn from a letter written by du Lion to Colbert under date of April 8, that this ceremony was followed, as at Martinique, by drinking and feasting: "We left the hall to gather in the square, where several barrels of wine had been tapped, and there we had the honor to drink the health of the king amid the shouts of 'Vive le Roi!' and the booming of cannon. We then attended the banquet offered by the West India Company to the most important persons of the island. It was spread beneath an arbor which had been prepared at the Place d'armes. . . . There were eighty-two covers on each side which proved insufficient. . . . Courtesy, order, entertainment and rejoicing characterized the occasion." Arch. Nat. Col., C_7, I.

ceremony on purpose not to take it. The principal officers and planters assembled and drew up a series of ten articles, in which they sought a guarantee that the rights which they had enjoyed under the proprietorship of the Knights of Malta would be respected by the company.[19] The great majority of these articles concerned questions of taxation and feudal dues. Article 6 demanded that the relations with the English should continue unchanged, that is to say, that trade should be carried on freely between the two nations. The articles were presented to de Chambré and his response demanded. In reply to Article 6, he said that it would be impossible to recognize the principle of free trade between the two nations, but added: "Nevertheless, as it would not be reasonable to let the planters remain in need, the said agent agrees that, whenever there is not to be had in the stores of the company any articles of which the planters have need, they may demand a permit from the general agent, which shall be granted freely, and they may forthwith purchase the said articles either from English merchants, or wherever else they choose."[20]

At the coast of St. Domingo and the island of Tortuga, the company encountered long and bitter opposition. In spite of the heroic efforts of the able governor, Ogeron, whom the company had placed in command, the untamed spirit of the buccaneers and freebooters refused to submit to the rule of a commercial company.

At Guadeloupe the planters, although in a spirit of submission, viewed the departure of the Dutch with sadness. Du Lion wrote to Colbert on April 8, 1665: "The liason of the planters with the Dutch is still dear to them [the planters]. The oldest and well-to-do inhabitants are Dutch and have always maintained a correspondence with

[19] Du Tertre, III, 255.
[20] Ibid., p. 265.

THE COMMERCIAL POLICY OF COLBERT

Holland. I have already informed you that these islands received much aid from these foreigners. . . . Most of the excellent sugar-mills which we have here were built from capital furnished by the Dutch." Du Lion closed this interesting letter by expressing the hope that the company would send enough vessels to satisfy the needs of the planters.[21]

It was, however, at Martinique, the most important and the most central for trade with the islands, that the West India Company met with the spirit of greatest opposition. Its inauguration in the island, described above, was auspicious only in appearance. In reality there was much murmuring among the people. The very evening following the ceremony, the spirit of revolt against the company was manifest. Some shots were fired. De Tracy, however, persuaded that there was no immediate danger, sailed for Guadeloupe on the morrow. But the sails of his vessels had not long disappeared from view before a revolt broke out.

One of the chief clerks of the company, du Buc by name, went into the district, Prêcheur, situated immediately to the north of St. Pierre, to establish a warehouse for the sale and storage of merchandise. He found a very pronounced spirit of antagonism. There were murmurings against the company, because it sold its merchandise too dear. Soon after his arrival he was attacked by a little band of rebels, led by one Rodomont. He succeeded in gaining his boat and making his escape amid a shower of stones and the cries of rebellion: "Aux armes! Vive M. du Parquet! Narque de la compagnie!" Du Buc immediately reported the affair to de Clodoré, who at once took prompt action, fearing lest the revolt become general. He gave orders to different captains to hold their troops in readi-

[21] Arch. Nat. Col., C₇, I, April 8, 1665; also ibid., letter May 11, 1665.

ness and sent one, whom he trusted, into the infected quarter to learn the state of affairs. The captain reported at his return that Rodomont and some five or six of his immediate followers were preparing a general revolt and that for this purpose they were going from house to house to gain adherents. The governor sent de Laubière, his lieutenant, to take into custody the young du Parquet, in order to prevent the rebels from placing him at their head and from using him as a pretext for revolt against the company. Then de Clodoré, at the head of a small body of troops, marched against the mutineers.

The spirit which characterized the governor's actions during the first trying months of his service to the company may be very well illustrated by the following incident, occurring at this time and related by Du Tertre:

"A captain who apparently would not have been sorry to see the rebellion succeed, had the boldness to ask the governor, just before he started on his march, whither he was going, saying that everyone was in revolt, and asking if there were some enemies to fight in the island. The governor, who was not a man to be frightened by such questions, replied proudly: 'I am going to chastise the seditious and I'll fire a pistol at the head of the first person who fails to respond to his duty. As for you follow me!' Whereupon he forced the captain to follow him, which he did without daring to say a word."[22]

Thanks to the vigour and the promptness of attack, the resistance offered by the rebels was small. The principal leaders were promptly arrested. Rodomont was hanged and three of his companions were condemned to the galleys, another was banished, the rest were pardoned. Thus ended the first rebellion against the company. De Clodoré suppressed it before it had a chance to become well organized, and for this he received warm commendation

[22] Du Tertre, III, 189.

from Béchameil, in the name of the company, and from Colbert, in the name of the king.[23]

In the meantime, the company had not been idle in France. Special boards of directors were chosen at Rouen and La Rochelle. Agents or correspondents were established at Honfleur, Havre, Dieppe, St. Malo, Nantes, Bordeaux, and in Holland. Contracts were let for the construction of vessels in different ports of France. By early summer of 1665, "two very beautiful ships" had been launched, and two others were to be ready by the end of the year. At St. Malo another large vessel was being built for the company. On the eve of its completion, in November, 1665, fire destroyed half of its hull.[24] Many more vessels were purchased. Janon, the French consul at Middleburg, seems to have been charged with the purchase of vessels for the company. Thus, on April 17, 1665, he wrote to Colbert as follows: "There arrived here, two or three days ago, a French crew from Havre, sent to me by the West India Company to man a vessel, which, in accordance with its orders, will take cargo at St. Malo and sail thence for the West Indies."[25] A week later he wrote that some Flemish merchants had bought a vessel of 260 tons which he had intended to buy for the company.[26] One of the directors affirmed in a memoir that before the end of the year 1665 the company was in possession of fifty-two vessels.[27]

[23] Pierre Margry, Les Seigneurs de la Martinique in *Revue Maritime et Coloniale*, vol. 58, publishes a letter written by de Chambré; see Du Tertre, III, 192-193, for the texts of the two letters. De Chambré remarked that, in the opinion of all the islands, de Clodoré had conducted himself most admirably in the affair.
[24] Arch. Col., F_2, 17, Mémoire de la Compagnie des Indes Occid. sur l'Etat où elle se trouve, 1665; Bib. Nat. MSS., Mél. Colbert, 133, fol. 328, Letter from Béchameil to Colbert, November 14, 1665.
[25] Bib. Nat. MSS., Mél. Colbert, 128 *bis,* fols. 898-899.
[26] Ibid., fol. 1048.
[27] Arch. Col., F_2, 15, Mémoire, 1665.

TOWARD THE FRENCH WEST INDIES

All accurate records of the vessels sent out to the islands and of their cargoes has, perhaps, been lost for ever by the disappearance of the company's registers. The *Gazette* has preserved, however, some important information.[28] A dispatch of January 23, 1665, from La Rochelle, noted sailings for the island of vessels belonging to the company, as follows: one from Bordeaux on January 8, one from Texel (in Holland) about the same time, and two from La Rochelle on the 15th. The dispatch added that twelve more vessels were being equipped at La Rochelle for trade with the islands, "for," it remarked, "the company has undertaken a commerce which formerly gave

[28] In a dispatch of December 21, 1664, from La Rochelle, the following news is given: "A few days since, there sailed from this port with favourable winds, seven vessels for the Islands of America. They form a part of the vessels which the West India Company is having equipped here and in several other ports of France for its commerce. The Sieur Chambré, general agent of the said company, was aboard, as were also the governor, the lieutenant, and other officers which the company sent out to take possession of the islands and to establish trade. There was also a large number of passengers. Many, in fact, were obliged to remain behind, but will sail on the six large vessels which the same company is diligently preparing together with some of the most important merchants of this city who have an interest in it." *Gazette,* 1664, No. 156.

This will be recognized at once as the description of the sailing of the first fleet, which has been noted above. It will also be remarked that it differs very much from the information which has been reported from Du Tertre, for that historian states that only four vessels composed the first fleet and the *Gazette* says seven. Inasmuch as Du Tertre gives such definite details in regard to the tonnage, equipment and number of persons aboard each vessel, one would be inclined to suppose that the account given in the *Gazette* was purposely exaggerated in order to stimulate subscriptions to the company. If one adopted such a view, the reliability of later reports found in the *Gazette* would be seriously called in question and all information gleaned from that source would be of doubtful value. Fortunately a letter, written by de Chambré to Colbert, on the eve of departure of the fleet from La Rochelle, makes it possible to reconcile the two accounts. "There are ready to sail from this port several vessels belonging to the West India Company, *L'Har-*

THE COMMERCIAL POLICY OF COLBERT

employment to 100 or 120 ships. It will send out to the islands at least eight or ten each month."[29] From Dieppe came the news that on January 14 there sailed from that port two vessels which had been equipped by orders of the company's directors at Rouen. Other vessels, belonging to the company, it stated, had sailed from the same port only a few days before. Four more vessels would be prepared to sail at the end of the month.[30] There is thus indicated by the *Gazette* a total of eight ships sailing for the islands during the month of January, 1665.

The company had, however, allowed its expenditures to run far ahead of the amount of money subscribed to it or

monie, *Le St. Sebastien, Le Mercier* and *La Suzanne,* all of 300 to 400 tons. . . . There has already sailed a little vessel named *Le Cheramy,* to carry dispatches to M. de Tracy. She carried also a cargo of merchandise. Another vessel, named *Les Armes de la Compagnie,* which is almost laden and is of 500 tons, will sail in five or six days. This makes six vessels without counting the one belonging to the king, named *Le Terron.* Another vessel, named *La Marie,* of about 400 tons, which is being equipped in this port, will sail in about fifteen days." Bib. Nat. MSS., Mél. Colbert, 134 *bis,* fols. 454-455.

It is to be noticed that in the first part of this letter, the information which Du Tertre gives about the sailing of the first fleet is entirely confirmed. It remains to be seen if the report printed in the *Gazette* is also confirmed. The dispatch in the *Gazette* is dated at La Rochelle on December 21, a week after the sailing of the fleet. De Chambré remarked that *Les Armes de la Compagnie* would be ready to sail on December 18 or 19, which would make a total of six vessels going to the islands without counting *Le Terron,* which had sailed a few days before the fleet, and arrived at Guadeloupe on February 3. (Arch. Nat. Col., C₇, I, letter from du Lion, April 8, 1665.) It is possible that *Les Armes de la Compagnie* sailed before December 21, as de Clodoré thought it would do, and that the writer of the dispatch from La Rochelle included it and *Le Terron* in his count, so that he reported that seven vessels had sailed for the islands. This would seem to offer a plausible explanation of the lack of agreement between the dispatch printed in the *Gazette* and the account given in Du Tertre. It enables one to accept with more conviction the later reports which appear in the *Gazette.*

[29] Ibid., 1665, p. 109.
[30] Ibid.

placed at its disposal. It is necessary only to recall what has been recounted in a former chapter to know that the total subscriptions for the year 1664 amounted only to 983,000 livres, and that probably of this sum only about 500,000 livres, at most, represented funds which could be expended by the company. It was not with such a comparatively small sum that the purchase of many vessels and of many cargoes could be made.

The directors frankly admitted that their expenditures had been much larger than their funds. They justified their conduct to Colbert in the following way:

"Inasmuch as the first design in the establishment of the said company was to exclude from the islands the Dutch traders, who were in control of commerce, and as it was not possible to do that except by sending at once enough merchandise for the subsistence of the planters, the directors should not and could not have regulated their expenditures according to the sums actually subscribed to the company. . . . The letters of M. de Tracy, filled with complaints that not half of what was necessary was being sent to the islands, justified haste, and when he wrote that it would take at least eighty vessels and 3,000,000 livres worth of merchandise to satisfy the needs of the islands and drive out the Dutch (which is much exaggerated), the said directors were forced to make large expenditures for vessels and merchandise."[31]

These large expenditures alarmed the stockholders and made them fear that they would be held responsible for the debts of the company to an amount larger than that of their subscriptions. To allay this fear, an *arrêt* of December 16, 1664, was published which guaranteed shareholders in the company against any such responsibility.[32] In spite of this assurance, subscriptions came in very slowly. Thus,

[31] Arch. Col., F_2, 15, Mémoire des Directeurs de la Cie. des Ind. Oc. pour rendre raison à Mgr. Colbert de leur conduite, 1665.
[32] Arch. Nat., E, 1717, fol. 259.

for the first month of the new year, 1665, only five were received for a total of 53,000 livres. The king had not as yet contributed a cent. Colbert seemed too absorbed in the promotion of the East India Company to devote much attention to the affairs of the West India Company.

Colbert did open a small source of revenue for the company by granting it, on February 12, the farm for the collection of a special import duty of 6d. the pound, levied at Rouen on sugar and wax. The farm was granted on the condition that the company pay yearly 24,000 livres to the city of Rouen and 20,000 livres to the king, or a total of 44,000 livres. The surplus was to go to the profit of the company. With the exception of the year 1666, when the revenue was 1601 liv. 8s. 6d. less than the aforesaid 44,000 livres, the farm proved a source of profit, varying from 11,669 liv. 15s. in 1665, to 77,981 livres in 1672, and representing, for the years 1665 to 1672, a total profit of 372,478 liv. 8s. 3d. The company also profited from the fact that it was not forced to pay this tax on the sugar which it imported from the islands to Rouen. It is to be remarked, however, that although the farm later proved profitable, it offered no immediate relief to the company, for it yielded a gain of only 11,669 liv. 1s. in 1665, a loss of 1501 liv. 18s. in 1666, and a gain of 18,151 liv. 16s. in 1667, or a total gain for the first three years of less than 30,000 livres.[33]

The directors were forced to seek money elsewhere. They decided, in their meeting of February 11, to borrow 600,000 livres. An *arrêt* of February 14 authorized the company to borrow the said sum "for one year and at whatever rate of interest it chooses, for the pay-

[33] Arch. Nat., G$_7$, 1312, Extrait du grand livre de la Cie. des Ind. Oc. "Comptes des droits de 6d. pour livre sur les sucres et cires entrants en la ville et banlieu de Rouen." Chemin-Dupontès, pp. 37-38.

ment of which sum the directors may pledge all the effects of the company." It was from the *fermiers généraux des aides* that the sum was borrowed.[34] With these funds at its disposal the company was enabled to continue its shipments, which had been interrupted during the last two weeks in January and throughout the month of February. On March 3, three large vessels sailed from La Rochelle for the islands. Three others were being equipped in the same port and would be ready to sail within another week. On March 6, another sailed from Honfleur and according to the calculations of the directors at Rouen, two more would be ready to sail from Dieppe at the end of the month.[35]

In spite of the very praiseworthy efforts made by the directors, the company had not proved itself equal to the task of satisfying the needs of the islands. Thus, near the beginning of April, 1665, de Chambré wrote from Guadeloupe to de Clodoré: "We are in about the same state of affairs as you. The proof is that I should be obliged to drink water, if it were not for the fact that M. de Tracy is here. As for meat, five days from now there will not be a pound in our stores. It is for this reason that both you and we are in great need of the arrival of vessels. It must be that bad weather has prevailed, for according to the letters which I have received, eight or ten vessels should have arrived."[36] Du Lion, governor of Guadeloupe, wrote about the same date that the company was not sending more than half enough vessels to satisfy the needs of the planters.[37] Even the vessels which had been sent lately failed to contain in their cargoes one important article,

---

[34] Arch. Nat., E, 1717, fol. 259; Arch. Col., F$_2$, Mémoire sur la Cie. des Ind. Oc., 1667. Against 55,000 livres of this amount shares of the company's stock were issued.

[35] *Gazette*, 1665, p. 254, La Rochelle, March 6, 1665.

[36] Du Tertre, III, 195.

[37] Arch. Nat. Col., C$_7$, I, April, 1665.

THE COMMERCIAL POLICY OF COLBERT

a fact which, according to Du Tertre, aroused much discontent against the company. This article was shoes for the women. "This omission," remarks the historian, "was all the more dangerous, because it aroused natures more sensitive and vindictive than those of men. When the women saw that there was nothing for them in the company's ships and that some of them would have to go barefooted to mass, they lost patience. It is certain that the anger of the women who had thus been disappointed contributed much toward the rebellion of which we shall have occasion to speak presently, especially so, for in the islands women have much influence over their husbands."[38]

The company had also failed to provide enough small barks by which the transportation of crops from the plantations along the coast to centers of trade was made. The harvest in the islands gave promise in the spring of 1665 of being "so abundant that more than twenty vessels seemed necessary for its exportation."[39] Du Lion remarked that only about half enough vessels were in sight to take away the products of Guadeloupe. Letters from different ports of France to correspondents in the island brought the news that the West India Company refused to transport merchandise of individual traders in spite of the promises which had been made to the planters.[40] All of these things, together with the fact that the company sold its merchandise much dearer than the Dutch had been accustomed to do, caused a widespread feeling of discontent and of rebellion in the islands, and especially in that of Martinique, where rebellion shortly afterwards broke out.

First came word to de Clodoré from one of the company's agents that some rebels in Cabesterre had hoisted

[38] Du Tertre, III, 218-219.
[39] Ibid.
[40] Arch. Nat. Col., C₇, I, April 8, 1665.

TOWARD THE FRENCH WEST INDIES

the Dutch flag with the cry, "Vive les Hollandais et les Flamands!" The governor let the incident pass unnoticed for the moment in order to abide a more favourable season to reply. A few days later, the planters of Basseterre came in great numbers to present a petition to the governor, in which they complained that the company had failed to carry out the regulations established by de Tracy. The framers of the petition had been very careful to address de Clodoré as governor for the king, and not as governor under the authority of the West India Company. De Clodoré received the petition and read it. Thereupon, he harangued the crowd, urging patience and promising to send the petition to the company and to exert his own influence in obtaining satisfaction for them. He urged them to remain loyal in the meantime, and not to assemble again without his permission. Thanks to the spirit of moderation of some of the planters, the governor's words were heeded. Promises were made to be obedient to his requests, and the crowd dispersed, apparently in a spirit of submission.[41]

This was followed a short time afterwards by a similar demonstration on the part of the tobacco "stringers," who were the most turbulent class in the islands and who during about half the year were idle, spending their time roaming from plantation to plantation, from cabaret to cabaret, and who "under the shadow of bottles and mugs hatched out all the rebellions in the Antilles." They marched in great numbers to the governor. De Clodoré was indignant at seeing such a crowd and refused to listen to their grievances unless they chose some representatives to present them to him. The governor's wishes were complied with. Their representatives made the complaint that the agents of the company were insolent and that only about half of their needs were being satisfied

[41] Du Tertre, III, 217.

by the company. De Chambré urged patience, assuring them that in a short while the stores of the company would be adequately supplied to provide plenty for all. "To remove present disorders, they had only to place an honest planter in each store who could supervise the distribution of merchandise, with the understanding that if the clerks did not heed the orders given them, he [de Chambré] would either dismiss them, or punish them according to their merits. This gave satisfaction, and for the second time a band of rebels disbanded, apparently contented."[42]

Both de Clodoré and de Chambré were so alarmed over the spirit of the planters, however, that they decided to build a fort as a refuge in time of rebellion. Plans were accordingly drawn up, the foundations dug, the stones dressed, all the material collected and the construction actually begun, when orders arrived from the directors of the company to stop the work. It is to be remarked that the directors gave these orders on the recommendation of de La Barre, who had recently returned to France, and who made the recommendation apparently through hostility to de Clodoré. The fact is worth noting, because the hostility between de Clodoré and de La Barre became very pronounced in 1666 and was not without certain importance in the history of the company.

Béchameil seems to have recognized the importance of sending ships to the islands in order to quell the spirit of revolt, for he wrote to Colbert that it was necessary to send twenty vessels to the islands during the months of April and May.[43] It was undoubtedly to enable the company to accomplish this that Colbert decided at last to aid it financially. On March 16, he made a personal subscription of 30,000 livres, but much more important was

[42] Ibid., pp. 220-221.
[43] Bib. Nat. MSS., Mél. Colbert, 128, fol. 30.

TOWARD THE FRENCH WEST INDIES

the fact that he opened the royal treasury. Thus there were subscribed, in the name of the king, 187,000 livres on March 26; 100,000 livres on April 22; 100,000 livres on May 16; and 100,000 livres on June 22, making a total of 487,000 livres furnished by the royal treasury within the space of three months.

The company was thus enabled to send out immediately two expeditions. About May 15, a fleet of seven vessels sailed from La Rochelle for the islands, and on May 17, four others sailed from St. Malo.[44] None of these vessels arrived in time, however, to prevent a very serious rebellion at Martinique, which arose in the following way. In the regulations established by de Tracy at Martinique on March 17, 1665, it was provided that the ships of the company should transport into the ports of France sugar, tobacco, indigo, and other products for the planters at the rate of seven livres the hundredweight, all import duties to be paid by the company. The company refused to be bound by this agreement, for de Tracy, in establishing the rate, supposed that the exemption from the payment of one-half the import duties ordinarily levied in France on products of the islands was valid not only for goods belonging to the company but for all those imported in its ships, and therefore thought that the company would be obliged to pay only two livres as import duty and would have the remaining five livres the hundredweight as payment for transportation. This, however, was not the case, for the revenue-farmers demanded four livres per hundredweight on all products belonging to individuals and brought by the company's own ships. The company felt itself justified in interpreting the spirit of de Tracy's regulation by demanding five livres per hundredweight for freight and four livres instead of two for the import duty,

[44] *Gazette,* 1665, p. 510.

thus making a total of nine livres instead of seven.[45] An *arrêt* of the *conseil d'état* of June 6, 1665, sustained the company's decision and, when judgments were rendered in the admiralty courts of Dieppe and Rouen against the company in favour of individual merchants who refused to pay more than seven livres per hundredweight on goods consigned to them from the islands and transported in the company's vessels, another *arrêt* of November 26, 1665, annulled the decisions and ordered the *arrêt* of June 6 to be enforced.[46]

This refusal of the company to abide by the regulations of de Tracy was taken as an excuse by some planters at Martinique to stir up a rebellion. On June 1, in the district of Casepilote, one Guillaume Roy with ten or twelve companions attacked the agent of the company and forced him to flee for his life. They were joined by about a hundred other planters and sacked the company's store, with cries of "Aux armes!" They forced everyone to obey the cry and marched from plantation to plantation exciting all to rebellion. They attempted to win as their leader Sieur de Merville, a lieutenant, assuring him that they were in communication with all the other parts of the islands and that by the morrow all would be in their hands. At his refusal they attempted to win Sieur de Lisle, who in his turn refused the command by feigning a case of gout, and went straightway to inform the governor.[47]

Again the courage and promptness of de Clodoré saved the day for the company. "The diligence which the governor showed is almost inconceivable. It was one o'clock in the afternoon when he received news of the outbreak of the rebellion. Casepilote was a distance of ten long miles over a very difficult mountain road. Nevertheless, he

[45] Arch. Nat., E, 1717, No. 297.
[46] Arch. Col., F$_2$, 17, Extrait de Reg. du conseil d'état.
[47] Du Tertre, III, 226-227.

TOWARD THE FRENCH WEST INDIES

assembled his troops and arrived there before nightfall, which comes before six o'clock."[48] On the point of departure, de Laubière, the lieutenant-governor, informed him that rebellion had also broken out in the district of Carbet at three miles distance from St. Pierre, and that there were signs of a general rebellion. De Clodoré commanded the ships in the harbour to draw as close as possible to the shore in order that their cannon might be utilized in case of emergency. He then set his troops in march to attack the rebels of Casepilote.

On arriving in the district of Carbet, he found that the rebels had taken flight and returned to their homes. At Casepilote, a loyal lieutenant, de Valmenière, had persuaded many rebels to return to their allegiance. The rest fled to the woods at the appearance of the governor with his armed force. De Clodoré was firmly resolved to punish the leaders of the revolt and yet was afraid that he would frighten them farther into the woods. Sharp practice was resorted to. He had an interview with the curate of the district in which he said that it was necessary for everyone to return to his post of duty and employed other ambiguous expressions, so that good curate inferred that the governor would pardon everyone, and so announced it in the church on the morrow. This announcement gave assurance to all those whom fear had driven into hiding and even the most guilty, except two, returned to their homes. But the two were captured by a sergeant who was implicated in the rebellion, and who thereby gained his pardon. All the leaders were then arrested and imprisoned.[49]

No sooner had this rebellion been put down than the news came of the preparation of a more serious uprising in Cabesterre. It presented the most difficult task which

[48] Ibid., III, 226.
[49] Du Tertre, III, 229.

the governor had yet encountered, because it was the district the farthest distant from St. Pierre and the most inaccessible of the whole island. Promptness and shrewdness again proved effective. De Clodoré at once sent to Cabesterre, du Chesne, a lieutenant, with twelve soldiers of his own troops. In order to disguise the real purpose of the act he commanded du Chesne to arrest Planson, the West India Company's agent in the district, against whom the planters were making violent complaints. At the same time he wrote a letter to de Vepré, one of the commanding officers in Cabesterre, to send him full information of the rebellion, and to conduct into his presence his father-in-law, Sieur de Massé, one of the chief planters and also one of the leaders of the rebellion. It was in this way that the rebellion was suppressed before it had a chance to break out.

Fortune again played into the governor's hands. This time he received news in advance of a plot being formed at Canonville. A Jesuit priest appeared, conducting into his presence a woman who was the wife of one of the conspirators in a plot. On being assured that her husband would not suffer, she disclosed to the governor that the night before some fifty men had come to her house and had a prolonged conference with her husband and that it was there agreed that on the morrow at nightfall, two hundred armed men would assemble to march straight against the governor. Again the principal leaders were arrested and another revolt was nipped in the bud.[50]

It is necessary to reflect only for a moment to recognize in these rebellions and plots of rebellions a spirit of unrest and discontent which was all but universal at Martinique, and which had not proved disastrous for the authority of the company, because an energetic and courageous governor held the reins of power.

[50] Du Tertre, III, 231.

TOWARD THE FRENCH WEST INDIES

De La Barre, who was actually at Martinique en route from Cayenne to France, was requested by de Clodoré to give his opinion as to the punishment which should be meted out to the leaders of the late rebellions. He replied in writing under date of June 20:

" . . . Before expressing my opinion on this matter, I deem it necessary to consider two things of importance. The first is the condition of the islands and the state of mind of the planters; the second, the interests of the company. As to the first, one should recognize that the planters are composed of two classes, namely those who have property and hence interests at stake, and those who have none nor the means of acquiring any. Both classes are sore from the fact that His Majesty has prohibited the commerce of the islands to foreigners. They are both convinced that they will be made to suffer losses in their commerce, in the value of their property and in their affairs in general. . . .

"As to the interests of the company, it is undeniable that from its début the company has not been able to furnish the islands with supplies in the same abundance as foreigners had been accustomed to do for more than twenty years. It is to the interest of the company to silence complaints, to appease the troubled spirits, and to break up the factions of do-nothings who would be able in course of time to win the more influential planters to their cause, who might join them either from a desire to protect their own interests or from fear of seditions. It is thus clear that it is to the company's interest to calm the spirit of rebellion and to make it possible for every one to return to work. . . . To accomplish this two things, I believe, are necessary, namely, a prompt settling of all cases now pending before the courts and an assurance of pardon for all those who have reason to fear. Let matters be conducted in such a way that . . . punishment may fall on a few and fear on all."[51]

De Chambré expressed the opinion that the rebellions at Martinique were being caused by two classes of people,

[51] Du Tertre, III, 234-237. See also *Relation de l'Amérique,* I.

the riffraff, and the merchants, who as a consequence of the company's monopoly remained without employment and with their stores empty and their fortunes wrecked.

"To tell the truth as I see it," remarked Du Tertre, "one must seek for the real cause of all these rebellions in the inveterate hatred of the people against the name of a company and its agents. This hatred has always been stimulated by the adroit employment of two bugbears which have been dangled before the eyes of the planters by those who have wished to be masters of the commerce. The first is the small amount of succour furnished by the first two companies and the tyrannical and capricious spirit of their agents, the second is the high price at which supplies are sold by companies."[52]

Whatever may be the principal causes of this spirit of rebellion, it is certain that affairs at Martinique were in a bad way in this summer of 1665, and that the West India Company, more than a year after its creation, had not proved itself equal to the task of satisfying the needs of the planters, of stimulating the growth of industry and of building up a thrifty trade. It must not escape notice, however, that the spirit of rebellion seems to indicate that the monopoly of trade was being asserted by the company and that Dutch vessels were no longer bringing merchandise from Holland. If this be true, it means that a part of Colbert's plan in creating the company had been, at least temporarily, realized.

It may be recalled that according to the dispatches contained in the *Gazette*, the company sent out eleven vessels during the month of May. It apparently sent no more until the month of July. During the first week of that month, three of its vessels sailed from Havre for the islands. They were all three captured by the English frigates, searched for Dutch goods, but allowed to con-

[52] Du Tertre, III, 238.

TOWARD THE FRENCH WEST INDIES

tinue their way.[53] Béchameil wrote to Colbert on July 23, 1665, that 200 soldiers would be sent to Martinique "aboard vessels which will sail during the month of August."[54] But no records have been found of the sailing of vessels either during the month of August or during the months following. One of the company's vessels arrived from the islands at Dieppe about July 1, and on the 6th another at Havre with a cargo valued at 150,000 livres. On July 15, there arrived at Dunkerque "one of the first vessels which the West India Company had sent out to the islands of America. It had a cargo of tobacco and sugar."[55]

No evidence has been found, however, which makes it possible to say that the number either of vessels sent out to the islands, or of those received in France, was of importance. One of the directors asserted in a memoir that the company received but small returns from the large outlay of capital in the islands. This explains why the company was in its chronic state of lack of funds. Its books were still open for subscription, but no appreciable sums were subscribed. Colbert was forced to provide funds. On July 31, the king subscribed 100,000 livres, 300,000 livres on September 4, and finally, 500,000 livres on December 4. This made a total of 1,387,000 livres subscribed by the king within ten months. The large subscription of December 4 was perhaps made in order to

[53] *Gazette*, 1665, p. 699. These three vessels were probably those referred to in the following extract from the Calendars: "Warrant to the commissioners for Prizes at suit of the French West India Company, the three ships of Dieppe, the *Jonas*, the *Hercules*, and *Florissant*, laden with goods for Barbary and Martinique which will spoil if they wait the usual forms of the Admiralty Court." *Cal. St. Pap., Dom., 1664-1665*, p. 476, July 14, 1665. The *Jonas* was captured near Brest, on its return, by English corsairs.

[54] Bib. Nat. MSS., Mél. Colbert, 130 *bis*, fol. 905.

[55] *Gazette*, 1665, p. 699.

THE COMMERCIAL POLICY OF COLBERT

aid the company in the crisis of an approaching war with England.[56]

The company's commerce became considerably embarrassed by English corsairs. During the summer and fall of 1665, although France and England were yet nominally at peace, they captured five vessels belonging to the West India Company.[57] In order to offset these losses, an *arrêt* of February 24, 1666, authorized the West India Company to seize, either on land or on sea, English goods to the value of 620,000 livres, notwithstanding the three months

[56] Arch. Nat., G$_7$, 1312.

[57] Arch. Nat., E, 1733, fols. 93-95. Arrêt portant represailles contre les Anglais pour la Cie. des Ind. Oc., February 24, 1666; *Gazette,* 1666, No. 897; Arch. Col., F$_2$, 15, Mémoire importante pour la Cie des Ind. Oc., 1667. *La Fortune,* 250 tons, captain J. Thomas, laden in July, 1665, at the island of Martinique with a cargo of 8000 rolls of tobacco, of which 5800 belonged to the company and the rest, together with a certain quantity of sugar, ginger and other goods, to planters of the said island, en route for France, was captured by some English vessels under the pretext that the vessel was of Dutch construction and in spite of the protests of the captain, was taken to Nevis and afterwards to Jamaica. Loss, 120,000 livres to the company and 40,000 to individuals.

The *St. Jean d'Hambourg,* Nicolas Billiet, captain, laden at Hamburg with a cargo of masts, tar, clay, lumber and other merchandise for the company, was captured by English corsairs, in September, 1665, taken to Dover, ordered released, recaptured and taken to Plymouth. After a delay of six weeks, the Admiralty Court ordered its release, but merchandise to the value of 60,000 livres was seized under the pretext that the king had need of it. No payment had yet been made for the said merchandise in February, 1666.

The *St. Pierre* of La Rochelle, Pingault, captain, was captured in the English Channel in October, 1665. It had a cargo of sugar, tobacco and other products laden at Guadeloupe, and belonging to the company and planters of said island. It was taken to Plymouth and declared good prize. Loss to the company, 100,000 livres and "much more to individuals." . . .

The *St. Jean de Dieppe,* 300 tons, Le Moyne, captain, which had sailed from Dieppe in May, 1665, for Cape Verde and Senegal, on its return voyage was forced by stress of weather to put into Waterford, Ireland. In spite of the assertion of the captain that his vessel and cargo were French, it was seized and searched. "Many letters were

TOWARD THE FRENCH WEST INDIES

grace which had been granted English merchants at the declaration of war in January.[58] The British Admiralty Courts granted the West India Company £10,639 9d. sterling for its claims in regard to the *St. Jean* of Hamburg, the *Jonas* and the *St. Jean* of Dieppe. They declared the *St. Pierre* good prize and refused to pronounce judgment on the *La Fortune* before receiving news from Jamaica.[59] The directors of the company asserted that the total loss sustained from these captures amounted to 465,900 livres.[60]

Navigation became so dangerous that an embargo was laid which forbade French vessels, without special permission, to go into the English Channel, or to carry on commerce with England, Scotland, or Ireland.[61] Béchameil addressed a memoir to Colbert in November, 1665, to explain the very serious embarrassments which the company faced in the present crisis. "The company," he said, "has at present twenty vessels in the ports of the Channel and in Holland, which already have their cargoes or are ready to take them."[62] In addition it had two vessels char-

found in her directed to merchants in Amsterdam and to others of the United Province. Many Dutch were also found aboard." The vessel with her cargo was therefore ordered confiscated. Loss to the company, 50,000 livres. *Cal. St. Papers, Ireland, 1663-1665*, p. 669, contains a letter from the Earl of Orrey to Secretary Arlington, of November 15, 1665, in which the news is given of the capture of the *St. Jean*. Id. 1666-1669: "Copy of the note of the appraisement of the *St. John* of Dieppe, her apparatus and goods."

Le Jonas was captured near Brest in the fall of 1665, and confiscated at Tangier. Her cargo, according to the estimates of the British authorities, was about 60,000 livres.

[58] Arch. Nat., E, 1733, fols. 93-95.

[59] Arch. Aff. Etrang., Mém. et Doc., Amérique, V, fol. 268.

[60] Arch. Col., F_2, 17, Mémoire des pièces touch. les navires pris par les Anglais avant la déclaration de la guerre.

[61] Bib. Nat. MSS., Mél. Colbert, 133, fol. 328.

[62] They were as follows:

At Havre:
  Le Mercier, 400 tons, with a cargo for Cayenne. It will take 120 young women together with a certain number of servants.

THE COMMERCIAL POLICY OF COLBERT

tered. Of these twenty-two vessels, fourteen were actually taking, or prepared to take, cargoes for the West Indies; one, the *St. Pierre*, had been captured on its return from Guadeloupe. There were thus fifteen out of a total of twenty-two occupied with the trade of the islands. To these must be added the three vessels indicated in the memoir as being ready to sail for the coast of Guinea, whence they were to carry cargoes of slaves to the islands, making thus a grand total of eighteen. Only one vessel was destined for Cayenne and one for Senegal, and none for Canada. This is quite a striking indication of how completely the affairs of the company were centered in the islands. Béchameil

> *Le St. Michel* with a cargo for the islands. It is to call at Madeira.
> *Le Marsouin*, 300 tons, with a cargo for the islands. It is to call at Madeira.
> *La Marie*, 350 tons, with a cargo for the islands. It is to call at Madeira.
> At Honfleur:
> *St. Jean*. Is taking cargo for the islands.
> At Dieppe:
> *L'Espérance*, 300 tons, with cargo for Cape Verde Islands and Senegal.
> *La Bergère*, 250 tons, to take cargo for the islands.
> At Dunkerque:
> *Les Armes de France*, 350 tons, with cargo for the islands.
> *St. Antoine*, 130 tons, to take cargo for the islands.
> At St. Malo:
> *Le Grand St. Jean*, with cargo for the islands.
> *La Pucelle*, 260 tons, with cargo for the islands.
> *Le Lion d'Or*, 250 tons, to take cargo for the islands.
> In Holland:
> *La Justice*, 300 tons, ready to sail with cargo for Guinea.
> *L'Angélique*, 350 tons, ready to sail with cargo for Guinea.
> *Le St. Guillaume*, 350 tons, ready to sail with cargo for Guinea.
> *L'Yrondelle*, 160 tons, ready to sail with cargo for the islands.
> *Le Comte François*, 300 tons, ready to sail with cargo for the islands.
> *Le Dauphin*, to take cargo in France for the islands.
> [These last two were chartered by the company.]
> In Zealand:
> *La Lucorne*, 250 tons, ready to sail with cargo for the islands.

TOWARD THE FRENCH WEST INDIES

informed Colbert that the four vessels at Havre were waiting for the six from Holland in order to sail in company with them, but added that "unless they were escorted by some armed vessels, it would be very dangerous to let them risk the voyage." He requested that a suitable escort be provided by the king.[63]

How many of these vessels really sailed it is not possible to say. The *Gazette* fails to indicate any sailings for the West Indies between those of the month of July, 1665, which have been noted above, and the month of March, 1666. An order was issued on December 14 to the Admiralty officials of St. Malo to permit three vessels, *Le St. Jean, La Pucelle* and *Le Lion d'Or*, to sail from that port for the islands.[64] Janon, French consul at Middleburg, wrote to Colbert, under the date of December 4, 1665, that two vessels had recently sailed for the islands from that port by way of the north of Scotland, but had been forced to return on account of bad weather.[65] Were these vessels two of those belonging to the West India Company mentioned in the memoir of November, 1665? If so, it would seem to indicate that the plan of sending the vessels in Holland with those actually at Havre by way of the Channel had been abandoned, either because suitable escort

At Gothenburg:
Le Chariot d'Or, with a cargo of masts for La Rochelle.
In England:
Le St. Pierre, 260 tons, with a cargo from the islands.
    The vessel referred to above as being captured by English corsairs.
At Hamburg:
    A flyboat with a cargo for France. Arch. Col., F$_2$, 17, Mém. de la Cie. des Ind. Oc., Besoin des Isles et Terre ferme de l'Am. et la nécessité de pourvoir à la seureté des pais de ladite compagnie tant pour lesd. Isles que pour la Guinée dans la conjoncture de la rupture avec les Anglais.
    [63] Ibid.
    [64] Arch. Aff. Etrang., Mém. et Doc., Amérique, V, 193.
    [65] Bib. Nat. MSS., Mél. Colbert, 134, fol. 131.

THE COMMERCIAL POLICY OF COLBERT

could not be furnished by the king, or because prudence dictated such a course. If this be true, it is more than probable that the vessels from Havre did not sail. There is a passage in a memoir presented by the directors to Colbert in May, 1666, which seems to indicate the same thing:

"The company has at present, in the ports of Holland, of Zealand, Dunkerque, Dieppe, Havre and St. Malo, fifteen of its vessels freighted for Cape Verd, Senegal, Cayenne and the West Indies, which have been waiting for three months for the Channel to be free. There is more than 600,000 livres worth of merchandise in these vessels. . . . The company can very well stop making new purchases, as it has actually done, for it is well supplied with vessels, but it cannot afford to stop its expeditions to the islands for, besides the fact that the planters would suffer, it would be unable to market in France all the merchandise which it has on hand to the value of 1,000,-000 livres."[66]

Of the twenty-two vessels enumerated by the memoir of November, 1665, the *St. Pierre* was being detained in England as a prize, *Le Chariot d'Or* was at Gothenburg, and a flyboat was at Hamburg. The other nineteen were in the ports of Holland and of northern France. Of these nineteen we have already indicated that the passports were issued on December 14 to three vessels, *Le St. Jean, La Pucelle* and *Le Lion d'Or*, to sail from St. Malo for the West Indies. *La Pucelle* and *Le Lion d'Or*, however, did not proceed at once to the islands, for both were at La Rochelle in April, and they formed part of de La Barre's fleet which sailed from that port in June.[67] *Le St. Jean* did continue its way to the islands, for its presence at St. Christopher on April 27, 1666, is noted by the *Gazette*.[68]

[66] Arch. Col., F$_2$, 17, Estat prés. des affaires de la Cie. des Ind. Oc. de France, mai, 1666.
[67] Du Tertre, IV, 116.
[68] *Gazette*, 1666, p. 975.

TOWARD THE FRENCH WEST INDIES

Thus we know positively that three of these nineteen vessels sailed. This leaves sixteen vessels of which we have no information up to the beginning of May, 1666. The memoir of May, 1666, says that fifteen of the company's vessels had been waiting for three months to set sail. It is more than probable that the phrase "depuis trois mois" does not state, or did not attempt to state, with precision the time which the vessels had been kept waiting. We know, as a matter of fact, that this is true in regard to *La Justice* and *Le St. Antoine*, for the former is indicated in the memoir of 1665 as being in Holland ready to set sail, and the latter at Dunkerque also ready. These vessels, however, did not set sail from Holland before May 25. They turned the north of Scotland and arrived at Martinique on July 28.[69] We have no less than four long dispatches written from the islands and published in the *Gazette* of 1666. They bear the dates of April, May and August, 1666. None of the other sixteen vessels in question is mentioned as being in the islands.[70] It seems highly probable, therefore, that the West India Company's commerce, so far as the important northern ports were concerned, was almost completely blocked during a period of several months. We have no positive evidence of any important aid at all being sent to the islands by the company between July, 1665, and June 7, 1666, the date of the departure of the expedition sent out from La Rochelle under de La Barre's command, of which an account will be given in the following chapter.

The close of the year 1665 marks the end of the first period of the West India Company, for, shortly after the beginning of the following year, the war with England began, which, as we shall see, had an important influence

[69] *Gazette*, 1666, p. 752, and No. 138, p. 1166. Letter from Martinique to the directors of the West India Company.
[70] Ibid., 1666, Nos. 106, 115, 138, and 157.

THE COMMERCIAL POLICY OF COLBERT

upon its history. One naturally pauses to ask what the company had been able to accomplish. We are fortunate in having had preserved for us, in the few papers of the company which have survived, a memoir presented by the directors to Colbert, very probably in the month of November, 1665, and containing a statement of the things which the company had done. The most interesting passages are the following:

"After a year or a little more, the company has, to the astonishment of all nations, placed upon the sea sixty vessels of 200, 300 and 400 tons, of which it has bought, or had built, forty representing an outlay of 1,200,000 livres. . . . It has laden vessels for 1,500,000 livres worth of various sorts of merchandise for the islands, 150,000 livres for Canada, 200,000 livres for Senegal, Cape Verde and the coast of Guinea. Returns are beginning to come in from the islands, but in such small measure that the company has not as yet received any revenue of importance, for it has received only tobacco, for which there is no sale on account of the Dutch war. The only profit gained is that from freight. It has been spent for the repairing of vessels in order that they might return promptly to the islands. . . . The pressing need to supply food-stuffs and furnishings in order to prevent a recurrence of the deplorable state of affairs of last year, has forced the directors to stock all of the warehouses, situated in the ports where the company has subdirectors and correspondents, with a supply of these articles . . . so that the company has in these several warehouses goods to the value of more than 600,000 livres, without counting the contracts which it has made for the delivery of salt meat.

"Inasmuch as the number of vessels which the company has at present cannot satisfy the needs of commerce in all of the countries which His Majesty has conceded to it, the said directors have made contracts for the construction in France of several more, which are actually being built. Two of these vessels, large and beautiful, have already been launched and two more will take the water before the end of the year.

TOWARD THE FRENCH WEST INDIES

"The company has also amassed a supply of lumber, flax, cordage, tar, masts and other things necessary for the calking, equipment and armament of its vessels. Thus by its orders two large flutes have come from Hamburg with full cargoes of these articles, the value of which amounts to 20,000 or 25,000 écus.

"Besides all of this . . . it has taken possession of the different lands of its concession, or rather restored them to the allegiance of His Majesty. For this it has had to make large expenditures, as in the case of Cayenne, of Cape Verde and of Senegal, and besides to buy the several islands from proprietors, for which it assumed large obligations, amounting to more than 1,000,000 livres, of which sum it has actually paid 154,000 livres and must pay the remainder on the dates exacted by the contracts.

"This is but a short résumé of the things which the company has accomplished since its establishment."[71]

The West India Company had, in fact, as this memoir asserts, done much to deserve praise. It had occupied with varying success different parts of its concession. Thus, near the beginning of 1665, it sent Sieur Jacquet to Senegal as the director of its commerce.[72] By the end of the year, according to the claims of its directors, it has established there a post of sixty men and merchandise to the value of 250,000 livres. It has already been noted that it sent out one of its vessels, *Le St. Jean*, from Dieppe, in May, 1665, which on its return was captured with its cargo in November, 1665.[73]

Efforts had been made to develop trade on the coast of Guinea in order to supply the islands with slaves. Thus, on February 8, 1665, a contract was made with Sieur Carolof, " heretofore commander for the West India Com-

[71] Arch. Col., F₂, 17, Mémoire de la Cie. des Ind. Oc. sur l'état où elle se trouve et les secours qu'elle attend du Roy, 1665.
[72] Labat, *Nouvelle Relation de l'Afrique,* I, 16.
[73] Arch Col., F₂, 15, Mémoir, 1665.

pany and at present a naturalized French citizen, assisted by Jean André, Baron de Woltrogue, a German gentleman and his brother-in-law." This contract gave Carolof command for six years of all posts which he might establish in the kingdoms of Luango, Congo, Angola, and all others situated on the coast of Africa between the equator and the Cape of Good Hope. It bound him to carry to the French islands all negroes captured or gained by trade. He was given full freedom to sell these negroes freely in the islands, on condition that the company's agent be permitted to choose seven per cent of them before they were offered for sale. All products received in exchange were to be brought directly to La Rochelle, Dunkerque, or any other port of France. All sugar was to be delivered directly to the company at the rate of eighteen livres per hundredweight net. The company assumed the obligation to pay all import duties and the expense of unloading the cargo. Of all merchandise sent to France directly from the coast of Guinea, Carolof was to pay seven per cent to the company. Finally, Carolof was permitted to fly the company's ensign on all vessels which he employed in this commerce. In November of this same year, 1665, the company had three vessels in Holland ready with cargoes to sail for the coast of Guinea. Whether these vessels had been equipped by Carolof in fulfillment of the above contract, or by the company on its own account, the writer is unable to say. In a later chapter it will be shown that Carolof commanded an expedition equipped by the company in 1670 and sent to Martinique with cargoes of slaves. He was also in Guadeloupe in 1672, engaged in the same trade.

The company had also taken possession of Canada in 1665. It sent three large vessels there during the course of that year.[74]

[74] Arch. Col., F_2, 15, Mémoire sur le Canada par les directeurs de

TOWARD THE FRENCH WEST INDIES

Most important of all, the company had taken possession of the several West India islands and thereby had brought to an end the period of proprietary rule, and had restored these islands to the national domain. It gained for itself, thereby, a rich field for the development of its commerce, and it was in this field that it expended its most important efforts.

What had the company done in equipping vessels and establishing commerce? It is necessary to correct an error which has been repeated time after time in endeavoring to answer this question. The *Dictionnaire du Commerce* of the *Encyclopédie méthodique*, in its article on the West India Company, remarks: "The funds to maintain such an extensive commerce were proportional to the enterprise and were so considerable that in less than six months the company equipped more than forty-five vessels, by means of which it took possession of all the lands of its concession and established trade with them."[75] This statement has been accepted by Bonnassieux and repeated from him by Chemin-Dupontès.[76] We have already seen that the first expedition of the company was not sent out before December 14. That is to say, the West India Company, far from being able to arm "more than forty-five vessels in less than six months," armed seven at the most before the end of the year 1664, which was nearly eight months after its letters-patent were granted. It has also been shown that the company was not able to take possession of the islands before February and the months following of the year 1665. Furthermore, the directors of the company claimed in the memoir, written probably in November, 1665, and quoted above, that the company had at that

la Cie. des Ind. Oc., 1666; *Cal. St. Pap., Am. and W. I.*, 1661-1668, No. 1227.

[75] Tome I, p. 641.

[76] Bonnassieux, *Les Grandes Compagnies de Commerce*, p. 371; Chemin-Dupontès, pp. 36-37.

time at its disposal some sixty vessels, of which forty were owned by it, and the remainder, it is to be presumed, chartered. It is nowhere claimed in that memoir that the company had actually equipped and sent out that number of vessels. On the contrary, as has been seen, at the end of 1665 the company had some twenty vessels locked in the Channel ports and in the ports of Holland, unable to sail on account of the danger of being captured by English corsairs. It has also been shown that almost all these vessels were still at anchor in these ports in May, 1666. But May, 1666, is two years after the establishment of the company. So that it is more than probable that it had not, even at that date, actually equipped forty-five vessels for voyages to the islands, and that, therefore, the statement quoted from the *Encyclopédie méthodique* is entirely inaccurate.

According to the sailings reported in the *Gazette* in 1664 and 1665, fifteen of the company's vessels sailed from La Rochelle, one from Nantes, one from Bordeaux, four from St. Malo, three from Havre, two from Dieppe, and one from Honfleur, and one from Texel (Holland), which makes a total of twenty-eight. One cannot be sure, of course, that the reports in the *Gazette* contain a complete list of all sailings for the two years, but it is probable that they indicate the approximate activity of the company. If so, it is a most creditable showing, especially when one considers that the company's capital was small, and that it did not succeed in sending its first expedition to the islands before December, 1664, and that consequently the above figures would represent the sailings for the year December, 1664, to December, 1665. Furthermore, the list of vessels which the company had ready to send out in November, 1665, shows that it was well on the road to increase the trade which it had begun. As compared with what the French East India Company had

TOWARD THE FRENCH WEST INDIES

accomplished within the same period, results were very encouraging. It is the most creditable showing that any commercial company had ever made in France.

There can be but little doubt that the directors had worked conscientiously against great odds for the accomplishment of the gigantic task of driving out the Dutch and of supplying the islands. There can also be but little doubt that they had fallen far short of attaining this goal. Even if it be supposed that the company had actually sent out the sixty vessels said to be at its disposal in November, 1665—the most favourable estimate which was made of its activity—it would still be far short of supplying the place of the hundred or hundred and twenty vessels which the Dutch had been accustomed to send to the islands annually according to the estimate of de Formont. The cries of "Vive les Hollandais!" which resounded through Martinique told their story of the company's failure to supply the needs of the planters.

In spite of the 1,387,000 livres contributed by the king during the last ten months, the end of the year 1665 found the company deeply in debt. To the total of 2,587,000 livres of subscription was opposed an indebtedness of more than 4,000,000 livres. Its deficit amounted, in January, 1666, to more than 2,000,000 livres.[77] To aid the company to escape from its financial embarrassments, the directors made a most interesting suggestion:

"The directors, in searching for every means to sustain the company, cannot refrain from proposing to Monseigneur [Colbert] a suggestion which he entertained at one time himself, of uniting the two companies [the East and West India Companies] and thus place the funds of the East India Company at the disposal of the West India Company. . . . Or one might consolidate a part of the capital of the former, say for 1,000,000 or 1,500,000 livres, with that of the latter and

[77] Arch. Col., F_2, 17, Mémoire de la Cie. des Ind. Oc., 1665.

place two or three of its directors on the board of the West India Company."[78]

This suggestion was not adopted, but it is most interesting in disclosing to us the fact that Colbert had at one time thought of uniting the two companies and thus bringing into existence a company even more gigantic in its scope, and offering to it the world for its conquest.

The West India Company faced the outbreak of a war, which was destined to occur in the following year, heavily burdened with debt and with its ships locked in the ports of northern France. It was highly regrettable that just at a moment when it seemed prepared to advance upon the road of commercial expansion, the affairs of state dictated a declaration of war with England which called into play all the company's capital and all of its resources for the military defense of the islands, and thus made it impossible to use them for the development of its commerce.

[78] Arch. Col., F_2, 15, Mémoire des Directeurs de la Cie. des Ind. Oc., mai, 1666.

CHAPTER V

THE WEST INDIA COMPANY, 1666-1667

THE year 1666 dawned beneath the clouds of an approaching war. It has already been seen that the company's commerce suffered from the captures operated by English corsairs and that the English Channel was considered too dangerous to risk the cargoes of merchant vessels in its waters. The directors seem to have entertained at first some hopes of maintaining neutrality between the two nations in the islands. "The orders of the court and of the company to the governors to maintain the principle of neutrality," says Du Tertre, "were so explicit that they considered it as a matter which had been agreed upon." One of the directors of the company, Pocquelin by name, seemed so convinced of the fact, that, so late as May 2, 1666, he sent out a vessel with a cargo of wine under instructions to call at Barbadoes to trade, before proceeding to Martinique.[1] De Sales, the French governor at St. Christopher, seems to have renewed the treaty with the English governor that peace would be maintained between the two nations in that island, in case of a declaration of war in Europe.[2] These hopes, however, proved vain. The war was destined to prove more violent in the islands than in Europe.

No attempt will be made here to follow the events of the war. The reader will find a detailed account thereof in Du Tertre. It will be attempted to give an account only of those events in which the interests of the company were

[1] Du Tertre, IV, 10.
[2] Ibid., p. 4.

THE COMMERCIAL POLICY OF COLBERT

affected and in which it was called upon to expend its energy in the defense of the islands.

The official declaration of war against the English was signed at St. Germain-en-Laye, on January 26, 1666. Du Tertre makes a very serious charge against the West India Company in regard to notifying the islands of this fact. "The English governors," he says, "received the news of the fact by the middle of April, whereas the West India Company displayed such small diligence in informing our governors that Captain Forant, commanding the *St. Nicolas*, which bore the dispatches of the court, did not sail from France before the month of March, so that the commander, de Sales, was killed [in the first battle at St. Christopher] before learning from France the news of the declaration of war."[3]

We have, however, a letter from de Clodoré to Colbert, dated at Martinique, May 23, 1666, in which he says: "I received on March 19, the letters which His Majesty and you did me the honour to write on February 2 and 6, and by which I was informed of the declaration of war against England."[4] It seems very evident from this letter that either Du Tertre was misinformed or that there was some unexplained negligence on the part of de Clodoré at Martinique in sending news to St. Christopher. The latter is highly improbable. On the contrary, either the government or the company showed promptness in communicating the news to the islands. The declaration of war signed on January 26, letters written on February 2 and 6, received at Martinique on March 19, is a most respectable schedule for the seventeenth century.

De Clodoré, before the arrival of the news, became convinced of the bad faith of the English and made preparations for the conflict. Thus he sent a special warning to

[3] Du Tertre, IV, 13.
[4] Bib. Nat. MSS., Mél. Colbert, 138 *bis*, fol. 684.

TOWARD THE FRENCH WEST INDIES

de Sales, governor of St. Christopher, to be on his guard. Du Lion, the governor at Guadeloupe, was warned personally by de Chambré, and the governors of the other islands by letters. De Clodoré completed the forts and batteries which were under construction at Martinique, increased his forces and put everything in such good order that all approaches to the islands were well guarded against attacks by the enemy. Du Lion likewise placed Guadeloupe in a state of defense. The governors of St. Christopher, Marie Galante, Grenada and St. Domingo, in response to the warnings given by de Clodoré, prepared their forces of varying strength for the conflict.[5]

The company, however, had not made adequate provision for the protection of the islands. Ammunition was exceedingly scarce. There was not enough in all the islands to sustain a battle of two hours' duration. This was partly relieved by the fact that the Dutch brought 800 pounds of powder to Guadeloupe. Furthermore, there was a scarcity of food supplies which made the planters murmur against the company. It was not wholly responsible for this fact, however. The vessels which were ready with their cargoes to sail for the islands in November, 1665, did not do so, because suitable escorts could not be furnished by the king to conduct them beyond the zone of danger. Béchameil had distinctly stated the necessity for such escort. Colbert seems to have made no response to this request and, in failing to do so, he must be held at least partially responsible for the lack of ammunition and food supplies which the company's vessels would have brought.

Fortunately the islands did not suffer seriously from these facts, because the English were not prepared to take the offensive. They seemed to think that the French were in an excellent state of preparation. Thus Governor Wil-

[5] Du Tertre, IV, 4 ff.

THE COMMERCIAL POLICY OF COLBERT

loughby wrote to the king on May 12, 1666: "The French spare no cost to supply their plantations with shipping, men, arms, and ammunition, all from home, and keep garrisons in every island, well paid and disciplined, all done by a company."[6]

The edition of the *Gazette* for September 3, 1666, was devoted entirely to the description of the first important event of the war in the islands. The headlines announced: "The details of the defeat of the English and of the capture of their forts, arms and standards in the island of St. Christopher in America effected by the French under the command of M. de Sales, commander under the authority of the West India Company."[7] It told the story of the victory gained by the French in April preceding. The English had been reinforced by some 600 or 700 men, principally buccaneers under the command of Captain Morgan from Jamaica, so that they greatly outnumbered the French, in the proportion of six to one, according to Du Tertre, of two, three and four to one, according to various English accounts as given in the Calendars.[8] They furthermore had the advantage of position, for they occupied the center of the island and were united, whereas the French occupied the two extremities and were disunited. In spite of these advantages, the courageous and well-directed attacks of the French leaders, de Sales and St. Laurent, won a rapid and decisive victory. The English claimed that their defeat was due to cowardice shown by their leaders.[9] The French account in the *Gazette* reported

[6] *Cal. St. Pap. Col., Am. & W. Ind., 1661-1668*, No. 1204.

[7] *Gazette*, 1666.

[8] *Cal. St. Pap., Am. & W. Ind., 1661-1668*, No. 1179, Relation of the loss of St. Christopher.

[9] Thus a band of refugees, on arriving in a small vessel at Swansea in September, reported that St. Christopher had been lost by reason of the cowardice and indiscretion of the governor, Watts, and the other officers. Ibid., No. 1278. See also other accounts, Nos. 1204 and 1206.

TOWARD THE FRENCH WEST INDIES

that Governor Watts was accused of treason by Morgan and forced at the point of a pistol to march to battle.[10] Captain Morgan and his buccaneers, on the other hand, seemed to have shown much courage. Thus out of a total of 360, there remained only about seventeen of them who had not been killed or wounded. Captain Morgan himself was among the killed. "This victory," says Du Tertre, "is beyond doubt one of the most remarkable and noteworthy of this century, for the French, with 800 or 900 men, killed more than 1000, disarmed or made prisoners more than 3000, captured five standards and conquered with all of its forts one of the most beautiful islands of the Antilles."[11]

By the articles of surrender the English ceded all forts, artillery and firearms. Vagabonds and persons not possessing plantations were forced to leave the island at once. Owners of plantations could remain or retire, as they chose. If they chose to retire, they could dispose of their real estate, slaves and live stock to the French and embark with their families and movables. If they chose to remain, they would be forced to take the oath of allegiance to the French king and to the West India Company. They would be granted religious liberty, provided they did not exercise it in public assemblies.[12]

Most of the English refused to take the oath of allegiance and their expulsion began. The task of superintending their transportation was performed by St. Laurent and de Chambré, the general agent of the West India Company, who had come to St. Christopher with reinforcements from Guadeloupe on learning of the victory. From May 8 to June 8, no less than 8000 persons, according to

[10] *Gazette,* 1666, p. 912.
[11] Du Tertre, IV, 45.
[12] *Cal. St. Pap., Am. & W. Ind., 1661-1668,* No. 1180; and Du Tertre, IV, 47.

Du Tertre, were transported to various places. Some were sent to Montserrat and Antigua, others to Jamaica, Bermuda and St. Domingo, still others to Virginia. Some 800 or 900 Irish were sent to St. Bartholomew to cultivate the plantations which the French planters had left, in order to strengthen the colony at St. Christopher. Three or four hundred more were sent to Martinique and Guadeloupe. No less then 400 contracts of sale were registered for the transfer of plantations by the English to the French, which represented a total value of 3,000,000 pounds of sugar or 450,000 livres of money.[13]

The news of this victory was received with joy in France. The king, Colbert, and the directors of the company, wrote most eulogistic letters to St. Laurent. Colbert informed him that the king, as a mark of his appreciation, granted him 1000 écus. The directors informed him that they had chosen him to succeed the late de Sales as governor of St. Christopher.

The first battle had ended decidedly in favour of the French and the whole of St. Christopher passed into the hands of the West India Company. The burden of defense thereby became greater. The victory meant an increase of responsibility and an additional drain upon its resources.

The company had faced the crisis of a foreign war in a very embarrassing financial condition. The directors consequently hesitated to engage the company's credit by further expenditures. But conferences, held at the beginning of 1666 with de Laubière, lieutenant-governor of Martinique, who had been sent to France by de Clodoré to depict the deplorable condition of affairs at Martinique and to urge them to send relief, made the directors decide to equip another expedition. De La Barre, who was in Holland occupied with the affairs of the company, was

[13] Du Tertre, IV, 62-63.

TOWARD THE FRENCH WEST INDIES

summoned to Paris to give his advice. The directors had not yet given up hope that a treaty of neutrality could be made with England and thought that the expedition of two or three vessels would be sufficient. De La Barre, on arriving at Paris, quickly destroyed this illusion by assuring them that the English were waiting only for the outbreak of a war in order to attempt the conquest of all the French islands. In accordance with his advice it was decided to equip a strong fleet and send it to the islands under his command.[14]

Preparations were immediately begun at La Rochelle. The king, in response to a request by the directors, granted permission to levy four companies of 100 soldiers each and to place in command Sieur de Léon, captain of a company of the regiment of Navarre. Haste was made to put the fleet in readiness to sail. The vessels were laden with ammunition for the defense of the islands and with supplies for the relief of the planters. Troops, passengers, and cargoes were all embarked and the fleet set sail from La Rochelle on May 26, 1666.[15]

It was a mistake, as events proved, to place de La Barre in command. Even before the sailing of the fleet, Colbert de Terron warned Colbert of the danger: "M. de La Barre is impatient to sail. . . . It is very easy to see that his thoughts are not of warfare, for which he has no disposition. He has no thought than that of establishing at Cayenne a part of his family which is to accompany him. . . . Under the smallest pretext, he will change his route and proceed to Cayenne with the women and best

[14] Du Tertre, IV, 116-117.
[15] Ibid., pp. 118-119. It was composed of ten vessels, *Le St. Georges,* 25 cannon, flying the admiral's pennant, *Le St. Christopher,* 26 cannon, *Le Mercier,* 24 cannon, *L'Hirondelle,* 14 cannon, *Le Lion d'Or,* 14 cannon, *La Dorothée,* 8 cannon, *Le Cher Amy,* 10 cannon, *La Pucelle,* 14 cannon, a galiot and a bark of 50 tons.

THE COMMERCIAL POLICY OF COLBERT

men whom he has on board."[16] Most prophetic words, which should have served as a warning to Colbert and to the directors of the company!

The fleet sailed with favourable winds, but encountered such a rude southwester that it was forced to return almost immediately to La Rochelle. The flagship, *Le St. Georges*, was found so badly damaged that it was considered unfit to make the voyage. Fortunately another of the company's vessels, *Le Florissant*, armed with twenty-eight cannon, was found near La Rochelle and substituted. The fleet sailed again on June 8. This time the *St. Christopher* was fouled by one of the other ships and so badly damaged that it was forced to return to La Rochelle. The rest of the fleet continued its way. It arrived at the Madeira Islands on June 27, where de La Barre learned that war had already broken out in the islands and that, furthermore, a squadron of twelve English vessels had sailed from the Madeiras on June 6 for the West Indies. Instead, however, of making haste to carry relief to the islands, as duty commanded him to do, he decided to direct his whole fleet to Cayenne.[17]

De La Barre himself explains the reason for this decision by saying that after his arrival at the Madeiras, he took counsel with the most experienced navigators in his fleet, who said that inasmuch "as it was not possible to sail from the Madeiras before July 10, by reason of the cargoes which they were compelled to take aboard, it would not be possible to arrive in the islands before the first days of August which is the season of the greatest danger on account of storms and during which only rash and imprudent sailors dare approach near the coasts of the islands; . . . that thus the fleet in arriving in the islands at such a season would be obliged to take

[16] Bib. Nat. MSS., Mél. Colbert, 137 *bis,* fol. 649.
[17] Du Tertre, IV, 124.

TOWARD THE FRENCH WEST INDIES

refuge in the cul-de-sac of Martinique, which was a very unhealthy anchorage and where the greater part of the crews might die from sickness; that it could not render any service to the islands at such a season. . . . These considerations, after being discussed, influenced Sieur de La Barre to change the plan, which had been agreed upon with Sieur Colbert de Terron, to sail directly to the islands, and made him decide to go first to Cayenne in accordance with the first orders which had been given him."[18]

This explanation is not convincing. One naturally asks why it was necessary for de La Barre to go all the way to the Madeiras before learning that it would be dangerous to arrive in the Antilles toward the first of August. It is evident that de La Barre did not act in good faith and that he gave this explanation only as a pretext to hide the truth, which Colbert de Terron had already divined, namely that he had his heart set on building up the colony at Cayenne and was willing, at almost any cost to the Antilles, to sidetrack the expedition for the profit of that colony.

In accordance with his decision, de La Barre reprovisioned his ships in the Madeiras, made a stop of another ten days at Santiago in the Cape Verde Islands to buy live stock, and finally sailed on July 25 for Cayenne. He was separated on July 27 and 30 from the rest of his vessels, all of which arrived at Cayenne between October 6 and 12, except one, which did not arrive until the last of October.[19] They were thus nearly three months on the way from Santiago to Cayenne. Their cargoes were so badly damaged that they furnished small aid to the colony. Much surprise was felt at the failure to find de La Barre at their arrival. For forty-eight long days he had

[18] *Relation de l'Amérique*, I, 72 ff.
[19] Ibid.

struggled against head winds and unfavourable tides. At the end of that time, finding himself separated from his fleet and still far from his destination and without a supply of water to drink, he at last gave up hope of reaching Cayenne and turned his lone vessel toward Martinique.

In the meantime, the colonies had been suffering and the spirit of rebellion had reappeared, which might have been prevented, had de La Barre obeyed orders and arrived in season with his fleet. After the defeat of the English at St. Christopher, the planters, who had shown themselves courageous and loyal subjects in combating the enemy, grew impatient at the unfulfilled promises of the company's agents. Many found their plantations damaged by the war, and poverty seemed greater than ever, in spite of the brilliant victory. A sedition would have broken out, but for the prompt action of de St. Laurent in arresting two of the most rebellious leaders. In Martinique, a revolt of some importance did break out against the company.

On July 13, de Clodoré received word that some planters in Cabesterre had refused to obey his orders to aid in strengthening the fortifications of the islands, complaining that they did not have food to eat. A little later in the day, he received additional news that all the planters of the district were in open revolt and were moving towards the district of Prêcheur which was to serve as a rendezvous with other rebels. De Clodoré was thus forced to turn his attention from defense against the enemy to the quelling of a rebellion against the company. Only four days before, yielding to the urgent requests of de Chambré and de St. Laurent, he had sent his own picked troops to St. Christopher. He, however, gave orders promptly to the commanders of the different districts to hold their troops in readiness. He commanded de la Calle, chief agent of the West India Company in the

TOWARD THE FRENCH WEST INDIES

island, to assemble his troop of sixty clerks and employees of the company and to use it as a guard for the fort.

Father Forcade, a Dominican, was sent to Cabesterre in order to persuade the planters to desist from rebellion, or, persuasion failing, to attempt to frighten them by assuring them that God would not desert the governor and that the larger planters would march with him against them. The leaders refused either to be persuaded or to be frightened. The two leading rebels, La Rivière and Daniel Jousselin, assured the good father that they were determined to perish rather than to submit to the company longer; that they were in intelligence with the planters of Basseterre, but that, nevertheless, they would send some one to confer with the governor. The rebels had already made the two commanding officers of the district prisoners. Father Forcade returned and reported to de Clodoré that he was convinced that the rebels were determined to make good their threats.

De Clodoré found very little enthusiastic support among the commanding officers. When he assembled some of them to take counsel, he found many of the opinion that it would be wise to yield to the rebels or at least to satisfy them temporarily. He refused, however, to listen to the expression of such ideas, saying that such a course would mean the ruin of all and put the island in danger of being taken by the English. Delay in attack meant a rapid spread of the rebellion. Success of a rebellion meant savage treatment of the officials and of the rich planters. As for him, he was resolved to march directly against the insurgents. He summoned those who loved him and their duty to follow him.

The plan of the rebels of Cabesterre was to traverse Mt. Pélée in order to join those of Prêcheur. De Valmenière, one of the most trusted officers, was sent with a body of troops to capture the mountain and combat them at their passage. At dawn of July 15, he set his troops in march and arrived at the summit of Mt. Pélée about ten o'clock. The rebels had anticipated his movements and were firmly entrenched. They fell victims, however, to their own stupidity and lost their vantage. They had forced the two commanders, Perière and Bouillon, whom they had taken prisoners before leaving Cabesterre, to accompany them. As quickly as these two officers realized that the troops commanded by de Valmenière were those sent by de Clodoré, they very adroitly made use of their situation to defeat and rout the rebels. They persuaded them that the troops in sight were none other than their friends from Prêcheur, who had come to join them. Under this pretext, Perière and Bouillon, who had gained some fifteen or twenty wavering rebels to their plot, were able to join de Valmenière and inform him of the situation. They returned straightway to the band of insurgents and informed them that de Clodoré was not present and they could confer with de Valmenière in all security. The rebels fell at once into the trap. They deserted their posts of vantage and went down to the point which de Valmenière occupied. The two officers quickly rallied about them those whom they had won over and demanded of the others whether they did not recognize them as their officers, and at the same time began to shout: "Vive le Roi et M. de Clodoré!" The most of the insurgents were so surprised by these cries that they began to cry the same thing. An energetic attack was made upon the others. A volley was fired and some fifteen or sixteen of the mutineers lay dead or wounded. Perière sprang upon Jousselin, smote him with his sword and captured him. This quick turn of affairs spread terror among the rebels. They took to their heels and escaped into the woods. Some, however, in their flight encountered the troops led by de Clodoré himself, who had marched

TOWARD THE FRENCH WEST INDIES

straight into Cabesterre, and were captured. The leaders were captured, thanks to rewards offered by the governor. Jousselin was hanged and Rivière severely punished. Some of the rest were condemned to three years of service to the company, others to the payment of large fines.[20]

"Such were the misfortunes caused by the dishonesty of the West India Company's agents and by the scarcity of supplies which prevailed. One must admit that the company was very fortunate on this occasion in having a governor, who was loved and respected enough by the planters to make them fight and destroy their brothers, who were in revolt, as they themselves believed, only by reason of motives which they could not condemn. The design of the rebels was, after uniting themselves with those of Prêcheur, to march against St. Pierre, where they would force the governor to surrender his commission, to overthrow the company and to establish himself governor under the proprietorship of M. D'Esnambuc, provided that he permitted the Dutch to trade in the island. They were nevertheless divided as to the choice of a governor, some desiring de Valmenière, others de Clodoré. But God willed otherwise."[21]

It can easily be imagined with what impatience de Clodoré awaited relief from France. But de La Barre failed to appear. Some aid arrived shortly afterwards from another quarter. Three of the company's vessels which had sailed from Holland on May 25 arrived at Martinique on July 28. They were *Le Lys, La Justice* (300 tons) and *Le St. Antoine* (130 tons). They brought with them two small English prizes, one with a cargo of salt fish and the other with a cargo of tobacco from Virginia.[22] About the same time, there arrived three Dutch vessels with

[20] Du Tertre, IV, 82 ff.
[21] Ibid., IV, 12.
[22] *Gazette,* 1666, No. 138 and pp. 752 and 1166.

cargoes of supplies.[23] Some two weeks later, on August 9, arrived the *St. Christopher*, which, it may be recalled, formed a part of de La Barre's fleet, but was forced to put back into La Rochelle for repairs. It had aboard a hundred soldiers of the regiment of Poitou under the command of Sieur de l'Alou and de Laubière, the lieutenant-governor of Martinique. The latter raised high the hopes of all by telling them that their suffering would soon be at an end, for a strong, well-equipped fleet, under the command of de La Barre, well laden with provisions, was on its way, that it had already touched at the Madeiras and should arrive shortly.[24]

Every eye was turned toward the horizon to see some sign of the approaching fleet. If that horizon had not been so limited, they might have seen a sight to turn them mad, for, thanks to the obstinate selfishness of de La Barre, the precious cargoes of supplies which they awaited were wasting away in mid-ocean in a struggle against adverse winds and unfavourable tides.

At the arrival of the news of the victory at St. Christopher, the king resolved to send, at his own expense, another expedition to the islands. Orders were issued for the levying of 400 soldiers in Normandy and Navarre. The following vessels were equipped by the king: *Le St. Sebastien* (28 cannon), *L'Aigle Noir* (26), *L'Aurore* (16), *Le Cher Amy* (8), *L'Eglise* (16). "Two or three other vessels belonging to the West India Company were joined to this squadron."[25] This fleet sailed from La Rochelle on July 27 and arrived at Martinique on September 15, two weeks before the arrival of de La Barre. The troops brought by this fleet remained only a very short

[23] Du Tertre, IV, 95.
[24] Ibid., pp. 100-101.
[25] Du Tertre, IV, 122-123. See also Bib. Nat. MSS., Mél. Colbert, 138 *bis*, fols. 812 and 936, for letters from Colbert de Terron in regard to the expedition; also vol. 140, fols. 1084 and 161. The last

TOWARD THE FRENCH WEST INDIES

while at Martinique as they were shortly transferred to St. Christopher. Finally de La Barre arrived, on October 1, not with his fleet, but with one lone vessel. The disappointment of all must have been great, as they saw this poor remnant of the strong fleet which they had awaited so impatiently and on which they had placed so much hope.[26]

De La Barre was forced, soon after his arrival, to deal with a problem which he had done much to create and which demanded an immediate solution. The principal officers and planters of Martinique assembled and drew up a petition which they presented to him. Their principal demands were: that the articles of de Tracy's ordinance be respected; that foreigners be admitted to trade in the islands; and that they be not discouraged from doing so

reference contains a statement of the expenses of equipping the fleet which was as follows:

For levying 400 men	4,800 livres.
400 swords	4,800 livres.
280 muskets	2,250 livres.
150 guns	1,800 livres.
4 standards	160 livres.
300 shoulder straps	375 livres.
600 lbs. fuses	172 livres.
600 lbs. powder	300 livres.
A quantity of flints	6 livres.
A quantity of lead	100 livres.
400 belts	600 livres.
800 shirts	1,400 livres.
400 uniforms	2,400 livres.
400 pairs stockings	240 livres.
800 pairs shoes	2,200 livres.
400 hats	900 livres.
800 cravattes	240 livres.
Salaries for soldiers	3,720 livres.
For their board and lodging	28,380 livres.
Total	50,568 livres.

[26] The other vessels of de La Barre's fleet, after having discharged most of their damaged cargoes at Cayenne, set sail for the islands on November 13. See *Relation de l'Amérique*, I, 376.

by excessive duties laid on their merchandise; that the planters might bargain freely for the transportation to Europe of their sugar, indigo and tobacco without being forced to ask permission of the company's clerks, provided they were not indebted to the company; and that the maximum rate of transportation be fixed at ten deniers (money of France) the pound. The other demands concerned minor details of regulating and distributing merchandise. Among others the following regulations were made by de La Barre, de Clodoré and de Chambré:

"All Frenchmen shall enjoy the right to trade freely in the island of Martinique. They may import into the island whatever merchandise they wish and may export, into whatever country in alliance with France which they choose, the products received in exchange. For the said privilege they shall pay to the company an import duty of 2½ per cent and an export duty of 2½ per cent.

"Likewise foreigners, at peace and in alliance with France, shall enjoy the same privilege on the condition of paying 5 per cent on cargoes imported into the island and 5 per cent on cargoes exported therefrom."[27]

The directors of the West India Company in France, some three or four weeks previously, had come to a similar decision. They agreed to admit the Dutch to trade in the West Indies on condition of paying ten per cent both on incoming and outgoing cargoes, and private French traders on paying five per cent.[28] On learning of the terms of the regulations made at Martinique, the directors sent instructions that the regulations which they had made should have precedence over the latter.[29] This action by the directors in admitting private French and Dutch traders was of course an abnegation of the company's monop-

[27] Du Tertre, IV, 135-139.
[28] Arch. Nat. Col., F₃, 52, September 24, 1666.
[29] S. Daney, *Hist. de la Martinique*, II, 135.

oly, but was regarded as a temporary expedient to relieve the crisis created by the war.

After this, the attention of de La Barre and of all was turned to the struggle with the English. It was decided to make an attack upon the enemy and first upon the island of Antigua. All ships, belonging to the West India Company actually in the islands, were commanded by de La Barre to report for duty at Martinique. Eight responded to his call. The fleet sailed from Martinique for Antigua on November 2, and on the 4th an attack was made under the command of de La Barre. The resistance offered by the English was slight, for a landing was effected, the forts taken and the governor and his principal officers captured all on the same day. On the morrow de Clodoré and du Lion were sent with troops to complete the conquest of the island, which they did after some sharp fighting. Articles of surrender, essentially the same as those at St. Christopher, were signed. The conquest of the island seems not to have been thorough, however, due perhaps to the failure of de La Barre to grant the full quota of troops demanded for the purpose by de Clodoré. Three weeks later, at the refusal of the English to abide by the treaty, de Clodoré was compelled to return to the attack.[30]

De La Barre attacked and took Montserrat in February, 1667. Du Tertre states that he had no less than twenty-five vessels under his command when he quit Martinique. The French for the moment "were masters of the sea."[31] This was changed, however, by the arrival in April, 1667, of a strong English fleet which chose Nevis as the base of operations and captured five Dutch merchant vessels trading at Guadeloupe and blockaded effectively the island of St. Christopher.

[30] Du Tertre, IV, 173.
[31] *Cal. St. Pap. Col., Am. & W. Ind., 1661-1668*, No. 1273.

THE COMMERCIAL POLICY OF COLBERT

De La Barre returned to Martinique and made preparations to attack the fleet. He united under his command the following vessels: *Le Lys Couronné* (38 cannon), *La Justice* (32), *La Concorde* (32), *Le Florissant* (30), *Les Armes d'Angleterre* (24), *Le St. Christopher* (26), *L'Harmonye* (32), *L'Hercules* (26), *Le St. Sebastien* (34), *L'Hirondelle* (14), *La Nostre Dame* (10), *Le Mercier* (24), *Le Marsouin* (12), and two fireships. All these vessels belonged to the West India Company.[32] In addition there were four Dutch vessels armed with 108 cannon. In spite, however, of most elaborate preparations in the details of the order of battle, the fight with the English fleet off Nevis on May 20 was indecisive. De Clodoré attributed the lack of victory to the cowardice shown by de La Barre. De La Barre in turn attributed it to the failure of de Clodoré to obey orders.[33] The Dutch seemed to have been disgusted with the poor seamanship of the French. De La Barre withdrew to St. Christopher and a few days later the whole fleet returned to Martinique to await the attack of the English. They did not have to wait long, for the English fleet, under the command of Sir John Harman, began a series of attacks upon the island, which lasted from June 29 until July 6, and which proved of much consequence to the West India Company.

After three unsuccessful attacks the English fleet entered the road of St. Pierre on July 6. On that day, after five hours of cannonading, an English fireship succeeded in attaching itself to *Le Lys Couronné*, the French admiral, and setting her afire. *Le St. Jean*, an unnamed vessel, and two large flutes, *Le Mercier* and *Le Lion d'Or*, the last two named laden for Holland with cargoes valued

[32] Du Tertre, IV, 242-243.

[33] See on this controversy a pamphlet, entitled *Plaintes et griefs présentés à Mgr. de Colbert par M. de Clodoré*, and de La Barre, *Relation de l'Amérique*, and finally Du Tertre, IV, 243-260.

TOWARD THE FRENCH WEST INDIES

at 1,200,000 livres, also took fire and were "reduced to ashes, nothing being saved aboard them." The crews leaped into the sea and many were drowned.[34] Terror spread to the other vessels, soldiers and sailors jumped into the water, believing that all would be burned. Besides, they were no longer able to resist the cannonading of the enemy which was riddling their ships. But for a change of wind, all the other twenty-eight vessels might have been destroyed by fire, for they were all anchored close together. "The fire and the booming of cannon and the slaughter of our forces so frightened those who escaped from the vessels that it was almost impossible to stop them in their flight."[35] Only by heroic efforts was de Clodoré able to check their rout, restore their courage, rearm them and offer resistance to the enemy. Heroism saved the day from complete disaster.[36] The English, apparently disheartened by the stubborn resistance, or else satisfied with the damage which they had wrought, retired at the moment when they seemed to have a complete victory in their grasp. At their withdrawal, de La Barre gave orders that all vessels which remained should be entirely unladen, and that portholes be made so that they could be easily sunk, if the enemy returned.

The English fleet reappeared on the morrow for a final attack. Again the heroic efforts saved Martinique from capture, but the English did not retire without forcing the French to sink their vessels near the shore in order to save them from capture or destruction. "Sir John Harman has burned nineteen or twenty great French ships in

[34] Du Tertre, IV, 286-287; *Relation de l'Amérique*, II, 261.
[35] Du Tertre, IV, 287.
[36] "A woman, named Madeleine d'Orange, whose husband was gunner at the battery of St. Sebastien, remained unflinching by his side during the combat, bringing courageously ammunition to aid in the conflict." See du Motey, *Guillaume d'Orange et les Origines des Antilles Françaises*, Chap. XXXI.

Martinico road,"[37] was a rather exaggerated English account of what happened, but it told the story of the great disaster which had been inflicted upon the French. The significance of the victory was that it gave the English control of the sea and made commerce almost impossible for the French, and that it inflicted a most serious financial loss upon the West India Company, for the directors estimated that the vessels destroyed by fire alone represented a loss of 400,000 livres.[38]

St. Christopher remained effectively blockaded, but the English seemed unable to capture it. Cayenne was captured easily. The French settlement was pillaged, farmhouses were burned and sugar-mills destroyed.[39] Thus much of the work for which the company had expended such large sums was undone and the losses were heavy.

The proclamation of peace alone seems to have saved the French from greater disaster. The treaty of Breda was signed on July 31, 1667. The *status ante bellum* was restored so far as the islands were concerned.[40]

The war had proved disastrous to the West India Company. Before the outbreak of the war, as we have seen, the company lost no less than five vessels from capture by English corsairs. This represented a loss of some 272,000 livres, deduction being made for the sums awarded by the English admiralty courts. It lost during the course of the war: by shipwreck in the islands, *Le St. Sebastien*, a vessel of 250 tons, and *L'Angélique* of 350 tons; by capture, *La Suzanne* (350 tons) and an unnamed vessel; by destruction at the hands of the enemy in "Martinico road," *Le Lys Couronné*, *Le St. Jean*, an unnamed vessel, *Le Lion*

[37] *Cal. St. Pap. Col., Am. & W. Ind., 1661-1668*, No. 1520. Willoughby to Williamson, July 19, 1667. Id., 1521 and others. See index.

[38] Arch. Col., F$_2$, 15, Mém. sur l'état des affaires de la Cie. des Ind. Oc., November, 1667.

[39] Du Tertre, IV, 313.

[40] Du Tertre, IV, 318-325, prints the text of the treaty.

TOWARD THE FRENCH WEST INDIES

d'Or (250 tons) and *Le Mercier* (400 tons), the two last named containing cargoes of sugar for France. Furthermore, the company had been forced to expend its funds, or rather to sink itself deeper in debt, not for the advancement of its commerce, but for the defense of the islands against the enemy. What this meant is clearly understood, when one recalls such an attack as that of de La Barre against Antigua in November, 1666, where all the vessels of the company in the islands were put in battle array and thus called from the peaceful pursuits of commerce into the exacting duties of warfare, or when one remembers that many of the cargoes sent out to the islands were composed entirely of ammunition and of provisions for soldiers. The loss to the company from the fact that production was virtually arrested during the war is incalculable. The planter had been forced to turn his face to the battlefield and his back upon his plantation, with the result that there was not enough tobacco or sugar or indigo at the close of the war to lade the company's vessels. To the devastation and privation of war had been added, in the case of St. Christopher, the ravages of a violent storm. There on the first of September, storehouses and sugar-mills had been overturned, trees uprooted, sugar-cane blown down and the plantations all ruined.[41]

It is interesting to note the estimate made by the directors of how much the war had cost the company. In a memoir,[42] addressed by them to Colbert in November, 1667, they remarked: "It is evident from the company's books that without the expense of the war and the losses incurred therein, which together amount to more than 2,000,000 livres, it would have gained during the first four years of

[41] Du Tertre, IV, 298-299.
[42] Arch. Col., F$_2$, Mémoire sur l'état des affaires de la Cie. des Ind. Oc., November, 1667.

its existence 500,000 livres. . . . Thus without the burden of a war which the company has sustained for two years and in which it has employed all of its vessels and during which its agents and even all the planters of the islands have had time to think of nothing except their defense, the company would not have been forced to appeal constantly to His Majesty for aid." The directors estimated the losses as follows:

Expenses of the war . . .	1,000,000 livres.
Captures by the English before the war	272,000 livres.
Sundry losses caused by the war .	250,000 livres.
Destruction by fire of five vessels and their cargoes at Martinique .	400,000 livres.
Depreciation of value of vessels which served in the war . . .	300,000 livres.
Total	2,222,000 livres.[43]

The actual deficit of the company in November, 1667, was 1,639,860 livres. If, said the directors, one compared these two sums, it would be seen that the losses caused by the war were greater by 581,140 livres than the deficit.

The company very naturally found itself, at the close of the war, in serious financial embarrassments, for Colbert had responded very feebly to the appeals for aid during the course of the war. Thus in May, 1666, the directors had informed him that the company was forced to meet pressing obligations amounting to 650,000 livres (300,000 livres at Lyons, 150,000 livres at Rouen, and 200,000 livres at Paris), and that it would be forced to go into bankruptcy, if some funds were not placed at its disposal. They estimated that the sum of 2,000,000 livres was neces-

[43] The directors remarked that to this should be added the losses sustained by the company by reason of cessation of commerce, which were incalculable.

sary to enable the company to meet those obligations and to continue its commerce. But the royal treasury remained closed. Colbert attempted to satisfy temporarily these needs, however, by commanding the farmers of the taxes imposed for non-pursuit by the Chambre de Justice, to pay to the company sums amounting to 1,084,000 livres.[44] The total sum realized from this source for the year 1666 amounted to only 245,400 livres and this seems to be the entire amount placed at the disposal of the company during the year.[45] The income from the farm at Rouen was in deficit to the sum of 1601 liv. 8s. 6d. Colbert did not aid the company directly until 1667. On April 27, 230,000 livres, and again on September 4, 192,000 livres from the royal treasury were placed at its disposal. But it was another case of "a drop of water on the tongue of a man with a fever."

In November, 1667, the financial state of the company was as follows:

DEBIT.

Funds furnished by the king at different times August 17, 1664, to September 4, 1667		1,922,000 liv.
The Fermiers gén. des Aides paid in 1665 . . .	600,000 liv.	
For which stock in the company was issued for .	55,000 liv.	
	545,000 liv.	545,000 liv.

[44] Thus Sieur Coquille was ordered to pay for the généralité of Paris, 45,000 livres in ten equal payments at intervals of three months, the first payment to be made on March 1, 1666. Arch. Col., F$_2$, 17, Mém. de ce qui doibt estre payé par les soubstraitans des taxes faicts pour la descharge des recherches de la Chambre de Justice dans les généralités de ce royaume.

[45] Arch. Nat., G$_7$, 1312.

THE COMMERCIAL POLICY OF COLBERT

Stock subscribed . .		1,784,000 liv.
Farmers of taxes of Chambre de Justice, paid, 1666-67	607,000 liv.	
For which stock in the company was issued for .	72,940 liv.	
The Company owes	534,060 liv.	534,060 liv.
To Correspondent at Amsterdam . . .	84,000 liv.	
To different individuals .	930,000 liv.	
Deficit in cash account .	70,000 liv.	
	1,084,000 liv.	1,084,000 liv.
Total		5,883,860 liv.

CREDIT.

32 vessels, estimated value .		600,000 liv.
Small boats in the islands .		20,000 liv.
Goods sent to islands on which agents have not made report—for 2,262,000 livres. Adding estimated profit of 50 per cent, this should yield	3,393,000 liv.	
Returns already received, 393,000 liv., plus probable expenses during the war, 1,000,000 liv., equals .	1,393,000 liv.	
	2,000,000 liv.	2,000,000 liv.
The Company has paid on the sums due for the islands .		179,000 liv.
It has effects:		
At Tortuga for . .		30,000 liv.
At Cape Verde and Senegal		200,000 liv.
In Canada . . .		260,000 liv.
In warehouses in France .		285,000 liv.
In Madeira . . .		20,000 liv.

TOWARD THE FRENCH WEST INDIES

Its establishments at Cayenne have cost . . .	600,000 liv.
Total	4,194,000 liv.

The Company, therefore, was in arrears for 1,639,860 livres.[46]

An examination of the credit sheet will show that the company's assets were of doubtful value. It is hard to accept, for instance, the calculation that from 2,262,000 livres of merchandise sent to the islands, the company would realize 2,000,000 livres after the expenses of the war had been deducted. It is much more probable that a very large part of this sum would be and was lost in debts, especially when one takes into account the reckless way in which the company's agents granted credit to the planters. Again, among the company's assets one finds the value of the colony at Cayenne estimated at 600,000 livres. It is very evident that news had not yet been received of the pillage wrought by the English in that island. Much of the amount expended by the company for the establishment of that colony had been undoubtedly lost.

At the end of November, Colbert opened the royal treasury and placed 713,000 livres at the disposal of the company. On December 26, the *fermiers généraux des aides* paid 200,000 livres and the *fermiers généraux des gabelles* paid 150,000 livres. The total sum received by the company for the year 1667 was 1,601,040 livres, of which His Majesty alone had contributed 1,134,000 livres. It was proposed to employ these new funds, half for the payment of pressing debts and half for the maintenance of commerce.[47]

The directors informed Colbert that the company had thirty-two vessels with an aggregate tonnage of 7610

[46] Arch. Col., F₂, 15, Memoir by the directors, November, 1667.
[47] Ibid.

THE COMMERCIAL POLICY OF COLBERT

tons.[48] It is to be noticed that in comparison with the number of vessels owned by the company at the close of 1665, which was estimated at forty, the company's fleet had decreased; that instead of having a large number of vessels well equipped and laden ready to sail for the islands, as in November, 1665, nearly half of its fleet, namely fourteen, were in the islands awaiting cargoes—many of them perhaps in much worse condition than the directors of the company realized. Of the vessels actually in Europe, two were being prepared to be sent to Cayenne, one to Santiago (Cape Verde Islands) to take a cargo of live stock, one to the coast of Guinea for a cargo of slaves, and ten to the islands. It is to be remarked in passing how completely the commerce of the islands was still absorbing the company's attention. It is also to be noticed that out of fifteen vessels in France eleven were at La Rochelle, for in 1665, it will be remembered, the great majority of the company's vessels were in the ports of northern France. Attention is called to this fact here, because the continual wars of Louis XIV's reign almost destroyed commerce between the Antilles and the northern ports and left it

---

[48] They were distributed as follows:

In the islands: *Le St. Antoine* (130 tons), *La Marye* (350), *L'Harmonye* (350), *La Concorde* (380), *Les Armes de France* (350), *L'Hercules* (300), *L'Angélique* (350), *La Justice* (300), *La Nostre Dame* (150), *Le St. Nicolas* (250), *L'Hirondelle* (160), *Le St. Paul* (250), *La Licorne* (250), *Le St. Georges* (400).

In Holland: *La Bergère* (250 tons), ready to sail for the islands.

At Havre: *Le Marsouin* (300 tons), *Le Florissant* (350), *Le St. Guillaume* (50), *Le Marchand* (an English prize, 30).

At La Rochelle: *Les Armes de L'Angleterre* (prize, 180 tons), *La Vierge* (120), *Le Postillon* (120), *La Pucelle* (260), *La Ste. Dorothée* (250), *L'Oranger* (250), *L'As* (250), to take cargo at Bordeaux, *Le Soucy* (50), *Le Chasseur* (200), *La Catherine* (180), *Le St. Christopher* (300).

On the sea: *L'Espérance* (300 tons), en route for Cayenne, *Le St. Louis de Bayonne* (300), coming from Senegal.

almost entirely in the hands of the traders of Bordeaux, La Rochelle and Nantes.

Thus ended the second period of the company's history. Its finances were in a deplorable state, its commerce was in a state of decadence, its monopoly of trade was broken, for foreigners had been re-admitted to the privileges of commerce, and private French traders were permitted to trade freely. Between the two the company had been cheated out of the few crumbs which had fallen from the table of the planters during the war. It had a most difficult task to gain its feet after such an enfeebling struggle. "It passed from a period of embarrassment into the period of its downfall."[49]

[49] Chemin-Dupontès, *op. cit.*, 64.

CHAPTER VI

THE WEST INDIA COMPANY, 1668-1670

IT was the general opinion in the islands at the close of the war, according to Du Tertre, that the West India Company was totally ruined and that its restoration could be effected only at the expense of much suffering to the planters. Houel would soon be back at Guadeloupe and du Parquet at Martinique. The Dutch ships would soon be coming freely, well laden as before with all sorts of merchandise to satisfy their needs.[1] There was much to justify such an opinion. The company was heavily in debt; a large number of its ships lay idle in different ports of the islands, some of them being much the worse for the service which they had been called upon to perform during the war. It was but an easy step backwards for the company to retire and yield the place to the former proprietors, because it had as yet paid only a small part of the sums due them for the islands. The Dutch, re-admitted to the privileges of commerce during the war, were already trading with increased freedom, even without permits from the company. Thus the cry of the rebels, *"Vive les Hollandais,"* and the dream of all the planters to see the return of the old days of comparative prosperity seemed well on the road to realization.

There was, however, the indomitable will of a great minister, which had not been fully reckoned with or fully understood. Colbert never debated for a moment the plan of taking a backward step by restoring proprietary rule. Least of all did he think of permitting the Dutch trader to reconquer the commerce of the French islands. A spe-

[1] Du Tertre, IV, 335-336.

TOWARD THE FRENCH WEST INDIES

cial chapter will be devoted to the study of the persistent and uncompromising fight which he pursued against him and no further attention need be paid to the subject here.

As to the belief that the company was ruined and would be dissolved, some modern writers have misunderstood Colbert's attitude toward the company at this time. M. Pigeonneau, for instance, remarks: "From the commencement of 1668, Colbert retained very few illusions as to the future of the West India Company. He regarded it henceforth as a *pis aller* and awaited a propitious day to dissolve it."[2] This opinion has been accepted by M. Chemin-Dupontès.[3] There are several facts, however, which show that this opinion is erroneous. Colbert placed almost a million livres at the disposal of the company near the end of the year 1667. No less than 713,000 livres of this sum were granted as late as November 30. This fact was regarded by the planters of the islands as ample evidence that the company was to be continued and would receive the support of Colbert.[4] Again in the autumn of 1667, His Majesty ordered a squadron of his vessels to be sent for a year's cruise in the West Indies and in the Gulf of Mexico. It was placed under the command of Sieur de La Rabesnières de Treillebois. He was commanded to remain three months in the islands, and was ordered to direct his attention principally to the maintenance of order and to the exclusion of foreigners from trade and to the protection of the interests of the West India Company. In regard to the last point, his instructions were very definite:

"His Majesty wills that Sieur de Treillebois make it clearly known to the planters that he intends to maintain the West

[2] Pigeonneau, La Politique coloniale de Colbert, in *Annales de l'École des Sciences Politiques*, 1886, p. 800.
[3] Chemin-Dupontès, *Les Compagnies de Colonisation en Afrique Occid. sous Colbert*, pp. 66-67.
[4] Du Tertre, IV, 335.

India Company in possession not only of the islands which he has granted them, but also of all the commerce thereof; that he will see to it that the said company treat them well and that he will always be disposed to listen to their complaints."[5]

In the instructions to de Baas, on the eve of his departure for the islands in 1668 to succeed de Clodoré as governor at Martinique, there is another very clear expression of the same policy:

"M. de Baas should know that the interests of the king and those of the West India Company are one and the same. He should be thoroughly persuaded that everything which he can do to advance these interests will be very agreeable to His Majesty."

De Baas was further instructed to act in concert with the directors of the company in order to promote their trade.[6]

When Béchameil suggested in a memoir that subscriptions to the company be closed on January 1, 1669, Colbert remarked: "I do not believe that it is necessary to close the books of the company."[7] In fact, during the course of 1669, Colbert subscribed from the royal treasury half a million livres to aid the company.

At the beginning of 1668, Colbert himself made out a plan of reform for the administration of the company.[8] He continued to keep in very close touch with the administrators of the company's affairs, especially by correspondence with Pélissier, one of the directors, who was sent out to the islands in 1670 to look after the company's affairs. Even as late at February 26, 1670, he seems to have had in mind a possible restoration of the company's

[5] Clément, III, 2, p. 400.
[6] Ibid., p. 410.
[7] Arch. Col., F$_2$, 17, Mémoire, 1668.
[8] Arch. Col., F$_2$, 17, Projet de reglement proposé par M. Colbert le 7 déc. 1667, et adopté par la Cie.

TOWARD THE FRENCH WEST INDIES

monopoly. In a memoir which he addressed to the directors at that date, the following passage is to be found:

"So long as the company grants permission to trade to French private traders, it will suffice merely to grant the freedom to those who trade in the islands to sell their goods to whatever persons and in whatever way they wish, on the condition that they complete their sales before the lapse of one month after their arrival, under penalty of having them seized and sold at public auction. *When, however, the company ceases to grant such permission and will hold all of this commerce in its own hands,* the only policy to be adopted is that the company act in good faith in its relation with the planters."[9]

It is very clear from these facts that Colbert had not reached the point at the beginning of 1668 or even much later, where he planned to abolish the West India Company. On the contrary, the maintenance of that company was still an essential part of his policy.

There was one point, nevertheless, where one might say that Colbert's attitude toward the company had changed. He was unwilling that its monopoly of trade be restored to the exclusion of the French private trader. Béchameil remarked that a large number of private traders were going to the islands at the beginning of 1668, and that, if it continued, the Dutch could soon be driven out. In the margin of the memoir containing this remark, Colbert made the following comment: "There is nothing so important as to influence the French to send ships to the islands and to exclude all the Dutch from this trade."[10] By an *arrêt* of the *conseil d'état* of September 10, 1668, the directors of the company were forbidden to grant any passports whatever to the Dutch, but were specifically

[9] Clément, III, 2, pp. 472-476.
[10] Arch. Col., F₂, 15, Mémoire, January, 1668.

153

THE COMMERCIAL POLICY OF COLBERT

ordered to grant them freely to all Frenchmen.[11] Measures were passed, and instructions constantly given to the governors of the islands and to the directors and agents of the company to insure the largest possible freedom to the French private trader.

This did not mean necessarily any hostility on Colbert's part toward the company. It meant rather that he believed that the company needed help in its conquest of the islands. In this he was in accord with Béchameil, the most active director of the company, who remarked: "If that continues [the trade by individual Frenchmen], there is every reason to believe that we shall be able to take this trade out of the hands of the Dutch."[12] The essential point in Colbert's mind was that the traders in the islands be French. This, let it be recalled, was the real reason of the creation of the company itself, and the directors were heartily in sympathy with this view. Thus in the memoir to Colbert under date of November, 1667, they said:

"If individual French traders, by sending vessels to the islands after the manner of the Dutch, could carry on all of this trade, the company would willingly consent to yield it to them in order that the kingdom might profit from it, but it cannot think of yielding it to the Dutch, who were driven from the islands during the first year of the company's existence."[13]

It is therefore much more accurate to say that the West India Company began the year 1668 with the sincere support of Colbert and that the limitation of its monopoly was not intended as a step towards its dissolution, but rather to give it an ally in building up its trade.

[11] Moreau de Saint-Méry, I, 174-175.
[12] Arch. Col., F_2, 15, Mémoire, 1668.
[13] Arch. Col., F_2, Mémoire important, November, 1667.

TOWARD THE FRENCH WEST INDIES

The company had just passed through two very trying periods; the first was a period of organization, during which it had insufficient capital to solve a tremendous problem whose solution was imperative, with the result that it was forced to plunge itself into the embarrassment of heavy debts; the second period was more embarrassing still, for the company had to defend its possessions against the attacks of a foreign foe by the expenditure of large sums and had to suffer a cessation of its commerce. It is not surprising that during these two periods, as Béchameil asserted, the directors had not been able to pursue a well-defined policy, and that they had often lost heart, when they saw so many interruptions to the carrying out of their plans. But the war was now over and peace had come. Prospects seemed much more favourable for success.

Some reforms were made. One was in the organization of the board of directors, adopted in accordance with the plan drawn up by Colbert himself, whereby each director was given definite work to do. All were required to report for duty at the company's office "every Tuesday, Wednesday, Friday and Saturday at four o'clock and remain until seven." It was hoped that in this way the indifference of many directors to the interests of the company would disappear.[14] A governor-general was placed in command of all the islands. They had been governed for the first four years of the company's rule separately by individual governors. The choice for the first governor-general fell upon Jean Charles de Baas, a lieutenant-general in the army of the king. After instructing the new governor in the duties which he had to perform—the maintenance of law and order, encouragement to early marriages, promotion of clearing new lands and increased

[14] Arch. Col., F_2, 17, Projet de reglement proposé par Colbert; ibid., Mémoire, January 1, 1668.

production—Colbert specifically commanded him to act conjointly with the directors to re-establish the trade of the company. De Chambré, who had served as general intendant since 1664, was replaced by Sieur Cartier, who had been serving the company as its agent at Bordeaux. It was decided to dismiss the great body of agents and clerks in the islands and to limit the company's activity to wholesale trade. It was planned to maintain henceforward two large warehouses in each island, from which individual traders and merchants might supply themselves with goods at a price that would assure a profit of ten, twelve and fifteen per cent by retailing them to the planters. Béchameil expressed his belief that after these reforms were inaugurated, success was assured.

With perhaps the double purpose of encouraging old stockholders and attracting new investors, Colbert decided to have the company declare a dividend—the first in its history. All those who had voluntarily subscribed as much as 3000 livres before December 1, 1665, and those who had supplemented such subscriptions by a sum of 1500 livres or more were to receive a dividend amounting respectively to four per cent and five per cent annual interest on sums subscribed, the time to be reckoned from December 1, 1665, to December 1, 1668.[15] To make the payment of such a dividend possible, 300,000 livres were furnished from the royal treasury on January 9, 1669, and later an additional sum of 104,545 liv. 8s. 6d. Toward the close of the year some fifteen new subscriptions were made, which yielded a total of 540,000 livres.

In spite, however, of efforts to bolster up the company by reforms and by the subscription of new funds, its affairs seem to have drifted from bad to worse. No material has been found which enables one to estimate even approximately the amount of commerce carried on by the

[15] Arch. Nat., E, 1753, Arrêt, January 9, 1669.

TOWARD THE FRENCH WEST INDIES

company during the years 1668 and 1669. A letter written by de la Cale, the company's agent at Martinique, to Sieur Cartier, the general agent for the islands, reported the sailing of the *St. Pierre* for Dunkerque in June, 1669, with a cargo of 3078 rolls of tobacco, valued at 190,280 livres, for the West India Company, and 729 rolls of tobacco and 58½ hogsheads of sugar for private traders. Likewise in a letter of July 3, he noted the sailing of the *St. Joseph* for St. Malo.[16] But these cases do not indicate anything more than that the company was still carrying on some trade. Du Lion, in a letter of December, 1669, remarked that the number of vessels which the company was sending to the islands at that date was small.[17] Later events show that the company's commerce was declining at this time and that it was far from being in a prosperous condition. It is very clear that its affairs were being managed very poorly. Its general agent, Sieur Cartier, proved to be both a thief and a smuggler. He not only appropriated some of the company's property for his own personal use, but accepted bribes freely from the Dutch for the permission to introduce slaves, live stock and merchandise in the islands. He also kept up a smuggling trade with the English at Antigua. He kept the vessels of the West India Company "wasting away in the roads while those of the Dutch received payments for their smuggled goods and sailed away promptly with full cargoes." The Dutch were also given preference in the collection of debts.[18] Du Lion made similar charges of corruption against other agents

[16] Arch. Nat. Col., C$_7$, I.
[17] Ibid.
[18] Arch. Nat. Col., C$_7$, I, a long and interesting letter by du Lion of December 1, 1669. The charges against Cartier were substantiated by de la Cale, who was charged by the company with the investigation of Cartier's conduct. Arch. Nat. Col., C$_8$, 2nd series, I, letter from de la Cale to directors, November 18, 1669.

of the company, notably against Sieur Royer, the agent at St. Christopher, and even against de Baas, the governor-general.

It was perhaps to remedy this situation that the directors decided to choose a new general agent and in addition, perhaps at Colbert's suggestion, to send out to the islands one of their own number to protect the company's interests and to introduce some necessary reforms. For the former position it chose Bertrand Pallu, Sieur du Ruau, a former officer of justice at Tours. He remained in the islands until January, 1674, the eve of the company's dissolution, and it is to be supposed that he gave satisfaction in his service. The director selected to represent the company in the islands was Pélissier, a titular secretary of the king.

Colbert de Terron demanded at the time of Pélissier's selection that the powers of intendant be conferred upon him during his sojourn in the islands. To this demand Colbert made the following response:

"The demand which you have made in regard to M. Pélissier is very difficult to grant, and in any case I can do nothing before the return of the king. I do not believe, however, that His Majesty will be willing to confer upon him the power which you ask, all the more so, because it is hardly practicable to confer upon a member of a commercial company the same power as that conferred upon intendants in the provinces of the realm. In addition I am not at all informed as to the way in which justice is administered in the islands and I do not know Sieur Pélissier well enough to confer upon him such extensive power. But if, after having informed himself of the general practices in the islands, he sends me an excellent account thereof, more extensive powers can be conferred upon him with more certainty of success."[19]

[19] Clément, III, 2, p. 482, May 5, 1670.

TOWARD THE FRENCH WEST INDIES

Although no record has been found which shows that the powers of an intendant were formally conferred upon Pélissier, yet Colbert certainly charged him in his letters with the duties of an intendant. In one letter, for instance, he instructed him to study the means "of establishing order in matters of religion, justice, and police."[20] Furthermore, he regarded Pélissier as directly subject to his orders. Thus on December 20, 1670, he wrote him:

"I am very much surprised that you have not replied article by article to the instructions which I gave you and that you have not answered my letters. Do not fail to do so as soon as you receive this letter. Inasmuch as the company is in accord with the orders which I have given it in the name of the king and with all the suggestions which I make for its advancement and welfare, you must conform your conduct to what I write. You may rest assured that the company will give you orders to do the same thing."[21]

The original instructions to Pélissier present very clearly Colbert's views as to the particular duties of a director and as to the principles which should guide the West India Company in its efforts to build up trade. He was instructed to inform himself thoroughly before his departure of the complete history of the company's activities and policy. After his arrival in the islands, he was to examine carefully the accounts of agents, to listen to the complaints of the planters against them, and, in general, to examine thoroughly their conduct. In case they were found guilty, they were to be dismissed and punished. The most interesting passages of these instructions are the following:

"As the interests of the company are purely commercial, the conduct of the directors should be governed by three unvarying maxims, namely, freedom in trade, honesty, and content-

[20] Ibid., pp. 486-496.
[21] Ibid., p. 503.

THE COMMERCIAL POLICY OF COLBERT

ment with a small profit. ⟨As to freedom in trade, although it may prove difficult, if the company monopolizes commerce, it is nevertheless certain that some expedient can be found which will give satisfaction to the planters on this point. It is very important to maintain this principle, as it is the only thing which will promote the cultivation and the development of the islands . . . for liberty is the soul of commerce and alone can work its increase.⟩ As everything which is contrary to it will retard the development of the colonies some means of establishing it must be found. So long as the company grants permission to French private traders, it will be sufficient merely to grant the liberty to those who send merchandise to the islands of selling to whomever they wish and for whatever price they wish. . . . When, however, the company ceases to grant such permission and assumes a monopoly of this commerce, one will be compelled to trust to the good faith of the company in establishing storehouses in each of the islands, where an abundance of all sorts of merchandise will be on sale, and in selling its merchandise at auction to the highest bidder, in order in this way to make it possible for a large number of people to carry on a retail trade.

⟨ "In regard to sugar and the other products of the islands, their price will be regulated by the sale of merchandise at public auction.⟩ But if it is found that the introduction of specie, recently made, interferes with the system of exchange, and that merchandise is being bought for cash, it will be necessary to find some means of limiting liberty of sale or at least of regulating the price in such a way that both the company and the planters will find an honest gain. The profit and development of the company depend on the considerable increase in the number of inhabitants in all the islands, because such an increase brings with it an increase both in the demand for the merchandise and in the quantity of products in the islands. These two sources of increase should prove instrumental in enriching the company. The company, therefore, must work for the comfort of the planters, so that their friends in France may be attracted to the islands. Thus it should sell its goods at low prices and leave as much liberty as possible in trade. It should choose two seaports, such as La Rochelle and Havre, with some others such as Honfleur or Dieppe, where it can load and unload its vessels. In these ports it should maintain its dépôts well filled with all merchandise for which there is a demand in the islands.

. . . Vessels on arriving in France should be unloaded, repaired and reloaded and sent back to the islands with all diligence. The same rule should be observed by the company's agents in the islands. The company should strive to pay all debts and begin a new record.

"The king desires that Sieur Pélissier remain an entire year in the islands. He is not to return to France without an express order from the king, or before another director will have arrived to replace him."[22]

Pélissier arrived in the islands at the beginning of July. His credentials were formally registered at Martinique on the 14th.[23] He spent about two years in inspecting and supervising the affairs of the company. During this time Colbert was in constant correspondence with him. He instructed him to work at the larger task of promoting the interests of the islands. "Remember that I count upon it," he wrote in one letter, "that during your sojourn in the islands you will pay much attention to the enforcement of the king's orders that foreigners be entirely excluded from trading and that French private traders enjoy complete liberty to trade. Inasmuch as upon these two points depend the advancement of the company's interests, the prosperity of the islands and the increase of the colonies, bend your energy to their enforcement."[24]

In other letters he urged Pélissier to reduce the amount of sugar produced in the islands by persuading the planters to undertake the culture of other products; to see to

[22] Clément, III, 2, pp. 472-476.
[23] Daney, *Histoire de la Martinique*, II, 195.
[24] Arch. Nat. Col., B, 2, fol. 121 verso, October 12, 1670.

THE COMMERCIAL POLICY OF COLBERT

it that wise regulations were made for the preservation and increase of live stock in the several islands; to urge the inhabitants to build ships and to engage in commerce; to make a census of the island; to try to settle the dispute between the governors of Guadeloupe and St. Christopher; and in general, to consider what would be "the most advantageous and wisest thing to do for the police of the islands and particularly to establish an entire freedom of commerce to all French traders, to drive out foreigners, to establish public fairs and markets, to insure full liberty to creditors, to compel their debtors to pay them, and finally, to perfect the manufacture of tobacco and sugar."[25]

Pélissier does not seem to have carried out the spirit of Colbert's instructions that the company work for the comfort of the planters and sell goods at small profit. Thus du Lion complained to Colbert, "that M. Pélissier, a short time after his arrival at Martinique, ordered the company's agents to sell at prices as high as 9000 and 10,000 pounds of sugar each, horses and mares of Poitou for which the company had paid forty of fifty écus."[26] Likewise de Baas complained that Pélissier had given instructions to the company's chief agent at Martinique to sell at 4000 pounds of sugar slaves for which the Dutch used to demand only 2000 pounds. "That is certainly hard," remarked de Baas, "and it is not a means to make the planters love the company."[27] Colbert was forced to interfere by ordering that this exorbitant price be lowered.[28] Pélissier does seem to have made some efforts in accordance with Colbert's suggestion to study the needs of the islands with a view of increasing

[25] Clément, III, 2, pp. 526 ff.
[26] Arch. Nat. Col., C$_7$, II, March 15, 1672.
[27] Arch. Nat. Col., C$_8$, I, de Baas to Colbert, March 29, 1671.
[28] Ibid., February 28, 1672.

TOWARD THE FRENCH WEST INDIES

commerce, for, in a letter of July 8, 1671, he enclosed a memoir regarding "the trade which can be carried on with the French Antilles by the merchants of Marseilles and of other French ports of Provence and the Mediterranean coast." Detailed information was given as to the articles which the islands needed and the current prices there.[29]

Material is entirely too scanty to permit any estimate of what Pélissier really accomplished in the islands. Colbert's letters to him would seem to indicate that he had much confidence in him and was more or less satisfied with what Pélissier was doing. His mission, however, certainly failed to restore the West India Company to a prosperous condition, or to check it on the downward road to bankruptcy.

The more Colbert laboured to build up the commerce of the French West Indies, the more he realized that all efforts to make the company prosperous were proving fruitless, and that much more hope was to be placed in the employment of the private trader as an agent in the realization of his plans. He seems, however, to have entertained one last hope that the West India Company could be utilized in the solution of his important problem. He endeavoured to make it useful by forcing it to concentrate its forces upon the importation of special articles which the private trader was not supplying satisfactorily and which were very essential to the welfare of the planters. "The king orders me to inform you," he wrote to the directors on November 10, 1671, "that it is his will that the West India Company engage in no other commerce

[29] Thus the common wine of Provence was sold in the islands for 700 or 800 pounds of sugar the cask, brandy for 600 to 650 pounds the barrel, salt fish at 550 to 600 the barrel, salt beef at 200 to 250 the barrel. Colbert in his letter of December 8, 1670, acknowledged the receipt of Pélissier's memoir on "the price of sugar, the trade in slaves and live stock," but no trace of the memoir has been found.

THE COMMERCIAL POLICY OF COLBERT

in the countries of its concession than that of importing into the islands slaves from the coast of Guinea and live stock and salt meat from France."[30]

This short letter, which has been quoted entire, is an important document in the history of the company, and marks a milestone in the history of the commercial policy of Colbert, for it is proof positive that the great minister had realized that the instrument which he had chosen in 1664 to carry out his plans for establishing commerce with the West Indies was no longer suited to that end in 1671. It remains to see in the succeeding chapter how far the company succeeded in accomplishing the smaller task which Colbert had assigned to it and to trace briefly the events which led to its dissolution.

[30] Arch. Nat. Col., B, 3, fol. 97, letter to the directors of the W. Ind. Company, November 3, 1671; fol. 99, circular letter to the officials in the ports, November 10, 1671.

CHAPTER VII

THE WEST INDIA COMPANY, 1670-1674

ITS TRADE IN SLAVES, SALT BEEF, LIVE STOCK. ITS DOWNFALL

THE West India Company apparently made its first attempt to establish, on its own account, trade on the coast of Guinea at the end of the year 1669. It is particularly fortunate to have an account of this attempt written by Sieur Delbée, the captain of one of the vessels sent out by the company.[1] The expedition was composed of two vessels, *La Justice*, a frigate of 250 tons, under the command of Sieur Delbée, and *La Concorde*, under the command of Captain Jasmin. They were both laden with everything necessary for the establishment of trading posts and for the commencement of trade. On board *La Justice* were Sieur du Bourg, who was to become commander for the company at the coast, and Sieur Carolof, with several clerks and passengers. We have already had occasion to make the acquaintance of Carolof, for it was to him, it may be remembered, that the company granted in 1665 the privilege of trading on the western coast of Africa.[2]

They set sail from Havre on November 1, 1669, doubled Cape Verde on the 26th, and, having passed before the English settlement at Gambia, were becalmed nearly two

[1] Delbée (le Sieur), *Journal du Voyage du Sieur Delbée, commissaire général de la Marine aux Isles, dans la coste de Guinée pour l'establissement du commerce en ces pays en l'année 1669*, Paris, 1671.

[2] He had apparently been engaged in the slave trade during the intervening years, for Delbée speaks of him as "one who had traded at this coast and who had great knowledge of the practices of trade there." *Journal*, p. 387.

weeks at the mouth of the Sierra Leone. On December 21, the Cape of Palms was rounded and on the 26th anchor was cast before Assenay,[3] where an English ship was trading with the natives, but set sail immediately on perceiving that the incoming vessels were French. "A short time afterwards a number of negroes came in a canoe to our vessels. The moment that they saw we were French, they plunged into the sea, daring not to come near us, for the English had told them, as we learned afterwards, that we were not to be trusted and that we kidnapped all the negroes who came to trade with us along the coast."[4] Seeing that it was impossible to trade with these negroes, the vessels set sail on the 27th, and after encountering light winds, rounded the Cape of Three Points on the 30th, and anchored before Chateau de la Mine, "where resides the Dutch general who is in command of all those of his nation who frequent the coast."[5] As the French possessed no fort there and realized that it would be difficult to establish one, they sailed farther to the eastward. Carolof learned from the directors of the Danish post that the Dutch had long since known of the West India Company's plans and were making preparations to prevent their realization. Acting under instructions from Holland, they "were resolved to spare no pains to keep us from trading or at least to render our trade so unprofitable that our voyage would prove unfruitful."

[3] On the coast between Cape of Palms and Cape of Three Points.
[4] *Journal,* p. 369.
[5] "It is a place well fortified with a good garrison, where all the Dutch ships take water and wood and receive their orders. The Dutch pay a water tax to the king of the country who has never permitted them to dig a cistern in their chateau, employing this means to hold them in subjection. Cape Corse is about twelve miles from this chateau, where the fort of the English general is located. Five miles farther to the east is the chateau of the Danes, which is called Fredericksburg. Still farther on are three forts, two of which belong to the Dutch and one to the English." Ibid.

TOWARD THE FRENCH WEST INDIES

La Justice anchored at the gold coast in the kingdom of Ardres on January 4, 1670. Four Dutch vessels were already anchored there and were joined by a fifth a few days later. On January 5, Carolof debarked and went to Offra, "a burg about five miles from the seashore where were situated the trading posts of all foreigners who traded with the king of Ardres." He had an interview with the *fidalque*, who was charged with the commercial affairs of the kingdom. Carolof at once perceived that the Dutch were using shrewd and underhanded means to thwart his mission, but succeeded, nevertheless, in obtaining a promise from the *fidalque* to demand an audience of the king for him. He also sent a messenger to the king on his own responsibility. Four days passed without a word of reply, which was very surprising, "because Carolof had hoped that the news which he had sent the king of his arrival, in recalling to his memory the confidence which he had honoured him with in former years, and the fact that they had drunk '*bocca à bocca*' together would produce some extraordinary effect in his favour and shorten the delay which newly arrived foreigners are forced ordinarily to endure."[6]

On the 9th, a coach all gilded and a set of harness, with gilded trimmings and gilded bridles, were brought from the ship and set ashore. It was the present of the West India Company to the king of Ardres. All was put in preparation for the reception by the king, but the French were kept waiting until the 16th, when an officer came to Offra with a message from his master to Sieur Carolof. The king, said the message, had not forgotten his ancient friendship for Sieur Carolof, and as a proof of his esteem for him he would not require presents in advance, as he had the habit of doing with others; he was favourably disposed to grant to the French the same

[6] *Journal*, p. 388.

THE COMMERCIAL POLICY OF COLBERT

privileges as he had already granted to those who were actually engaged in trade in his kingdom. On the 18th, the prince and the grand captain of commerce arrived at Offra to conduct Carolof into the presence of the king. The 19th and 20th were passed in exchanging compliments. On the latter day the prince had a great tent pitched on the seashore, whither he came with his invited guests, du Bourg, Carolof, the chief agent of the English, and a sub-agent of the Dutch, and there a feast was spread.[7]

On the 26th, du Bourg was invited to lodge in the royal palace in an apartment to be henceforth reserved for the French. He was received by the king on the morrow. He paid his compliments to the monarch in the name of the West India Company and begged him to accept the chariot as a present from it. He then asked permission to build a trading post at Offra, promising to send four ships yearly to trade. The reply was made that the Dutch were in the habit of sending more vessels than could be supplied and that during the last year some were compelled to sail without cargoes; that there were at present six Dutch vessels at the coast and four more were at Chateau de la Mine near by, which awaited word from their agents to come and take cargoes; that thus there was no scarcity either of vessels or of merchandise; furthermore that the Dutch had made very attractive offers to establish a close alliance with the king and to have a monopoly of trade which the king would perhaps find advantageous to accept, inasmuch as the English seemed to have neglected his coast last year, and as the French, who used to come in former years, did not keep their word or fulfill their promises, of which no one could with justice

[7] Delbée has recorded his impressions of the feast which may be consulted with interest by all those who love the curious. *Journal,* p. 394.

TOWARD THE FRENCH WEST INDIES

accuse the Dutch; but that notwithstanding all of these reasons, "the great things which he had heard of the king of France and of the love which one of his principal ministers had for commerce . . . made him desire to gain the friendship of such a great monarch by treating his subjects with favour; that accordingly he had given orders to his great captain of commerce to construct a post for the French at Offra and to protect them in all things, and to favour their commerce." Thereupon were brought before the king the chests which contained the most precious merchandise which had been brought. The king chose "all the pearls and the large red and blue beads, the *carnavacques*, crystals and the fine cottons of India, because the Dutch did not bring such merchandise."[8]

Carolof made an agreement that slaves should be delivered to the West India Company's agent at the rate of eighteen bars of iron each, although the former price had been only twelve.[9] He then went to Assem, where he traded with the prince and some important officials for 260 slaves. He returned to Offra on January 30, and spent the month of February trading. By March 1, *La Justice* had aboard a cargo of 434 negroes and was ready to sail for the West Indies. When she was on the point of sailing, *La Concorde* arrived. Carolof was unwilling to sail before provision had been made for its cargo. Much to the detriment of the cargo of slaves aboard *La Justice*, many days were spent in new interviews with the king and the prince. Delbée reports a very interesting conversation which he pretends to have had with the king during the course of these new interviews:

"The king remarked that he was somewhat surprised that

[8] *Journal*, p. 409.
[9] "He had reason for that which I do not know and as he had been given direction of all that which concerned trade, du Bourg permitted him to do this without interfering." Ibid.

we brought only merchandise similar to that which the Dutch for a long time had been in the habit of bringing. To this I replied that the Dutch being our neighbours carried on an important commerce with France and were in the habit of choosing those articles which were the best suited and would prove the most agreeable to the king; and that inasmuch as we had no knowledge ourselves of what would prove most useful to the king, we brought those articles which the Dutch were in the habit of bringing; but that if we had known that had he desired other things, we would not have failed to bring them. Whereupon the king asked me to bring him, on my next voyage, a sword of silver *à la française,* a large knife, two large mirrors, some fine cloth, lace suitable for making two vests, two pairs of slippers, which I promised to do."[10]

La Justice set sail on March 13 for the islands and arrived at St. Pierre (Martinique) on June 7. De Baas wrote to Colbert on June 25, 1670, as follows:

"I found on arriving here [Martinique] the vessel, named *La Justice,* commanded by Sieur Delbée, with a cargo of 310 negroes or thereabouts. More than a hundred died during the voyage and certain others after they were landed. I gave orders for an equal distribution to be made between the three islands, Martinique, Guadeloupe and St. Christopher. Two-thirds were set aside for the last named islands, but as Captain Delbée assured the general clerk [of the company] that there would be a cargo of slaves for each island, and that his own was meant for Martinique, the whole cargo was sold here."[11]

The vessel had taken two months and three days to make the voyage from Havre to the coast of Guinea and

[10] *Journal,* p. 424.

[11] Arch. Nat. Col., C_8, I, de Baas to Colbert, June 25, 1670. Du Lion in his letter of July 18 likewise notes the arrival of the vessel. As to its cargo, he simply says that the vessel "had a cargo of slaves." Du Lion notes in this same letter, however, the arrival of another vessel belonging to M. de Formont "with a considerably less cargo of negroes." Ibid., C_7, I.

TOWARD THE FRENCH WEST INDIES

from there to Martinique, two months and twenty-three days. After having spent a little more than three months in trade at St. Pierre, *La Justice* set sail for France on July 21 with a cargo of sugar and tobacco. Cape Lizard was sighted on September 16, and on the 20th the vessel anchored at Havre. The voyage from the islands was made in two months, less a day. The whole voyage, therefore, had taken ten months and twenty days.[12]

La Concorde, which we left at the coast of Ardres, traded successfully and sailed for the islands with a cargo of 563 slaves. It arrived at Martinique on September 22, 1670, with 443, having lost 120 en route.[13] Aboard her was Matheo Lopez, sent by the king of Ardres as his ambassador to the French king. He was received with great pomp at Martinique by de Baas and Pélissier. He was sent to France aboard *La Bergère*, one of the company's vessels, which sailed from Martinique about October 1. The arrival of this ambassador with three of his wives, three children and several slaves created a sensation at Versailles.[14]

This initial expedition of the company to the coast of Africa seemed auspicious, for it had yielded good profit. Colbert seems to have had a large vision of what might be accomplished. Thus we find him instructing Pélissier to "consider carefully what advantage there will be for the company if, after having furnished some 2000 negroes to meet the demand in the islands, it can obtain 2000 more to sell to the Spaniards of *Terre Ferme*, for these Spaniards never refuse to buy slaves and pay very dear for them to the Dutch of Curaçao."[15] Encouragements were offered to continue the trade. An *arrêt* of the *conseil d'état* removed all duties from merchandise exported from

[12] *Journal*, p. 473.
[13] Ibid., p. 474.
[14] *Le Commerce de l'Amérique par Marseille*, II, 159.
[15] Clément, III, 2, p. 485, June 21, 1670.

THE COMMERCIAL POLICY OF COLBERT

the kingdom to the coast of Guinea,[16] and a bounty was offered of thirteen livres per head for all slaves imported into the islands.[17]

The company seems to have continued to send vessels to Guinea. Carolof arrived at Guadeloupe near the beginning of 1672 with a cargo of 350 slaves. One of the company's vessels, the *St. François* (captain, Mallet) of Dieppe, brought a cargo of over 200 slaves to the same island at the close of the year. At the same time, *La Justice* was being expected with another cargo from the coast of Guinea.[18] The energetic measures which Colbert took to keep the Dutch out of the islands, especially during the years 1670-71, by maintaining patrol about the Windward Islands, probably gave the West India Company and private French traders licensed by it a monopoly of this trade. Pélissier tried to take advantage of this fact by putting the price of slaves at 4000 pounds of sugar, which was 100 per cent dearer than the price formerly demanded by the Dutch.[19]

[16] To prevent frauds captains of vessels were forced to deposit at their return a certificate of discharge of cargo signed by the agents of the company at the coast. Arch. Nat., AD,vii, 3; *Le Commerce de l'Amérique par Marseille*, II, 303, arrêt of September 18, 1671.

[17] Moreau de Saint-Méry, I, 259-260, January 13, 1672; ten livres of this sum were to be paid by His Majesty to merchants who sent the ships with cargoes of slaves and three livres by the West India Company to the captains of ships.

[18] Arch. Nat. Col., C₇, II, du Lion to Colbert, December 5, 1672.

[19] Colbert attempted to encourage the individual French trader to share the slave trade with the company. Thus an *arrêt* of August 26, 1670, removed the tax of 5 per cent laid by the company on them for the privilege of trading at the coast of Guinea. Moreau de Saint-Méry, I, 197. They were also admitted to the benefits of the *arrêt* which granted exemption from duties on cargoes exported to Guinea and of that which granted a bounty of thirteen livres per head of slaves imported into the islands. No large results, however, were obtained from this policy. Very few individuals seemed to have been attracted to the trade. Colbert himself expressed his disappointment. Arch. Nat. Col., B, 3, fol. 137, Colbert to the directors.

TOWARD THE FRENCH WEST INDIES

But no important results seem to have been realized from the efforts of the company. It was approaching too near to its *débâcle* to be able to accomplish the task set for it. Du Lion wrote in 1672 that the company was no longer making efforts to satisfy the needs of the islands, for the vessels it sent brought only cargoes "of planks, coal and barrels in order to carry away the sugar received in payment of debts which the company was demanding with utmost vigour."[20]

It is to be recalled that Colbert commanded the company to direct its attention also to the importation of salt beef and live stock. He was not satisfied with the fact that the large amount of salt beef consumed in the French islands came almost entirely from Ireland and was often imported by foreign traders. He was particularly anxious that France be made to produce the supply necessary and most of all that it be carried to the islands by French traders. This was why he wished the West India Company to devote special attention to the matter.

His correspondence with Brunet, one of the directors of the company, is very instructive in showing the persistence with which Colbert attempted to realize his wishes. On October 27, 1670, he wrote:

"I note by your letter the application which you are giving at present to carry out the principal points of the instructions which I gave you, and especially in regard to the purchase of French beef to send to the islands in place of that of Ireland. As you know how very much I cherish the success of the plan, you will understand how happy I am to learn of the hopes which you have of success. . . . Bend your energy in that direction and be very sure that you can do nothing which could prove more agreeable to me."[21]

[20] Arch. Nat. Col., C$_7$, II, du Lion to Colbert, July 22, 1672.
[21] Depping, *Correspondance,* III, 522.

THE COMMERCIAL POLICY OF COLBERT

On November 13, he wrote:

"In regard to the matter of beef, do not let yourself be discouraged by difficulties which you encounter at first and continue without exception to buy French beef. In order to let you know how very much I have the matter at heart, I shall tell you that I have informed the directors who are at Paris that if the company will ship during the year 4000 barrels of French beef to the islands, I shall have the king pay to it 4000 écus.[22] During your sojourn at La Rochelle take measures which will be necessary for the shipment of the said amount to the islands during the year 1671. Take care, however, that this be done in good faith, and that only beef of France be furnished. . . . Let me know every two weeks how much beef you have bought and the number of barrels which you have in condition to send to the islands."[23]

To the objection that French beef was too dear, Colbert wrote Brunet that is was necessary to convince traders that it was of superior quality. When Brunet found that merchants resorted to smuggling, Colbert wrote:

"Continue always to buy French beef. . . . In order to force merchants who trade in the islands to buy French beef, you can forbid them to use Ile de Ré as an *entrepôt* for the purchase of Irish beef. In case that you have need of an *arrêt* of the *conseil d'état* to aid you in the matter, let me know and I shall send it to you promptly."[24]

Such an *arrêt* was published on August 17, 1671, which formally annulled the right of *entrepôt* for "beef and other

[22] Bonnassieux, *Les Grandes Comp. de Commerce*, p. 374, states that the sum of 3012 livres was accorded to the West India Company as a bounty on salt beef which it had shipped to the islands.
[23] Depping, *Correspondance*, III, 523; see also other letters in regard to the same subjects, pp. 524, 525, 526.
[24] Ibid., p. 527, February 26, 1671.

TOWARD THE FRENCH WEST INDIES

meats from Ireland."[25] This was followed by a royal ordinance which forbade the importation into the islands of all beef and bacon from foreign countries under penalty of confiscation and 500 livres fine for the first offense, and of bodily punishment in case of repetition.

Brunet seems to have made some purchases of beef for the company in upper Guyenne.[26] Colbert encouraged him to continue: "I see already from news which reaches me from the provinces around La Rochelle that the fact that you are buying cattle has aroused interest. I am counting on you to arrange matters in such a way that in the future it will not be necessary to buy Irish beef."[27]

In spite, however, of Colbert's determination "to succeed in the project at any cost," he was doomed to disappointment. De Baas wrote to him in February, 1672, that French ships were bringing no beef and that, as a consequence, suffering was great.[28] The West India Company thus met with even less success in supplying the islands with salt beef than in furnishing them with slaves.

It met apparently with another failure in trying to supply live stock. Brunet received instructions to purchase live stock during his sojourn at La Rochelle and to ship it to the West Indies. He seems to have made some shipments, for we find Pélissier arousing protests, because he demanded the exorbitant price "of 9000 to 10,000 pounds of sugar for horses of Poitou," which the West India Company was shipping to the islands. No evidence has been found, however, which shows that these shipments were of any considerable importance.

It was the failure to perform these tasks, together with the fact of an increasing number of private French trad-

[25] Moreau de Saint-Méry, I, 230.
[26] Depping, *Correspondance*, III, 528.
[27] E. Jourdan, *Ephémérides de la Rochelle*, II, 32, 33.
[28] Arch. Nat. Col., C$_8$, I, de Baas to Colbert, February 28, 1672.

ers, that brought Colbert to the resolution to abolish the West India Company. On October 11 he wrote to the directors:

"Inasmuch as the commerce of the West India Company is diminishing every day by reason of the number of vessels which private traders are sending to the islands and to the coast of Guinea, and consequently as some of the company's vessels may remain idle, the directors may charter such vessels to the Company of the North, which will pay them five livres per ton more than they pay to foreign vessels."[29]

On December 20, Colbert informed the directors that it would not be necessary to maintain any longer the special boards of directors at La Rochelle and at Rouen, but only correspondents, such as the company maintained at Bordeaux, Nantes and other ports.[30]

Although the revocation of its charter did not occur until December, 1674, for all practical purposes, as Chemin-Dupontès remarks, the West India Company ceased to exist after 1672.[31] On April 9, of that year, Menjot, *conseiller*, and Guillaume Mesnager, a stockholder and former director, were instructed to prepare the liquidation of the company's effects,[32] and on January 21, a commission was named to make a thorough examination of the company's books and further prepare its liquidation. This commission was composed of Mess. Hotman, le Vayer, Menjot, de Senteuil, de Manse, de Formont and Denison.[33]

[29] Arch. Nat. Col., B, 3, fol. 135.
[30] Ibid., fol. 137, December 20, 1671.
[31] Chemin-Dupontès, *op. cit.*, p. 82.
[32] Arch. Col., F_2, 17, arrêt du cons. d'état qui commet les srs. Menjot et Mesnager intéressés en la Cie. des Ind. Oc. pour pourvoir à l'utilité employ. des effets de ladite Cie. April 9, 1672.
[33] Ibid., Extrait des Reg. du conseil d'état, January 21, 1673.

TOWARD THE FRENCH WEST INDIES

On February 21, 1674, a report was made on the state of affairs of the company, of which the following is a summary:

CREDIT.

	liv.	s.	d.
In good debts	155,464	6	8
In bad debts	26,475	1	8
Vessels	3,000	0	0
Effects in the islands	695,717	15	1
Effects at Cayenne	96,309	12	9
Effects at Tortuga, St. Domingo	16,407	4	3
Furnishings and other effects in stores at Paris	2,423	0	1
Value of taxes levied at the entry of the port of Rouen on sugar, wax, etc.	800,000	0	0
Estimated value of land, seigneurial rights and taxes levied in the countries of its concession	1,473,000	0	0
Total	3,268,797	16	5

(Estimated value of the above, according to the opinion of Mess. Bellinzani and Dalier, 3,074,000 livres.)

DEBIT.

Sums owed to various persons	514,730	8	0
To François Le Gendre or to notes held by him	700,000	0	0
To His Majesty	5,382,628	8	6
Total	6,597,350	16	6
Indebtedness of the company	3,328,553	0	1[34]

[34] Arch. Col., F₂, 15, Procès verbal sur les affaires de la Cie. des Ind. Oc.—Etat officiel des comptes de lad. Cie. fait suivant les ordres de Sa. Majesté; also Arch. Nat., G₇, 1316.

THE COMMERCIAL POLICY OF COLBERT

From its origin the company had received from:

Voluntary subscribers	1,297,000 livres.
Sums yielded from taxes of Chambre de Justice	2,000,000 livres.
Total paid by the king	3,337,000 livres.
Sums paid by revenue farmers	700,000 livres.
Total	7,374,000 livres.[35]

In addition the revenue farm at Rouen had yielded for the years 1665-72 a total profit of 372,478 liv. 8s. 5d. That is to say, the West India Company had made use all told of a capital of nearly 8,000,000 livres.[36]

The liquidation of the company went forward rapidly. Its effects yielded the sum of 1,047,195 livres which served for a partial reimbursement of voluntary subscriptions. The king supplied 250,000 livres necessary to make this reimbursement complete and assumed responsibility for all the debts of the company.[37] The right to collect taxes and duties in the islands was farmed out. This revenue-farm became known henceforth as *Domaine d'Occident*. Of the 350,000 livres, the annual rent paid by the farmer, 250,000 livres were set aside for the payment of the company's debts. In the following year the company's possessions in Senegal were sold to the first Company of Senegal. All of its other possessions were reunited to the royal domain and opened freely to all Frenchmen.

[35] Arch. Col., F_2, 15, Mém. sur les avantages procurez par la Cie. des Ind. Oc.

[36] Chemin-Dupontès, *op. cit.*, 68, somewhat exaggerates matters when he asserts that the company had absorbed a capital of 10,000,000 livres.

[37] Arch. Nat., G_7, 1312, Mémoire touchant la Cie. des Ind. Oc. par MM. Mesnager and Dalier—"les Hollandais ayant fait offre de 24,000,000 livres pour ce que de Roy a eu par le moyen de ladite compagnie quoyque le tout n'en couste pas 6,000,000 à Sa. Majesté."

TOWARD THE FRENCH WEST INDIES

The edict of revocation was issued in the month of December, 1674,[38] and thus came to an end the famous West India Company. It had been founded by Colbert in 1664, apparently with high hopes, certainly with gigantic plans for it to realize, and here it was ten years later in a state of hopeless bankruptcy.

It is precisely this fact about the company which has received most attention, and which is the reason why it is considered one of the failures of Colbert's ministry. It is perfectly true that the company did not realize the hopes which both its mission and its opportunities justly raised. Its funds were not always wisely expended, for they were sometimes foolishly wasted, as we have seen. It was often the victim of the dishonesty and ignorance of its agents and clerks. It failed to satisfy more than half the needs of the islands. It sometimes abused its monopoly by imposing unreasonable prices and impossible conditions upon the planters. It was constantly in debt and was forced to appeal frequently to the royal treasury for support. Many of these points of failure can be explained by adverse conditions, some of which, as we have had occasion to see, were quite beyond the power of the company to control. There is one phase of its history, however, which presents the West India Company in a totally different light and which must not escape attention. It is presented in the preamble of the edict of revocation:

"The situation of our kingdom between the Mediterranean on one side and the Atlantic on the other facilitates the lading and discharging of merchandise and has made possible many commercial enterprises. Success has not always crowned such enterprises, because most of the armaments have been made by individuals and have not been supported by sufficient force to insure their success. . . . We were prompted by the affection which we had for our subjects to undertake to estab-

[38] Arch. Col., F₂, 17; Moreau de Saint-Méry, I, 283-289.

lish trade with the islands and mainland of America, which foreigners had usurped for sixty years, in order to preserve for our people the advantages which their courage and their industry had given them the right to enjoy from the discovery of a great expanse of land in this part of the world. For this end we formed the West India Company. . . . Our plan, both useful and glorious, has attained the success which we could expect, and this company has happily taken possession of the lands of its concession, . . . which are inhabited at present by more than 45,000 persons, . . . which furnish trade to more than 100 French ships of 50 to 300 tons, giving employment to a great number of pilots, sailors, gunners, carpenters and other artisans, and which furnishes a market for many articles produced in this realm."

One might be inclined to dismiss this language as official jargon, common to nearly all public documents of the period, but it may be asked if this bit of official jargon does not contain many grains of truth. There is a great difference between 1664 and 1674 in the number of French vessels going to the West Indies. We have seen that in the former year there were practically none, whereas in the latter year there were 131 of private traders alone. The difference is notable. It means that during the ten years a comparatively large commerce had been built up. We can not, of course, credit the West India Company with a very large per cent of the vessels sent to the islands during the last five years of its existence. After October, 1666, private traders became more and more important. But how is one to explain the somewhat rapid rise of the private trader? Was it not from the fact that the organization of the West India Company made possible a concentrated attack upon Dutch traders? Its capital and its resources, together with its centralized administration, made possible a kind of *tour de force* both in closing the doors to foreigners and in re-opening the way for French merchants and French merchandise. The comparatively

TOWARD THE FRENCH WEST INDIES

large number of vessels which it collected during the years 1665 and 1666, created in a sense the nucleus of a merchant marine with which to carry on this trade. The monopoly of the company existed in reality only for two years, and after that time private traders could and did profit from the work of preparation which the company had done.

Thus the West India Company was the means of transition from the period of Dutch commercial supremacy to that of the growth and development of French commerce. It was constantly stated by Colbert and by the directors themselves that the mission of the company was to substitute French trade for Dutch trade. As early as 1667 the directors affirmed in a memoir to Colbert that the moment private French traders grew strong and numerous enough to carry on the entire trade of the islands, the company would willingly cede the whole field to them. This moment had come in 1672 and the company's fall should not be regarded as a failure or as a check in Colbert's commercial policy, but rather as an indication that enough progress had been made to render the employment of such a company no longer necessary. In short, the West India Company rendered a definite service and its fall marks a post of progress in the history of Colbert's policy.

CHAPTER VIII

THE EXCLUSION OF FOREIGN TRADERS

IT has already been remarked that de Tracy, at his departure from France in February, 1664, was charged with the enforcement of an *arrêt* which forbade the Dutch to trade in the islands during the period of six months. Although the fact that a pest was raging at Amsterdam was given as the reason for this action, there can be but little doubt that this was only a pretext and that the measure indicates that Colbert had already reached the decision to exclude Dutch traders and that he thereby laid the first stone in the construction of the solid wall which he intended to build around the French islands. We have just seen that one of the chief tasks imposed upon the West India Company at its creation was to maintain its monopoly of trade to the exclusion of all foreigners. The outbreak of the war with the English, however, forced the company to expend so much of its energy in the defense of the islands and in carrying on war against the enemy, that it was forced to forego its monopoly by admitting both private French traders and the Dutch to the commerce of the islands. The necessity for this is proved by the fact that the directors of the company in France and the administrators in the islands, acting independently of one another, took the step almost simultaneously.

But in spite of the fact that the admission of foreign traders during the war was made necessary by the inability of the West India Company to supply the islands with food, the practice of admitting them did not cease at the close of the war in July, 1667. For over a year after that date the Dutch continued their efforts to draw the commerce of the French islands back into their control and they were so successful that Colbert was forced to begin a long and difficult campaign to drive them from the French possessions. An *arrêt* of the *conseil d'état* of September 10, 1668,[1] formally forbade the West India Company "to grant permission to foreigners to trade within its concession, under penalty of being deprived of the privileges which the king had granted it." The reasons for taking this action were very clearly set forth in the preamble:

"Whereas the king has been informed that contrary to the intentions which he had in organizing and establishing the West India Company, the chief of which was to draw into the kingdom all the commerce of the French islands of America, then in the hands of foreigners, the said company during the late war with England has granted permission to a number of foreigners to trade in these islands in consideration of a certain tax levied on their cargoes; and that since the war the said company has continued the same practice; that the said foreigners, incited by the desire to regain entire possession of this trade, have not remained satisfied with sending vessels for which they had obtained permission from the said company, but have sent vessels without any such authorization; furthermore, that the governors of the said islands, in spite of orders which have been given them to permit no vessels to trade without the company's permission, have received all vessels indiscriminately and have permitted them to barter their cargoes freely; that foreigners take away all the sugar and tobacco and other products of the said islands to the detriment of the sums due by the planters to the West India Company, so that its directors have been forced to appeal to His Majesty; His Majesty, therefore, taking into consideration how important it is for the welfare of the state and for the commerce of the realm that the trade of the islands of America, which gives employment to a large number of vessels and furnishes a market for a large quantity of articles

[1] Arch. Nat. AD,xi, 48; Arch. Nat. Col., A, 24, fol. 93; Moreau de Saint-Méry, I, 174.

produced in the provinces, remain in the entire possession of the French and that foreign traders be excluded in accordance with the practice which other nations follow in regard to their colonies, and His Majesty having for this very purpose placed such large funds at the disposal of the company and lately accorded extraordinary sums in order to repair the great losses which it sustained during the late war with England, and being resolved to grant to the said company additional sums to enable it to regain the greater part of its commerce . . . wills that the commerce of the islands of America and of the other lands granted to the West India Company be carried on by the said company alone and by French traders authorized by it."

This is a most clear statement of the motives which Colbert had had in establishing the West India Company and it gives expression to his large unchanging purpose to permit no compromises with foreign traders and to march with determination straight to the commercial conquest of the French West Indies.

Colbert was still willing, however, to leave in the hands of the company the power of granting passports. He was satisfied for the present with a formal prohibition to the company to issue passports in favour of foreigners. In spite of this, the company continued to allow the Dutch some liberty of trade, for the directors instructed de Baas, at his departure from France in the fall of 1668 to become governor-general of the French West Indies, to admit foreign vessels which brought cargoes of slaves and live stock.[2] In addition the report reached Colbert's ears that the Dutch were obtaining passports in the name of Frenchmen and were continuing to trade in the islands. He thereupon established, on June 12, 1669, the following regulations: (1) that all passports bearing permission to trade in the islands should be granted by His Majesty

[2] Arch. Nat. Col., C$_8$, I, de Baas to Colbert, December 26, 1669.

on certificates of recommendation issued by the West India Company; (2) that the said passports be granted only to Frenchmen; (3) that the passports should be valid only for eight months; (4) that all to whom passports were granted should give bond, either to the directors of the West India Company or to the officers of the Admiralty, that they should take their cargoes to the port specified in the passport and make their returns either to the port from which they had sailed or to some other port of the realm; and (5) that certificates of discharge and of lading of cargoes, properly signed by Admiralty officers, should be deposited at the Admiralty bureau where the passport was issued, otherwise obligations imposed by the bond should still be considered binding.[3] On December 30, 1670, the *arrêt* of June 12, 1669, was restated with the following additions: (1) it was prohibited to trade in the islands without passports; (2) all captains of vessels on arriving in the islands should present to the Admiralty officers their passports and bills-of-lading, properly signed by the Admiralty officers of the port from which they had set sail; and (3) failure to comply with these regulations subjected one to the penalty of confiscation of vessel and cargo and of 1500 livres fine for the first offense, and to corporal punishment in the case of repetition.[4]

Colbert did not content himself with controlling the issue of passports and with making regulations. On September 12, he addressed a circular letter to the governors of Martinique, Guadeloupe, St. Domingo, St. Christopher, Grenada and Cayenne on the subject of foreign commerce:

"Having resolved that all the commerce of the islands of America under my obedience shall be carried on by the French

[3] Moreau de Saint-Méry, I, 178-179. The last clause of the regulation seems not to have been promptly complied with, for an *arrêt* of July 1, 1670, commanded obedience to this regulation. Arch. Aff. Etrang., Mém. et Doc., France, 2007, fol. 127 verso.

[4] Arch. Nat. Col., B, 3, fol. 117; Moreau de Saint-Méry, I, 206-207.

THE COMMERCIAL POLICY OF COLBERT

West India Company, and by my other subjects with permission of the directors of the said company, who have been commanded by me to grant no permission to foreigners, . . . I forbid you very expressly to admit into the island under your command or into the ports which depend upon it any foreign vessels to trade there."[5]

Special instructions were sent to de Baas on June 13, 1669:

"Of all things which you have been commanded to do, there is absolutely nothing to which I desire that you devote your attention so much as to drive out foreign vessels from the islands and in every way possible to prevent them from trading there, without suffering a single exception under whatever pretext that may arise. I desire that you enforce this order with all the precision and with all the severity which are merited by an affair of such importance to the well-being of my subjects."[6]

Colbert wrote to de Baas again on July 31: "In regard to commerce, His Majesty wills that above everything else you devote all of your attention and employ all of your industry and every means at your command to exclude foreigners from trade in the islands, either by punishing inhabitants who aid them or by destroying all their ships and barks which frequent our islands. Keep special watch on the Dutch established at St. Eustatius, who will miss no opportunity to employ every means to sell their merchandise in the French islands and to carry away the products thereof."[7] These instructions were repeated with the same

[5] Arch. Nat. Mar., B$_2$, 7, fol. 128; ibid., Col., F$_3$, 67.
[6] Arch. Nat. Col., B, 1, fol. 153, the king to de Baas, June 13, 1669. On the same day instructions were addressed to Comte d'Estrées, who was in command of a squadron of vessels on a cruise in American waters, to remain in the islands six months longer and "to prevent in every way possible foreign vessels from trading in the islands under any pretext or for any cause whatever." Ibid., fol. 154.
[7] Ibid., fol. 159.

TOWARD THE FRENCH WEST INDIES

emphasis in letters to de Baas on August 8, September 15, and October 4.[8]

In order to give greater publicity to the orders which had been issued to exclude the foreign trader from the islands, a royal ordinance was issued on June 10, 1670, which was as follows:

"His Majesty, having already ordered Sieur de Baas, lieutenant-general in his armies, in command of the islands of America inhabited by his subjects, as well as the particular governors of the several islands, not to suffer any foreign vessel to anchor or to traffic there, and having sent a squadron of three ships of war to seize and capture all foreign vessels found in the ports and roads of the said islands, or in their neighbourhood, and being informed that the said prohibitions have not been executed as rigidly as the welfare of the state and the interests of his subjects demand and that even vessels after confiscation have been repurchased by proprietors for trifling sums; in order to put an end to these abuses, His Majesty expressly forbids any foreign ship or vessel to enter the ports, or anchor in the roads of the said islands, or sail near their shores, on pain of confiscation, and at the same time he expressly forbids his subjects who are inhabitants of the said islands, or who go to trade there, to receive any foreign merchandise or any foreign vessel, or to have any relations with them, on pain of confiscation of said merchandise, 500 livres fine for the first offense and corporal punishment in case of repetition. His Majesty wills that the proceeds from the confiscation of ships and merchandise taken at sea shall be divided, one-tenth to the commander of His Majesty's squadron, another tenth to the captain of the ship that has made the prize, a third tenth to the lieutenant-general in command of the islands, and the rest, half for the crew of the vessel, and half to the West India Company, to be employed by it for the establishment and maintenance of hospitals in the said islands; and that of the proceeds from prizes made on land, one-third shall go to the informer, another third shall

[8] Ibid., fols. 164 and 170; ibid., March 27, October 4, 1669.

be equally divided between the lieutenant-general and the particular governor of the island, and a third shall be given to the aforesaid company for the establishment and maintenance of hospitals. His Majesty hereby commands and orders Sieur de Baas, lieutenant-general in his armies and in command of the said islands, the several governors, the officers of the *conseils souverains* and all of his officers and subjects whom these presents concern, to obey and to enforce the present ordinance."[9]

A copy of this ordinance was sent with special letters to the various governors and officers in the islands.[10] Other letters and instructions, sent by Colbert and the king during the year 1670, show the immense importance which was attached to its enforcement. Out of nineteen letters written to de Baas in that year, no less than twelve were devoted largely to the exposition of the two principles of freedom of trade to all Frenchmen and of rigid exclusion of all foreigners.[11]

Both the ordinance and the instructions were so clear that they should have left no doubt in the minds of governors as to the intentions of the minister. The habit, however, of relying upon the Dutch for a supply of certain articles, such as slaves and live stock, was of such long standing that de Baas seems not to have understood at first that the Dutch should be prevented from bringing these articles. His confusion was quite natural, for, in the first place, although on leaving France to begin his administration in the islands he was ordered to maintain the principles of exclusion of foreigners, he was specifically instructed by the directors of the West India Company

[9] Arch. Nat. Col., B, 2, fols. 85-86; Arch. Nat., AD,vii, 2A; Moreau de Saint-Méry, I, 195-196; Dessalles, I, 516 (Note 2). See also *Cal. St. Pap. Col., Am. & W. Ind., 1669-1674*, No. 104, for a translation, which has served as a base of the present translation.

[10] Arch. Nat. Col., B, 2, fols. 86, 86 verso, 95, 95 verso, 98, 100, etc.

[11] Arch. Nat. Col., B, 2, fols. 88-89, 94, 114 and 115-119.

TOWARD THE FRENCH WEST INDIES

to admit Dutch ships which brought cargoes of negroes and live stock; and, in the second place, he failed to see that any special provisions were being made by Frenchmen to supply these two articles of such prime importance in the cultivation of the islands. He could not understand that such vital interests could be sacrificed for the maintenance of the principle of exclusion of foreigners:

"In regard to commerce with foreigners, Monseigneur, I must say to you that inasmuch as the efficiency of the planters depends upon the number of slaves and of horses which they have, the directors of the West India Company instructed me, when I sailed from France, to receive foreign vessels which brought these two articles. I have acted in accordance with these instructions up to the present. But since receiving the orders of His Majesty, I have forbidden all foreigners to trade and shall continue to do so until I receive instructions from you as to the king's will in the matter. It may be well, nevertheless, to inform you that the planters will suffer very much from the maintenance of such a policy, for the Dutch have been accustomed to bring every year horses from Curaçao and Ireland—a thing which French merchants will not do—and if the planters cannot replace the negroes and horses which die, they will suffer seriously."[12]

Colbert's reply to this letter left no doubt as to the policy which he meant to pursue: "The West India Company has taken such excellent measures to furnish the number of slaves and horses necessary for clearing and cultivating lands in the islands that any brought by foreign vessels would prove superfluous. I desire, therefore, that you receive no foreign vessel under any pretext whatsoever."[13] A formal order was addressed to Pélissier to forbid the clerks of the West India Company to continue

[12] Arch. Nat. Col., C$_8$, I, de Baas to Colbert, December 26, 1669.
[13] Arch. Nat. Col., B, 2, fol. 19 verso, the king to de Baas, March 25, 1670.

THE COMMERCIAL POLICY OF COLBERT

the practice of receiving slaves and horses brought by Dutch ships. A similar order was addressed to the general directors of the West India Company.[14] It was at this time that Colbert commanded the company to limit its commerce to the importation of live stock and slaves. We have dealt elsewhere with the measures which it took in obedience to his orders. In addition, Colbert attempted to make a partial provision for the supply of live stock by requiring every vessel going to the islands, to take two mares, or two cows, or two she-asses.[15] Although the results of these measures were not encouraging, a strict exclusion of all foreign vessels was constantly urged. Thus a letter was written to de Baas on October 12, 1670:

"I shall say to you, in short, that nothing which you can do in the discharge of the duties which I have imposed upon you could prove more agreeable to me than a rigourous enforcement of my orders to exclude foreigners from the trade of the islands. You are not to admit them under pretext that there is need of slaves, or of live stock, or of furnishings of sugar-mills, or of any other sort of merchandise, however pressing such a need may be. I repeat that you are not to admit any foreign vessel or permit any commerce with foreigners. I shall take pains to insure a supply of things necessary for the islands and especially of slaves and live stock."[16]

Again, de Baas did not seem to be sure that French ships should be prevented from trading with foreign islands:

"M. de Gabaret has sent here [Martinique] the bark of a French merchant, named Dartiagne, which he ordered seized when he arrived at Guadeloupe. The merchant, who hails from St. Jean de Luz, confessed that the merchandise which

[14] Ibid., fols. 21, 22.
[15] Arch. Nat. Col., B, 2, fol. 145, December 20, 1670.
[16] Arch. Nat. Col., B, 2, fol. 111, the king to de Baas, October 12, 1670.

TOWARD THE FRENCH WEST INDIES

he had on board had been bought from the English at Nevis. That's why I condemned him to a fine of 4000 pounds of sugar. . . . To tell the truth, I imposed this fine against my own feelings, for I do not know whether or not the king intends that a French merchant who goes to trade in New England and comes back to barter his goods in Barbadoes and in Martinique, for instance, be punished. The *arrêt* of the *conseil d'état* prohibits foreigners to trade in the islands. I understand nevertheless that if a French merchant enjoyed the liberty of going to the English islands, he could, with permission of their governor, transport our sugar to St. Eustatius and load it on Dutch ships. As I thought that Dartiagne had done this, I imposed a fine upon him. Otherwise I should have had scruples in punishing him at all."[17]

Colbert's response could not have left any doubt as to his intentions. He commanded de Baas to prohibit with the utmost rigour "absolutely all foreign commerce in the islands, whether carried on by foreigners themselves or by French subjects. That is to say, that every foreigner importing merchandise into the islands from whatever source it may be, unless he has a passport from the king,

[17] Arch. Nat. Col., C$_8$, I, de Baas to Colbert, March 22, 1670. Du Lion, governor of Guadeloupe, in a letter to Colbert on March 29, mentions the capture of this vessel. He says that Dartiagne had permission from St. Laurent to pass from St. Christopher to Martinique and that en route he was becalmed off Guadeloupe where he was captured by de Gabaret. Du Lion adds that Dartiagne had traded with an English vessel which he had met on his way probably by appointment. Ibid., C$_7$, I, du Lion to Colbert. In another letter de Baas shows that he did not understand at first the earnestness and thoroughness with which Colbert intended to make his fight against the foreign trader. "Two inhabitants of this island who own a bark have applied for permission to trade at Barbadoes two or three times a year in order to buy provisions of which the planters are in such need at present and thus to bring some welcomed relief. I refused to grant the permission and shall continue to do so unless you should see fit to make an exception of an affair of such small consequence, as it assuredly is." Ibid., C$_8$, I, de Baas to Colbert, January 16, 1670.

THE COMMERCIAL POLICY OF COLBERT

should suffer the penalty of confiscation, and that every Frenchman, importing merchandise from foreign countries and even from the nearest foreign islands, should likewise suffer the same penalty, and besides that, all foreign vessels, and particularly those belonging to the Dutch, which are found sailing near the coasts of the French islands are to be seized."[18]

Colbert made only two small exceptions in his rigid system of excluding foreigners. One was in regard to trade between the English and French inhabitants of St. Christopher, and the other, in regard to trade with the Spanish Main. As to the former, he defined his position very clearly in a letter to de Blénac, governor-general of islands, under date of June 2, 1680:

"I note what you write me of the difficulties encountered at St. Christopher to prevent commerce between the English and French. In regard to the commerce of that island, you should distinguish between trade by sea, carried on between the two nations, which should be prohibited just as it is in the other islands, and trade by land, which cannot and should not be prevented in this island."[19]

As to commerce with the Spanish Main, Colbert, true to the ideas of his age and to his own, naturally welcomed any trade which brought returns in gold and silver. He seems to have thought at one time of establishing an *entrepôt* at Grenada for contraband trade with the Spaniards, and at another, he instructed Pélissier to consider the advisability of having the West India Company send 2000 slaves to the Spanish Main, "for these Spaniards never refuse to buy slaves and always pay the Dutch of Curaçao

[18] Arch. Nat. Col., B, 2, fols. 87-89, Colbert to de Baas, June 22, 1670.

[19] Arch. Nat. Col., B, 10, fol. 2, letter to de Blénac, June 2, 1680; also fol. 18, letter to Patoulet; also B, 9, fol. 34, letter to Blénac, April 19, 1679.

TOWARD THE FRENCH WEST INDIES

very dear for them."[20] When, however, Colbert saw that no commerce sprang up with the Spanish Main, he forbade the islands to trade with the Spaniards:

"The exclusion of all commerce with foreigners should be maintained in all the islands. Trade even with Spaniards is to be prohibited, for His Majesty is of the opinion that no Spanish vessels are likely to come from the Spanish Main and he is unwilling that any commerce be carried on with the Spaniards of Porto Rico and the other islands belonging to Spain."[21]

These two small exceptions in the system of excluding foreigners are very readily understood and need not make one stop to qualify the statement that Colbert's exclusion of foreign traders was in theory complete.

If the planters were hungry, barefooted and in rags, they must count these things as a bit of temporary suffering to be endured for the upbuilding of French commerce. They must wait for the law of supply and demand to operate and bring them, sooner or later, an abundance from France. If these same planters were in need of slaves and of live stock to cultivate their cane and turn their sugar-mills, they must await the *"bons ordres"* which the West India Company had given to supply their needs. Such was the system of exclusivism which Colbert wished to impose upon the islands. Such were his demands upon the planters. Their realization would mean the growth of a valuable commerce for the kingdom and thus the realization of one of his fondest dreams. But he was demanding too much. What meant the noble idea of restoring French commerce and the upbuilding of a mighty colonial empire to the planters in the West Indies, whose empty bellies were crying for food, whose nakedness demanded to be clothed, whose sugar-cane, like time and tide, tarried for

[20] Clément, III, 2, p. 485, June 10, 1670.
[21] Arch. Nat. Col., B, 9, fols. 1-8, letter to de Blénac, July 6, 1682.

no man, but ripened for the harvest in its season? Under the shelter of the night in the little inlets and creeks, or in the open day, thanks to the corruption of the officials, foreign traders came and bartered wine, salt beef, slaves and live stock for tobacco, sugar, ginger and dye-woods. The great Louis and his determined minister might thunder commands from Versailles with a voice of Sinai, and the governors might be obedient, or they might not, but one thing was certain, such a rigid system could be enforced only at the cannon's mouth and only by a long and determined struggle could the subjects of the far-away West Indies be brought into subjection to it.

CHAPTER IX

THE FIGHT AGAINST THE DUTCH

A SQUADRON of His Majesty's vessels under the command of Sieur de Treillebois was sent for a cruise in the West Indies and the Gulf of Mexico at the end of 1667. De Treillebois was commanded to remain in the islands for three months, during which time he was to prevent all foreign vessels from trading.[1] At the close of the following year, the Count d'Estrées, vice-admiral, was sent in command of a squadron on a similar mission. He arrived at Martinique about February 1, 1669,[2] and was commanded by an order dated June 13 to remain six months longer in the islands in order to prevent "in every manner foreigners from coming into the roads of the islands and from carrying on trade there under any pretext, or for any motives whatever."[3] No evidence has been found which shows that either de Treillebois or d'Estrées maintained any systematic patrol or succeeded in any large measure in preventing foreign traders from violating the strict orders which had been given for their exclusion. It may have been for this reason that Colbert decided in July, 1669,[4] to send to the West Indies three vessels charged with the special duty of enforcing regulations by maintaining a strict patrol.

In accordance with this decision, *Le Normand, Le Galant* and *L'Aurore* were equipped and sent to the West Indies under the command of de Gabaret. De Gabaret was given special orders, in the name of the king himself, "to

---

[1] Clément, III, 2, p. 398, October 1, 1667.
[2] Dessalles, *Histoire générale des Antilles,* I, 506.
[3] Arch. Nat. Col., B, 1, fol. 154, June 13, 1669.
[4] Clément, III, 2, pp. 456-459, Colbert to de Baas, July 31, 1669.

sink or take or capture all foreign vessels, sailing in the waters about the islands, or attempting to anchor in the roads or harbours of said islands, for whatever cause and under whatever pretext which may be given, under penalty of disobedience to the king."[5] He was commanded to keep his vessels "constantly cruising around the islands," and to keep his plans secret, so that "he could surprise foreign traders in every inlet and harbour where they might attempt to trade."[6] He was ordered to make special efforts to interrupt contraband trade between the Dutch at St. Eustatius and the colony at St. Christopher.[7] De Gabaret received during the year no less than fourteen letters either from the king or from Colbert.[8] Both the frequency and the contents of these letters bear testimony to the importance which was attached to his mission.

De Gabaret arrived with his three vessels at Martinique on January 19, 1670.[9] He straightway sent one of his ships, *L'Aurore*, to Grenada to capture a Dutch vessel which he had heard was trading there. The vessel in question was the *Queen Esther*, of 300 tons, Drik Jansen, captain. In spite of the fact that the captain had a passport, issued by the French West India Company on November 9, 1668, which gave him permission to trade in the islands, and in spite of the fact that the governor of Grenada had given him permission to sell slaves in that

[5] Arch. Nat. Col., B, 2, fol. 47, the king to Capt. de Gabaret, April 9, 1670. The seriousness with which de Gabaret regarded the last phrase of these orders was shown, when he refused near the close of the year to obey the orders of de Baas to go to St. Domingo to quell a rebellion, on the grounds that he had been commanded by the king to perform the task of patrolling the islands and was responsible to the king for the thoroughness of his work. Ibid., de Baas to Colbert, October 19, 1670.

[6] Arch. Nat. Col., B, 1, fols. 89, 98 verso.

[7] Ibid., fol. 47.

[8] Ibid., *passim*.

[9] Arch. Nat. Col., C_8, I, de Baas to Colbert, February 24, 1670.

island, his vessel was seized and taken to Martinique.[10] De Baas wrote the facts to Colbert and awaited instructions. They came under date of June 22, and were very brief: "I believe that I have already said enough for you to know that in all cases where there is any doubt, the king wishes that they be decided against the foreigner."[11] The case must have been considered, for de Baas informed Colbert, in a letter of March 29, 1671, that the vessel had been restored to its captain, but that the sums due him for his negroes were yet to be collected at Grenada.[12] About the same time another small Dutch vessel with a cargo of wine was captured. From November 5 to November 9, five Dutch vessels were seized near St. Christopher.[13]

De Baas complained that de Gabaret was showing too much zeal in his efforts to capture Dutch vessels. Thus he reported his capture of a Dutch bark with a cargo of wood which it was taking from Dominica to Curaçao: "I am sending you, Monseigneur, an inventory of its cargo

[10] Arch. Nat. Col., C$_8$, I, de Baas to Colbert, March 22, 1670. The passport granted to the *Queen Esther* is to be found ibid., C$_{10}$, La Grenade, 1654-1729. The said passport was granted on condition of paying to the company 5 per cent on negroes and live stock imported into the islands and 10 per cent on products exported. The incident was recounted by the English governor of Antigua as follows: "I cannot omit one ignoble passage of the governor of Grenadoes. A Dutchman from Guinea falling in with the islands with 200 negroes was invited by the governor to trade and security assured him, but no sooner were the negroes landed than the governor dispatched a shallop to La Barret [Gabaret] who sent up his vice-admiral and immediately seized poor Hans suspecting no danger, being of twenty-four guns, carried him to St. Kitts and keeps him as a prize till the business be decided in France." *Cal. St. Pap., Am. & W. Ind., 1669-1674,* No. 508, W. Byam, governor of Antigua, to Willoughby.

[11] Arch. Nat. Col., B, 2, fol. 94.

[12] Ibid., C$_8$, I.

[13] Arch. Nat. Col., C$_8$, I, Mém. des prises faites à St. Christopher par M. Gabaret, commandant l'escadre des vais. du Roy.

THE COMMERCIAL POLICY OF COLBERT

and a copy of the captain's commission in order that you may see for yourself that excessive zeal is causing M. de Gabaret to seize all vessels which he can lay his hands upon. He says that he is doing so in accordance with orders to handle the Dutch brutally."[14] To this complaint Colbert made the following reply:

"In regard to the Dutch or the Flemish, as they are called in the islands, His Majesty commands me to say to you that we have the right to capture and confiscate their vessels, when they are found trading or even cruising in the waters of our islands, and that he orders you to enforce with the utmost vigour this right against them. You cannot render a service which would prove more pleasing to him than to trouble them in their commerce and even to chase them from the West Indies entirely, if it can be done without openly violating our treaties, as could be done, for instance, by secretly aiding the Caribs against them in case of a war, or by secretly inciting them to attack the Dutch by furnishing them firearms and ammunition. It will be necessary, however, to be very cautious, so that the Dutch can not make any complaints which could be justified by proof of an unfriendly act."[15]

Colbert stated in another letter that he wished to make the Dutch "lose the habit" of coming to the French islands, and that they would never lose it until the news of confiscation and of destruction of vessels and cargoes produced its effect in Holland.[16]

De Baas' reply has something of the sarcastic in it and shows a disapproval of treating the Dutch with such severity:

"Inasmuch as the first instructions to me to exclude the foreign trader did not specify or explain the policy which the court wished to be followed, I supposed that in case the Dutch

[14] Arch. Nat. Col., C$_8$, I, same to same, March 22, 1670.
[15] Clément, III, 2, p. 487, Colbert to de Baas, July 3, 1670.
[16] Arch. Nat. Col., B, 2, fol. 115, October 12, 1670.

TOWARD THE FRENCH WEST INDIES

came into our roads to trade, they should simply be sent away without listening to their offers and not be treated as enemies. M. de Gabaret, however, who was better informed than I, as he had been enlightened by some rays from the sanctuary, began to treat the Dutch in a fashion which he knew would prove more agreeable to you. I made objections to his brutal treatment, and was so shrouded in darkness as to your intentions, that I myself was groping toward the abyss of error into which I thought he was already falling. It is thus that the ignorant err and are lost. Nevertheless since receiving the orders of His Majesty and your own, Monseigneur, I see the error of my way. . . . You may rest assured that I shall henceforth treat the Dutch with the utmost severity."[17]

The strict exclusion of foreigners from the French islands brought a protest from the English government. Colbert replied to it in a very interesting letter to the French ambassador at London:

"In reply to your letter of the 20th of the last month, I shall say that the ambassador of England at this court has filed the same complaint as the English government has with you in regard to the ordinance of June 10 last, which forbids foreigners to trade or cruise in the waters of the French islands of America under penalty of confiscation. His Majesty orders me to say that he was forced to issue this ordinance in order to drive out the Dutch, who have become so accustomed to carry on all of this trade (in which they are especially favoured by all the planters) that it was impossible to get rid of them without the employment of extraordinary measures; that for this purpose His Majesty is forced to maintain a squadron of armed vessels in the islands. As the same causes of complaint did not exist against the English, who are contented, as we are informed, to carry on trade with their own islands, His Majesty would have been glad to make any exception in their favour in the enforcement of the aforesaid ordinance, but he was obliged to make the terms of the regulation general in regard to all nations on account of the

[17] Arch. Nat. Col., C$_8$, I, March 29, 1671.

treaties which he had with Holland. He has given orders to Sieur de Baas, who is in command of the islands, to enforce the regulation with the utmost rigour against the Dutch, but at the same time to treat the English differently by reason of the fact which I have already noted, that they have never engaged in this trade nor at present are attempting to do so. You can, therefore, assure the king of England and his ministers that nothing will be done in the enforcement of the present regulation contrary to the good relations which the king wishes to be maintained between the two crowns and between their subjects; and that English vessels will receive in all of the waters and lands of His Majesty good treatment and all the aid which his own vessels and those of his subjects receive from the English, on condition, however, that they attempt to carry on no trade in our islands, as they pretend that they do not do and in accordance with the regulations which the king of England orders to be enforced in the islands under his own obedience."[18]

It is to be noticed that although it was promised here that the English would not be treated with severity as were the Dutch, Colbert made no exception in their favour as to the privileges of trading in the islands. De Gabaret, in fact, captured a French vessel which attempted trade with the English islands.[19]

The effect of de Gabaret's activity seems to have been felt at once, for de Baas wrote on November 10, 1670: "The Dutch have stopped coming to our coasts. As long as there are vessels of the king here they will flee from them as from dangerous reefs. M. de Gabaret is continually trying to surprise them by laying traps. I believe that in the future he will be able to see them only from afar off. They are greatly frightened."[20] The work of patrolling,

[18] Clément, III, 2, pp. 491-493, Colbert to Colbert de Croissy, August 5, 1670.

[19] Arch. Nat. Col., C_8, I, de Baas to Colbert, March 22, 1670.

[20] Arch. Nat. Col., C_{10}, St. Christophe, I, de Baas to Colbert, November 10, 1670.

TOWARD THE FRENCH WEST INDIES

however, had to be interrupted in order to quell a rebellion which had broken out in St. Domingo.

When Ogeron took command at St. Domingo as governor for the West India Company, the inhabitants said frankly that they would never submit to the company and that they would obey him only as governor for the king, and that although they intended to be obedient to the king, there was one point in which they would never yield, namely, in regard to trade with the Dutch, "who had never let them lack for anything at a period when the presence of French at Tortuga and St. Domingo was unknown in France."[21] There was a spirit of too much independence and too great a habit of not being subjected to any other law than that of force for these inhabitants to submit peaceably to any such system as that which Colbert was attempting to impose upon them.

About the first of May (1670), Ogeron, on returning to Tortuga from the coast of St. Domingo, sighted two large vessels, which, on seeing him, pretended to be going to Coridon, where the English were accustomed to go to get salt. Consequently he believed them to be English vessels from Jamaica and did not give chase. On arriving at Tortuga, however, he learned that the two vessels were Dutch, armed with twenty-eight and thirty-two guns, and commanded by Peter Constant and Peter Marcq; that during his absence these vessels had traded with filibusters at Bayaha and then had anchored on the northern coast of St. Domingo at Port de Paix, where they had remained trading during eight days. They had not only traded with all comers, but had sent a boat to Tortuga, and although the West India Company's agents forbade them to trade, Peter Constant replied that some one stronger than he would have to keep him from doing so.

[21] Charlevoix, *Histoire de l'Isle Espagnole*, II, 61.

THE COMMERCIAL POLICY OF COLBERT

Two days later, having learned that all the inhabitants of Léogane were in rebellion, Ogeron embarked on the vessel, *Les Armes de la Compagnie*, and sailed thither. On arriving at Nippes four days later, he found the same two Dutch vessels anchored there, and learned that the rebellion had spread to the whole western coast. The rebels had sent messengers to the northern coast in order to win the co-operation of the filibusters and buccaneers there. An attempt was made to prevent the two Dutch ships from continuing their trade and when they sent two boats ashore they were ordered seized. The Dutch forthwith attacked the governor, retook the boats by force, and sent Renou and another commander, de Ville Neufve, on board their vessels as prisoners. Ogeron himself was forced to leave Nippes before the attack of a hundred armed men. He sailed and arrived two days later at Petit Goave. There the inhabitants pretended to welcome him. As a bit of caution, however, he first sent a messenger with letters addressed to some of the principal inhabitants. The messenger had hardly set foot ashore before he was arrested. No less than two thousand shots were fired at the governor's vessel and he was forced to retire to Tortuga. He learned on arriving there that the rebels of the west coast were marching to unite themselves with those of the north and that they were planning to attack him at Tortuga.

He straightway dispatched Renou, a lieutenant, to the Windward Islands in order to inform de Baas of the revolt and to demand aid. Renou fell sick en route and did not reach Martinique before September 25.[22] De Baas gave orders to de Gabaret to proceed at once to St. Domingo in order to quell the rebellion. De Gabaret, however, refused to obey the order, on the grounds that he was under special orders from the king to patrol the Windward

[22] Arch. Nat. Col., C₇, I, du Lion to Colbert, September 30, 1670.

TOWARD THE FRENCH WEST INDIES

Islands. Consequently a special order from France had to be waited for before aid was sent to Ogeron.

In the mean time the revolt continued. Ogeron was attacked by three hundred rebels, but succeeded in holding his ground at Tortuga.[23] St. Domingo, however, was entirely in control of the rebels and foreigners were trading there with the greatest freedom. The hatred against the company was so great that the planters asserted, according to Ogeron, that they would rather have their goods perish than see them loaded upon one of its vessels. The governor was powerless to assert his authority, because he found no support among the planters. He was so discouraged, in fact, that he proposed to Colbert the establishment of a colony on the coast of Florida with the few who remained faithful to him.[24]

On receiving news of the revolt, Colbert acted promptly. He first filed complaint with the Dutch government against the conduct of the two vessels at St. Domingo, and at the same time gave warning that all Dutch vessels found cruising near Tortuga and the coast of St. Domingo, would be sunk or confiscated.[25] He then sent orders to de Gabaret to go to St. Domingo, to restore Ogeron, and to capture or sink all Dutch vessels found near the coast.

In obedience to orders, de Gabaret arrived in Tortuga on February 7, and tried, in co-operation with Ogeron, to quell the rebellion. The planters of Tortuga were persuaded without difficulty to take a new oath of allegiance to the king. De Gabaret and Ogeron then sailed, on February 9, for the western coast of St. Domingo. They arrived at Léogane on the 14th. De Sourdis, captain of *L'Aurore*, was sent ashore with a summons to the rebels

[23] Bib. Nat. MSS., Franç. Nouv. Acq., 9325, fols. 176-178, Ogeron to de Baas, October 9, 1670.
[24] Charlevoix, II, 89.
[25] Arch. Nat. Col., B, 2, fol. 127, Colbert to Ogeron, November 6, 1670.

to lay down their arms and to acknowledge Ogeron as their governor. In reply to his appeals they said that although they were good subjects to the king, they would not submit to the West India Company or acknowledge Ogeron as their governor. De Gabaret then came ashore himself to endeavour to persuade the rebels to change their mind. He found before him 600 of them armed. He received the same reply. When he tried to frighten them by threats, he was greeted with cries of derision. He then tried to deal directly with one of the leaders, but he no sooner began to talk with him than the rebels crowded about in great numbers and shouted that this leader had no more power to treat than anyone else. De Gabaret returned to his vessel to confer with Ogeron as to the best measures to be taken. An immediate attack seemed imprudent, because the landing of troops would prove exceedingly difficult on account of the marshes. Accordingly they sailed on the 16th and arrived at Petit Goave the following day. Here they found also all the inhabitants armed and drawn up in battle array. Ogeron addressed a letter to them, but they refused to listen to its contents, and began to cry, "*Vive le Roy, point d'Ogeron!*"[26] They announced their intentions to do as the inhabitants of Léogane had done, and asserted that they would be re-inforced by the rebels from there on the morrow. In spite of these threats an attack was made upon them and they fled into the woods. The royal troops, after burning a few houses, were re-embarked and sailed away. The same thing was repeated at Nippes. No thorough

[26] An explanation of the hostility of the inhabitants of St. Domingo towards Ogeron is perhaps to be explained by a letter written by du Lion to Colbert on September 30, 1670: "The people of St. Domingo say that since Ogeron has participated in commerce with the West India Company, he no longer governs them as a father, but as a man who is promoting his personal interests. I don't know whether these reports are true or not." Arch. Nat. Col., C₇, I.

TOWARD THE FRENCH WEST INDIES

campaign seems to have been attempted. De Gabaret and Ogeron both decided that it was best to return to Tortuga, where they arrived on the 25th. From February 27 to March 4, the inhabitants of Port de Paix and Port Français were visited and finally persuaded to take the oath of allegiance. With this de Gabaret seems to have been contented and straightway sailed for France.

After de Gabaret's departure, Ogeron, on returning to the west coast of St. Domingo, found that the spirit of rebellion had lost much of its zest. He agreed that no prosecutions would be made on account of the recent rebellion, but said that all French vessels would be permitted to trade at Tortuga and the coast of St. Domingo, but that foreigners would be excluded. The inhabitants thereupon returned to their obedience to the governor. Renou was sent on a special mission to France with a letter to Colbert to demand pardon for the rebels. The letter bore the date of May 7, 1671. Colbert replied under date of October 21, expressing entire satisfaction with the conduct of Ogeron, and informing him that the king had granted general pardon to all. The terms of the pardon stated that it had been granted because Ogeron had affirmed that all acts of hostility had ceased; that arms had been laid down, and that there was sincere regret for the acts of rebellion.[27]

De Gabaret and Ogeron were both in agreement as to the cause of this rebellion. "This rebellion occurred," said Ogeron, "only by reason of the regulation which forbade trade with foreigners. Thus it is certain that if the two Dutch vessels had not come to trade and made strong appeals to the inhabitants to do so, the rebellion would not have occurred."[28] De Gabaret affirmed that the rebel-

[27] Arch. Nat. Col., B, 3, fols. 75-78, 79.
[28] Arch. Nat. Col., C₉, I, Proces verbal de la Revolte arrivée à la Coste de St. Dom., August 12, 1670.

lious and insolent spirit of the inhabitants came from the fact that they were too sure of trade with foreigners. Suzanne, a former agent of the West India Company at St. Domingo, had established himself at Jamaica and offered good prices to the inhabitants of St. Domingo for all their products. He had, in fact, made a contract with them by which he agreed to take all they produced and transport it to Holland, for which purpose he would furnish a vessel of 300 tons armed with twenty-two guns, and in return to bring every year a quantity of negroes and all sorts of merchandise for a reasonable price. This agreement had made the planters believe that they could be quite independent of France and resist all attacks against them.[29]

In the following year, Ogeron demanded a vessel of twenty or thirty guns to serve as a patrol,[30] but his demand seems not to have met with a favourable response, for he wrote in the following year, on the eve of the outbreak of the war with Holland, that he had neither vessels nor armed soldiers nor ammunition, and that it would be impossible for him to defend himself in case of a foreign attack or to prevent foreign commerce.[31]

The revolt at St. Domingo seems to have awakened some echo in the other islands, but beyond a bit of murmuring there was no overt act of rebellion.[32]

De Gabaret's sojourn in the islands had meant much toward the enforcement of the regulations against foreign traders. The presence of three armed vessels which captured at the cannon's mouth Dutch vessels and confiscated them before the eyes of the planters must have made, as Colbert hoped it would do, a big impression both upon the Dutch and upon the planters. The show of such force

[29] Charlevoix, II, 94; Arch. Nat. Col., C$_9$, I, Ogeron to Colbert, March 4, 1671.
[30] Arch. Nat. Col., C$_9$, I, September, 1671.
[31] Charlevoix, II, 97.
[32] Arch. Nat. Col., C$_7$, I, du Lion to Colbert, September 30, 1670.

TOWARD THE FRENCH WEST INDIES

proved much more effective in a frontier community like the West Indies than ordinances and commands. The spirit of revolt was hushed and the planters were held in subjection. The governor of a neighbouring English island remarked that, although the French were "thus huffing it at sea," the poor planter was suffering within the islands.[33] The Dutch fled before such force and seem to have suffered. Thus du Lion wrote to Colbert on March 29, 1670:

"The quantity of merchandise is so great at St. Eustatius that the Dutch do not know what to do with it and are forced to sell it at very low prices to the English at Nevis, Montserrat and Antigua. . . . The Dutch will certainly be ruined so far as the islands are concerned, if the policy of excluding them is strongly enforced, for they will be obliged to see their merchandise perish or to send it back to Europe, and in addition they will be forced to send away their vessels without any cargo whatever."[34]

The results upon French shipping seem to have proved rather satisfactory to Colbert. He wrote to de Baas on October 10, 1670, as follows:

"I'll tell you for your own satisfaction that since you have turned your attention to the enforcement of the laws against foreigners, we notice that a much larger number of French vessels demand permission to go to the islands and we see also that the number of refineries is increasing constantly in the realm. Foreigners no longer bring us sugar. We have begun since six weeks or two months to export it to them."[35]

It would be a mistake to suppose, however, that the problem of excluding the foreign trader had been definitely solved, for the presence of armed vessels was still necessary. De Gabaret was commanded to leave at his depart-

[33] *Cal. St. Pap., Am. & W. Ind., 1669-1674.*
[34] Arch. Nat. Col., C₇, I, March 29, 1670.
[35] Arch. Nat. Col., B, 2, fol. 115.

ure one of his vessels, *L'Aurore*, a frigate, to continue the work which he had begun.[36] Another squadron under the command of d'Aplemont was sent to Martinique at the beginning of 1672. De Baas was ordered to use it for the protection of French commerce and "in order to prevent any foreign vessel from trading in the French islands."[37] In 1673 three vessels, *Le Belliqueux*, *La Fée* and *La Sibille*, were on patrol duty, and at the close of the year three others were sent out, *L'Alcion*, *Les Jeux* and *La Friponne*, "which were to be employed for no other purpose than to give chase to all foreign vessels which attempted to come into the roads of the islands."[38] Throughout the course of the Dutch war, ships were constantly sent to the West Indies, both to defend them and to keep out foreign traders.[39]

But Colbert was not contented with the ground which he had gained from de Gabaret's work in 1670. Reports reached his ears that some vessels, purported to have been built in Canada and in the West Indies, were taking cargoes to foreign ports under the claim that they were not subject to the regulations which governed vessels built and owned by merchants of France. To meet this situation, a royal ordinance was proclaimed on July 18, 1671, which forbade such practice.[40] In this same year he advanced to another point in his fight by attempting to exclude Irish salt beef.

Salt beef was indispensable at this time for feeding slaves, and a large quantity was necessary to West India planters. The supply had almost from the beginning been

[36] Arch. Nat. Col., B, 2, fol. 149, order to de Gabaret, December 28, 1670.
[37] Arch. Nat. Col., B, 4, fol. 29, Colbert to de Baas, March 24, 1672.
[38] Ibid., 5, fol. 47, Colbert to de Baas, September 5, 1673.
[39] Ibid., 6, fols. 15 verso, 16.
[40] Arch. Nat. Col., B, 3, fols. 62-64; Moreau de Saint-Méry, I, 227.

TOWARD THE FRENCH WEST INDIES

brought either from Ireland directly, or indirectly through Holland or the ports of France.[41] But one of the cardinal points in Colbert's economic policy was independence so far as possible of foreign markets. He saw no reason why the French should seek a supply of salt beef in Ireland, when it might be produced in France. The privilege of *entrêpot* in France was annulled for Irish salt beef by an *arrêt* of August 17, 1671.[42] Another ordinance of November 4, 1671, forbade the importation of salt meat, purchased in foreign countries, under penalty of confiscation of vessel and 500 livres fine for the first offense and corporal punishment for the second.[43] Bounties were also offered for the exportation to the islands of French salt beef. Salt beef, however, became so scarce that governors were forced to permit trade with foreigners to save slaves and planters from suffering. "I saw people at Guadeloupe," wrote one official, "come to thank their commander for the permission which he had given to the English to sell 200 barrels of beef, swearing to him with tears in their eyes that it had been more than a year since they or their families had had a morsel of meat to eat."[44] Two Jewish merchants of Martinique were permitted to import from Barbadoes, a cargo of codfish, cheese, butter, bacon, beef, candles, cloth and shoes.[45] Permission was likewise granted to four English vessels to trade, one, a ketch with a cargo of provisions for Guadeloupe, the other three with

[41] Du Lion states, in a letter of July 25, 1670, that de Formont, a French merchant, was preparing a quantity of salt beef and live stock in Ireland for shipment to the islands. Arch. Nat. Col., C₇, I. A further discussion of trade in salt beef will be found in a succeeding chapter.

[42] Moreau de Saint-Méry, I, 130. Its enforcement was postponed until February 1, in order to enable those merchants who had a stock of Irish beef on hand to dispose of it.

[43] Ibid., p. 253.

[44] Arch. Nat. Col., C₈, I, du Clerc to Colbert, January 20, 1675.

[45] Ibid., de Baas to de Bléor, February 6, 1674.

similar cargoes for Martinique. Among the latter was a "ketch coming from the city of Boston."[46] De Baas permitted another foreign vessel to bring some salt beef to St. Pierre, to enable the labourers to continue the work on the fortifications which they had been compelled to quit because they had nothing to eat.[47]

Colbert sternly rebuked this conduct and forbade any exceptions being made to the regulations regarding trade with foreigners.[48] He was forced, however, by conditions in the islands in 1673, to restore the right to import Irish beef and never renewed the fight.[49]

De Baas wrote on February 8, 1674, in most emphatic terms that all foreign commerce had ceased:

"I do not know, Monseigneur, what can be your thoughts on the subject of foreign commerce after the repeated assurances which I have given you that there is none at all. If anyone has written you differently and can convince me that what he writes is so, I shall submit to punishment without asking for mercy. It is true that on the eve of my departure for Curaçao a small English vessel which asked permission to take water in this harbour [St. Pierre] aided me by bartering a small quantity of codfish, herring and biscuits for French wine. Lately a bark brought seven or eight barrels of beef, which were bartered for French brandy. The beef was needed to feed the workmen who are engaged in fortifying the harbour and who had been forced to abandon their work on account of a lack of food. It is perhaps of these facts that you have been told. If beyond these two cases any foreign commerce has been carried on in the French islands with my knowledge, I wish very much that the king punish me with the utmost rigour. Thus, Monseigneur, your mind can be at

[46] Arch. Nat. Col., C$_8$, I, du Clerc to Colbert, January 20, 1675.
[47] Ibid., de Baas to Colbert, February 8, 1674.
[48] Arch. Nat. Col., B, 6, fols. 32, 34-39, Colbert to de Baas, May 15, 1674.
[49] Arch. Nat. Col., B, 5, fol. 45, September 5, 1673.

TOWARD THE FRENCH WEST INDIES

rest on the subject of foreign trade, for the truth is as I have represented it."[50]

And yet in the same letter de Baas wrote near its close that as the price of sugar was exceedingly low, the planters had begun to cultivate indigo and ginger, and that they had devised "other means for their subsistence by raising stock and poultry of every description, which they sell at good profit, especially to foreigners."[51]

The letter raises a question of some importance. What did de Baas mean by affirming most categorically that commerce with foreigners had ceased, and yet adding that stock and poultry were being sold to them? He could not have been ignorant of the fact that the regulations prohibited all trade with foreign islands, even when carried on by Frenchmen, for he had raised the question himself in a letter to Colbert in 1670 and had received most definite and clear-cut instructions on the point.[52] The same difficulty occurs elsewhere in the correspondence of de Baas. Thus only a few months later he wrote Colbert that commerce with the Dutch had ceased and that regulations were being strictly enforced,[53] and yet he was at that time, according to one of his own letters, trying to establish trade with the Dutch:

"I should tell you, Monseigneur, that during my stay at St. Christopher, I wrote to a Dutch merchant, named Doukre, who lives at Curaçao and whom I knew here at Martinique some three years ago, to send me information in regard to the price of sugar, ginger and indigo at Curaçao in order that I might have some idea of their value. I shall send him a large enough quantity of these articles to yield to both of us an honest profit. I had been thinking of this scheme for some

[50] Arch. Nat. Col., C$_8$, I, de Baas to Colbert, February 8, 1674.
[51] Ibid.
[52] See preceding chapter.
[53] Arch. Nat. Col., C$_8$, I, March 29, 1671; C$_{10}$, St. Christophe, I, de Baas to Colbert, November 10, 1670.

time, but I did not wish to take the risk of sending a vessel to Curaçao without receiving in advance some assurance that it would be permitted to return. Some six days ago I received a reply not only from the merchant to whom I had written, but also from the governor, Otterinck, who informed me very civilly that M. Doukre had informed him of my intentions and assured me that foreigners received the same treatment at Curaçao as the Dutch. His letter is dated at Fort Amsterdam, Curaçao, December 10, 1671. I believe, Monseigneur, that after this assurance that you will not raise any objections, if I send a small bark, belonging to the king, which is still here, and carry on a little trade with Curaçao. . . . I shall do so in about fifteen days."[54]

Furthermore, de Baas informed Colbert from time to time, as has been noted above, that he had admitted in some cases trade with foreigners and justified his conduct by saying that it was necessary in order to prevent suffering. The motive given for sending a vessel to Curaçao, however, was not the relief of suffering, but personal gain.

Did de Baas tell Colbert of these few instances in order to hide from him a larger number where he was permitting foreigners to trade? Did he profit from his situation by sharing in the profit with foreign traders? Du Lion, the governor of Guadeloupe, asserted in many letters that de Baas was doing so. In one very long letter he gave an account of the corrupt practices of Cartier, the West India Company's general agent, in admitting the Dutch, and cited specific instances where de Baas had aided him and profited personally from trade with the Dutch.[55] In another letter, du Lion said that de Baas was embarrassed by the presence of the king's vessels:

"MM. de Gabaret and de Sourdis, captains of the king's vessels, have stated to me that M. de Baas is not pleased with

[54] Arch. Nat. Col., C$_8$, I, de Baas to Colbert, January 20, 1672.
[55] Arch. Nat. Col., C$_7$, I, du Lion to Colbert, December 1, 1669, a long and extremely interesting letter.

TOWARD THE FRENCH WEST INDIES

the way in which they have been capturing foreign vessels in the roads of Martinique and Grenada, where they were wont to trade. They turned over their prizes to him and had difficulty enough in obtaining receipts from him. They are of the opinion that this arises from the fact that M. de Baas wishes to have more leeway in granting favours to foreigners, to whom he must have made promises, for, since he is unable to grant them freedom to trade on account of the presence of the king's ships, they have complained that he has not kept his promise to them. . . . These captains are determined, however, to capture as many Dutch vessels as possible. Notwithstanding this, M. de Baas has granted three permissions to land cargoes brought from Holland. I notified him that I would not permit the cargoes to be landed in Guadeloupe, unless he gave a written order forcing me to do so. I urged him to remember that you had given me orders to destroy a Dutch vessel rather than let it trade in this island. M. de Baas has another way of regarding the matter."[56]

Du Lion, the author of these charges, seems to have been a jealous, meddlesome busybody and gossiper. His letters leave the impression that their author was one of those unfortunate self-righteous individuals who are quick to see the faults in others and gloat upon them. Colbert saw fit more than once to rebuke him, as for instance:

"I am writing you only a few lines, in response to all the letters which I have been receiving from you for a long time, to tell you that I find them too long, too tedious and of too small importance to spend my time reading them. . . . M. de Baas is your enemy, the West India Company is trying to destroy you, Pélissier is also your declared enemy, as is also du Ruau Pallu and the rest. Their enmity toward you is a creation of your own imagination, for as a matter of fact, none of them has ever tried to play you a bad turn. Your own letters prove to me that you would like to be omnipotent in the government which the king has confided to you, as well

[56] Arch. Nat. Col., C$_7$, du Lion to Colbert, March 8, 1670.

as in all of the other islands. Judges fail to do their duty, if their decisions are not in accord with your views. The West India Company does nothing worth while if it does not meet with your approval."[57]

In another letter he rebuked du Lion for insubordination,[58] and in still others he told him that it was needless for him to keep watch on what de Baas did, as for the most part he was commanded to do many things against which he was making complaint.[59] It must be stated also that du Lion was decidedly hostile to de Baas, because he had been forced by de Baas to leave Guadeloupe and sail for France in 1669.[60]

But one cannot read carefully the charges made by du Lion without being on the whole convinced that they were based partially at least on facts. Colbert stated himself that he "continually found de Baas conniving with foreign traders and pardoning them too easily."[61] Furthermore, Colbert did not accept the statement which de Baas made in the letter quoted above that all commerce with foreigners had ceased, for he wrote under the king's name in reply as follows:

"I receive complaints from merchants every day to the effect that when they send their vessels laden with merchandise for the use and consumption of the inhabitants of my islands, they find vessels of the English and of other foreigners admitted under various pretexts—a fact which is utterly ruining the commerce of the French. It is this which forces me to

[57] Arch. Nat. Col., B, 5, fols. 51 verso, 52.
[58] Clément, III, 2, p. 538, May 1, 1672.
[59] Arch. Nat. Col., B, 2, fols. 49 verso, 50, April 9, 1670; and fol. 100, July 3, 1670.
[60] Arch. Nat. Col., C₇, I, June 27, 1670, and Clément, III, 2, p. 457, July 31, 1669.
[61] Arch. Nat. Mar., B₂, 14, Colbert to Colbert de Terron, January 2, 1671.

TOWARD THE FRENCH WEST INDIES

write you that it is my will that my ordinances which forbid foreigners to trade in the islands be promptly enforced."[62]

It seems on the whole probable that de Baas was guilty of admitting foreign traders and perhaps that he even did so with corrupt purposes. De Baas' actions, however, are to be explained in part by the fact that he yielded in some cases to necessity and admitted foreign ships to relieve suffering, and it must be added that on the whole de Baas made an excellent governor, and was retained in his position until his death on January 24, 1677.

How far French governors of the West Indies were guilty of bribery in the matter of foreign trade it is impossible to state. There is one case of conviction of an official at St. Christopher in 1670,[63] and about the same time, St. Marthe, governor of Martinique, was convicted of carrying on illicit trade with the English.[64]

The year 1677 was marked by two formal renewals of the regulations against foreign commerce, one on September 11, 1677, by the proclamation of a royal ordinance,[65] and the other by an *arrêt* of the *conseil d'état* of October 16, 1677.[66] The latter was necessitated by the fact that the *conseil souverain* of St. Christopher had interposed its authority to prevent the penalty of confiscation from being enforced in two cases of conviction for trade with foreigners. The circumstances were as follows. At the liquidation of the West India Company, the right of collecting duties and taxes in the islands had been trans-

[62] Arch. Nat. Col., B, 6, fol. 17 *bis*, May 10, 1675.

[63] It is spoken of in the correspondence between de Baas and Colbert as the "affair Royer." See Clément, III, 2, pp. 490, 500 and 673.

[64] See a full exposition of the case in Dessalles, *Hist. gén. des Antilles*, III, 194-197.

[65] Arch. Nat. Col., B, 7, fol. 41 verso, 49; Moreau de Saint-Méry, I, 304-305.

[66] Arch. Nat., G$_7$, 1313.

ferred into a farm called the *Domaine d'Occident*. The farmer in taking possession of the farm was commanded to instruct his agents to prevent foreign commerce. The agents, sent to St. Christopher, found on their arrival the inhabitants trading freely with foreigners. Several attempts at arrest proved fruitless, but two seizures were made, one of twenty-six barrels of sugar and another of six barrels of beef. Sieur Dupas, the judge of the island of St. Christopher, declared the seizures justified and ordered their confiscation according to law. The *conseil souverain*, however, annulled the decision and ordered the restitution of the goods in question. Oudiette, the farmer of the *Domaine d'Occident*, considered the case of enough importance to make appeal to the *conseil d'état* in France. It was in answer to this appeal that the *arrêt* of October 16 was rendered, sustaining the decision of the judge, and at the same time ordering the enforcement of the laws against foreign trade. In spite, however, of this *arrêt*, trade between the English and the French at St. Christopher continued. The task of preventing it was exceedingly difficult. A double frontier existed between the two peoples from the fact that the French occupied the two ends of the island and the English the middle. It was consequently only a matter of "one kick of the foot to roll a barrel of beef or a bale of cotton to the French, and another to roll a barrel of sugar in payment to the English."[67] Soldiers were posted along the frontier, but they proved entirely untrustworthy, for they profited from their situation by permitting foreign trade. Commercial agents also proved unfaithful. They stocked their stores with foreign goods and wrote to their employers in France that there was no sale for French goods in the islands, because the governors and intendants and agents

[67] Arch. Nat. Col., C₁₀, St. Christophe, I, Mémoire sur St. Christophe par Sr. Cloche, commis. du Dom. d'Oc., April 10, 1679.

of the revenue farmers permitted free commerce with foreigners. Only about one-fourth of the vessels which went to St. Christopher between July, 1678, and April, 1679, were officially reported.[68] Consequently the English imported much merchandise from Nevis and the Dutch from St. Eustatius. One effect of this was that beef at Martinique and Guadeloupe was twenty to forty per cent dearer that at St. Christopher.[69] St. Laurent, the governor of St. Christopher, wrote on July 2, 1679, that two companies of marines and twenty soldiers from the garrison had been posted along the frontiers at places indicated by Sieur Cloche, and that he had given all orders necessary to prevent foreign trade. Englishmen were forbidden to pass with merchandise through French territory without special permission.[70] The English governor objected, however, to such a regulation, maintaining that all harbours and roads were free to them for the transportation of all of their goods according to treaty between the two nations. This constituted a very serious difficulty.

"It is not at all easy," St. Laurent wrote, "to prevent foreign commerce at St. Christopher, so long as the roads and harbours remain common to both nations for the transportation of merchandise. . . . If we forbid the English to anchor in our harbours of Basseterre and Cabesterre, whence they transport provision to their quarters of Cabesterre and Cayonne, and to which they bring their goods to be embarked, they will have the right to forbid us to pass across their territory and

[68] Ibid.
[69] Ibid., Cloche proposed among other things the following remedies: (1) A strict enforcement of the orders of His Majesty in confiscating all foreign vessels found in French waters; (2) a visitation of stores and of vessels and the confiscation of foreign goods found in them; (3) a reward of three écus to soldiers for every barrel of sugar which they intercepted in passing into English territory; (4) a prohibition for soldiers to board foreign vessels.
[70] Arch. Nat. Col., C_{10}, St. Christophe, I, Mémoire sur le commerce étranger à St. Christophe par St. Laurent, July 2, 1679.

THE COMMERCIAL POLICY OF COLBERT

thus interrupt commerce between our two settlements. In case of war with the English or another power, the French governor would not be able to unite the inhabitants of the two colonies or to send aid from one to the other in case of danger."[71]

Another very serious objection was that there was no adequate supply of water in the French territory for the supply of ships and that the French had always been forced to go into English territory where there was a small river. Matters remained in this state until the arrival of de Blénac, the governor-general of the islands, and of Patoulet, intendant, in 1679. They proposed a treaty with the English containing the following clauses: (1) a delimitation of the harbours with a prohibition for one nation to frequent the waters of the other; (2) free passage across the territories of each nation for persons without merchandise; (3) formal permission to be made obligatory for the transportation of colonial products or of merchandise from Europe across the territories of the other nation, and a bond to be given in order to insure good faith; (4) free access for the French to the sulphur mines on British territory; (5) free access for the English to the salt fields on French territory. The treaty, however, was refused by the English.[72] Colbert seemed to realize the impossibility of preventing trade between the English and French in the island, for he instructed de Blénac to remain satisfied with the prevention of commerce between the two nations by sea and not to attempt to prohibit it within the island.[73]

The Dutch attempted to send some vessels to the islands in 1678, on the pretext that the passports in blank which

[71] Ibid.
[72] Arch. Nat. Col., C_{10}, St. Christophe, I, Un project de traitté qui a esté envoyé aux Anglais, December 15, 1679.
[73] Arch. Nat. Col., B, 9, fol. 34, Colbert to de Blénac, April 19, 1679.

were given them by the treaty of Nymwegen authorized them to do so. Colbert, however, wrote letters to all the governors of the islands to respect no such passports and to enforce rigourously the regulations against all foreigners without exception.[74] De Blénac, who was sent out to the islands in 1678 to succeed de Baas, deceased, and Patoulet, who was sent out to become the first intendant of the islands in 1679, were both ordered to keep up the fight against foreign traders. In the instructions of the latter the following passage occurs:

"Inasmuch as His Majesty has forbidden all foreigners to trade in the said islands and has reserved the trade thereof for his own subjects, there is nothing to which Sieur Patoulet should devote more attention and on which he should concentrate more effort than to prevent all foreign vessels from entering into the harbours, bays and inlets of his islands and trading there under any pretext whatsoever. He is not to admit them even when the inhabitants are in need of some article of merchandise for their subsistence."[75]

When Patoulet wrote Colbert that he had permitted three French vessels to trade at Martinique, although they had no passports, and another one from Nantes which had called at Cadiz and taken part of its cargo there, Colbert rebuked him for his conduct and commanded him to act in concert with de Blénac in order to insure strict enforcement of regulations.[76]

On October 11, 1680, de Blénac and Patoulet issued an ordinance which forbade French vessels to bring cargoes of

[74] Arch. Nat. Mar., B₂, 38, fol. 498 verso, June 10, 1678; ibid., Col., B, 7, December 8, 1678.

[75] Arch. Nat. Col., B, 9, April 1, 1679.

[76] Bib. Nat. MSS., fonds français, 11315, fol. 54 verso. He instructed the same official a few months later that in case the officers of the Domaine d'Occident disobeyed the regulations regarding foreign trade, they be punished as all other subjects. Ibid., fols. 150-151, 125-134.

salt beef, bacon, cloth, and other merchandise from foreign countries.[77] About the same time a squadron of His Majesty's vessels was sent to the West Indies under the command of Count d'Estrées "to protect the commerce which my subjects carry on in the islands and prevent the foreigners from participating therein."[78] The following year order was given for two small vessels of 120 and 150 tons to be equipped at Rochefort and sent to the islands to serve as a patrol.[79]

Colbert made provision, in theory at least, for the importation of all goods from Europe of which the planters had need, for he asserted that the law of supply and demand would force French merchants to bring them. He did not, however, make provision for the marketing of the by-products of the sugar industry, namely molasses and rum. In proportion as the sugar industry developed, these by-products became more important. Their importance became especially great after the establishment of refineries in the islands. By 1681, Patoulet estimated their value at 100,000 écus. But neither molasses nor rum could be marketed in France, the former apparently because there was no demand for it, the latter because law forbade its importation, in order to prevent it from entering into competition with various distilled liquors manufactured by the vine-growers of the realm. This fact gave rise to a very interesting proposal made by the refiners in Guadeloupe and Martinique:

"Whereas his honour the intendant has urged the chief planters of the islands to undertake trade with the inhabitants of Canada and the coast of Acadia, the proprietors of the aforesaid refineries under the direction of Sieurs Bouteiller and Jamain, . . . offer conjointly to open commerce with the

[77] Moreau de Saint-Méry, I, 343.
[78] Arch. Nat. Col., B, 9, April 8, 1680.
[79] Ibid., second part, fol. 10.

inhabitants of Canada and of the coast of Acadia, which should be promoted in order to facilitate the sale of all syrups and rum made from cane, and to stop the mixture which is now being made of syrup with sugar, under the following conditions: (1) A monopoly of trade for ten years to be granted them with exemption from all import and export duties; (2) as Quebec and Acadia cannot consume all the syrup and the rum which are being made in the French islands and two-thirds of which is at present a pure loss, permission to be granted to barter these syrups with the English colonies, especially those in the neighbourhood of Boston, for salt meat and live stock for which there is such great need in the French islands."

In regard to the latter, the petitioners asserted that they would be able in this way not only to satisfy a need in the islands, but also find a market for a product which remained a pure loss upon their hands, that they would thus be able to obtain an adequate supply of salt meat by barter, for which they had been accustomed to pay money to the Irish. In order to insure their good faith in limiting their trade with the English colonies strictly to the articles enumerated, the petitioners offered to submit to a strict inspection by the customs officers and that in case any other merchandise were found they agreed to submit to whatever penalty His Majesty wished to impose.

"This trade would occasion no diminution in the revenue of the king as there is no duty on syrups and rum. It would increase considerably the earnings of the planter, would perfect the manufacture of sugar, and would encourage the establishment of refineries, for they are now forced to throw away their syrups, whereas the refiners of France sell theirs to the Dutch for seven livres a hundred, a thing which the refiners of the islands cannot do by reason of the great leakage and cost of transportation."

This petition received the approval of Patoulet, who

wrote to Colbert that he regarded the project as very commendable:

"I am convinced that if trade with the English colonies, close to Boston, can be established, as is proposed, the king and the colonies would derive great profit therefrom. I can hardly persuade myself, however, that the king of England will suffer his subjects to receive all of our syrup and rum, as they have an annual value of more than 100,000 écus. The proprietors of the refineries here believe the contrary, and have confidence in their project, because they have learned that the English islands cannot furnish a sufficient quantity of these articles to satisfy the demands of those colonies. The English who dwell near Boston will not worry themselves about the prohibitions which the king of England may issue, because they hardly recognize his authority."[80]

Three things are to be remarked about this document: First, it presents a very interesting and reasonable proposal on the part of the refiners, which throws light upon the need of the colonies to find a market for some important commodities outside of the French empire; second, it shows clearly that the profit in exchanging these products with the English North American colonies for commodities which these colonies were in turn forced to market outside of the British empire was great; third, that the New Englanders had already won a reputation among the French for a spirit of independence.

The petition was refused by Colbert, partly because he did not approve of the establishment of a monopoly of trade between Canada, Acadia and the islands, but chiefly because he did not wish to authorize a modification of his policy to exclude all foreign trade.[81] He thus main-

[80] Arch. Nat. Col., C$_8$, III, March 8, 1681. The text of this petition is to be found accompanying the letter of Patoulet. What appears to be the original, however, is found in the correspondence of Canada, Arch. Nat. Col., C$_{11}$, V.

[81] Arch. Nat. Col., B, 9, fols. 38-39, Colbert to Patoulet, July 13,

TOWARD THE FRENCH WEST INDIES

tained his fight to the end and refused to yield a jot or a tittle in the principles which he had striven so long to maintain.

As we draw to the close of the ministry of Colbert, we naturally ask how far his indefatigable efforts, his strict orders had borne fruit. Patoulet stated in a memoir of December 26, 1680, that he was "convinced that no foreign commerce is being carried on in the island."[82] De Blénac assured Colbert in 1681 that no foreign commerce existed in the islands, and, finally, in 1683, St. Laurent and Bégon in a joint memoir gave him assurance of the same fact.[83] Some three weeks after Colbert's death, the king wrote to these two officials that he was satisfied by the assurance which they had given him that foreign commerce had been effectively interrupted in the islands.[84] It is not necessary to conclude from these statements that absolutely all commerce with foreigners had been stopped, for later events proved that there was still some contraband trade, but the rapid increase in the number of French vessels trading in the islands indicates that Colbert's long and determined fight against foreign traders had borne fruit and that, on the whole, the great minister had won a signal triumph.

The enemy of 1669, the ubiquitous Dutch trader, had been defeated and the French islands were comparatively free of foreign traders. The eyes of a prophet might have seen, however, that the rapid development of the French sugar colonies with a constantly increasing supply of molasses and rum, for which there was no market in the mother country, and with their increasing demand for

1681; fol. 24, instructions to Sieur Bégon, May 1, 1682; Arch. Aff. Etrang., Amérique, V, 507.

[82] Arch. Nat. Col., C₈, III.

[83] Ibid., November 12, 1681.

[84] Arch. Nat. Col., B, 10, fol. 20, the king to St. Laurent and Bégon, September 24, 1683.

food stuffs, live stock, slaves and lumber, which France could not satisfy, and the growth of the thrifty New England trader who could find neither a satisfactory supply of the former articles, nor a sufficient market for his increasing quantity of the latter in the British West Indies, meant an inevitable trade between the two groups of colonies. It proved an economic fact of prime importance in the eighteenth century and was destined to have momentous consequences, both in overthrowing the "system" of exclusivism which Colbert had established, and in forming one of the chief economic causes of the American Revolution.

CHAPTER X

FREEDOM OF TRADE AND THE RISE OF THE PRIVATE TRADER

WITH the dissolution of the West India Company in 1674 came to an end the administration of the islands by a commercial company. With the exception of the slave trade, which was committed into the hands of contractors or of companies after 1673, the entire commerce of the French West Indies was henceforth entrusted by Colbert to private enterprise. Attention has already been called to the fact that the private trader was admitted to the trade of the islands during the English war (October, 1666) and that Colbert refused to close the door to him at its termination (July, 1667). That fact must be reconsidered here and the policy of the great minister stated with more precision.

By an *arrêt* of the *conseil d'état* of September 10, 1668, the privilege of trading in the islands was guaranteed to private traders. Heretofore it had depended upon the willingness of the company to grant them passports. By this *arrêt* they were accorded an equal right with the company to trade in the islands and to re-export from France, free of duty, colonial products which they wished to market in foreign countries.[1] For a while their vessels were subjected to a tax, imposed by the company, of six livres per ton on their registered tonnage, when they sailed for the islands, and of five per cent on their cargoes at their return to France. But Colbert forced successively the abolition of the tax of six livres (December 9, 1669) and the reduction of the five per cent to three per

[1] Moreau de Saint-Méry, I, 174-175.

cent (June 4, 1671). He also abolished the special tax imposed by the company on cargoes of slaves imported by private traders into the islands (August 26, 1670).[2] Even after the West India Company was forced to concentrate all of its efforts upon the importation of salt beef, live stock and slaves, the private trader was encouraged to enter into competition with it by being made a beneficiary of the same premium of four livres on every barrel of French salted beef, and of thirteen livres per head for slaves imported into the islands.

By an *arrêt* of June 12, 1669, Colbert took into his own hands the power of granting passports to private traders.[3] He gave an explanation of this action in a letter to Colbert de Terron a few days later: "I am resolved to grant henceforth all passports myself in order to prevent the company from diminishing this commerce by preferential treatment to its own ships and in order to encourage individuals to apply themselves to it."[4]

These measures, which favoured in such an unmistakable way the growth of the private trader, were accompanied by reiterated commands of their enforcement and repeated statements of the principle of freedom of trade. The correspondence between Colbert and de Baas, governor-general of the islands, is very instructive on this point.

De Baas seems to have had very little sympathy for the private trader. "I must tell you," he wrote to Colbert at the beginning of 1670, "that since private traders, coming from France, have begun to receive their passports directly from the king, they hold their heads too high and have become impertinent. They wish to sell their merchandise according to their own sweet wills without so much as paying the taxes usually levied on such cargoes

[2] Ibid., I, 187, 197.
[3] Ibid., I, 178.
[4] Clément, II, 2, p. 473.

in the islands."[5] He complained in another letter that French merchants were taking advantage of the fact that the king was assuring them a monopoly of trade, by demanding too high prices for goods, and that they were coming to the islands with no other idea than that of personal gain and without thinking of the real needs of the planters. Thus, in order to have cargoes of sugar, they were bringing fancy articles instead of the supplies which were really needed.[6] Furthermore, de Baas showed partiality toward the ships of the company, and recommended that its monopoly be restored.[7]

To these reflections and recommendations, Colbert replied by a restatement of his policy and a command of obedience in the name of the king in regard to it:

"It is really not necessary that you bother yourself with the consideration of the question as to whether it would be more advantageous or not for the company to carry on commerce with the islands to the exclusion of all others. You have nothing to do, in fact, except to attract French vessels which have my passports by the good and just treatment which you accord to them. . . . In regard to the company, when it becomes strong enough, and has a sufficient number of vessels to satisfy the needs of the islands, I shall then listen to the arguments which it has to advance why permission should be refused to other Frenchmen who wish to go to the West Indies to trade. . . . Be assured that it is only through liberty to all of my subjects to trade with these colonies that an abundant supply of everything can be obtained. This is especially true now, because my subjects are applying themselves much more than formerly to the pursuits of navigation and trade. They will surely go to trade where they receive good treatment and gain profit."[8]

[5] Arch. Nat. Col., C$_8$, I, February 24, 1670.
[6] Ibid., January 15, 1670.
[7] Ibid.
[8] Clément, III, 2, p. 477, note 1.

THE COMMERCIAL POLICY OF COLBERT

In regard to the refusal of private traders to pay taxes on their cargoes, Colbert wrote: "The custom which has been followed up to the present of levying duties on incoming and outgoing cargoes was a very good practice for the time, when foreigners and only a few Frenchmen carried on this trade, but at present, when foreigners have been entirely eliminated and only French traders remain, the custom must be abolished."[9] A royal ordinance was proclaimed on June 9, 1670, whereby it was forbidden to lay any tax upon merchandise brought in French bottoms from France, or upon sugar exported in the same manner to France.[10]

As to de Baas' complaint that French merchants were demanding too high prices for their goods, Colbert replied again in favour of the private trader by affirming that it was only an entire freedom to sell goods at whatever price one chose which could produce an abundant supply, and only an abundant supply which could produce cheapness. A royal ordinance was straightway proclaimed which ordered "that all merchandise brought in French bottoms into the French islands of America shall be sold, either wholesale or retail, at whatever prices and under whatever terms that are agreed upon between buyer and seller."[11] He rebuked de Baas for preferential treatment to the vessels of the West India Company and specifically commanded him "to leave entire freedom to all Frenchmen to ply their trade in accordance with their passports."[12] He appealed to de Baas' patriotism to guide him in the matter:

"I should say to you in regard to freedom of trade that we should not be surprised to find that the directors of the West

[9] Ibid., p. 478.
[10] Moreau de Saint-Méry, I, 194.
[11] Moreau de Saint-Méry, I, 194, June 14, 1670.
[12] Arch. Nat. Col., B, 1, fol. 156 verso, July 10, 1669.

TOWARD THE FRENCH WEST INDIES

India Company wish to keep for themselves a monopoly of trade, because they very naturally think only of their own interest and not of the general welfare or of that of the state. But as for you and me, we should raise ourselves above the plane of personal interests to that of public welfare, and plant ourselves squarely upon the principle of freedom of trade."[13]

In order that there might be no mistake as to what he meant by freedom of trade, Colbert took occasion to define it himself in most specific terms:

"The maxim of freedom of trade means that every French trader, holding a passport from the king, shall be received in all of the French islands and shall have an entire liberty to trade, to sell and to exchange goods at whatever price he chooses, and that the planter shall have the same liberty to dispose of his sugar in the same way. Any doubts which may arise in the application of this principle should be decided in favour of the trader, except where suspicions are entertained that the cargo contains articles purchased in foreign countries."[14]

Colbert is thus very clearly presented as the champion of freedom of trade, that is to say, of the principle of assuring to all Frenchmen the right of trading in the islands. He appears in this rôle only after 1668, and especially in his correspondence of 1669, 1670 and the years following. Only about five years previously he had apparently appeared in quite a different rôle. In 1664 he was active in the organization of the West and East India Companies. Although all Frenchmen and even foreigners were invited to become stockholders and thus the whole nation was free to share in the two enterprises, yet both companies were endowed with monopolies. The inference is natural that in 1664 Colbert preferred the employment of large companies, founded on the principle

[13] Clément, III, 2, p. 479.
[14] Clément, III, 2, p. 487, Colbert to Pélissier, June 21, 1670.

of monopoly of trade, to private enterprise, founded on the principle of freedom of trade, and that after five years of experience, he was converted from the error of his way and henceforth espoused the cause of the private trader and became a champion of the principle of freedom of trade. Some recent French historians have adopted the view that this inference is correct, and that a sharp line separates the commercial-colonial policy of Colbert into two periods, namely, that before 1669 and that from 1669 to 1683.[15]

But had a great change really gone on in Colbert's mind between 1664 and 1669? Had experience really proved to him that the principle of monopoly was really wrong and converted him to that of freedom of trade? Is one forced to conclude that the minister made a radical change in his commercial policy after 1669?

It must be said at the outset, that there is really no material for the period anterior to 1669 which enables one to say that Colbert established the two companies of 1664, because he believed in the principle of monopoly in preference to that of freedom of trade. Material throwing light upon Colbert's relations to the colonial problem previous to 1669 is exceedingly meagre. It is only for the period after that date, when Colbert was officially charged with the administration of the colonies and when correspondence became regular and was method ically preserved, that one has any very satisfactory material on which to base any assertions as to the motives or the principles on which any given action of the minister was based. One can, at best, only adopt some working hypothesis to explain his commercial policy previous to 1669.

[15] See especially E. Bénoit du Rey, *Récherches sur la politique coloniale de Colbert;* Chemin-Dupontès, *Les Compagnies de Commerce en Afrique Occidentale sous Colbert.*

TOWARD THE FRENCH WEST INDIES

But the adoption of the view that Colbert accepted freedom of trade as the principle governing his commercial policy after 1669 leads at once to difficulties. The East India Company continued to enjoy a monopoly of trade until Colbert's death in 1683. A monopoly of the slave trade in the islands was granted to individual contractors or to companies in 1675, 1679 and 1681. No less than five commercial companies—the Company of the North, the Company of the Levant, the Company of the Pyrenees, the first Company of Senegal and the second Company of Senegal—were organized after 1669, and to all of them either a partial or a total monopoly was granted. These facts do not tend to make one accept the view that Colbert had discarded the principle of monopoly. Furthermore, a strange confusion at once appears in his correspondence, if this view is accepted. Thus he wrote to de Baas on July 31, 1669:

"In regard to trade by the French, His Majesty desires that you accord an equal protection to the ships belonging to the West India Company and to those belonging to individuals who have passports, and he desires that you execute with promptness the terms of the said passports. . . . His Majesty is of the opinion that it is immaterial whether the company carry on this trade or not [trade between France and the islands]. This is all the more true because if it is freed from the necessity of carrying on this trade, it can undertake that of Guinea, or some other which will prove more profitable. . . . If the trade of the islands can be carried on in full liberty by all Frenchmen, it is certain that both the kingdom and the islands will be better off."[16]

Only seven months later, however, he addressed a memoir to the directors of the West India Company on February 26, 1670, which said:

[16] Clément, III, 2, pp. 456-457.

THE COMMERCIAL POLICY OF COLBERT

"As long as the company grants permission to private traders, it will suffice to permit all those who send cargoes to the islands to sell their goods to such persons and in such quantities as they wish. . . . But when the company ceases to grant such permission and asserts its monopoly, in order to avoid oppression the company must act in good faith toward the planters."[17]

But on April 9, 1670, only a little over a month later, he wrote to de Baas that "inasmuch as commerce was an act of the free will of man, it should be necessarily left free."[18]

Thus Colbert seems to be shifting from the thought of delivering the trade of the islands entirely into the hands of private traders to that of placing it again under the monopoly of the West India Company. De Baas complained of this fact as a cause of much unrest among the planters:

"The common complaint of the planters at present is that changes are continually being made in the manner of governing them and in the policy which controls their commerce. Yesterday, so they say, they were under the rule of individual proprietors, and today they are subjected to the rule of a company which they can not tolerate, for besides the bad treatment which they receive at its hands, it is responsible for the fact that the conditions of trade are ever changing so that they are at sea as to what to do. Sometimes the company endeavours to monopolize trade and drive out foreigners, sometimes foreigners are readmitted only to be driven out again a short time afterwards. Then private French traders are admitted. Such frequent changes confuse and disgust them so much that they would be glad to see the company decide something definite, either to carry on the trade all alone, or to admit foreigners."[19]

[17] Ibid., p. 472.
[18] Ibid., p. 477.
[19] Arch. Nat. Col., C$_8$, I, February 24, 1670.

TOWARD THE FRENCH WEST INDIES

The fact is, that if one studies the acts and correspondence of Colbert with the hope of making some dogmatic assertion as to whether he became after 1669 a convert to the principle of freedom of trade, he will find himself in about as much confusion as the planters of Martinique. One thing is certain, Colbert was a practical man, not a doctrinaire who stopped to study the advantages or disadvantages of monopoly or of freedom of trade as theories. He regarded a commercial company and a private trader in exactly the same light. They were both instruments to be used in the realization of a plan which meant the building up of French industry and French commerce. He never organized a commercial company or permitted the organization of one to which he did not commit some mission of national service. It was for this end that he subsidized and often entirely supported them, that he often charged some special officer or public official with their administration, and for this purpose that he gave so much of his own busy life to their direction. The dominating note of Colbert's industrial and commercial policy was patriotism. He worked so indefatigably for its realization, because he saw in it national prosperity and national greatness. It has already been shown what importance he attached to the establishment of commerce. For that end he was willing to seize any means at his command, were it a commercial company or a private trader, which gave promise of being an effective agent in accomplishing his work. If that is taken as a working hypothesis to study Colbert's commercial policy, it gives to it a unity from the commencement to the end of his ministry. He knew perfectly well that a régime of monopoly was oppressive and that one of freedom of trade was more natural and productive. "Commerce must be left free," he said, "*unless there is an indispensable necessity to commit it into the hands of a company or of a few contract-*

THE COMMERCIAL POLICY OF COLBERT

ors."[20] Colbert said this in 1670, but there is nothing to show that he did not hold the same view in 1664, when he created the East and West India Companies. At that date he saw the Dutch in control of practically all of the commerce of the French West Indies, which had been established by French settlers and bought by French blood. He set his hand to the task of driving them out and of laying fast hold upon their riches for the profit of France and of her people. But Colbert never did things by half measures. He saw that such or such a thing should be done and he ordered it done immediately. So in this case the Dutch must be driven out at once. De Tracy left France in February with orders to exclude the Dutch trader during the space of six months, and consequently the problem of sending a large number of ships with cargoes of supplies was very pressing. Some agent must be found which could supply without delay the place which the Dutch had been occupying in the islands. There were too few private traders in the ports of France to make it at all possible to leave to them the task of satisfying the needs of the planters. Obviously the formation of a company which would have enough capital to send enough cargoes of supplies to the islands at once was about the only means at hand. One is justified in saying that the "indispensable necessity of committing commerce into the hands of a company" had arisen, and perhaps it is not too much to add that Colbert was of that opinion when he created the company. It does not follow at all that as Colbert created the West India Company in 1664, and endowed it with a monopoly, he did so because he did not believe then, as he believed in 1670, that "commerce must be left free" wherever possible.

When he found at the close of the English war that a number of private French traders were going to the

[20] Clément, III, 2, p. 477, Colbert to de Baas, April 9, 1670.

islands, he protected them and encouraged them to continue. From 1669 to 1674, he insisted that the ships of the company and those of private traders should be treated alike. He offered to both the same premiums, the same freedom from import and export duties, and subjected them to the same laws. He knew that every French ship which went to the islands, whether it belonged to the company or to a private trader, was a gain for French commerce and was a step forward in the realization of his plans. He wished to see a large number of vessels carrying an abundance of French manufactures and merchandise to the West Indies and bringing back with them rich cargoes of colonial products.

"When the company becomes strong enough and has enough ships to carry on all of this trade alone, I shall then listen to arguments which it has to advance why passports should be no longer granted to private traders who wish to go to the islands."[21]

His only concern was that enough ships be sent to the islands and that they be French. The West India Company was discarded in 1674, simply because it had ceased to be an effective instrument in building up that trade. Private traders had become numerous and into their hands was committed the commerce of the islands. When in turn private traders showed themselves incapable of satisfying the needs of the planters for slaves, Colbert called back into play commercial companies and endowed them with a monopoly of the slave trade.

It seems much more accurate to say, therefore, that the so-called radical change in Colbert's policy in 1669, dividing his ministry into two halves, was not an important change at all. The only difference to be noted between the two periods, 1664-1668 and 1669-1674, is that

[21] Clément, III, 2, p. 427, note 1.

in the latter period he employed two instruments instead of one to realize his policy. In 1674 he discarded one of these instruments, because it had become too old and too weak to be of further service. Later he employed both commercial companies and private traders in the commerce of the islands.

The rapid growth of the number of private traders in the West India trade is one of the achievements of Colbert's ministry, and, it might be added, one of the most permanent achievements, if it be measured in the light of its influence on the development of French commerce in the eighteenth century. The number of private ships going to the West Indies rose from three or four in 1662[22] to 60 in 1670, 89 in 1672, 131 in 1674[23] and to 205 in 1683.[24]

This growth took place principally in the three southern ports of Bordeaux, La Rochelle and Nantes. The Norman and Breton ports of Havre, Honfleur, Dieppe, Rouen and St. Malo became considerably handicapped by the frequent European wars and profited much less from the increase of trade with the islands. Thus, out of a total of eighty-nine passports demanded by private traders in 1672, only eighteen were demanded by the ports of the north, and only twenty-four in 1674 out of a total of 131. Complete statistics are lacking for the later years, but it is certain that the trade of the northern ports with the West Indies continued to be of much less importance than that of the three southern ports mentioned.

The admiralty records of Bordeaux, although incomplete, enable one to follow with reasonable accuracy the growth in that port of trade with the West Indies. The

[22] Lavisse, VII, 2, p. 235, note 1.
[23] Arch. Nat. Col., B, 4, fols. 148-149; 4, fols. 107-114; 6, fols. 54-60.
[24] Arch. Col., F₂, 15, Memoir marked "Indes Occidentales," and endorsed "M. Morel."

TOWARD THE FRENCH WEST INDIES

registers for 1640 and 1651 indicate no sailings for or arrivals from the islands.[25] *La Justice*, 68 tons, of Amsterdam arrived on January 1, 1661, with a cargo of sugar from St. Christopher, and the *St. Joseph*, 70 tons, of La Rochelle, brought a similar cargo from the West Indies on February 28, 1667.[26] These two cases are the only sailings or arrivals indicated for the two years. In 1671, twelve ships, with an aggregate tonnage of 1115 tons, sailed from Bordeaux for the West Indies and six entered, all coming from Martinique except one, which came from St. Christopher.[27] Fifteen sailed in 1672, and twelve more (1087 tons) in 1673.[28] In 1674 passports were granted to twenty-four private vessels to trade in the islands,[29] and in 1676 nineteen vessels were recorded as sailing for the West Indies.[30] This number rose to twenty-six in 1682 and 1683.[31] Twenty vessels arrived at Bordeaux from the West Indies in 1684.[32] Of these twenty, six came from Martinique, of which one had touched at St. Domingo, six from St. Christopher, one from Guadeloupe, one from Cayenne, two from St. Domingo, and three indicated simply as coming from "the islands of America." The average tonnage of these twenty vessels was only fifty tons, and one *Le Pierre* of Royan, gauged only thirty tons. It made the voyage from Martinique with a cargo of sugar. The log of *La Marie*, fifty tons,

---

[25] Arch. Dépt., Gironde, B, 1640, and Malvezin, *Histoire du Commerce de Bordeaux*, II, 369. Malvezin consulted the admiralty records for 1651, 1671, 1672 (sailings only), 1676 and 1682 (arrivals only). His researches have been supplemented and the results offered in part here.

[26] Arch. Dépt., Gironde, B, 153, fol. 3, and 154, fol. 27 verso.

[27] Malvezin, *op. cit.*, II, 369.

[28] Arch. Dépt., Gironde, B, 186; Malvezin, II, 369.

[29] Arch. Nat. Col., B, 6, fols. 54-60.

[30] Malvezin, II, 369.

[31] Arch. Dépt., Gironde, B, 187, 188.

[32] Ibid., 159.

may be taken as typical. It sailed from Bordeaux on January 17, and arrived at Martinique on March 14. After trading there until May 7, it sailed for St. Domingo, arriving at Port de Paix on May 13. No mention is made of any cargo being taken at Martinique, but at Port de Paix, *La Marie* took 718 rolls of tobacco and two bales of cotton and sailed on August 9 for Bordeaux, where it arrived on November 13.[33]

The principal articles of export from Bordeaux to the West Indies were wine, brandy, staves, headings and hoops, flour and salt beef.[34] The majority of vessels went to the Windward Islands, Martinique, Guadeloupe, St. Christopher, and a few to St. Domingo. The cargoes from the former were composed almost entirely of sugar, with small quantities of indigo, ginger, roucou, and cotton, those from the latter, of tobacco, with small quantities of cotton, indigo and hides.[35]

This trade proved very beneficial to Bordeaux. Profit derived from it laid the basis for the fortunes of many successful traders. One, Darriet by name, equipped no

[33] Arch. Dépt., Gironde, B, 159.

[34] The details of cargoes are not often indicated in the registers for the period. Very frequently it is simply noted at the registration of a passport that the cargo of the vessels was composed of "wine and other merchandise," or "wine and victuals." The cargo of *Les deux Maries,* which sailed from Bordeaux for the West Indies on September 16, 1698, was as follows: 56 tuns of wine, 65 barrels of beef, 88 quintals of salt pork, 30 barrels of flour, 22 quintals fish oil, staves and hoops and headings for 100 barrels. *La Vierge,* 160 tons, which sailed on October 6 of the same year, had a cargo composed of 64 tuns wine, 100 gallons brandy, 53 barrels flour, 100 bundles hoops, staves, 200 pounds copper, 200 refining forms and pots, 6 guns, 300 tables, 10 dozen pair shoes, 2 dozen hats, 100 dozen drinking glasses, 400 yards cloth, 150 pounds olive oil. Arch. Dépt., Gironde, B, 197, fols. 72 verso and 75 verso.

[35] *Le Charles,* 60 tons, coming from St. Christopher in 1671, brought a cargo of 13 pipes, 95 hogsheads, 138 barrels sugar, 2 barrels indigo. Malvezin, II, 369.

TOWARD THE FRENCH WEST INDIES

less than five vessels for the West Indies in 1683, seven in 1682, and received five in 1684.[36] The registers of 1661 and 1667 show that Bordeaux had been receiving its sugar from Portugal and La Rochelle,[37] but henceforward its supply was obtained directly from the West Indies. A new refinery was established in 1670.[38] Thanks to the high tariff against foreign refined sugar, established in 1665,[39] and to the increase of trade with the French West Indies, the refining industry became prosperous. Trade with the West Indies became, in the eighteenth century, the most important factor in the economic life of Bordeaux. It is only in the light of that development that one can fully appreciate the importance to Bordeaux of the work which Colbert accomplished in the seventeenth century.

It is particularly unfortunate that the admiralty records, which would render it possible to state accurately the facts concerning the development of trade with the West Indies at La Rochelle, have not been preserved, for it is clear that La Rochelle was the most important port for that trade throughout the ministry of Colbert. The inquest of 1664 showed that there were only three vessels in this port engaged in trade with the West Indies.[40] In the list of passports granted to private traders in 1672 in all France, no less than twenty-seven out of a total of eighty-nine were demanded by its traders. In 1674, the proportion was thirty-five out of a total of 131.[41] In both cases La Rochelle heads the list in number of passports demanded. For 1682 we have found scattered rec-

[36] Arch. Dépt., Gironde, B, 187, 188, 159.
[37] Ibid., 153, fol. 19; 154, fols. 91, 94, 98, etc.
[38] Malvezin, II, 373.
[39] See below, the discussion of legislation regarding sugar.
[40] Bib. Nat. MSS., 500 Colbert, 199, fols. 37 ff.
[41] Arch. Nat. Col., B, 4, fols. 107-114; 6, fols. 54-60.

THE COMMERCIAL POLICY OF COLBERT

ords of thirty-four vessels sailing for the West Indies,[42] and forty-nine in 1685.[43]

Colbert seems to have especially favoured the Rochellais. Thus he wrote on January 23, 1671, to Brunet, one of the directors of the West India Company:

"Let me know exactly how many private traders are making preparations at La Rochelle to go to the islands of America. Inform the merchants that the moment I see that the number of their vessels is sufficient to satisfy the needs of the islands, the king will exclude those of Nantes and St. Malo, because I notice that the traders of those ports gain their profit from sugar which they sell to the Dutch, who take it away to refine in their own country."[44]

The average tonnage of twenty-five ships sailing from La Rochelle for the West Indies in 1674 was 144 tons, almost three times greater than that of the ships from Bordeaux in 1684, recorded above.[45] The cargo of *La Fortune*, 150 tons, which sailed in 1674, may be taken as typical. It was composed of 248 one-quarter barrels wine, 122 ditto brandy, 116 ditto flour, and 139 ditto salt pork.[46]

Since the establishment of the port of La Pallice, the picturesque harbour of La Rochelle is being neglected. Mud banks and sand-bars keep out all but small fisher boats and shallow-draft steamers which glide over them at high tide. But no one can roam about the ancient stronghold of the Protestants without seeing traces and hearing echoes of the great wealth brought by the sail vessels which, after their long voyage from the distant West Indies,

[42] Arch. Dépt., Char. Inf., B, 235, Roles d'équip., 1682-1696.
[43] Ibid.
[44] Jourdan, *Ephémérides de la Rochelle,* II, 32-33.
[45] Arch. Dépt., Char. Inf., B (unclassified), Rap. et Proc. Verbal, 1674.
[46] Only two cases have been noted for the year where cargoes contained any salt beef. One was three one-quarter barrels and the other sixty barrels. Ibid.

TOWARD THE FRENCH WEST INDIES

glided between the two watch-towered gateways to unload their rich cargoes of sugar. Colbert had pointed the way and the enterprising Rochellais were quick to follow it.

Results were also very encouraging at Nantes. According to the inquest of 1664, only two vessels were engaged in trade with the West Indies.[47] But after the admission of private traders to the privileges of trading, the merchants at Nantes seized the opportunity and established a regular commerce with the West Indies. Colbert became convinced, however, as we have seen, that some merchants of this port were lending their names to Dutch traders and that practically all of the raw sugar, imported from the French colonies, was being re-exported to Holland. He, therefore, in 1670, refused to grant any more passports to the traders at Nantes. He restored the privilege by an *arrêt* of the *conseil d'état* of December 14, 1671, on condition that the merchants of Nantes give up their former practices.[48] After this interruption, trade with the West Indies increased steadily and Nantes became a close rival to La Rochelle. In 1672 traders of Nantes demanded twenty-four passports,[49] and twenty-four again in 1683.[50] During the year, August 18, 1685, to August 18, 1686, no less than fifty-eight vessels, 5830 tons, sailed from Nantes for the West Indies.[51]

The principal exports were wine, brandy, salt pork, Irish and domestic salt beef, Irish butter, olive oil, fuel

[47] Bib. Nat. MSS., 500 Colbert, 199, fols. 225 ff. See also L. Maitre, Situation de la Marine du comté de Nantes d'après l'enquête de 1664 in *Ann. de Bretagne,* xviii, 326-343, and E. Gabory, La Marine et le Commerce de Nantes au xviie siècle et au commencement du xviiie, ibid., 1-44.

[48] Arch. Nat., G$_7$, 1313.

[49] Arch. Nat. Col., B, 4, fols. 107-117.

[50] Arch. Dépt., Loire Inf., B, 6, Reg. de sorties, 1679-1685. The aggregate tonnage of these 34 vessels was 3410 tons, the average being a fraction over 100 tons.

[51] Ibid., B, 7, Reg. de sorties.

THE COMMERCIAL POLICY OF COLBERT

oil, flour, peas, biscuits, staves, headings and hoops, cloths and clothes, etc., etc.[52] Imports were raw and refined sugar, cotton, indigo, ginger, syrup, etc.[53]

The admiralty records for the ports of northern France which carried on trade with the West Indies are almost wholly lacking and it is impossible to state more than superficial facts regarding their trade. The inquest of 1664 showed that there were no vessels at Honfleur engaged in trade with the islands,[54] or at Rouen.[55] There were at Havre one, at St. Malo three and at Dieppe six.[56] Up to the outbreak of the English war in 1666, the West India Company carried on a large part of its trade with the islands from these ports. In November, 1665, it may be recalled, it had about thirty vessels either ready or preparing to sail from them. But the war seriously interfered with commerce. During the years after its close, ships again sailed for the West Indies, for traders of Dieppe demanded nine passports in 1672; those of Honfleur, six; those of St. Malo, three; and in 1674, Dieppe demanded ten; Honfleur, nine; Havre, seven; St. Malo, six.[57] De Vanvré, general commissioner at Havre, stated in a letter of February 5, 1675, that there were fifteen vessels at Havre, Dieppe and Honfleur ready to sail for

[52] The cargo of *L'Africaine*, 250 tons, equipped by René Montaudouin, which sailed on January 18, 1675, was as follows: 41 tuns wine of Nantes, 30 barrels domestic beef, 200 barrels Irish beef, 900 sets of staves, hoops and headings, 6 hogsheads prunes, 5 casks of brandy, 4 hogsheads peas, 3 cases shoes, 8 one-quarter barrels flour, 8 cases hats, 15 bales cloth Bilbao style, 4 hogsheads and 6 cases cloth, 10 barrels glass. Arch. Dépt., Loire Inf., B, 3.

[53] *The St. François Xavier*, 100 tons, which arrived at Nantes on October 12, 1688, brought a cargo of 94 hogsheads raw sugar, 1 hogshead refined sugar, 20 bales cotton, 22 small barrels syrup. Ibid., B, 1, Long Cours, Rapports, 1686-1689.

[54] Bib. Nat. MSS., 500 Colbert, 199, fols. 113-116.

[55] Ibid., fols. 47-66.

[56] Ibid., fols. 101-108, 237-260, 69-83.

[57] Arch. Nat. Col., B, 4, fols. 107-117; 6, fols. 54-60.

TOWARD THE FRENCH WEST INDIES

the West Indies, and on March 3, that ten had actually sailed from Dieppe, five from Honfleur and four from Havre.[58] The northern ports suffered both from the existence of the Dutch war, 1672-1676, and from the superior advantages of the southern ports for trade with the islands. A memorialist of 1698, in noting the decline of trade of these ports, offered the following explanation:

"The Norman traders and those of La Rochelle, particularly, rendered possible the first establishment of the French in the West Indies. Those of Brittany also had relations with the islands up to 1664. . . . After the West India Company granted the privilege of trade to private traders, Normandy continued her commerce principally through the effort of Sieur Pierre Formont, who sent a considerable number of ships to the islands. It was through this trade that the refineries of Rouen were able to obtain a supply of sugar and supply Paris and other parts of the kingdom. But this commerce diminished and the Normans were in the habit of sending only a small number of vessels or none at all to the West Indies even before the outbreak of the last war [war of the Austrian Succession] and during that war. This change was due in part to wars during which danger of capture in the English Channel was great, and also, in part, to the growth of trade at Nantes, which had at hand a supply of all sorts of food-stuffs, products and merchandise necessary for the West India trade, whereas Normandy had neither wine nor brandy which were most important in making up cargoes for the islands."[59]

It would be a mistake to suppose, however, that trade with the West Indies ceased in the northern ports, for the second Company of Senegal equipped a number of its

[58] Arch. Nat. Mar., B_3, 19, fols. 183, 190. It seems certain that some of the vessels to which passports were granted in 1674 were the same as spoken of in these letters. See ibid., 17, fols. 215, 218, for letters from the same person in regard to these vessels.

[59] Arch. Nat. Col., C_8, 2nd series, II, Mém. sur le commerce et navigation des Isles de L'Amérique.

vessels at Dieppe in 1682,[60] and in 1683 five vessels belonging to Protestants, or belonging to Protestant captains, sailed from Dieppe to trade with the islands.[61]

The war with the Dutch, declared in April, 1672, interfered seriously with the West India trade in 1672, 1674 and 1676. At the opening of the war, Bellinzani stated in a memoir that inasmuch as the "commerce of the islands is of considerable importance to France, there being at present in the islands more than 100 French vessels, which should bring back very large quantities of merchandise," measures should be taken to protect it.[62] In accordance with this advice, vessels were forbidden to sail from the ports of France for the islands without an armed escort, and those in the islands were expressly prohibited from sailing for France "except after having assembled at the time and place indicated by the lieutenant-general" in order to be escorted by the king's vessels beyond the zone of danger.[63] Escorts were furnished in some cases, for mention is made in one letter from the islands of the arrival "of the king's vessels and the merchants ships which they escorted."[64] Royal vessels sometimes carried cargoes back to France. Thus du Lion noted in one of his letters the sailing for La Rochelle of "one of the king's flutes with a good cargo of sugar, much to the contentment of the merchants and planters who transacted affairs with the captain."[65]

In spite, however, of these precautions, Dutch corsairs at times wrought havoc with trade. Most of the fifteen vessels which sailed from Bordeaux for the islands in 1672

[60] Arch. Col., C₆, Cie. du Sénégal, I, Estat des vais. ap. aux bourgeois marchands de Dieppe.
[61] Ibid.
[62] Arch. Nat. Col., C₈, 2nd series, I, Mém. du Sr. Bellinzani sur le commerce des Isles, March 12, 1672.
[63] Moreau de Saint-Méry, I, 262, Ordon. du Roy, March 14, 1672.
[64] Arch. Nat. Col., C₈, I, letter from Jolinet, September 11, 1676.
[65] Arch. Nat. Col., C₇, I, March 22, 1672.

TOWARD THE FRENCH WEST INDIES

were captured by them so that "the chamber of insurance was bankrupt and many failures followed."[66] Ogeron, governor of St. Domingo, wrote to Colbert that he had neither vessels nor troops nor ammunition nor any means of defending the colony against their attacks or of keeping foreigners from trading there.[67]

An embargo was laid in all the ports of France by an ordinance of February 23, 1674, but special permission was given to sixteen vessels assembled at Belle Isle, three at La Rochelle, four at Bayonne, and three at Nantes, to sail for the islands.[68] The attack of Reuyter on St. Pierre (Martinique) in July, 1674, although unsuccessful by reason of the heroic defense maintained by the French, seemed to scatter terror among French shippers, for not a single vessel from France arrived at Martinique from the month of August until December 17.[69] The price of sugar, consequently, fell so low in 1674, that some planters in Martinique began to cultivate ginger and indigo, and "to raise stock and poultry which they sold very dear to foreigners, much to their relief and satisfaction."[70] In the following year, however, French traders "came in such large numbers that the planters lacked nothing and all supplies of which they had need were furnished them at very reasonable prices. This was an unexpected joy to them, for the previous year had been very hard because only a small number of vessels came from France and such high prices were demanded by merchants that they became intolerable."[71]

---

[66] Malvezin, *op. cit.*, II, 369.
[67] Charlevoix, II, 97.
[68] Arch. Nat. Col., B, 6, fols. 5, 6, 6 verso, and 11.
[69] Arch. Nat. Col., C_8, I, du Clerc to Colbert, January 20, 1675. On Reuyter's attack see ibid., 2nd series, I, de Baas to Colbert August 28, 1674; also Dessalles, *Hist. Gén.*, I, chap. 21.
[70] Arch. Nat. Col., C_8, I, de Baas to Colbert, February 8, 1674.
[71] Arch. Nat. Col., C_8, I, de Baas to Colbert, May 4, 1675.

THE COMMERCIAL POLICY OF COLBERT

Another Dutch squadron appeared in the islands in 1676 and interrupted trade again. In May it was at Marie Galante. Jacob Beinchk, its commander, demanded the surrender of the island. He contented himself, however, with sending a small band of his men ashore to sack a plantation. In July, Beinchk appeared at the coast of St. Domingo, and on the 7th addressed a letter to the French inhabitants, offering them generous treatment, if they would declare themselves subjects of the Prince of Orange.[72] On the 15th he attacked Petit Goave, where

[72] Arch. Nat. Mar., B$_4$, 7, fol. 179; Dessalles, *Hist. Gén.*, I, 544; Arch. Nat. Col., F$_3$, 164, contains a copy of the letter addressed by Beinchk to the inhabitants of St. Domingo. It is as follows:

"His Royal Highness, the Prince of Orange, has been informed several times of the strong desire which the French of the coast of St. Domingo have to trade with the Dutch. He knows also that His Majesty, the King of France, out of regard for the King of Spain, has never wished to recognize them as his subjects, with the exception of those who dwell at Tortuga. Besides, His Majesty does not permit in any way the inhabitants of St. Domingo to trade with any others than French merchants. He refuses to them the same freedom in this respect which he grants to his subjects in the Antilles to whom negroes are brought by foreigners and who trade freely with all Frenchmen. His Majesty, for special reasons, prevents negroes to be brought to St. Domingo. It is needless to describe the suffering imposed upon the inhabitants of St. Domingo by such narrow restrictions and by a host of burdens which are imposed upon them, such as excessive taxes and duties laid by His Majesty. It is useless to describe these things, because the inhabitants themselves have been made to feel the burden thereof. His Royal Highness, the Prince of Orange, believing that these hardships are unendurable and that the French of St. Domingo will take advantage of the existence of the war to throw off such a heavy yoke and to enter under the protection of our lords, the estates of Holland and His Royal Highness, and into the enjoyment of trade with all nations without any distinctions, and into that of other privileges which we will not specify in this letter, but which will undoubtedly prove advantageous to the said inhabitants. This generous offer of His Royal Highness is very favourable to the inhabitants of St. Domingo and of great consequence to them. Thus every one would be freed from the burden of work by the quantity of negroes imported into the island. . . . The majority of the planters would become in time very prosperous. We

TOWARD THE FRENCH WEST INDIES

he defeated and destroyed the few French vessels there. Moreau de Saint-Méry has preserved for us a list of no less than thirteen vessels captured by the Dutch between June 10 and July 17, 1676.[73] Beinchk next captured Cayenne.

Trade became more secure in the following year, for Comte d'Estrées was sent to the islands with a squadron of twenty vessels. He recaptured Cayenne on December 21, 1676, and took Tobago on December 25, 1677.[74] He was at St. Domingo in May, 1678. In the summer he attempted an expedition against Curaçao, but his squadron was shipwrecked on August 5. The Dutch took advantage of the catastrophe and captured several vessels with cargoes of tobacco at the coast of St. Domingo.[75]

are sure that the inhabitants will not refuse proposals which are so vital to their prosperity and well being, and that they will come aboard our vessels to confer with us more at length. We hereby give assurance to all in general, and to each in particular, that those who wish to come aboard, either to confer with us or for other things, will be freely returned ashore, whenever they wish. If the inhabitants, collectively, desire to delegate some representative who will go with us to Cul de Sac, empowered to act conjointly with the inhabitants of that quarter in treating with us, we shall be very glad to receive such representatives and will guarantee their safe return. To accomplish this His Royal Highness has sent this squadron of vessels hither and has commanded us to treat with the inhabitants of St. Domingo in the most friendly spirit. Awaiting a response, we are your humble servant,

"JACOB BEINCHK.

"Aboard *La Defense*, July 7, 1676."

[73] Arch. Nat. Col., F$_3$, 164, liste des Navires qui sont pris des Hollandais à la Côte de St. Domingue. The thirteen vessels had an aggregate tonnage of 1900 tons and had cargoes of 18,900 rolls of tobacco. Of the thirteen vessels four were from La Rochelle, three from Honfleur, two from Dieppe, one from Havre and one from Nantes.

[74] Arch. Nat. Mar., B$_4$, 7, contains much material on d'Estrées' voyage.

[75] Charlevoix, *Hist. de L'Isle Esp.*, II, 118-119.

THE COMMERCIAL POLICY OF COLBERT

Again the disturbance in trade was only temporary, for the French quickly regained control of the West India waters by the appearance at Martinique on May 8 of d'Estrées with another squadron, and they remained in control until the close of the war.[76] Treaties of peace were signed at Nymwegen on August 10, 1678.

With the exception of such interruptions occurring during the war, private traders steadily increased in numbers and carried on a constantly growing trade with the West Indies. An experienced merchant of La Rochelle remarked in 1679 that "so many vessels had never been seen at Nantes, La Rochelle and Bordeaux in preparation for the islands."[77] By 1683, the number of French ships trading with the West Indies had increased to 205.[78]

Freedom of trade seems to have worked miracles, but in reality it was the indomitable will and the wisdom of a great minister which had called the dormant forces of the nation to life, and endowed them with new prosperity.

[76] Arch. Nat. Mar., B$_4$, 8.
[77] Bib. Nat. MSS., fonds franç., 11315, fols. 19-22, letter from Anthoine Allaire to Patoulet, 1679.
[78] Arch. Col., F$_2$, 15, Memoir marked "Indes Occidentales" and endorsed "M. Morel."

CHAPTER XI

COLONIAL EXPORTS—TOBACCO

WE have had occasion in the preceding chapters to see the situation which confronted Colbert at the beginning of his ministry, to study the history of the West India Company from its origin in 1664 to its downfall ten years later, to follow the unrelenting campaign against the Dutch, and finally to trace the rise and development of the private trader. An important task still remains, for we have touched only superficially upon the legislation which Colbert framed, on the one hand, to control the production of colonial commodities and to regulate their exportation to the mother country, and, on the other, to stimulate French industry to furnish the articles demanded by the planters and to open the way for their importation into the islands. The royal edicts, ordinances, *arrêts* and letters, concerning these several problems, contain some of the least known and, at the same time, some of the most interesting phases of Colbert's commercial policy. But their number is so great that it would prove quite impracticable to present them in detail. We shall limit our study, therefore, to the most important. There were really only two commodities of importance produced in the French West Indies during the entire ministry of Colbert, namely, tobacco and sugar. Neither cotton, nor roucou, nor indigo, nor any other product, except the two staples mentioned, ever became important enough to be made the subject of special legislation. The study has been limited therefore to a discussion of the legislation relating to tobacco and sugar. As for articles imported into the islands, slaves, food-stuffs, live stock, lumber and manufactured goods were the most important, and it will be only with them that we shall concern ourselves.

It will be recalled that d'Esnambuc, at his first visit to St. Christopher, was enthusiastic over the quality of tobacco which grew there and took back with him to France a cargo of "excellent tobacco." The Dutch, too, were so attracted by its excellent quality that they established a regular trade with the island. It became the staple product at Guadeloupe, Martinique, St. Domingo, and the other islands, at their settlement by the French. Jacques Bouton stated in 1640 that tobacco was the only product carried to Europe from the French West Indies.[1] Its production became so extensive that de Poincy, governor-general of the French islands, resident at St. Christopher, made an agreement with the governor of the English that no more tobacco would be planted for seventeen months "in order to restore that merchandise to its former price." In accordance with that agreement, de Poincy issued an ordinance on May 6, 1639, ordering "everyone to pull up root and branch the tobacco already planted, without saving a single plant."[2]

Tobacco remained the staple product throughout the period of the first two companies and served, as in Virginia, as currency in the islands. It was not until near the middle of the century that the cultivation of sugar-cane became important enough to create a rival for it.[3] By the beginning of Colbert's ministry, the cultivation of tobacco had become secondary and during the course of his ministry the cultivation of sugar-cane became the all absorbing occupation of the planters. This was true only so far as the Windward and small Leeward Islands were concerned, for at French St. Domingo tobacco

[1] J. Bouton, *Relation de l'Estab. des Franç.*, pp. 80-81.
[2] Du Tertre, I, 143, prints text.
[3] Pelleprat, *op. cit.*, 8-9.

TOWARD THE FRENCH WEST INDIES

remained practically the only product of importance throughout the entire period.[4]

It was apparently Ogeron who first tamed the wild spirit of the freebooters of St. Domingo and led some of them to undertake the more gentle pursuit of cultivating the soil. He was so successful that by 1669 the production of the colony reached 1,200,000 pounds of tobacco,[5] and by 1674, 3,000,000 pounds.[6]

Previous to the ministry of Colbert, French colonial tobacco seems to have been admitted free of duty. Thus a royal proclamation of November 17, 1629, laid a duty of thirty sous the pound on tobacco imported from foreign countries, but specifically exempted that brought from the islands within the concession of the Company of the Isles of America.[7] By the tariff of 1664, framed by Colbert, an import duty of thirteen livres the hundredweight was laid on foreign tobacco and one of four livres the hundredweight on colonial tobacco.[8] The latter was re-

[4] A contemporary description of the coast of St. Domingo passes in review the different settlements thereof. On the section of the north around the Cape it is noted that "all the lands are planted in tobacco," and that a few of the inhabitants were buccaneers; on that of Port-de-Paix that the inhabitants were occupied with the production of tobacco and food-stuffs; on that of the west coast around Petit Goave it is remarked that "the occupation of all the inhabitants of this gulf is the cultivation of their lands in tobacco and the hunting of the wild boar." Arch. Nat. Col., C_9, 2nd series, I, Mémoire envoyé par Bellinzani sur les Boucaniers et sur l'état des establ. faits à St. Dom., 1677.

[5] Arch Nat. Col., C_9, I, Ogeron to Colbert, September 23, 1669.

[6] Arch. Aff. Etr., Mém. et Doc., Esp. 79, fols. 46 verso, Mémoire sur le commerce des isles franç., 1692. Arch. Nat. Col., F_3, 164, contains a list of vessels captured by the Dutch at the coast of St. Domingo between June 10 and July 17, 1676. There were thirteen captured, of which nine were laden with 18,900 rolls of tobacco (945,000 pounds). In a supplementary list are given the names of nine vessels which had sailed from St. Domingo for France with 13,900 rolls (695,000 pounds).

[7] Arch. Nat., AD,xi, 48; Sabatier, *La ferme du tabac*.

[8] Dessalles, *Hist. Gén.*, II, 31.

THE COMMERCIAL POLICY OF COLBERT

duced to two livres by an *arrêt* of December 10, 1670, but restored to four livres on May 24, 1675.[9] In addition, an import duty of three per cent was paid by private traders to the West India Company up to the date of its dissolution (1674), and then to the Domaine d'Occident throughout the remainder of the period. The right of re-exportation with drawback of import duties was provided by law throughout the period.[10]

Other legislation favoured the West India planter. Thus the cultivation of tobacco was forbidden in Canada on the ground that it would prove less profitable to the inhabitants than other occupations and that "the cultivation of this weed in Canada would be injurious to the interests of the islands of America."[11] Its cultivation in France was restricted to the *généralités* of Bordeaux and of Montauban and to certain districts around Montdragon, St. Maixant, Levy and Metz.[12]

But the most important act concerning tobacco taken during Colbert's entire ministry came in 1674. In that year the sale of all tobacco in France was transformed into a monopoly, controlled by the state. The monopoly was farmed out to Jean-le-Breton, whose bail bears the date of November 30, 1674. By the terms of the bail a monopoly was granted of the sale, wholesale and retail, of all tobacco, whether grown in France or imported from the French West Indies, from Brazil or from other foreign colonies or countries; consequently, all those who grew tobacco in France or imported it into the realm were forced to treat with the farmer or his agents; if, however, no agreement could be reached between the two contracting parties, the liberty of exporting or of re-exporting

[9] Moreau de Saint-Méry, I, 204, 292.
[10] Moreau de Saint-Méry, I, 208-209.
[11] Arch. Nat. Col., B, 4, Colbert to Talon, June 4, 1672.
[12] Arch. Nat., AD,xi, 48, *Arrêt du conseil d'état,* March 14, 1676.

tobacco to foreign countries was to be enjoyed by the seller, on condition that, in case of delay, his tobacco be placed in the warehouses of the farmer at the owner's expense until the time of shipment; the wholesale price of tobacco, grown within the realm and in the French islands of America, was fixed at twenty sous per pound, and of foreign tobaccos at forty sous and upwards; the retail price at twenty-five sous and fifty sous and upwards, respectively; and it was forbidden to import tobacco into the kingdom by land and by any other ports than by those of Rouen, Bordeaux, La Rochelle, for the ocean, and of Marseilles for the Mediterranean; although special permission was granted to import tobacco for Normandy by Dieppe and for Brittany by Morlaix, St. Malo and Nantes.[13] By an *arrêt* of January 25, 1676, exportation of tobacco was limited to the ports of Bordeaux, Sables d'Olonne, La Rochelle, Nantes, Morlaix, St. Malo, Rouen, Dieppe, St. Valery, Narbonne, Cette, Agde, Marseilles and Toulon.[14]

The marketing of colonial tobacco in France was thus made highly unprofitable by reason of the relatively high import duty laid upon it and by reason of the fact that its sale was placed in the hands of a monopoly. The fact that it was liberally protected against foreign competition was offset by the fact that in actual practice the privilege of its re-exportation to foreign countries was rarely enjoyed. Thus a well-known merchant of Nantes remarked that when tobacco arrived from St. Domingo, it was necessary to place it under the lock and key of the farmer. If the farmer wished to buy the tobacco, he sought all sorts of means to intimidate the trader. He objected to the quantity or to the quality, and offered

[13] Arch. Nat., AD,xi, 48, contains a copy of the bail which bears date of November 30, 1674.
[14] Ibid.

THE COMMERCIAL POLICY OF COLBERT

low prices. He tried to prevent re-exportation to foreign markets, for which provision was made by the law, by demanding a bond of twenty sous the pound as a guarantee that the tobacco would be carried to the port designated.[15]

The effect of this policy was felt at once in the colonies. Patoulet stated in 1680 that, whereas the cultivation of tobacco used to occupy in the Windward Islands 4000 or 5000 men, none was being cultivated then "by reason of its depreciation."[16] De Pouançay wrote about the same time from St. Domingo that he was compelled to employ all of his efforts in order to hold the planters within their allegiance, because "they are reduced to the last extremity on account of the great losses which they have suffered since the time that tobacco was placed in the hands of a monopoly. I have seen them in despair, and ready to withdraw among the English of Jamaica and among the Dutch of Curaçao." He added that he had persuaded them from doing so only by communicating to them a letter which he had received from Bellinzani and which held out the hope that the monopoly would be suppressed at the expiration of the bail, that is to say, in 1680, and that colonial tobacco would be subjected to a simple import duty as in former times.[17] De Pouançay gave warning that if conditions continued as they were, he would not remain responsible for what might happen in the colony.[18] He wrote again at the beginning of the following year that the cultivation of tobacco had become so unprofitable by reason of the quantity produced and of the low price offered by the monopoly in France that several plantations

---

[15] Boislisle, *op. cit.*, II, appendix, 497, Mémoire du député de Nantes.
[16] Arch. Nat. Col., C$_8$, 2nd series, I, Memoir by Patoulet, 1680.
[17] Arch. Nat. Col., C$_9$, I, de Pouançay to Colbert, March 20, 1680.
[18] Charlevoix, *Hist. de l'Isle Esp.*, II, 131.

TOWARD THE FRENCH WEST INDIES

had been abandoned.[19] In still another letter, a few months later, he remarked that the planters could no longer gain a living by cultivating tobacco.[20] Accompanying this last letter was a memoir addressed to Colbert by "the officers and principal planters of St. Domingo who had assembled in obedience to the orders of M. de Blénac, governor and lieutenant-general of the islands and *terre ferme* of America":

"The planters of the coast of St. Domingo find themselves reduced to the last extremity, being unable to derive any fruit from their labour, because the monopoly places such a low price upon the tobacco which they send to France, notwithstanding the fact that the same tobacco is sold at a very high price in the realm. The result is that they can no longer support themselves or maintain their plantations so that most of them have been forced to abandon their fields and become freebooters. It is therefore humbly begged of Monseigneur that he take some measure, agreeable to His Highness, which will prevent the destruction of the colony, either by abolishing the monopoly or by prohibiting, within the kingdom, the use of foreign tobacco with which the farmers of the monopoly are supplying themselves in abundance. . . . Monseigneur is also humbly begged to accord the privilege of re-exporting to foreign countries the tobacco imported from St. Domingo. The said officers and planters agree to furnish only a limited quantity of tobacco, properly weighed and of good quality, on condition that the monopoly be forced to purchase it at a price proportionate to the cost of production."[21]

This memoir had hardly reached France before the monopoly for the sale of tobacco was renewed in favour of Claude Boutet.[22]

[19] Arch. Nat. Col., C$_9$, I, de Pouançay to Colbert, January 30, 1681.

[20] Ibid., May, 1681.

[21] Arch. Nat. Col., C$_9$, I, Memoir of May 5, 1681.

[22] The bail was renewed on July 22, 1681. It is printed in full by Chambon, *Le Commerce de l'Amérique,* I, 482 ff. A printed copy is

THE COMMERCIAL POLICY OF COLBERT

But one measure was taken which theoretically freed the planters from the tyranny of the monopoly. This was the *arrêt* of April 8, 1681, which confirmed the right of re-exportation of colonial tobacco to foreign countries. Consequently all French subjects, importing tobacco from the "French islands of America and the coast of St. Domingo," were to enjoy this right on condition that a formal declaration be made of their intentions to do so.

The farmers of the monopoly apparently continued, however, to prevent the re-exportation of colonial tobacco, for a merchant guild of St. Malo made protest against their conduct, asserting that they were doing everything to control absolutely the price of colonial tobacco and that they were so successful that there was no longer any profit in the trade.[23] Complaints came also from the merchants of La Rochelle of the bad faith of the farmers in using every means to prevent the re-exportation of colonial tobacco and to force traders to sell them tobacco at prices which they offered.[24]

Whatever may have been Colbert's hope in the passage of the *arrêt* of April 8, 1681, or to whomever must be attributed the fault that the privileges accorded by it

to be found also in Arch. Nat., AD,xi, 48. Dareste, *Histoire de France*, V, 513, asserts that Colbert had the intention to abolish this monopoly. On what authority he makes the assertion, he fails to state.

[23] Arch. Nat., G$_7$, 1685, Sindic de la communauté des March. négoc. de St. Malo, November 28, 1685. Villebague Eon, one of the principal merchants of St. Malo, wrote to de Lagny, at that time director-general of commerce, asking permission to ship tobacco directly from St. Domingo to Holland. De Lagny replied that the request could not be granted, but that orders had been given to the farmer of the monopoly to grant without delay permission to re-export colonial tobacco. Arch. Nat. Mar., B$_7$, 58, II, fol. 98 verso, de Lagny to Villebague Eon, September 23, 1686.

[24] Boislisle, *op. cit.*, I, 358. The controller-general wrote to Arnoul, the intendant at La Rochelle, to inquire into the matter and report to him. Ibid.

256

TOWARD THE FRENCH WEST INDIES

were not enjoyed, one thing is certain, poverty continued at St. Domingo. Thus, de Pouançay wrote on September 25, 1682:

"They [the planters] live very well so far as food is concerned, but they are entirely destitute of cloth and garments for themselves, for their servants and their slaves, and are in need of other things necessary for their plantations. This is due to the fact that merchants are unwilling to barter merchandise for tobacco which is pure loss to them."[25]

De Cussy found on assuming the duties of governor as successor to de Pouançay in 1684, that his most difficult task was "to calm the planters on the subject of the tobacco monopoly which continued to ruin them, because the existence of this monopoly had so cheapened the price of tobacco, which had so long been the staple product of the colony and served as its currency, that those who had no other means of support than its cultivation were in danger of dying of starvation."[26] A priest wrote from St. Domingo somewhat later:

"I believe that you would like to know that the cause of discontent among the planters of the island is none other than the question of tobacco. It is only the well-to-do planters who can earn their living, as they have the means to cultivate indigo; the small planters who can cultivate nothing but tobacco are objects of pity, as they have no market for their tobacco. They are in extreme poverty. One can see whole families naked. I saw a poor young miss who was obliged to borrow a chemise from a negress to put on while she washed her own. I have seen women about to be delivered come and upon bended knee implore the governor to give them a small quantity of wool wherein to wrap their babes."[27]

[25] Arch. Nat. Col., C$_9$, I, de Pouançay to Colbert, September 25, 1682.

[26] Charlevoix, *op. cit.*, II, 150.

[27] Arch. Aff. Etrang., Doc. et Mém., Amérique, V, 565, Le Père Plumier to de Bonrepos, October 6, 1690.

THE COMMERCIAL POLICY OF COLBERT

If a contemporary estimate of 50,000 or 60,000 rolls (2,500,000 or 3,000,000 pounds) of tobacco as the production of the colonies in 1674 be accurate, the decrease in production in ten years was nearly fifty per cent, for the average production of St. Domingo for the six years, 1683-1688, was only 30,674 rolls (1,533,700 pounds).[28] A few years later the planters became so incensed at the low price of tobacco that they pulled up what they had planted and ceased to plant it altogether.[29]

This policy of sacrificing the interests of the planters to those of the monopoly in France forced the adoption of another means to gain a livelihood. De Pouançay tells us, in one of the last letters which he wrote before his death, that "the planters are devoting themselves to the cultivation of indigo and cotton, and a few to the cultivation of sugar-cane, some others to that of cacao and to the raising of cattle."[30] This was true, as Père Plumier remarked, only of the larger planters who had the capital necessary to begin the cultivation of new products. The

[28] Arch. Nat. Col., C₉, IV, Estat des quantités de rolles de tabac de St. Domingue entrez dans le Royaume pendant le bail de Fauconne, de celle qui en a esté acheptez, pour la ferme et le prix qu'ils ont esté payez le cent pesant. Sçavoir:

Année	Nombre des Rolles entrées	Ditto acheptées pour la ferme	Prix courant du centpesant
1683	47,822	8,913	600 rolles à 20 livres
			5,513 rolles à 25 livres
			7,800 rolles à 30 livres
1684	17,213	11,211	6,825 rolles à 25 livres
			d'autres rolles à 21 to 36 livres
1685	25,153	6,300	de 20 à 45 livres
1686	35,590	14,126	Moyenne à 30 livres
1687	45,500	6,381	Moyenne à 32 livres
1688	12,763	7,955	Moyenne à 22 livres

The "roll" usually contained 50 pounds.

[29] Boislisle, II, 497, Mémoire du député de Nantes, 1701.

[30] Arch. Nat. Col., C₉, I, de Pouançay to Colbert, September 25, 1682.

small planter was idling away his time in the sunshine with his hungry, naked children about him. Before him was his small tobacco field. As he gazed upon it, he doubtlessly thought of the days when the large green leaf, turning to a rich yellow for the harvest time, brought its reward for the days of sweat and toil. The bitterness of defeat and disappointment and rebellious anger must have been in his soul. The curse was writ upon his brow.

Colbert's ministry closed leaving poverty broadcast among the tobacco planters of St. Domingo, and the policy which had been pursued during the last ten years was directly responsible therefor. But one might have seen the first rays of a new dawn which was to transform the struggling colony of tobacco planters into the richest and most productive sugar colony of the world.

CHAPTER XII

Colonial Exports—Sugar

PELLEPRAT, who was in the islands in 1650 and again in 1654, and published an account of his voyage in 1655, remarked that the ordinary money of the islands was tobacco and sugar and that traders were exporting sugar. "I say that traders take away sugar with them, because of late sugar of excellent quality is being produced in the islands and particularly at St. Christopher."[1] De Rochefort, in 1658, in describing the plantation of de Poincy, the governor of St. Christopher, remarked that in the lot adjoining the dwelling-house, there were "three machines or mills suitable for crushing sugar-cane." Besides these, the same governor maintained three similar mills on another plantation in Cayonne. Following the example set by the governor, the chief officers and planters of St. Christopher also set up sugar-mills. De Rochefort gives a list of no less than fifteen planters who had done so.[2] Shortly afterwards Biët noted that the sugar industry at Guadeloupe was flourishing, thanks to the fact that the Dutch who had been driven from Brazil had settled in that island:

"After one of the principal Dutchmen had examined the soil of Guadeloupe, he found it so excellent that he assured the governor that even the soil of Brazil was not better adapted to the cultivation of sugar-cane. Immediately the governor granted him a plantation in Cabesterre where he employed his slaves in clearing the land, preparing the soil and planting sugar-cane. . . . The governor and all the planters followed his example with the result that according to report of those

[1] Pelleprat, pp. 8-9.
[2] De Rochefort, p. 312.

TOWARD THE FRENCH WEST INDIES

who come from the island, Guadeloupe is no longer what it used to be. . . . There are planters who manufacture 10,000 pounds of sugar a week. . . . All the planters are very well established and are little lords, whereas in former times they were very poor."[3]

In a memoir written in 1660, it was stated that the first trade of the planters of Martinique was in tobacco, which was still produced, and that indigo, cotton, ginger and roucou were also cultivated, but that in proportion as the planters become rich they began to plant sugar-cane and establish sugar-mills, of which, the author adds, there were many then in the islands.[4] De Tracy wrote to Colbert on October 24, 1664, that there was a scarcity of food-stuffs, not only for the soldiers, but also for the planters of all the islands, and especially of Martinique, because the planting of cassava had been abandoned for the cultivation of sugar-cane.[5] In another letter the same year he wrote to the same minister that it was useless to urge the planters to cultivate cotton and indigo, because much more profit was to be gained by the production of sugar.[6]

It is clear from these citations that by 1664 the production of sugar had become the chief industry of the French Antilles, except St. Domingo, where tobacco remained for more than two decades longer the chief produc-

[3] Biët, pp. 314-315.

[4] Arch. Nat. Col., C$_8$, 2nd series, I, Relation des Isles de l'Amérique.

[5] Du Tertre, III, 98.

[6] Arch. Nat. Col., C$_8$, 2nd series, I, Minute of a letter addressed by Colbert to the governor-general of the Antilles. In the margin is written in the hand of Colbert the following comment: "Quoyque le peuple trouvent (sic) plus d'advantage au sucre qu'au coton et à l'indigo comme il y a lieu d'esperer que les isles en se peuplant se défricheront et que cette augmentation de terre en culture pourroit rendre les sucres trop communs, il faut toujours s'appliquer et mainteuir la culture dudit coton et de l'indigo parceque la diversité des denrées et marchandises causera assurement l'abondance dans les Isles."

tion. But practically all of the sugar produced in the French islands was carried either directly or indirectly to Holland to be refined, for the refining industry in France was as yet in its infancy.[7] Colbert, therefore, had two problems: (1) the creation of the refining industry in France, and (2) the encouragement of production in the islands by legislation which would facilitate the sale of sugar in France.

Colbert formed the plan as early as 1664 of building up the refining industry in the realm, for he made provision in that year for exportation to foreign countries of sugar refined in France.[8] Shortly afterwards he encouraged Guy Terré, a merchant at Rouen, in the establishment of two refineries in that city. He even furnished part of the capital himself, "because he regarded the enterprise as very useful to the state, to the increase of navigation and to the development of the colonies of America."[9] On September 15, 1674, he ordered Gaspard Maurellet to establish a refinery at Marseilles "with the view of increasing and extending the commerce of the French islands of America to the ports of the Mediterra-

[7] As early as 1613 permission was granted to Jeremie Vualens to establish a refinery at Rouen and in 1620 he was authorized "to continue with his associates the refining of sugar." Gosselin, *Doc. authent. et inédits pour servir à l'histoire de la Marine Normande et du commerce rouennais pendant les 16e et 17e siècles,* Rouen, 1876, p. 131. Trezel, to whom was granted the privilege of establishing sugar mills in the islands, was also probably interested in the same industry at Rouen. But it is not probable that these refineries were of much importance.

[8] Article XVIII of the letters-patent of the West India Company of May, 1664, reads as follows: "The merchandise which will have been declared to be consumed in the kingdom and on which import duty will have been paid and which the company decides later to export to foreign countries will be subject to no export duty, nor shall the sugar, refined in France in the refineries which the said company will have established, be subjected to export duties with the condition, however, that the said sugar be exported in French bottoms."

[9] Chambre de Commerce of Nantes, C, 733.

TOWARD THE FRENCH WEST INDIES

nean and those of Provence, where it was not known, and to destroy in Provence and in the provinces, trade in Dutch sugar and the cassonades of Brazil."[10] Others were urged to make similar establishments at Dunkerque, Dieppe, Nantes, Saumur, Angers, Tours, Orleans, La Rochelle, Bordeaux and Toulouse. By 1683 no less than twenty-nine refineries existed in France, which consumed annually 17,700,000 pounds of raw sugar.[11]

Colbert protected refineries in France by putting, in 1664, a very high duty on foreign refined sugar of fifteen livres the hundredweight. This was increased by an *arrêt* of September 15, 1665, to twenty-two livres ten sous the hundredweight.[12]

The amount of sugar refined in the realm was important

[10] O. Teissier, *Inventaire des Archives Historiques de la Chambre de Commerce de Marseille*, p. 144.

[11] The document from which this information has been taken is of enough interest to be reproduced here: Estats des rafineries de France, 1683:

	Rafineries	Consommation de sucre brut
Dunkerque	2	1,500,000 livres.
Dieppe	1	500,000 livres.
Rouen	8	4,500,000 livres.
Nantes	3	2,000,000 livres.
Saumur	1	800,000 livres.
Angers	1	800,000 livres.
Tours	1	500,000 livres.
Orleans	2	800,000 livres.
La Rochelle	4	2,400,000 livres.
Bordeaux	3	2,000,000 livres.
Toulouse	1	400,000 livres.
Marseille	2	1,200,000 livres.
Totals	29	17,700,000 livres.
Aux Colonies	5	3,000,000 livres.
	34	20,700,000 livres.

Arch. Nat. Col., F_3, 142.

[12] Arch. Nat., AD,xi, 48.

THE COMMERCIAL POLICY OF COLBERT

enough by 1670 to raise a discussion between the revenue farmers, on the one side, and the West India Company and private traders on the other, to make it necessary for the king to settle the dispute. The dispute arose in the following way. By a royal declaration of September, 1664, a general provision was made whereby both French and foreign merchants were permitted to place in *entrepôt* foreign merchandise which they wished to export later into foreign countries. No export duties were to be laid upon such goods and even import duties paid upon merchandise which was at first declared to be for consumption in France were to be returned if the said goods were re-exported to foreign ports. This was confirmed by a royal edict of February, 1670.[13] It is to be inferred that colonial products brought by the West India Company and private French traders could thus be exported to Holland and other European countries. At any rate, the claim was made by the West India Company and private traders that raw sugar, brought from the French islands and refined in the kingdom and re-exported into foreign countries, fell within the law, and that therefore, duties paid on the raw sugar when imported, should be restored at its exportation after it had been refined. As it took two and one-half pounds of raw sugar to yield one pound of refined sugar, the duties paid on the two and one-half pounds should be restored for every pound of refined exported. The revenue farmers objected, however: (1) that the sugar brought from the islands came from a territory under the domination of His Majesty and did not fall within the law, which had to do only with merchandise imported from foreign countries; (2) that, besides, sugar after being refined changed its character; and (3) that it would be impossible to avoid confusion in attempting to restore duties collected on raw sugar, because raw

[13] Chambre de Commerce of Nantes, C, 730.

TOWARD THE FRENCH WEST INDIES

sugar imported by the West India Company paid only two livres the hundredweight, and that imported by private ships paid four livres, and that it would be obviously impossible to distinguish between the two after refining. An *arrêt* of September 29, 1670, settled this dispute by ordering the farmers to restore duties collected on raw sugar imported into the kingdom from the French islands at the rate of six livres the hundredweight on its exportation in the form of refined sugar. No distinction was to be made between sugar belonging to the company and private merchants. An interesting clause was added to this *arrêt* which said that no restoration of duty whatsoever was to be made on raw sugar re-exported to foreign countries.[14]

To the refiners of Rouen was granted, on every hundredweight of refined sugar exported, a special drawback of 100 sous, which represented a partial restitution of the special import duty of fifty sous per hundredweight laid at Rouen on raw sugar.[15]

This was a most distinct encouragement to the refining of sugar within the realm, both by the relatively high tariff imposed on foreign refined sugar, and by the encouragement given to exportation of refined sugar by granting a drawback. There was after this no additional legislation to affect the refiners in France before 1682, "when they complained of the competition of the refiners in the islands." Before, however, considering that legislation, it will be well to see what measures were taken to promote the interests of the planters in order to understand how the dispute arose.

[14] Chambre de Commerce of Nantes, C, 730.
[15] Chambre de Commerce of Nantes, C, 730, *arrêt* of March 25, 1670. This duty had been imposed originally by the city itself in 1638 as a temporary source of revenue, but it became permanert and the right to collect it was farmed out. The West India Company possessed the farm and it was by it that the drawback was to be paid.

THE COMMERCIAL POLICY OF COLBERT

By the tariff of 1664, all refined sugars which entered France by the ports of the *Cinq Grosses Fermes* were to pay fifteen livres the hundredweight, all other sugars four livres the hundredweight. Included in the last named was all sugar imported from St. Christopher. It is thus seen that French colonial sugar, that is to say, raw sugar, for as yet there were no refineries in the islands, received no preferential treatment. Colbert, however, quickly remedied this by an *arrêt* of September 15, 1665, by which all refined sugars imported from foreign countries were forced to pay twenty-two livres ten sous the hundredweight; cassonades and muscovado from Brazil, fifteen livres and seven livres ten sous, respectively; paneles and sugar from St. Thomas, six livres; and all sugar from the French colonies, four livres.[16]

This schedule remained in force for all foreign sugars throughout the entire period and for French colonial sugar until an *arrêt* of December 10, 1670, by which the import duty was reduced fifty per cent, that is to say, to forty sous the hundredweight. The motive for this reduction was stated in the preamble to be the fact that the import duty was so large in proportion to the price of sugar in France that the planters could no longer gain any profit in its production. Colbert remarked in a letter to Colbert de Terron, inclosing a copy of this *arrêt*, that "there is justification for the hope that, with such a great concession, the French will carry on all the commerce of the islands to the exclusion of the foreigner."[17] This new schedule on raw sugar from the islands was maintained, however, only until May 24, 1675, when the old schedule of four livres the hundredweight was restored. It remained thus fixed until the close of Colbert's ministry.

These duties were applicable only to the ports within

[16] Arch. Nat., AD,vii, 3.
[17] Arch. Nat. Mar., B$_2$, 14, January 2, 1671.

TOWARD THE FRENCH WEST INDIES

the *Cinq Grosses Fermes*, that is to say, so far as commerce with the islands was concerned, in the ports of Normandy. They were later extended to Bayonne and Bordeaux but did not apply to the Breton ports of St. Malo and Nantes. Sugar imported into Rouen was subject to a special local import duty of six deniers the pound or fifty sous the hundredweight. That imported into other ports likewise was subjected to local duties, but they were of small importance.

The increased production in the islands, stimulated no doubt by the new activity of French traders after the English war, seems to have been accompanied by a corresponding decrease in the price of sugar. De Baas repeatedly expressed the opinion in his letters of 1670 that the increasing production of sugar would shortly result in such low prices that the planter would no longer find profit in cultivating the soil.[18] Du Lion asserted in a letter of September 30, 1670, that the price of sugar in France was so low and the cost of freight so high that the planters were losing hope of gaining any profit from its sale.[19] The duty of four livres the hundredweight on colonial sugar was reduced to two livres by the *arrêt* of December 10, 1670, as we have just seen, because its low price made it impossible "for the planter to export it to France or to continue the cultivation of his plantation."[20] The same conditions continued at the close of the Dutch war, when the price of sugar in the islands fell to two livres ten sous and three livres the hundredweight.[21]

[18] Arch. Nat. Col., B, 2, fol. 135, the king to de Baas, December 21, 1670.

[19] Arch. Nat. Col., C_7, I, du Lion to Colbert, September 30, 1670. Du Lion stated that the price of sugar at Dunkerque was fifteen francs the hundredweight and that the planters were forced to pay sixteen deniers a pound for freight.

[20] Moreau de Saint-Méry, I, 204.

[21] Arch. Nat. Col., C_8, III, Mémoire de l'intendant Patoulet pour M. Bégon, December 20, 1682.

THE COMMERCIAL POLICY OF COLBERT

Three very obvious means could be employed to bring relief to the planter: (1) To limit the production of sugar in the islands so that the supply would more nearly correspond to the demands of the refineries in France;[22] (2) to permit a free exportation of raw sugar to foreign ports, either directly from the islands or indirectly by way of France; and (3) to permit the establishment of refineries in the islands.

Colbert seems to have favoured the principle of limiting production. To the remark made by de Tracy, in a letter from Martinique in 1664, that the planters found much more profit in the cultivation of sugar-cane than in that of cotton or of indigo, Colbert made the following reply: "Although the planters find more profit in the production of sugar than in that of cotton or indigo, it is necessary to maintain the cultivation of the latter, inasmuch as there is reason to expect that the islands, in proportion as their lands are cleared and put in cultivation, will produce too large a quantity of sugar. Variety in cultivation is more conducive to their welfare."[23] But to the letters of de Baas expressing fears that an over-production of sugar was imminent and might prove disastrous to the islands, the following reply was made:

"You can assuredly relieve your mind of the uneasiness which is expressed in all of your letters that the islands will produce so much sugar that it will be difficult to find a market for it and that consequently its price will be so cheapened

[22] P. Leroy-Beaulieu, *De la Colonisation chez les peuples modernes*, 5th edition, Paris, 1902, I, 166, states that the production of sugar in the islands was 27,000,000 pounds. He cites, however, no authority for this statement. Patoulet estimated the production at 18,000,000 pounds. Arch. Nat. Col., C_8, III, Mém. pour M. Bégon, December 20, 1682, and Moreau de Saint-Méry made from some source the estimate that the seventeen refineries in France consumed 17,700,000 pounds of raw sugar. Arch. Nat. Col., F_3, 142.

[23] Arch. Nat. Col., C_8, 2nd series, I, Minutes de lettre ad. par Colbert au gouv. gén. des Antilles.

that the planters will suffer a loss in its production and will no longer be able to cultivate their plantations. . . . Trust to me that I shall guarantee to my subjects who are engaged in this trade every means and facility to transport sugar to foreign markets."[24]

In spite, however, of this very clear evidence that Colbert did not wish at that time to limit the production of sugar, because he believed that there was a better solution to the problem, we find him writing in less than a year to Pélissier, a director of the West India Company in the islands:

"As the abundance of sugar seems to be exceedingly great in the kingdom, it would be wise for you to take into consideration whether or not you could influence the planters to decrease the amount of land devoted to the cultivation of sugar-cane, and to cultivate some cotton, indigo, and ginger. Try some experiments in the planting of spices such as pepper, nutmegs, etc."[25]

But no measures were taken to enforce such a plan upon the planters. Colbert regarded it as unwise because he believed that "a decrease in the production of sugar meant a decrease in the development of the islands."[26]

The expediency of permitting the exportation of raw sugar directly from the islands was never seriously considered, because "he [Colbert] knew that it would foster the growth of the Dutch refineries, which he wished to destroy."[27] The question arises as to whether the raw sugar of the islands could be exported from France to foreign countries. It seems that according to clause

[24] Arch. Nat. Col., B, 3, fol. 135, the king to de Baas, December 21, 1670.

[25] Clément, III, 2, pp. 526-527, Colbert to Pélissier, November 4, 1671.

[26] Arch. Nat. Col., C_8, III, Mémoire by Patoulet, December 20, 1682.

[27] Arch. Nat. Col., C_8, III, Mém. by Patoulet, 1682.

THE COMMERCIAL POLICY OF COLBERT

XVIII of its letters-patent, the West India Company had the right to re-export any sugar imported from the islands. The act of September 10, 1668, which forbade the company to grant passports to foreigners, said explicitly:

"The said company and the said private traders shall arm their vessels, and make their returns in the ports of France, where they shall have the privilege of discharging their cargoes of sugar, tobacco, and other merchandise coming from the company's colonies, and may re-export them into foreign countries without being obliged to pay duties thereon, on condition, however, of making a declaration of the fact before the proper officers."[28]

Colbert wrote on November 28, 1670, to Brunet, one of the directors of the West India Company: "In regard to muscovado, I shall not change my policy of requiring duties to be paid upon it when it is re-exported from the realm"; and again on January 23, that "His Majesty desires that all sugar imported from the islands of America be refined in the realm."[29] It was also about this time that the privilege of trading in the islands was taken from traders at Nantes and not restored until a formal promise had been given by them that no raw sugar would be re-exported to foreign countries, under penalty of confiscation of vessel and cargo, and that they would refine their sugar.[30]

Schérer[31] states that an ordinance of 1682 prohibited the re-exportation of raw sugar imported from the islands. Boizard and Tardieu[32] refer vaguely to a law of 1681 which forbade the same thing. The latter add that the same

[28] Moreau de Saint-Méry, I, 175.

[29] Depping, *Correspondance*, III, 524, 527.

[30] Arch. Nat., G₇, 1313; AD,xi, 48, *arrêt du conseil d'état*, December 14, 1671.

[31] *Histoire du Commerce*, II, 493.

[32] *Histoire de la Legislation des Sucres, 1664-1891*, p. 3.

TOWARD THE FRENCH WEST INDIES

law imposed a duty of eight francs the hundredweight on refined sugar in the islands and imported into the realm. But this last action was taken apparently for the first time by the enactment of the *arrêt* of April 18, 1682, which will be discussed below, and it seems probable that it is to this *arrêt* that reference is made. It contains, however, no prohibition to re-export colonial raw sugar. Although two very excellent collections of acts relating to sugar have been examined, no legislation of 1681 or 1682 containing such a prohibition has been found.[33] Apparently it was not until September 28, 1684, that the re-exportation of colonial raw sugar to foreign countries was formally forbidden.[34] It is to be remarked, however, that this date is posterior to that of the death of Colbert. All that can be said, so far as the records which we have consulted are concerned, is that Colbert expressed the wish that all raw sugar be refined within the realm before re-exportation, but that he never formally required it except in the case of traders of Nantes. The importance of this consists in the fact that colonial raw sugar was never placed by Colbert entirely in the control of the French refiner. The law permitted its sale in foreign markets. In actual practice, however, the refiner in France enjoyed a monopoly of colonial raw sugar, for it was found to be so unprofitable to sell it in foreign markets, after import duties had been paid in France and the expense of unloading and reloading had been met, that it was not done. Thus Patoulet explained the excessively low price of sugar in the islands in 1679, which was two livres ten sous or three livres per hundredweight, by saying that the refiners of France agreed among themselves to fix the price to be paid for raw sugar.[35]

[33] Arch. Nat., AD,xi, 48, Chamb. de Commerce of Nantes, C. 730.
[34] Moreau de Saint-Méry, I, 402.
[35] Arch. Nat. Col., C_8, III, Mémoire, December 20, 1682.

271

THE COMMERCIAL POLICY OF COLBERT

Obviously the only means left to save the planters from the tyranny of the French refiner was to encourage the establishment of refineries in the islands. The refining of sugar had already been begun in the islands in fact. Thus Claude Gueston, a director of the East India Company, and residing at Caen, established in 1667, at great expense to himself, a refinery in the island of Guadeloupe in order "to do something agreeable to His Majesty."[36] We learn from a letter by de Baas to Colbert of March 4, 1670, that the superior-general of the Jesuits, R. Père Brion, had begun the refining of sugar at Martinique and that he hoped to refine 10,000 pounds. De Baas added that it would be wise for the West India Company to encourage him in every way possible in order to stimulate others to follow his example in establishing refineries, for it was a matter of great importance to the welfare of the islands.[37] At the beginning of 1672, de Baas wrote that the planters were convinced of the advantage of refining their own sugar, but that there were several things which prevented them from doing so. In the first place, the planters were heavily indebted to private merchants and to the West India Company and wished to pay their debts, but their creditors wished to receive refined sugar on the same basis as raw sugar; in the second place, a considerable capital was necessary for the establishment of refineries; and in the third place, there were not enough refiners in the islands to teach the process of refining to the planters. In regard to the last point, de Baas suggested that the West

[36] Chamb. de Commerce of Nantes, C, 730, Extrait des Reg., July 4, 1682. The purpose of the act was to grant exemption from import duties for 200,000 pounds of sugar refined at this refinery and imported into France, as an import duty of eight livres per hundredweight had been laid by an *arrêt* of April 18, 1682, on sugar refined in the islands.

[37] Arch. Nat. Col., C$_8$, 2nd series, I, de Baas to Colbert, March 4, 1670. De Baas wrote again some few days later (March 22) that Father Brion was still persisting in carrying out his plans. Ibid.

TOWARD THE FRENCH WEST INDIES

India Company send out six refiners, two for each of the islands of Martinique, Guadeloupe and St. Christopher.[38] Du Lion wrote on November 16, 1671, that he was planning to establish a refinery at Guadeloupe and that he was trying to induce others to follow his example.[39]

Colbert pursued the policy of encouraging such establishments. He wrote to de Baas on November 29, 1672:

"You know how important it is for the commerce of the islands of America to persuade the planters to refine their sugar themselves and thus to gain a more ready and more assured market for their sugar. The West India Company has given orders and instructions to Sieur de Loover, planter of Guadeloupe, and supplied him with all implements necessary for the instruction of planters in the method of refining sugar and of making cassonades. You should not only aid him in every way that you can, but acquaint all with the undertaking and especially convince the planters of the advantage to be gained in refining their sugar."[40]

He wrote similar letters to du Ruau Pallu, agent-general of the West India Company, and to du Lion, governor of Guadeloupe.[41] In 1674, Colbert wrote again to de Baas instructing him "to urge the planters to purify and refine their sugar."[42]

Furthermore, Colbert protected colonial refiners by forbidding the revenue farmers to collect more than four livres the hundredweight on sugar refined in the islands

[38] Arch. Nat. Col., C$_8$, I, de Baas to Colbert, February 28, 1672.
[39] Arch. Nat. Col., C$_7$, II, du Lion to Colbert, November 16, 1671.
[40] Arch. Nat. Col., B, 4, Colbert to de Baas, November 29, 1672.
[41] Ibid., fols. 102, 102 verso.
[42] Ibid., 6, fol. 32, May 15, 1674. We have a bit of evidence in the admiralty records of La Rochelle which rather implies that a refinery was established in one of the islands a few months later. *L'Angélique,* whose passport was registered on December 22, 1674, had in her cargo "320 barriques de charbon, 1800 pots et formes à rafiner sucres." She was bound for Guadeloupe. Arch. Dépt. Charente Inf., B, unclassified, Rap. et Proc. Verb., 1674.

and imported into the realm. He thus placed the same import duty on it as that levied on raw sugar.[43]

By 1679, two refineries had been established at Martinique and three at Guadeloupe, but they seem to have been small and rather unimportant.[44] Thus Colbert's efforts had as yet borne small fruit. This was possibly due in part to the Dutch war. At any rate, the very low price of sugar in 1679 necessitated renewed activity.

Patoulet's arrival in the islands in the summer of 1679, to become the first intendant-general, marks an epoch in the growth of refineries. A memorialist of 1692 referred to him as the one who had proposed their establishment and fostered their growth.[45] It was inaccurate to affirm that Patoulet had originally proposed their establishment, as is evident from what has been said above, but it is strong proof of his activity during his intendancy in contributing to its success. Shortly after his arrival he wrote to Colbert that plans had been made for the establishment in Martinique of two large refineries which would be able to refine annually 800,000 or 900,000 pounds of raw sugar. These two refineries were to be ready by the beginning of 1680. Permission had been asked to construct others. Patoulet wrote to Colbert in regard to the matter as follows:

"As I do not know exactly what are your intentions toward such enterprises and as they might be unfavourable, I have postponed my reply to the very pressing demands of certain other planters who wish to construct two new refineries and asked my permission to do so. This delay which I imposed, together with the report which comes from the refiners at Bordeaux to the effect that a supplementary import duty of four livres had been laid on sugar refined in the islands, has

[43] Moreau de Saint-Méry, I, 294.
[44] Arch. Nat. Col., C$_8$, II, Patoulet to Colbert, September 22, 1679.
[45] Arch. Aff. Etrang., Mém. et Doc., Esp., 79, fol. 61, Mémoire sur le commerce des Antilles.

so alarmed every one that those who asked permission to establish the two refineries no longer talk of carrying out their plan."[46]

The reply which Colbert wrote to this letter, although brief, can leave no doubt as to the policy which he intended to pursue. "You should work to increase by every means the number of refineries."[47] Shortly afterwards he wrote again: "You should persuade the planters to establish refineries, for it is certain that it can contribute much to the increase of commerce."[48]

In accordance with these instructions, Patoulet became very active in promoting the refining industry. He wrote in 1680 enthusiastically, that the two large refineries of which he had written in a previous letter had brought forty good workmen from France and that the advantage of such establishments was already evident, for the price of sugar had already risen thirty-three and one-third per cent. "I shall exert all my efforts to persuade others to construct new refineries." He added that he had almost completed a company which would erect a new refinery and that he had written to the Company of Senegal to urge it to establish another. If these plans materialized he was sure that enough sugar could be refined in the islands to supply the entire kingdom.[49] Patoulet became personally interested in one refinery for a three-eighths interest,[50] and he seems to have carried on a regular trade in sugar with Anthoine Allaire, a merchant of La Rochelle.[51]

[46] Arch. Nat. Col., C$_8$, II, Patoulet to Colbert, September 22, 1679.
[47] Arch. Nat. Col., B, 9, fol. 24, June 2, 1680.
[48] Bib. Nat. MSS., fonds franç., 11315, fol. 133, May 4, 1681.
[49] Arch. Nat. Col., C$_8$, 2nd series, I, Mém. de Patoulet, December 20, 1680.
[50] Arch. Nat. Mar., B$_3$, 45, fols. 31-33, Patoulet to Seignelay, March 7, 1684.
[51] Bib. Nat. MSS., fonds franç., 11315, fol. 19 verso, contains a

The growth of these refineries produced immediate results, for the price of raw sugar rose in 1682 to five francs and later to six francs ten sous per hundredweight.[52] The refineries of the realm felt the competition and appealed to the government against this new force which had arisen to dispute their monopoly and to threaten their destruction. Colbert had been responsible, as has been shown, for the growth of the refining industry in France and those interested in it had a right to claim his protection. He was equally responsible for its growth in the islands, as has just been seen. There is, however, a difference to be observed in his attitude toward the two enterprises. There can be no doubt that his original plan was for the islands to produce raw sugar and to have it refined in the realm. When, however, the establishment of refineries in France was not sufficiently rapid to make it possible for all of the raw sugar of the islands to find a ready market in France and to prevent a serious depreciation thereof, he was forced to find some expedient to save the planter from ruin. He refused to permit the exportation of raw sugar direct from the islands to foreign markets and distinctly discouraged its re-exportation from France, and he was not willing to limit the production of sugar by forcing the planters to plant a certain per cent of their lands with other crops. He was thus forced in a sense to encourage the establishment of refineries in the islands. He thus seems to have favoured their establishment more as a temporary expedient than as a permanent policy.

The experiment had proved highly successful and advantageous to the planters. There were many sound reasons why the policy of encouraging colonial refineries

letter of October 29, 1679, from this merchant to Patoulet, contracting for 50,000 pounds of raw sugar at four livres the hundredweight.

[52] Arch. Nat. Col., C₈, III, Mémoire pour M. Bégon par Patoulet, 1682.

should be continued. Raw sugar lost in transportation from the islands to France about one-fourth, whereas refined sugar lost nothing.[53] By refining their own sugar in the islands the planters would gain, according to an estimate by Patoulet, 600,000 francs annually, for, he argued, 18,000,000 pounds of raw sugar at an average of five francs the hundredweight would yield only 900,000 francs, whereas the same, when refined, would yield 1,500,-000 francs (price twenty-five francs the hundredweight). This incidentally would mean a net gain for French traders, as the planters would have this additional sum with which to purchase French merchandise. An increase in commerce meant an increase in navigation, hence an increase in the number of vessels and sailors, which would be a source of strength to the kingdom. Vessels would not be obliged to wait such a long time for their cargoes. "At present," said Patoulet, "vessels are forced to wait a whole year for a cargo of raw sugar, whereas a cargo of refined sugar could be had in three or four days." It would produce another advantage for traders. A vessel of 150 tons, bringing a cargo of merchandise valued in France at 15,000 francs and yielding in the islands 22,500 francs, could receive payment in 90,000 pounds of refined sugar which could be obtained from a refinery in three or four days. If, however, the cargo were bartered for raw sugar, it would yield 450,000 pounds. As the vessel could not carry more than 300,000 pounds, one-third of the amount would have to be left in the islands. Furthermore, the establishment of refineries created a livelihood for the *petits habitants*. Thus Patoulet stated that the three refineries at Martinique consumed 12,000 francs worth of eggs. The effect of this was already seen in the fact that the *petits habitants* who had lately been seeking

[53] Arch. Nat. Col., C$_8$, IX, Memoir by Robert, intendant of the islands, April 21, 1696.

THE COMMERCIAL POLICY OF COLBERT

some way to return to France were planning to remain. Patoulet admitted frankly that the growth of the refining industry in the islands meant a destruction of that in France. "But," said he, "I am of the opinion that that would not be a bad thing [*un grand mal*]. It is true that one would thus destroy the profit made by thirty or forty individuals who are either foreigners or protestants, but the benefit thereof would be enjoyed by a large number of people."[54]

In spite of such sound arguments Colbert sided with the refiners of France by imposing a special import duty of eight francs the hundredweight on sugar refined in the islands. This was done by an *arrêt* of April 18, 1682. After having recalled the *arrêt* of May 31, 1675, by which the import duty on sugar refined in the islands was maintained at four livres the hundredweight, the same as that on raw sugar, the preamble says:

"Whereas His Majesty has been informed that when the said *arrêt* was rendered, there existed only a very small number of refineries in the islands and the planters were accustomed to send their sugar to France to be refined, but that at present a large number of refineries have been established in the islands by different individuals; that this fact is proving very prejudicial to His Majesty's customs, after having heard the recommendation of Sieur Colbert, councilor in his royal council, controller-general of his finances, and being in his council, he has ordered and hereby orders that sugar refined in the French islands and colonies of America shall pay, commencing with the first day of May next, the sum of eight livres the hundredweight."[55]

It is to be noticed that the reason given for laying duty is one of revenue. It is very clear, however, that the real

[54] Arch. Nat. Col., C_8, III, Patoulet to Colbert, December 20, 1682.
[55] Arch. Nat., AD,xi, 48; Moreau de Saint-Méry, I, 368-369. White sugar imported from Cayenne was exempted from this by an *arrêt* of September 19 following. Chamb. de Commerce of Nantes, C, 730.

TOWARD THE FRENCH WEST INDIES

reason was one of favouritism for the refiners of France, for the establishment of new refineries in the islands was definitely prohibited by an *arrêt* of January 21, 1684.[56] There the reason given for the action is stated very frankly and clearly:

"Whereas the king has been informed that the planters of the French islands and colonies of America . . . having devoted themselves almost entirely to the plantation and cultivation of sugar-cane, have established a large number of refineries in the said islands; that almost all of the sugar produced is being refined there; and that consequently the refiners established in France have almost ceased work and that men and refiners employed in them who have no other means of gaining a livelihood are leaving the kingdom, he, being in his council, has forbidden and forbids by these presents all of his subjects of the aforesaid French islands and colonies of America, planters, as well as merchants and traders, to establish any new refineries in the said islands and colonies under penalty of 3000 livres fine."

Patoulet, who in the meantime had been made intendant at Dunkerque, protested energetically against this measure.[57] But his protest was in vain. The mind of the government was clearly made up to sacrifice the general interests of the planters to the special interests of the refiners in France.

Such was the policy which Colbert pursued in promoting the production of sugar in the islands and the establish-

The duty was made permanent by an *arrêt* of September 28, 1674. Moreau de Saint-Méry, I, 402.

[56] Moreau de Saint-Méry, I, 395. Curiously enough a copy of this important act is not to be found in Arch. Nat., AD,xi, 48. A copy is found, however, in Chambre de Commerce of Nantes, C, 730.

[57] Arch. Nat. Mar., B$_3$, 45, fol. 30. Patoulet to Seignelay, letter and memoir of March 7, 1684. Patoulet there related the history of the refining industry in the islands and of the encouragement which had been given by Colbert to it. He demanded at least exemption from import duty for sugar refined in the refinery at Martinique in which he owned a three-eighths interest.

THE COMMERCIAL POLICY OF COLBERT

ment of refineries both in the islands and in France. There were three very important results: (1) an increase in the production of sugar, (2) the growth of the refining industry, and (3) France began exporting instead of importing refined sugar.

If we accept the estimate made by a memorialist of 1691, that the amount of sugar produced in the islands in 1674 was 12,000,000 pounds,[58] and that of Patoulet that it was 18,000,000 pounds in 1682,[59] an increase of fifty per cent is to be noted for the last eight years of Colbert's ministry.

The rise and growth of the sugar-refining industry was even more noticeable. Colbert stated in 1664 in his memoir on commerce that the Dutch were furnishing almost all of the refined sugar consumed in the realm. By 1683, no less than twenty-nine refineries existed in France and five in the islands, making a total of thirty-four, which refined annually 20,700,000 pounds.[60]

At the beginning of Colbert's ministry, as has just been stated, refined sugar was imported into France from Holland. But in 1670, Colbert wrote to de Baas: "Foreigners no longer bring us sugar. We have begun in the last six weeks or two months to export it to them."[61] No material has been found which makes it possible to state what amount of sugar France exported to foreign countries by the end of Colbert's ministry, but it is certain that the French had begun by that time to march forward in that road which led in the eighteenth century to their supremacy over the English as furnishers of sugar in the markets of Europe.

[58] Arch. Nat. Col., C$_8$, III, Mémoire pour M. Bégon, 1682.

[59] Arch. Nat. Col., C$_8$, 2nd series, II, Mémoire touchant le commerce des Isles, 1691.

[60] See above.

[61] Arch. Nat. Col., B, 2, fol. 115, Colbert to de Baas, October 10, 1670.

CHAPTER XIII

Colonial Imports—Indentured Servants and Slaves

IN the early history of the French West Indies the indentured servant played an important part. Large numbers of them were drafted in the Norman ports and sent out to the islands. During the years of 1637, 1638 and the first six months of 1639, more than 500 were sent from the single port of Honfleur.[1] Considerable numbers were also sent from Havre and Dieppe.[2]

The usual form of contract was three years of service on the part of the servant to the one who paid his passage and fed, clothed and housed him during his term of service.[3] The master had the right of selling to another any portion of the unexpired term of service. It was not unusual for a servant to have seven or eight masters during the three years.[4]

This form of contract proved so profitable to planters that they were willing to pay to ship captains 1000 to 1200 pounds of tobacco for servants. Even higher prices were paid for artisans.[5] Captains of La Rochelle, St. Malo, Dieppe and Havre engaged regularly in the trade. In order to obtain servants "they take advantage of the naïveté of many people whom they persuade that life in the islands is a bed of roses, that the land flows with milk and honey and that one works little and gains

[1] C. Bréard, *Les documents relatifs à la marine normande*, p. 187.
[2] Du Motey, *Guillaume d'Orange et l'origine des Antilles françaises*, chap. XIII.
[3] Both Bréard and du Motey publish the texts of several contracts made at Honfleur and Havre.
[4] Du Tertre, II, 454.
[5] Ibid., p. 464.

much. They not only deceive the ignorant, . . . but also debauch young children in order to kidnap them. Some have been mean and knavish enough to entice children aboard their vessels under various pretexts and force them to go to the islands where they were sold to masters who fed them poorly and made them work so excessively and treated them so inhumanely that many of them died in a short time."[6] Abuses of this nature grew so flagrant that de Poincy complained to the home government of one case where 200 young Frenchmen, some of whom were of good family, had been kidnapped, concealed at St. Servan for three months and then taken to be sold at Barbadoes.[7]

But after the establishment of the sugar industry and of the regular trade in slaves, the trade in indentured servants decreased. Colbert was forced to take measures to encourage and to compel the importation of servants into the islands. He first attempted to encourage it by making the terms of the contract more attractive to the servant. Thus by an *arrêt* of February 28, 1670, the term of service was reduced from three years to eighteen months.[8] This *arrêt* was re-enacted on October 31, 1672.[9] Colbert made efforts to force their importation by an *arrêt* of January 22, 1671, which required all vessels of 100 tons or more, going to the West Indies, to carry two cows or two mares, and those of less than 100 tons to carry two indentured servants in place of each cow or mare.[10] To prevent too large a growth of slave population in proportion to the white, a regulation was made which required all planters of St. Domingo to have a number of servants

[6] Pelleprat, p. 21.
[7] Du Tertre, II, 465.
[8] Moreau de Saint-Méry, I, 190; Arch. Nat. Col., B, 2, fol. 54, letter to *conseils souverains* of Martinique and St. Christopher to register the said *arrêt*.
[9] Ibid., p. 264.
[10] Ibid., p. 207.

TOWARD THE FRENCH WEST INDIES

equal to that of their slaves.[11] After the close of Colbert's ministry, regulations required that vessels of sixty tons or less should take three servants, those of sixty to 100 tons four, and those of more than 100 tons six.[12]

There were two facts, however, which militated against the success of any plan to supply labour in the islands by the importation of indentured servants from France. The one was that the supply was not large enough to keep pace with the demand for labour after the introduction of the cultivation of sugar.[13] The other was that slave labour was more reliable and much cheaper.[14] The slave became the planter's property and his labour was available throughout his lifetime, whereas the indentured servant offered only a temporary service and became his own master at the end of three years. This explains why the slave trade developed in the French West Indies, and it seems idle to argue, as does M. Peytraud,[15] that these islands might have been cultivated entirely by white labour.

There seems to be some evidence that d'Esnambuc found some slaves in the small French colony at St. Christopher in 1625.[16] Du Tertre informs us that in 1635 a Dutch trader, Pitre Cotté, brought to St. Christopher a "quantity of slaves" which he had captured from the Spaniards.[17] In 1643 the Company of the Isles of America made a

[11] Arch. Nat. Col., C$_9$, I, Ord. du Roy, September 30, 1686; Moreau de Saint-Méry, I, 434. The proportion was later changed to one servant to twenty slaves. Peytraud, *L'esclavage aux Antilles françaises,* p. 15.

[12] Moreau de Saint-Méry, I, 581, Ordre du Roy, February 19, 1698.

[13] This assertion seems warranted by the practices to which the traders were forced to resort in order to have a number of servants. See passages cited above from Pelleprat and Du Tertre.

[14] Arch. Nat. Col., C$_9$, I, Memoir by de Pouançay, governor of St. Domingo, 1681, speaks of indentured servants as "costing much more than slaves."

[15] *L'Esclavage aux Antilles françaises.*

[16] Peytraud, p. 5.

[17] Du Tertre, I, 59.

contract with a Captain Drouault to deliver sixty slaves at Guadeloupe for 12,000 livres.[18]

The supply of slaves did not as yet become very abundant, however, for Maurile de St. Michel remarked that slaves were being imported to the islands in 1646, but that they were very dear, the price at St. Christopher being 4000 pounds of tobacco for a male and 3000 pounds for a female. But the next ten years saw a considerable increase in the trade. In 1655, Pelleprat remarked that the planters "employed in tilling their land neither oxen nor horses, but only slaves which were brought from Africa or the coasts of America," and that well-to-do planters possessed twenty-five or thirty slaves. [19] De Poincy, the governor-general, had between six and seven hundred on his several plantations.[20] Pelleprat said that several ships came yearly to the islands with cargoes of slaves and that in 1654, between six and seven hundred had been brought to Martinique alone, the price having dropped to 2000 pounds of tobacco or 100 écus. By 1655 the slave population of the islands had reached 12,000 or 13,000.[21]

The French trader had apparently played a very small part in supplying these slaves. Du Tertre records that during the sojourn of de Tracy in the West Indies, from June 1, 1664, to April, 1665, the Dutch imported into Guadeloupe and Martinique no less than twelve or thirteen hundred negroes.[22] De Tracy wrote to Colbert from

[18] The contract was carried out by Drouault. We find him in October of the same year demanding payment for the sixty slaves and for two others which he had delivered to the company's agent at St. Christopher. Arch. Col., F$_2$, 19, fols. 444, 462, Records of the meetings of the directors for February 4, and October 7, 1643.

[19] Pelleprat, p. 54.
[20] Ibid.
[21] Ibid.

[22] Du Tertre, III, 201. The same historian records the arrival at Martinique in October, 1664, of a Dutch vessel bringing a cargo of

TOWARD THE FRENCH WEST INDIES

the islands in 1664 that the slave trade would prove profitable to the French, as it yielded a profit of 266 per cent.[23]

It will be recalled that the West India Company had all the west coast of Africa included in its grant and that it attempted to make provision for a supply of slaves to the planters by ceding to Carolof, in 1665, the right of trading on the coast of Guinea and importing slaves into the islands.[24] In 1667 a treaty was made by Villaut de Bellefond in behalf of the West India Company, with certain tribes on the coast of Guinea for trading privileges, which implies that the company was not satisfied with the results attained by Carolof and that it was taking other measures to supply slaves to its West India colonies.[25] Material is lacking to show what the company did to take advantage of this treaty, but it is very probable that it did nothing and that the Dutch still supplied slaves to the planters, for de Baas was instructed by the directors at the beginning of 1668, to admit Dutch ships which brought slaves from Curaçao,[26] and on November 7, 1668, permission was accorded by the company to a Dutch trader to import slaves into the islands.[27] In 1669, Cartier, the general agent of the company, was freely admitting into

300 slaves. He states that the price demanded was 3000 pounds of sugar per slave, which was reduced by de Tracy to 2000 pounds. Ibid., p. 101.

[23] Arch. Nat. Col., C$_8$, I, Abrégé de la corresp. de M. de Tracy. Letter de juillet, 1664.

[24] See Chapter IV.

[25] Arch. Col., C$_6$, I, Traité fait avec le Roy de Comendo en la coste de Guinée. The treaty was made on March 15, 1667, aboard L'Europe, a vessel belonging to a Dutchman, Van Teitz by name.

[26] Arch. Nat. Col., C$_8$, I, de Baas to Colbert, December 26, 1669.

[27] Arch. Nat. Col., C$_8$, I, de Baas to Colbert, March 22, 1670; C$_{10}$, La Grenade, 1654-1729, contains a copy of the passport. The trader, Drik Jansen by name, agreed to pay to the company five per cent on all slaves and horses imported into the islands and ten per cent on commodities exported therefrom. Jansen was captured by one of de Gabaret's ships. See a discussion of the case in Chapter IX.

THE COMMERCIAL POLICY OF COLBERT

Guadeloupe and Martinique Dutch vessels which brought slaves. For the slaves he was demanding as high as 4000 pounds of sugar per head.[28] Slaves were being imported also into Marie Galante from Curaçao in this same year.[29]

It will be noticed that we have reached the date when Colbert began his determined fight to exclude all foreign traders from the islands and attempted to supply absolutely all the needs of the planters by French commerce. He assigned to the West India Company, as one of its special duties, the task of furnishing a supply of slaves to the planters. It was most probably in accordance with Colbert's instructions that the company equipped and sent out, at the close of 1669, two vessels to the coast of Guinea.[30] Carolof, who was in charge of the company's interests, succeeded in establishing trade relations with the king of Ardres and the two vessels sailed for the West Indies with 997 slaves on board. Of this number there was landed at Martinique a total of 753, the remainder having died during the voyage. The results seemed so auspicious that Colbert at once had large visions of the company being able not only to furnish 2000 slaves annually to the French, but also to send 2000 more to the Spanish colonies.[31]

In order to encourage private traders, the special tax of five per cent levied by the company on slaves imported by them was removed in 1670.[32] In the following year (1671) all duties were removed from goods exported from France to the coast of Guinea,[33] and in 1672 a bounty of

[28] Ibid., C_7, I, du Lion to Colbert, December 1, 1669.
[29] Ibid., Témericourt to Colbert, December 14, 1669.
[30] A full account of this expedition will be found above in Chapter VII.
[31] Clément, III, 2, p. 485, Colbert to Pélissier, June 21, 1670.
[32] Arch. Nat., AD,vii, 3; Moreau de Saint-Méry, I, 97, *arrêt* of August 26, 1670.
[33] Arch. Nat., AD,vii, 3; *Le Commerce de l'Amérique par Marseille*, II, 303, *arrêt* of September 18, 1671.

TOWARD THE FRENCH WEST INDIES

thirteen livres per head was granted on all slaves imported into the islands.[34]

From the beginning de Baas expressed doubts as to the ability of the French traders to furnish the number of slaves necessary to the development of the islands and added the warning that "if enough were not furnished to take the place of those that died, the planters would suffer seriously."[35] Colbert, however, remained deaf to de Baas' doubts and warnings, and ordered a strict enforcement of the regulations against the foreign trader. The slave trade was thus left in the hands of the West India Company and of private French traders.

The activity of neither seems to have been great. We find mention of the arrival in 1672 at Guadeloupe of two vessels belonging to the company with about 550 slaves, and another of its ships, coming from Guinea, was expected to arrive in December.[36] But the company's commerce practically ceased after 1672. Its dissolution in 1674 formally removed it from the field. Private traders seem to have shown but small interest in the slave trade and it is very probable that their activity was even less than that of the company. The result was that the supply of slaves was very inadequate. Du Lion stated in 1672 that the clearing of new lands was being retarded for this reason.[37] Du Clerc, secretary to de Baas, informed Colbert in a letter of January 20, 1675, that it was impossible to

[34] Moreau de Saint-Méry, I, 259-260, *arrêt* of January 13, 1672. Of this sum, ten livres were to be paid by His Majesty to the *armateurs* and three livres by the West India Company to the captains commanding the vessels. After the dissolution of the company, the three livres were paid by the *Domaine d'Occident*.

[35] Arch. Nat. Col., C_8, I, de Baas to Colbert, December 26, 1669.

[36] Arch. Nat. Col., C_7, II, du Lion to Colbert, December 5, 1672. Du Lion states in a letter, eod. loco, of November 16, 1671, that he had become associated with Carolof in an enterprise to clear land at Guadeloupe for which Carolof was to furnish slaves.

[37] Ibid., du Lion to Colbert, March 15, 1672.

replace the slaves who were dying, because "no one is bringing slaves to the islands."[38]

Colbert, doubtless disappointed at the failure of the private trader to respond to his liberal policy, shortly afterwards committed the slave trade into the hands of a monopoly and continued to do so until his death.

By a contract of November 8, 1673, the West India Company ceded to a private company, composed of Maurice Egrot, François François and François Raguenet, all the western coast of Africa, lying between the rivers Senegal and Gambia, with all the privileges of trade which had been granted to it in its letters-patent and with all furnishings, utensils, arms, munitions and everything belonging to it at the said coast except the slaves in its possession, which were sold to Thouret, a merchant of La Rochelle.[39] This contract was approved by an *arrêt* of November 11, by which was granted to the new company a monopoly of trade for thirty years, the unexpired term of the West India Company, and all others were forbidden to encroach upon its monopoly under penalty of confiscation of vessels and cargoes and of a fine of 3000 livres.

Only a small part of this coast had ever been actually in control of the West India Company. The Dutch were in possession of a good strategic base in the island of Gorée,[40] and would have to be reckoned with before the Company of Senegal could enter with advantage into the exploitation of its grant. The war with Holland furnished the occasion to dispute with them the control of Senegal. In 1677, Jean d'Estrées attacked the Dutch at Gorée, destroyed their forts, and took possession of the island, thus preparing the way for the conquest of the coast south of

[38] Arch. Nat. Col., C₈, I, du Clerc to Colbert, January 20, 1675.

[39] Arch. Col., C₆, I, contrat de vente du Sénégal et dépendances aux Sieurs Egrot, François et Raguenet, November 8, 1673.

[40] D'Elbée, *Journal*, p. 351, states that the Dutch used the island as an *entrepôt* for trade with the tribes of the mainland.

TOWARD THE FRENCH WEST INDIES

Cape Verde.[41] Du Casse, who was later to win fame as governor of St. Domingo, and still later as admiral of France, had recently been appointed governor of the coast by the Company of Senegal. He at once took advantage of d'Estrées' victory. In command of *L'Entendu,* a royal vessel mounted by forty guns and with a crew of 250 men, he occupied Gorée and placed some agents in command for the company. He then made treaties with the princes of Rufisque, Portudal and Joal. In the following year, 1678, he continued the work of conquest. The Dutch, driven from Gorée, had concentrated their forces at Arguin, a well-fortified island off the coast near Cape Blanco. Du Casse first captured, without difficulty, their trading posts on the mainland opposite the island. The defense of the island itself proved so stubborn, however, that he was forced to return to Saint Louis for more ammunition and reinforcements. After sustaining seven days of bombardment, the Dutch were finally forced to surrender and evacuate the island. The French entered into possession on September 2, 1678.[42] Shortly after this a Dutch vessel appeared and succeeded in stirring up a rebellion among the natives on the coast between Cape Verde and Gambia, so that du Casse was forced to land troops and march against them. He met with small resistance and forced the natives to sign treaties, by which full trade privileges were accorded to the French.

These conquests made by d'Estrées and du Casse were sanctioned by the treaty of Nymwegen.[43] The Company

[41] P. Chemin-Dupontès, *Les Compagnies de colonisation en Afrique occidentale sous Colbert,* pp. 93 ff.; P. Cultru, *Histoire du Sénégal du XVe siècle à 1870,* Paris, 1910, pp. 58-59.

[42] Robert du Casse, *L'Amiral du Casse,* Paris, 1876, pp. 9 ff.

[43] The conquest of Arguin was in reality posterior to the signing of the treaty, but it remained effective by reason of the fact that the treaty provided that all conquests, made south of Cape St. Vincent within ten weeks after date, would be recognized.

THE COMMERCIAL POLICY OF COLBERT

of Senegal was thus placed in actual possession of the coast from Cape Blanco to the Gambia. It established several trading posts[44] which apparently became prosperous.[45] But no record has been found that the company even attempted to carry slaves to the West Indies. It is to be remarked that the company's concessions extended only to the Gambia and did not include the coast of Guinea, which furnished the supply of choice slaves and where the West India Company had carried on some trade.

No immediate disposition was made of the coast of Guinea, and the planters had to depend for a while longer upon private traders to supply them with slaves. The report came from the islands in 1675, that none were being brought.[46] It was perhaps for this reason that an attempt was made in this same year to make definite provision for a supply.

On October 16, 1675, the liquidators of the West India Company signed a contract with Jean Oudiette, the farmer-general of the *Domaine d'Occident*, whereby the latter agreed to import into the French West Indies 800 slaves a year for four consecutive years. Oudiette was probably granted a monopoly of trade.[47] He was certainly to enjoy the bounty of thirteen livres per head on all slaves imported into the islands.[48] De Baas was informed

[44] Cultru, *op. cit.*, 60.

[45] Arch. Col., C$_6$, I, Traité fait entre les Sieurs directeurs généraux du Dom. Roy. d'Occid. et la Comp. du Sénégal, March 21, 1679.

[46] Arch. Nat. Col., C$_8$, I, du Clerc to Colbert, January 20, 1675.

[47] No copy of the contract has been found. The fact of the contract and a part of its provisions are to be found in the avant-propos of the letters-patent creating the Company of Senegal of 1679. Moreau de Saint-Méry, I, 314.

[48] This had been originally provided, it will be recalled, by an *arrêt* of January 13, 1672. This meant probably only ten livres to Oudiette, because three livres were to be paid by the *Dom. d'Occident*, of which he was the farmer.

TOWARD THE FRENCH WEST INDIES

of the contract and instructed to aid Oudiette in every way possible. The king wrote him in part as follows:

> "As there is nothing which can contribute so much to the increase of my islands of America as the importation of a quantity of negroes, I am very glad to inform you that a contract has been made with the Sieur Oudiette, farmer of my Domaine d'Occident, to carry on this trade. As it is important for him to enjoy freely the privilege which I have granted him by the *arrêt* of which I am enclosing a copy, do not fail to aid him in every way you can."[49]

Oudiette for some reason did not carry out the contract and it was annulled on March 25, 1679.[50] Four days previously, on March 21, Bellinzani and Mesnager, in quality of liquidators of the defunct West India Company, had made another more important contract with the Company of Senegal.

The preamble of this contract stated that the Company of Senegal, "which had established large trading posts on the coast of Africa, was on the point of making contracts to furnish slaves to the Dutch and Spanish," and had offered to transport to the French West Indies 2000 slaves annually for the space of eight years.[51] It was apparently in excellent shape to make a contract to do so. Of its three original directors, François, Raguenet and Egrot, the first alone remained. Raguenet was dead. His widow and Egrot had ceded their interests to Bains and

---

[49] Arch. Nat. Col., B, 7, fol. 30, the king to de Baas, May 27, 1676, cited by Dessalles, *Hist. gen. des Antilles*, I, 546, and Peytraud, *op. cit.*, p. 42.

[50] Arch. Nat., AD,vii, 3; Moreau de Saint-Méry, I, 314.

[51] The company had apparently already begun to send some slaves to the islands, for in a letter written from Martinique on August 16, 1677, the arrival "of a vessel belonging to the Company of Senegal with eighty slaves" is noted. Arch. Nat. Col., C_8, II, Jolinet to Colbert, August 16, 1677.

le Brun.[52] Under the new directors the company had made considerable progress in its commerce and in 1679 was in a prosperous condition.[53] Within six years, thanks to the conquest of d'Estrées and du Casse and the wise direction of the latter, it had occupied a large territory and established a rich trade.[54]

It is to be remarked, however, that the company's prosperity had been gained most largely by trade in rubber, ivory, wax, and other articles from Senegal, and very little in the slave trade. Success in trade north of Gambia did not necessarily augur success in the slave trade on the coast which stretched to the southward. However, the offer of the company was accepted and a contract was signed on March 21.[55]

The number of directors was straightway increased by the addition of six new associates, namely, Duvivier of Paris, Thouret and Duport of La Rochelle, Petit Saint-Louis of Bordeaux, Sieur de Richemond, who had aided du Casse in his conquests, and Ballade at St. Domingo.[56] Chemin-Dupontès' remark that the company was thus composed of the "*principaux armateurs français de l'époque*," is perhaps a conjecture, but one is impressed with the distinctly national character of the company and with the fact that most of them were probably merchants. The new company was capitalized at approximately 1,000,000 francs, about one-fourth of what it really needed to carry out the plans which it had undertaken.[57]

The contract was officially approved by an *arrêt* of

[52] Arch. Col., C₆, II, Mémoire concernant le commerce du Sénégal, 1695.
[53] Ibid.
[54] Chemin-Dupontès, p. 99.
[55] A copy of the contract is to be found in Arch. Col., C₆, I.
[56] Chemin-Dupontès, p. 104.
[57] Chemin-Dupontès, p. 105, makes this estimate, based on an interesting calculation.

TOWARD THE FRENCH WEST INDIES

March 25, 1679, and letters-patent were issued in June, whereby the company was granted a monopoly of trade for twenty-five years (the unexpired time of the West India Company's grant) on the whole coast of Africa from Cape Verde to the Cape of Good Hope, and was also given a full monopoly of the slave trade in the West India colonies for the same period. All other French subjects were excluded from both these branches of commerce, under penalty of confiscation of vessel and cargo to the profit of the company, and of a fine of 3000 livres, to be divided between the company and His Majesty. Full freedom was accorded to sell slaves at any price agreed upon between the company's agents and the planters. The bounty of thirteen livres was granted on all slaves imported by the company into the islands. Exemption from all duties on goods exported to the coast of Guinea or to the islands, and from half the duties on goods imported into France from Africa or from the West Indies was to be enjoyed. The company assumed the obligation to import into the French West Indies 2000 slaves annually for eight years and in addition to furnish to "His Majesty at Marseilles such a number as he shall need for his galleys," on terms to be agreed upon later.[58]

Efforts seem to have been made at once to carry out the contract, for by May 20, 1679, the company had upon the sea, twenty-one vessels of an aggregate tonnage of 5580 tons. Of these, sixteen were occupied in the slave trade, four of which were to carry cargoes of slaves to Marseilles for His Majesty's galleys; four, cargoes to Spain to trade at the arrival of the galleons from America, and eight to carry slaves to the West Indies. Of the remaining five, three were to bring cargoes of hides, rub-

[58] Arch. Nat. Col., B, 9, fol. I, contains the *arrêt* of March 25, 1679; Arch. Col., C_6, I, contains the letters-patent. They have both been printed by Moreau de Saint-Méry, I, 314-317, and 325-326.

ber and ivory to France from Senegal, and two were to bring cargoes of sugar and tobacco from the islands.[59]

But misfortunes were encountered from the beginning. During the course of the first year no less than four of the company's vessels suffered shipwreck.[60] By April, 1680, the company had lost no less than 2000 slaves who died on board its ships during the voyage from Guinea to the West Indies.[61] Its total losses were estimated at 400,-000 livres. Furthermore, the company experienced the same difficulty which the West India Company had met with, in being unable to receive from the planters prompt payment for its slaves. It was thus unable to meet the heavy obligations which it had assumed in order to equip its vessels and carry out its contract. Even before the first fiscal year had closed, the debt of the company amounted to no less than 1,200,000 livres.[62] Large sums had to be borrowed, but they only added to the burden without creating any additional income.

A crisis came in the spring of 1680, with the failure of de Kervert and Simonnet, bankers. In the credits of the bankers, which amounted to 2,000,000 livres, the Company of Senegal figured for an indebtedness of 1,500,000 livres. Immediate bankruptcy of the company seemed inevitable. An appeal was made to the king by its directors "to grant

[59] Arch. Col., C_6, I, Estat des Navires appart. à la Cie. du Sénégal, May 20, 1679. Seventeen of these vessels belonged to the company, the other four were chartered. All were equipped with from six to forty guns. It is to be noticed that the company was sending as many vessels to Marseilles and Spain with slaves as to the West Indies.

[60] The *St. François,* 400 tons, was wrecked on the coast of Brittany and its cargo of tobacco and sugar from the islands lost. *La Paix,* 400 tons, was wrecked in the West Indies with a cargo of tobacco. *La Fortune* was lost in the Canaries, and *Le Soleil* on the coast of England with a cargo from the coast of Senegal.

[61] Arch. Col., C_6, I, *arrêt* of April 9, 1680, preamble.

[62] Chemin-Dupontès, p. 107.

them his protection in order that they might be able to continue their commerce, for which they have more than twenty vessels upon the sea." They promised that in a short while they would be able to pay all of their debts. After the approval of Colbert, a favourable reply was made to the petition. An *arrêt* of April 9 forbade the creditors to make any seizures against the company under penalty of invalidation of their claims and 3000 livres fine.[63] The persistence of the creditors was so great, however, that the *arrêt* had to be re-enacted on April 16. Finally, on May 14, an agreement was reached by which the creditors accepted the following settlement. De Kervert and Simonnet were to pay one-fourth of their debts within the space of three months. The remaining three-fourths were to be paid by the Company of Senegal, one-twelfth in eleven months, one-fourth in one year, one-twelfth in sixteen months, one-twelfth in two years, and for the remaining one-fourth, shares in the company were to be issued. This agreement was sanctioned by the king on May 26.[64]

But misfortunes continued to pursue the company. Shortly afterwards two vessels were lost by shipwreck and one was captured by pirates.[65] Storms in the West Indies destroyed much of the sugar and tobacco harvests and delayed payments upon which the company had counted. It was consequently unable to make the settlements which it had agreed to make with its creditors. By June 30, 1681, its liabilities exceeded its assets by 1,184,569 liv. 13s. 7d.[66] The Company of Senegal was bankrupt. It formally came to an end on July 2, 1681.

[63] Arch. Col., C₆, I, *arrêt* of April 9, 1680, cited by Chemin-Dupontès, p. 109.
[64] Chemin-Dupontès, p. 110.
[65] Ibid., p. 114.
[66] Arch. Col., C₆, I, Estat général des effets de la Compagnie du Sénégal, June 30, 1681. Among its chief assets were eight vessels in

THE COMMERCIAL POLICY OF COLBERT

The question naturally arises as to what success the company had met with in furnishing slaves to the West India colonies. We seem to have some evidence in the accounts of the *Domaine d'Occident*. Under the sixth title of the credit sheet of its accounts for 1680, 1681, 1682, 1683, the entry is made of thirteen payments made to "François for the thirteen livres per head of slaves imported into the islands of America." The total of these payments amounts to 49,424 liv. 10s.[67]

"This sum at thirteen livres per head, represents," says Chemin-Dupontès, "the bounty for 3810 slaves imported by the Company of Senegal from March 25, 1679, to July 1, 1682, in reality during the space of two years, . . . showing that the Company of Senegal, bankrupt as it was, was the company which did the most for the develop-

---

France valued at 73,000 livres and eleven upon the sea valued with their cargoes at 375,345 liv. 11s. 7d. and sums due in the West Indies amounting to 174,164 liv. 18s. 6d.

[67] Arch. Nat., G$_7$, 1312, Extrait de la Récepte et dépense du compte du Sr. La Live cy-devant caissier du dom. d'occident par luy faitte pendant les années 1680-1683. The portion in question is as follows:

Dates	Sixiesme Chap. de dépense	
14 sept. 1680. A François pour les 13 livres par teste de nègres portés aux Isles de l'Am. ord. du 11 fév. 1680	. .	7,059 liv.
14 dec. 1680 à luy ord. du 2 dud. mois	. .	2,907 liv.
15 avril 1681 à luy ord. du 12 dud. mois	. .	963 liv.
15 juin 1681 à luy ord. du 31 mai	. . .	4,515 liv.
27 fév. 1682 à luy ord. du 26 dud. mois	. .	1,212 liv.
21 nov. 1682 à luy ord. du 29 juin 1682	. .	3,051 liv.
31 nov. 1682 à luy ord. du 21 dudit	. . .	5,981 liv. 10 s.
Signature en blanc:		
Servant de quitt luy ord. du 29 desdit, mois et an	.	864 liv.
3 fév. 1683 à luy ord. du 3 jan. 1683	. .	1,971 liv.
5 avril 1683 à luy ord. du	. .	2,268 liv.
14 dec. 1680 à luy ord. du 2 déc. 1680	. .	5,733 liv.
13 juin 1681 à luy ord. du 2 dudit	. . .	10,000 liv.
7 oct. 1682 à luy ord. du dudit jour .	. .	30,000 liv.
		49,524 liv. 10 s.

TOWARD THE FRENCH WEST INDIES

ment of the slave trade with the West Indies."[68] This would be most interesting, if our data could be interpreted in such a way. Unfortunately a close analysis of the document, together with other evidence which apparently escaped the notice of M. Chemin-Dupontès, will not permit it. In the first place, the list of payments shows that of the thirteen payments made, only six, representing an aggregate of 31,177 livres, were made between June, 1679, the date when the privilege of the slave trade was accorded to the Company of Senegal, and July 2, 1681, when it was replaced by a reorganized company. François, to whom all payments were said to be made, was also a director of the reorganized company.[69] Now, payments after the date of July 2, 1681, would certainly represent bounties paid to the second company. Even upon M. Chemin-Dupontès's supposition that the sums represent bounties paid on slaves, we should be compelled to reduce the number of slaves imported by the Company of Senegal during the two years of its existence from 3810 to 2398. This would still represent a respectable activity by the company, as the average would be 1199 slaves a year. Our suspicion is aroused, however, by the fact that only two of the thirteen sums paid are divisible by thirteen. The total is also indivisible by that number. A possible explanation might be offered by saying that the thirteen livres "*par tête*" really meant thirteen livres "*par pièce d'Inde.*"[70] This would immediately introduce an element in

[68] Chemin-Dupontès, p. 111.

[69] Bib. Nat. MSS., fonds franç., 11315, fol. 152, letter of the directors to Patoulet, October 22, 1682. François' name occurs among the seven signatures of the directors.

[70] This suggestion has been made to me by Prof. P. Cultru of the University of Paris. The practice grew up of making contracts for the delivery of so many "pièces d'Inde," which served as a standard by which to measure the value of a slave. In the Spanish trade the "pièce d'Inde" was a slave seven "quartas" high (about 182 centimeters), between thirty and thirty-five years old and without any

THE COMMERCIAL POLICY OF COLBERT

the reckoning which we could not control from the data given in the document. It would obviously, however, increase the actual number of slaves sent to the islands, which would mean that the Company of Senegal sent more than 2398 slaves to the islands during the two years of its existence. It is not necessary to search farther for some key to unlock the mystery, for it is more than probable that the sums do not represent at all *bona fide* bounties paid on slaves imported into the islands. Just at the close of the document is to be found a most interesting note which reads, "*Nota, le Sieur Bellinzani a profité de la moitié des susdites sommes,*" and this is corroborated in another document, contained in the same carton, which states that Bellinzani himself had confessed the fact.[71]

With the name of Bellinzani enters upon the scene a person of more than passing interest. Taken into service by Colbert in 1654, he was named in 1669 to the important post of general inspector of manufactures. On February 19, 1670, he was made one of the directors of the West

physical defect. "On measurait les adultes qui n'avaient point cette hauteur, les enfants et l'on obtenait ainsi, en divisant le total obtenu un certain nombre de pièces d'Inde dans une cargaison." G. Scelle, *La traite négrière aux Indes de Castille,* Paris, 1906, 2 vols., I, 506. In a contract made at Nantes by the French Assiento Company in 1702, for the delivery of 4000 slaves, the following definition was given:

"La pièce d'Inde sera homme et femme depuis quatorze jusqu'a quarante ans au plus, ainsy qu'il paraistra par la veue, réglée par gens indifferens, choisis de part et d'autre, filles et garçons seront réglés à prorata de leur grandeur huit pour sept, six pour cinq et enfin quatre pour trois. On ne pourra rebuter ancun nègre que ceux qui passeront quarante ans qui n'auront qu'un œil ou qui seront rompus à leurs parties ou qui seront malades. On sera obligé de recevoir ceux à qu'il manquera un ou deux doigts à la main ou au pied, ou ceux qui seront maigres, pourveu qu'ils se portent bien, car maigre n'est pas un défaut." Chamb. de Commerce, Nantes, C, 739.

[71] Arch. Nat., G₇, 1312, Extrait de la dépence du compte du Sr. de La Live des 150,000 livres qu'il a receu par chacun an de M. Jean Oudiette, fermier du Dom. d'Occident, etc.

TOWARD THE FRENCH WEST INDIES

India Company at Colbert's recommendation.[72] It was in this way that he became actively associated with West India affairs. He became personally interested in the commerce of the West Indies. In 1671 we find a record of a cargo of slaves being sold at Guadeloupe "for the account of M. Bellinzani."[73] He wrote to de Baas in 1675 instructing him to permit four English vessels to trade in the islands, stating that permission had been granted by His Majesty.[74] Yet the letter which Colbert wrote to de Baas on receiving the news that these vessels had traded in the islands implies that no such permission had been granted.[75] At the dissolution of the West India Company, Bellinzani was named by Colbert as one of the three charged with the liquidation of its affairs.[76] A very long and detailed indictment was made against Bellinzani, by no less a personage than Jacques Savary, in which he was accused of dishonesty in the discharge of his duties in the direction and liquidation of the West India Company, specific cases being given where he had embezzled funds.[77] After Colbert's death he was thrown into the Bastille on charges of embezzlement and died there.

It is very possible that the sums entered in the accounts of the *Domaine d'Occident* as payments to the Company of Senegal for bounties on slaves imported into the islands represent, in part at least, sums embezzled by Bellinzani. In that case they give no clue to the number of slaves imported into the West Indies. Besides, we have some very positive evidence to show that the number of slaves,

[72] Arch. Nat. Col., B, 2, fol. 5.
[73] Arch. Nat. Col., C_7, II, du Lion to Colbert, November 16, 1671.
[74] Arch. Nat. Col., C_8, I, du Clerc to Colbert, January 20, 1675.
[75] Ibid., B, 6, fols. 34-39, Colbert to de Baas, May 17, 1675.
[76] Moreau de Saint-Méry, I, 290, *arrêt* of December 4, 1674.
[77] Arch. Nat., G_7, 1312. The exact title of the document has not been recorded in my notes, but it is easily found by its size, being the longest document in the carton.

THE COMMERCIAL POLICY OF COLBERT

corresponding to the bounties represented as having been paid, is much too large for the number actually imported. Thus de Blénac, the governor-general of the islands, wrote on July 13, 1680, that within the last sixteen months no more than 600 or 700 slaves had been imported into all the islands, including St. Domingo.[78] The "sixteen months" covered exactly the period of the obligation of the Company of Senegal to carry slaves to the islands. The company was probably less active during the last year of its existence, which followed these sixteen months, for de Pouançay stated in a memoir of 1681 that the company was not bringing a large number of slaves to St. Domingo,[79] and Patoulet wrote that an adequate supply was not being sent to Martinique.[80] A letter was written to the latter in May, 1681, explaining that the small number of slaves being sent was due to the embarrassments of the company, and that better results were expected from the new company soon to be organized.[81] So that on the basis of de Blénac's statement it is not probable that a large number of slaves were ever imported into the islands by the Company of Senegal.

All of this evidence points to the conclusion that the number of slaves imported into the West Indies by the Company of Senegal was much smaller than that for which bounties were purported to have been paid. The inference is natural that some fraudulent measures had been resorted to in order to collect bounties which were in reality not due. The point is of some importance because the conclusion here adopted shows that the success which

[78] Arch. Nat. Col., C$_8$, II, de Blénac to Colbert, July 13, 1680: "Depuis seize mois il n'est venu dans toutes les Isles ny à St. Domingue que 600 à 700 nègres."

[79] Arch. Nat. Col., C$_9$, I, Mémoire par de Pouançay, 1681.

[80] Ibid., C$_8$, II, Patoulet to Colbert, August 14, 1680.

[81] Bib. Nat. MSS., fonds français, 11315, fol. 133, the king to Patoulet, May 4, 1681.

TOWARD THE FRENCH WEST INDIES

M. Chemin-Dupontès attributes to the first Company of Senegal is fictitious. It means further that the efforts which Colbert made to supply slaves to the islands by the employment of a commercial company, endowed with a monopoly, were not highly successful. This failure imposed upon Colbert anew the burden of providing some means to supply slaves to the West India planters.

A tentative company offered to enter into a contract, provided it be entirely exempt from the liabilities of the former company. This proviso was rejected by Colbert, who insisted that all the debts, contracted by the old company since the *arrêt* of *supersedeas* of April 9, 1680, and in part those contracted before that date, be paid by the new company.[82] This retarded affairs for some months. But Colbert began to employ the same means which he had employed in the organization of the East and West India Companies, by informing certain parties that to participate in the enterprise "would be a thing very agreeable to His Majesty," and promised "to unite the *Domaine d'Occident* to the new company."[83] The result was that a company was formed composed for the most part of officials of various ranks,[84] "who entered it only for the sake

[82] Arch. Col., C₆, I, Memoir marked "La Compagnie du Sénégal," and endorsed "Envoyé à M. Morel, le 20 aoust 1685."

[83] Ibid.

[84] Arch. Col., C₆, I, Contrat de vente du privilège, habitations, effets de la Cie. du Sénégal et côte de Guinée, July 2, 1681. The original members are given as follows:

"Claude d'Appougny, conseiller, Séc. du Roy, Maison de couronne de France et de ses finances et Guillaume de Kessel, . . . Conseiller du Roy, maitre ordinaire en sa chambre des comptes.

"Guillaume Ménager, conseiller du Roy, directeur general du Dom. Roy. d'Occid.

"Réné de Larré . . . Conseiller, sécretaire du Roy, receveur général de finances à Caen.

"Paul Acéré, écuyer, Sieur des Forges. . . .

"Jean Massoit, le jeune, Marchand à la Rochelle demeurant à présent à Paris.

THE COMMERCIAL POLICY OF COLBERT

of pleasing the king and Monseigneur Colbert."[85] The name of only one merchant appeared in the list of stockholders. The point is worthy of notice, because it shows that the merchant class had not been attracted by the enterprise and that Colbert was forced to browbeat enough officials in order to form a company to which he wished to commit the performance of an important task in his plan of building up the commerce of the West Indies.

By a contract of July 2, 1681, the new company agreed to assume 1,010,015 livres of the debts of the old company and in return it received all the latter's effects and privileges.[86] Letters-patent were issued in the form of an edict in this same month of July, 1681.[87] A complete monopoly of trade was accorded on the same terms as to the former company.

A capital of only 600,000 livres was subscribed by the new stockholders, because it was hoped that this sum, together with the cargoes of returning vessels, which were upon the sea, would be sufficient to satisfy pressing obligations and to meet the expenses of carrying on trade.[88]

The directors chose J. Massoit, the younger, a stockholder, to manage the company's affairs at La Rochelle; a new director, Dancourt, was sent to Gorée;[89] du Casse

"Jean Faure, écuyer, Prieur de Valfrey et de Notre Dame, depuis Serviant.
"Jean du Casse.
"Claude Céberet."

[85] Ibid., Estat des affaires de la Cie. du Sénégal et costes d'Afrique en oct., 1687. "La plupart de ceux qui la composent n'y étant entrez que pour plaire au Roy et à feu Monseigneur, votre père." The memoir was addressed to Seignelay, the son and successor of Colbert.

[86] Arch. Col., C$_6$, I.

[87] Moreau de Saint-Méry, I, 356-359.

[88] Arch. Col., C$_6$, I, "La Cie. du Sénégal," 1685.

[89] An account of Dancourt's voyage is to be found in *Les Voyages du Sr. le Maire aux iles canaries, Cap Verd, Sénégal et Gambia*, Paris, 1695. Bib. Nat., G, 33098. No record has been found of an agent having been sent to the coast of Guinea.

TOWARD THE FRENCH WEST INDIES

was placed in charge of affairs at Martinique, du Clerc at Guadeloupe and Pinel at St. Christopher.[90] A special appeal was made to the intendant Patoulet to take measures to improve the quality of sugar, complaint being made that sugar lately arrived from Martinique was saturated with syrup and sold for three livres per hundredweight less than the sugar from the other islands.[91] The company promised to furnish an abundance of slaves, if he would do so.

No material has been found which enables us to trace the company's activity during the first years of its existence, but the company appealed to the king in 1683 to protect it against a contraband trade in slaves being carried on in the islands, and an ordinance was issued on September 23, 1683, which read in part as follows:

"His Majesty being informed of the damage which the Company of Senegal is suffering from the fact that the inhabitants of the islands of America and St. Domingo trade with the inhabitants of the Main and with the Caribs for slaves, captured from the English and Dutch, and wishing to maintain the company in the enjoyment of the privileges which he has granted to it alone of importing slaves into the islands, has forbidden and forbids by these presents all of his subjects to buy negroes from the said natives or to import them into the French islands of America and the coast of St. Domingo, under penalty of confiscation of negroes and of vessels and of a fine of 1000 livres."[92]

It is very probable that this ordinance attempted to stop the contraband trade in slaves of which the directors had complained to Patoulet in the previous year.[93]

[90] Bib. Nat. MSS., fonds français, 11315, fol. 152-153, the directors to Patoulet, October 22, 1682.
[91] Ibid.
[92] Moreau de Saint-Méry, I, 386.
[93] Bib. Nat. MSS., fonds français, 11315, fol. 152.

THE COMMERCIAL POLICY OF COLBERT

In a memoir dated August 14, 1684, it was asserted that the company had at that time nine vessels *en voyage* and four others which would be ready to sail some time before the month of October. Of these thirteen vessels, four were to carry negroes to the West Indies, three to bring cargoes from Senegal to France, and six to fetch cargoes of sugar from the islands. Besides these vessels, one had already carried a cargo of 290 slaves to St. Domingo and still another would carry 100 negroes to Cayenne. "If all of these vessels," added the memoir, "arrive happily at their destination, a sufficient number of slaves will be furnished to the planters."[94]

It seems reasonably certain, however, that the company did not import 2000 slaves annually to the islands, as it had contracted to do, for a memoir was written in 1684 to explain why it had not done so. The memoir is anonymous and undated, but it was very probably written by d'Appougny or one of the other directors, and it is easy to fix the date of 1684 from internal evidence.

"Two reproaches are made against the company," it said, "one that it is weak and cannot develop its trade as it should, the other that it does not furnish to the islands of America the number of slaves necessary to satisfy the terms of its contract. . . . In regard to the latter it seems that the reproach against the company is well founded, because the new company in succeeding the old assumed the obligation of importing 2000 negroes annually. The following considerations should be taken into account: (1) The promise was originally made on the supposition that this number of slaves could be sold in the islands and that a failure to carry out the promise imposed no penalty; (2) it is very easy to show that the present company has imported into the islands many more negroes during the past three years than was done during the six preceding;

[94] Arch. Col., C$_6$, I, Mémoire de la Cie. du Sénégal, August 14, 1684.

TOWARD THE FRENCH WEST INDIES

(3) it is a fact well known by all those who are well acquainted with the affairs of the islands that not more than 1200 negroes should be imported, if prompt payment is desired, for if this number be surpassed, a risk of a total loss or of not being paid for a long time must be taken. . . . [In support of this, the intendant, Patoulet, was quoted to the effect that if 2000 slaves were imported into the islands, more than one-half and almost two-thirds of the sugar produced would be required to pay for them]; (4) the company has found by actual experience that the reasoning of M. Patoulet is sound, not only as to importing 2000 slaves, but also a smaller number, for, having imported about 1200 slaves annually, it finds that the sums due it have accumulated so rapidly that at the commencement of the present year, 1684, they amounted to 6,000,000 pounds of sugar, and that the year preceding even three of its vessels were unable to obtain enough sugar for cargoes, one being forced to return empty."[95]

It is to be remarked that in neither of these memoirs is the claim even made that the company had ever tried to import 2000 slaves a year into the colonies, that, in fact, it is distinctly stated that only about 1200 had been sent there annually. One is therefore somewhat surprised to find the assertion made by Labat that "the company had not failed to meet its obligations, for it had sent to the American colonies 4561 negroes in less than two years and a half."

Labat states that the directors of the company made this assertion in a protest against the *arrêt* of September 14, 1684, which took away from them a large part of their grant to confer it upon the new company of Guinea about to be organized.[96] No record has been found among the papers of the company of Senegal of any such assertion.

[95] Arch. Col., C$_6$, I, Mémoire de la Compagnie du Sénégal et coste d'Afrique sur le droit qu'elle a de faire seule le commerce, etc.
[96] Labat (Le Père J. B.), *Nouvelle Relation de l'Afrique occidentale,* edition of 1722, I, 27-28.

THE COMMERCIAL POLICY OF COLBERT

A recent writer[97] has shown that Labat was not only guilty of plagiarism in writing the *Nouvelle Relation*, but also of careless handling of his material. It is possible, and even probable, that we have here but another case of inaccuracy on Labat's part. The fact that we have two memoirs, both of 1684, in agreement as to the company's activity, is rather conclusive against the accuracy of Labat's statement.

The company had certainly made progress over its predecessor by importing a larger number of slaves into the islands, but it had not kept pace with the needs of the planters. Patoulet stated in August, 1680, that Martinique alone had need of 1000 slaves per year for the next two years, and 1200 or 1300 for the third year. Now, Martinique was the most productive colony of all at the time and doubtless needed the greatest number of slaves, but both Guadeloupe and St. Christopher were well cultivated and must have needed many. The demand for slaves at St. Domingo was increasing. The amounts owed the first Company of Senegal by the planters of the several islands on June 30, 1681, gives a clue, perhaps, to the distribution of its trade and consequently some idea of the relative numbers of slaves which they demanded. The statement of debts owed the company at that time shows 67,018 liv. 1s. owed by planters of Martinique, 47,466 liv. 8s. by those of St. Christopher, 30,214 liv. 17s. 6d by those of Guadeloupe and 30,065 liv. 12s. by those of St. Domingo.[98] By making use of these figures to establish a proportion, it would not, perhaps, be far wrong to say that if Martinique needed 1000 to 1200 slaves annually, the others combined needed at least 1500 to 1800, making a total of 2500 to 3000 slaves for them all.

[97] P. Cultru, *Histoire du Sénégal du XVe Siècle à 1870*.
[98] Arch. Col., C₆, I, Estat gén. des effets de la Cie. du Sénégal, June 30, 1681.

TOWARD THE FRENCH WEST INDIES

From these estimates it seems very probable that the second Company of Senegal was importing only about enough slaves to satisfy the demand of Martinique alone and hence was not satisfying the total demand in the islands. A letter written by Patoulet from Dunkerque on October 18, 1684, seems to point clearly to this same conclusion. "I have urged," he wrote, "some merchants of Dunkerque and of Lille to undertake to import from Guinea into the islands 1000 slaves annually on terms much more advantageous to the king than those which are being proposed at Paris." Patoulet added that full liberty to all Frenchmen to import slaves would be beneficial to the islands.[99] No such suggestions would have been made, if the Company of Senegal had been furnishing an adequate supply of slaves. A still stronger piece of evidence is to be found in the *arrêt* of September 12, 1684, which revoked the monopoly of trade for that part of the company's concessions lying between the Gambia and the Cape of Good Hope. The act is explicit in giving the reason for such a step:

"Whereas His Majesty has been informed that the company has not only not satisfied the contract of importing 2000 slaves annually into the islands, but has imported even so few that most of the planters are planning to abandon the Windward Islands for the coast of St. Domingo and other places, a thing which would destroy both the colonies and the trade thereof; besides that as the concession made to the company in the letters-patent of June, 1679, which gave it the monopoly of trade for the whole coast of Africa from Cape Verde to the Cape of Good Hope, is too vast, it has not been able to equip enough vessels or furnish enough funds to carry on the trade of both Senegal and the coast of Guinea . . . the king, being in his council, has revoked and revokes by these presents

[99] Arch. Nat. Mar., B₃, 45, fol. 115, Patoulet to Ambleteuze, October 18, 1684.

THE COMMERCIAL POLICY OF COLBERT

the privilege accorded to the Company of Senegal by the contract of March 21, 1679."[100]

The monopoly of the company was henceforth limited to trade on the coast from Cape Verde to Gambia, trade on the coast between the Gambia and the Cape of Good Hope being left open to all Frenchmen. The period of leaving this latter trade open to all was of short duration, for letters-patent were issued in the month of January (1685) to the Company of Guinea, which granted it a monopoly of trade on the coast from Sierra Leone to the Cape of Good Hope, and conjointly with the Company of Senegal, a monopoly of slave trade in the French West Indies.[101]

Thus the history of the slave trade during the ministry of Colbert falls into three distinct periods: (1) 1661-1668, during which slaves were supplied to the planters by the Dutch; (2) 1669-1675, during which Colbert attempted to direct the energy of the West India Company to the trade and to stimulate both the company and private traders, by removing export duties on all articles used in the trade, and by providing a liberal bounty of thirteen livres per head on all slaves imported into the islands; and (3) 1675-1685, during which the slave trade was placed under a monopoly, granted successively to Oudiette (1675), first Company of Senegal (1679), the second Company of Senegal (1681), and finally conjointly to the last named company and the Company of Guinea (1685).

In no one of these periods had French enterprise shown itself equal to the task of satisfying the needs of the planters. The development of the islands was probably somewhat retarded as a consequence, but the policy pursued by Colbert had brought a distinct increase to French commerce. Many new trading posts had been founded on

[100] Moreau de Saint-Méry, I, 400-401.
[101] Moreau de Saint-Méry, I, 409-414. An account of the formation and history of this company will be found in a later volume.

TOWARD THE FRENCH WEST INDIES

the coast of Africa, trade relations had been definitely established and the ways of the slave trade known. The basis had been laid for the building up of a prosperous trade.

CHAPTER XIV

Colonial Imports—Food-Stuffs

ONE of the most pressing problems in the maintenance of prosperous colonies in the West Indies was to furnish an adequate supply of food-stuffs for both master and slave. This became more and more true as the large sugar plantations supplanted the small tobacco farms and as the larger planter with many slaves replaced the small farmer with his small number of indentured servants.

In their early history the planters of the French West Indies produced a large share of their own food supply. Maurile de St. Michel, in describing the life of the colonies in 1646, remarked:

"Here, instead of bread made from wheat, we eat bread made from the cassava plant which is very common and abundant. Instead of beef we eat lamantin, which is a sort of sea cow caught along the shore. Instead of chicken, we eat lizards, from which a very good soup is made and the meat of which is very delicate. I have often eaten them. . . . One of the principal articles of food is peas which grow here in abundance. I have seen many kinds, Roman peas, haricots brought from Virginia by the English, peas from Angola in Africa, which resemble our lentils. I have also seen large beans. The ordinary dinner of the average man consists of pea soup, cassava bread seasoned with red pepper, lemon juice and a small piece of bacon."[1]

With the exception of bacon, all the articles of this menu were produced in the islands and the planter was almost independent of foreign food supplies.

As trade increased, however, the planter found it much more advantageous to expend the labour of his slaves

[1] Maurile de St. Michel, *op. cit.*, 31, 64.

upon the production of sugar and tobacco and to barter these commodities to traders for food supplies. Pelleprat remarked in 1655 that "the grapevine was exceedingly productive in the islands, bearing fruit almost uninterruptedly," and that, if cultivated, three harvests could be gathered yearly and excellent wine made. "But," he added, "the planters of America find more profit in the production of tobacco and of sugar than in that of grapes. It is true that the traders of Europe supply them, so that there is an abundance of wine and flour in the islands."[2] Du Tertre stated that observing days of abstinence was exceedingly difficult in the islands and was not practiced by many families. "This is not because the seas are not full of fish, but because every one is so occupied with his plantation that it is only the well-to-do who have a savage or a negro to send a-fishing."[3]

It was then not so much a question of what the planters might and could produce to supply themselves with food, as of what they found it to their interest to do. The law of larger returns for amount of labour expended guided very naturally the course of production on the plantations.

The ordinary bread, both for master and slave, was made from the cassava plant, which flourished in the islands. The root of the plant was pressed so as to remove the poisonous juice and then made into a small loaf and cooked.[4] Only the richest planters ate bread made from flour imported from Holland and France and some of them preferred cassava bread.[5] The demand for European flour was great only when the crop of cassava was ruined by storms or drouth, as in 1670.[6] It seems to have

[2] Pelleprat, *op. cit.*, 5-8.
[3] Du Tertre, II, 458-459.
[4] Pelleprat, p. 5.
[5] Du Tertre, II, 457.
[6] Arch. Nat. Col., C_7, I, du Lion to Colbert, March 29, 1670, and ibid., C_8, I, de Baas to Colbert, March 22, 1670.

THE COMMERCIAL POLICY OF COLBERT

increased somewhat during the second half of Colbert's ministry, due no doubt to the increasing number of rich planters.[7] But no evidence has been found to show that the importation of wheat flour ever became permanently important or was made the subject of legislation by Colbert. With the exception of salt beef and bacon, this is true also of all other articles of food which were exported to the islands in only very small quantities.[8]

But the importation of salt beef became a matter of immense importance. De Baas stated that salt beef was more essential to the welfare of the islands than any other commodity "because it is the meat fed to the slaves and the consumption of which is so great that 30,000 barrels (6,000,000 pounds) are not sufficient."[9] The same governor stated in 1672 during a period of scarcity of salt beef that the slaves would starve, unless some measures were taken to guarantee a supply.[10] Du Tertre tells us that it was the custom for the planter to obtain from the ships which came to trade in the islands a supply of salt beef, of which he retained a part for his own table and the remainder he distributed to his slaves at the rate of about one-half pound a day for each,[11] whereas de Baas stated that it was the custom to feed the slaves on "three kinds of roots, potatoes, yams and cassava," to which was added two pounds of salt beef per week for each working slave.[12] Only the rich had fresh meat for their own table.[13] Salt beef was thus the common meat food of slave and master.

[7] Arch. Nat. Col., C$_8$, I, de Baas to Colbert, June 26, 1675.

[8] The cargoes sent out from Nantes in 1673 and 1675 contained only small quantities of flour, biscuits, prunes, olive oil, stockfish and codfish. Arch. Dépt., Loire Inf., B, 1, 4, "Declarations de Sorties," passim.

[9] Arch. Nat. Col., C$_8$, I, de Baas to Colbert, February 28, 1672.

[10] Ibid., November 20, 1672.

[11] Du Tertre, II, 457.

[12] Arch. Nat. Col., C$_8$, I, de Baas to Colbert, November 20, 1672.

[13] Ibid.

TOWARD THE FRENCH WEST INDIES

The demand for it increased in proportion as the number of planters and slaves grew. It was, therefore, imperative to provide an adequate supply.

Previous to the ministry of Colbert and during its opening years, this supply had always been obtained in Ireland and imported by Dutch and French traders. These traders not only went to the Irish coast for cargoes of beef, butter and horses, but bought "under the name of Irishmen, a certain number of acres to serve as a pasture for cattle, some of which they killed, salted and carried to the West Indies."[14]

After the Dutch had been excluded from the trade of the islands, Nantes and La Rochelle, especially the former, became the principal *entrepôts* for Irish beef. Paul Parfouru, late archivist of the archives of Ile and Vilaine, has called attention in a very interesting article[15] to the large number of Irish at Nantes and to the close relations between Ireland and that port during the eighteenth century. Unfortunately his article has very little to say about commercial relations. We have enough evidence, however, to state that commercial relations between Ireland and Brittany became important even during the ministry of Colbert.[16] Trade with Ireland, besides furnishing a valuable article of export for the West Indies, proved very profitable. A memoir written by some merchants at Nantes stated that the trade yielded a profit of forty-three per cent.[17]

[14] Arch. Nat. Col., C$_8$, 2nd series, I, Mémoire contenant les avis et sentiment de diff. capit., etc., 1661.

[15] *Annales de Bretagne,* IX, 524-533, Les Irlandais en Bretagne aux XVIIe et XVIIIe Siècles.

[16] The cargoes of vessels sailing to the islands contained large quantities of Irish salt beef. Thus *La Marie,* a vessel of thirty-five tons, sailing from Nantes on May 7, 1673, carried fifty-seven barrels of Irish beef in her cargo and the *Ste. Anne,* ninety tons, sailing on July 3, took 322 barrels. Arch. Dépt., Loire Inf., B, 1, "Decl. de Sorties."

[17] Arch. Nat. Mar., B$_7$, 496, fols. 118-119, Mémoire des march. de

THE COMMERCIAL POLICY OF COLBERT

But it was not in accordance with the mercantilist idea to permit the importation of such an important commodity from foreign markets. The ideal solution would have been to obtain a food supply for the West Indies from a temperate zone colony within the empire. The compara-

Nantes sur le commerce d'Irlande, 1690. Included in the memoir is an estimate of the profit to be gained on the cargo of a vessel of 100 tons. The outgoing cargo was to be composed as follows:

67 tons of salt	540	livres.
10 tons of wine of Anjou	860	livres.
10 tons of wine of Nantes	400	livres.
10 tons of brandy of Nantes	1,300	livres.
3 tons of cloth, paper, hats, etc.	1,900	livres.
100	5,001	livres.
Insurance on cargo at sixteen per cent	800	livres.
Interest on capital eight months at four per cent	200	livres.
	6,000	livres.

The cargo would sell in Ireland for . . . . . . 16,500 livres.
Deduct for cost of freight . 4,000 livres.
Deduct for commission . . 800 livres. 4,800 livres.

11,700 livres.

With this sum could be bought for return cargo:

30 tons of salt beef in 240 barrels at 9 livres per barrel, F. O. B.	2,160	livres.
3 tons of tallow	936	livres.
5 tons of butter at 15 livres the hundredweight	1,500	livres.
2 tons of beef hides	480	livres.
35 tons of wool	6,000	livres.
Commission and other expenses	624	livres.
	11,700	livres.

This cargo would yield at Nantes . . . 15,400 livres.
Deduct:
Capital . . . . . 6,000 livres.
Freight from Ireland . . 4,000 livres.
Insurance on cargo . . . 1,872 livres.
Expense of unloading . . 928 livres. 12,800 livres.

Which represents profit of forty-three per cent   2,600 livres.

314

TOWARD THE FRENCH WEST INDIES

tively early and rapid development of the New England and middle colonies made possible such a happy solution for the British West Indies. Colbert attempted to find in French Canada the equivalent of the British continental colonies for the French West Indies. As early as September 27, 1664, he wrote to de Tracy who was at Guadeloupe:

"Order being established in the islands, as it is now, it will prove a great advantage, if, in the course of a year as you hope, trade can be established between them and Canada by sending to the islands fifteen or sixteen vessels with cargoes of staves, hoops and headings for hogsheads which will find a ready market there and by sending, after the land has been cleared, cargoes of wheat flour, dry-salted eels, codfish and other fish."[18]

The establishment of trade between Canada and the West Indies seems to have been one of the cherished plans of Talon, who became intendant of Canada in 1665. In a letter of October 27, 1667, he informed Colbert that he had associated himself with a merchant in a plan to send a ship belonging to the West India Company with a cargo of salted fish, peas, lumber and other articles to the French West Indies "in order to make an experiment and open the road to a trade which the inhabitants of Canada have as yet not attempted."[19] In a memoir of November 10, 1670, he stated that Canada was producing a surplus of wheat, vegetables and fish, and that he had "laden this surplus on three vessels, constructed in Canada, to be carried to the West Indies, with the hope that this northern part of America will be able to furnish great aid to the southern part."

[18] Arch. Nat. Col., C_8, 2nd series, I, Colbert to de Tracy, September 27, 1664.
[19] Thomas Chapais, *Jean Talon, Intendant de la Nouvelle France*, p. 283.

THE COMMERCIAL POLICY OF COLBERT

"I hope," he said, "that the trade which I am opening up will prove of mutual benefit to the inhabitants of Canada and to the planters of the islands. My plan is for vessels to take a cargo [of food-stuffs] hence to the islands; thence a cargo of sugar to France and then to bring back here a cargo of merchandise suited to our needs. The realization of this plan will prove very advantageous to His Majesty's empire, for, in case of war, the Antilles can be supplied from Canada with food-stuffs and manufactures and they will thus not be made to suffer from having their supply cut off from Europe. Inasmuch as this consideration appears to me to be of some importance, my own feeling is that in order to encourage the inhabitants of Canada to construct vessels and employ them in this trade, it would be wise for His Majesty to offer a larger bounty than that which he offers to his other subjects for buying or constructing vessels, and in addition to reduce in their favour import duties on sugar which they bring from the islands."[20]

Colbert replied to this letter by saying that the king was delighted to learn that Canada was not only in condition to support herself, but even to send food supplies to the French West Indies.

"Inasmuch as His Majesty has furnished such large sums of recent years with a view of building up commerce between these two parts of his empire, there is nothing to which you should pay greater attention than to strengthen and to encourage the efforts which have been made this year in Canada to establish trade with the islands and to persuade the inhabitants to construct or buy vessels for the establishment of this trade. It is certain that there is no better means to make them prosperous and increase their numbers. I have not failed to render an account to His Majesty of the three vessels constructed in Canada and sent last year with cargoes to the West Indies.

[20] Arch. Nat. Col., C_{11} (Canada), III, fol. 94, Mémoire sur le Canada joint à la lettre de M. Talon, November 10, 1670.

TOWARD THE FRENCH WEST INDIES

The commencement of this commerce has proved very agreeable to His Majesty."[21]

As to Talon's demand that a special bounty be granted for the construction of vessels in Canada, Colbert replied: "I am very glad that the inhabitants of Canada are beginning to apply themselves to shipbuilding. Although those which you note are rather small . . . yet you may grant the bounty provided for in the *arrêt*, of which I am inclosing you a copy."[22] As to the reduction on sugar imported into France from the West Indies by Canadian vessels, Colbert extended to them the benefits of the reduction, made by the *arrêt* of December 10, 1670, on colonial sugar, from four livres to forty sous the hundredweight.[23]

Instructions were given to de Baas in 1668 to do everything to encourage trade with Canada.[24] Likewise, Pélissier was instructed to study the problem of establishing this trade. The latter submitted a memoir to Colbert, under date of December 10, 1670, suggesting that ships should plan to sail from Quebec by November 1, or November 11 at the latest, for the islands and pass thence to Bordeaux, La Rochelle, Nantes or to one of the channel ports, where a return cargo would be taken to Canada.[25] Blénac, governor-general of the islands, and Bégon,

[21] Arch. Nat. Col., B, 3, fol. 22, Colbert to Talon, 1671 (exact date not given—Clément, III, 2, p. 511, gives date of February 11).

[22] I have not been able to determine whether or not Colbert provided a special bounty by an *arrêt* of which I have found no record. It is more than probable, however, that the bounties here accorded were none other than those granted to ship builders in France, for in the margin of the memoir in which Talon demanded the special bounty is written in Colbert's hand: "Les graces que S. M. accorde sont si grandes qu'elles ne peuvent être augmentées. Il faut faire pour ces bâtimens reduction de quarante sols sur le sucre." Arch. Nat. Col., C_{11}, III, fol. 94.

[23] Arch. Nat. Col., B, 3, fol. 124 verso.

[24] Arch. Aff. Etrang., Doc. et Mém., Amérique, V, 237. Instructions to Sieur de Baas, September 15, 1668.

[25] Arch. Nat. Col., C_{11}, III, Mémoire touchant le commerce du

THE COMMERCIAL POLICY OF COLBERT

intendant, in a joint memoir to Colbert under date of February 13, 1683, stated that they were trying to encourage the planters to carry on trade with Canada, because they "could obtain there salted meats of better quality and cheaper than those of Ireland, as well as flour, peas, salted fish and lumber."[26]

A short time after Colbert's death, all duties were removed from sugar-cane brandy, sugar, tobacco, cotton, indigo, and other products imported into Canada from the French islands and from salted meats, peas, flour, fish, lumber, and other articles imported into the islands from Canada.[27] The encouragement of trade between the two groups of colonies continued to be a policy of the government throughout the reign of Louis XIV.[28]

These efforts yielded very meagre results. Talon lost two of the vessels sent to the islands in 1670, of which the estimated value with cargoes was 36,000 livres.[29] An intendant of the islands stated in 1691 that others who had made attempts to carry on this trade had made no profit.[30]

There were several obstacles to the success of the trade. Canada did not produce a sufficient quantity of foodstuffs or lumber to make the trade of large importance, nor was there a sufficient demand in Canada for West India products to make an independent trade between the

Canada aux Isles Antilles françaises de l'Amérique, December 15, 1670.

[26] Arch. Nat. Col., C$_8$, III.

[27] Arch. Nat. Col., B, 11, fol. 70, Extrait des Rég. du con. d'Etat, April, 1685.

[28] The history of this policy will be told in a succeeding volume. See Arch. Nat. Col., C$_8$, IV, Dumaitz de Goimpy to Seignelay, December 18, 1686; ibid., V, de Blénac and de Goimpy to the king, May 8, 1688; ibid., B, 24, Instructions to Desnos, February 9, 1701; ibid., B, 31, letter to d'Aguesseau, December 5, 1708, etc., etc.

[29] Arch. Nat. Col., C$_{11}$, III, fols. 274-279, Mémoire du Sieur Patoulet, January 25, 1672.

[30] Arch. Nat. Col., C$_8$, VI, letter from Dumaitz, February 16, 1691.

two groups of colonies possible.[31] It was necessary to establish a three-cornered trade between Canada, the West Indies and the mother country.[32] This meant a long and difficult voyage at great risks. A trader undertaking it had to wait a year for any returns from his capital.[33] Besides the British North American continental colonies furnished a much more accessible and much cheaper supply of food-stuffs. The petition of the sugar refiners of Guadeloupe and Martinique in 1681, quoted above,[34] for permission to establish a trade with these colonies is most significant.

Thus both Colbert and his successors failed in their efforts to obtain an adequate supply of food-stuffs for the West India planters by establishing trade with Canada. But Colbert was not willing to remain idle in presence of the fact that such a large part of that food supply came from Ireland, a foreign country. In 1670, he began to exclude Irish beef from importation into the islands and to substitute French beef. On October 27, he wrote to Brunet, one of the directors of the West India Company, who was at that time at La Rochelle, as follows:

"I note from your letter the efforts which you have made to carry out the instructions which I gave you, and particularly those concerning the purchase of beef in France to export to the islands instead of that of Ireland. As you know how very much at heart I hold this matter, you will understand why I am so happy to learn that you are hopeful of succeeding. . . . Bend your energies to the task and rest assured that you can do nothing which would bring me more pleasure than the success of the enterprise."[35]

[31] Arch. Nat. Col., C$_8$, V, Memoir by de Blénac and Dumaitz, May 8, 1686.
[32] Ibid.
[33] Ibid., IV, Dumaitz de Goimpy to Seignelay, December 18, 1686.
[34] Chapter IX.
[35] Depping, *Correspondance,* III, 522.

THE COMMERCIAL POLICY OF COLBERT

In order to induce the West India Company to devote special attention to the importation of French beef into the islands, he offered the directors a bounty of 12,000 livres for the importation of 4000 barrels during the year 1671.[36]

To the objection that French beef was too dear, Colbert replied that it was necessary to convince traders that it was of superior quality and he added:

"In order to force merchants who trade in the islands to buy French beef, you may forbid them to use Ile de Ré as an *entrepôt* for Irish beef. In that case you have need of an *arrêt* of the *conseil d'état* to do so, let me know and I shall send one to you promptly."[37]

Such an *arrêt* was published on August 17, 1671, which formally annulled the right of *entrepôt* in France for "beef and other meats brought from Ireland."[38] This was followed by a royal ordinance which forbade the importation into the islands of all foreign beef and bacon under penalty of confiscation thereof and 500 livres fine for the first offense and of bodily punishment in case of repetition.[39] A supplementary *arrêt* of December 21, 1671, granted the liberty of exporting to the islands all Irish beef actually on hand, if it were done before January 13, 1672.[40] Finally a bounty of four livres per barrel was granted on all beef salted within the kingdom and exported to the West Indies.[41]

[36] Ibid., p. 523, same to same, November 13, 1670.
[37] Ibid., p. 527, Colbert to Brunet, February 26, 1671.
[38] Moreau de Saint-Méry, I, 230.
[39] Arch. Nat., G7, 1313, *arrêt* of November 4, 1671; Moreau de Saint-Méry, I, 253.
[40] Arch. Nat. Col., B, 4, fols. 1-2; Arch. Aff. Etrang., Mém. et Doc., France, 2007, fol. 12 verso.
[41] Arch. Nat. Col., B, 4, fols. 4-5; Moreau de Saint-Méry, I, 259. Ordinance of January 13, 1672. In order to claim this bounty the captains were obliged to deposit a certificate, properly signed in the

TOWARD THE FRENCH WEST INDIES

There is but very little evidence to show that French traders made many efforts to take advantage of the bounty offered for salting beef in France and shipping it to the islands. The West India Company made some, but it has been shown above that it was too near bankruptcy to accomplish any important results. The cargoes of only a few vessels sailing from Nantes contained French beef and then the quantities were small.[42] In 1675, two years after the restoration of the privilege to export Irish beef to the islands, the quantities of French beef sent to the islands were still small.[43]

De Baas showed opposition to the policy from the first.

islands, certifying that the beef had been landed there. Ibid., fol. 22 verso.

[42] Thus *Le David,* 240 tons, captain, Chapelain, whose passport was registered on August 3, 1673, had in her cargo 23 one-quarter barrels, and *La Notre Dame de Mont Carmel,* 150 tons, captain, Castellier, July 3, had 64 barrels. Likewise, the cargo of *La Montagne,* 300 tons, captain, Hotman, had 179 barrels. The rest of the vessels for the year carried either Irish beef or none at all. Arch. Dépt., Loire Inf., Décl. de Sorties, B, 1, and 2. There is one case, *La Marguerite,* 50 tons, captain, Leroy, where the cargo contained a small quantity of beef from Hamburg.

[43] Of the ten vessels sailing for the islands from the port of Nantes in that year, the following is the record so far as beef contained in their cargoes is concerned:

			Beef French	Irish
Jan. 10, *L'Espérance,*	200 tons, Capt. Mezard,	70 bbls.	11 bbls.
Jan. 10, *St. François,*	120 tons, Capt. Gabillard,	39¼ bbls.	5 bbls.
Jan. 18, *L'Africaine,*	250 tons, Capt. Bernard,	30 bbls.	200 bbls.
Jan. 22, *La Montagne,*	300 tons, Capt. Allard,	274 bbls.	142 bbls.
Oct. 12, *St. Bernard,*	80 tons, Capt. D'Arquistad,	20 bbls.	75 bbls.
Jan. 23, *La Louise,*	40 tons, Capt. Lelois,	— bbls.	70 bbls.
Feb. 16, *St. Pierre,*	200 tons, Capt. Marston,	— bbls.	112 bbls.
Mar. 14, *La Tartaune,*	30 tons, Capt. Joubert,	— bbls.	18 bbls.
Oct. 2, *St. Nicolas,*	60 tons, Capt. Coillot,	— bbls.	64 bbls.
Dec. 23, *Le Charles,*	130 tons, Capt. Dubois,	¾ bbls.	— bbls.

Total, 434 bbls. 697 bbls.

Arch. Dépt., Loire Inf., Décl. de Sorties, B, 3 and 4.

THE COMMERCIAL POLICY OF COLBERT

On receiving notification of the *arrêt* excluding Irish beef, he wrote to Colbert:

"I shall obey orders, Monseigneur, but permit me to say that a supply of beef is more necessary to the islands than that of any other commodity, for it is the meat which is fed to the slaves. The consumption of it is so great that 30,000 barrels are not enough to satisfy the annual demand. I am not sure that France can furnish such a large quantity, and even if it could, the beef would have to be sold at double the price of Irish beef."[44]

After nearly a year of trial of the new regulation, the same governor wrote again:

"If the supply of salt beef fails, the planters will be without the services of their slaves. The stronger slaves will become robbers and runaways, and the weaker, the women and children, will grow faint and die, as they are already beginning to do. . . . I must say to you, with your permission, Monseigneur, that as beef is the meat given to slaves, a supply of it is absolutely necessary, if they are to be kept at work. It is impossible for French traders to bring a sufficient quantity from France, as the supply there is small and costs so much that beef, which has been selling here for 300 pounds of sugar per barrel, will cost 800. . . . None of the traders is importing any into the islands and there is none to be had here. The planters are murmuring because they see no means of feeding their slaves, who detest fat pork and eat it only by compulsion. . . . The slaves are forced to work twenty out of every twenty-four hours. If, then, these miserable wretches do not have beef to eat, how is it possible for them to endure so much work by eating only potatoes, yams and cassava bread? If Irish beef is not imported, it is certain that they will not be fed on French beef. . . . I confess, Monseigneur, that I have a great deal of weakness in the matter of carrying out your orders, for slaves are human beings and human beings

[44] Arch. Nat. Col., C_8, I, de Baas to Colbert, February 23, 1672.

TOWARD THE FRENCH WEST INDIES

should not be reduced to a state which is worse than that of cattle."[45]

De Baas added a postscript to say that he had been forced to interrupt the work of fortifying the harbour of Port Royal on account of not having a supply of beef and that he would have to discontinue the work, until some was brought from France, or until he could send to Barbadoes. A month later he wrote that beef and other provisions had become so scarce at St. Croix that the governor was sick and some of the chief planters had died.[46] One official reported that he had seen planters at Guadeloupe "swearing upon bended knee and with tears in their eyes to the governor that it had been more than a year since they or their families had had a morsel of meat to eat."[47]

De Baas seems to have taken the law into his own hands and, in spite of strict orders and instructions, permitted trade with the foreigner to relieve suffering caused by the scarcity of beef. Thus he permitted the planters at St. Croix to trade with the Danes during six months.[48] He permitted two Jew merchants of Martinique to fetch a cargo of food supplies from Barbadoes,[49] and likewise four English vessels to trade at Guadeloupe and Martinique. Among the latter was "a ketch coming from the city of Boston."[50] Colbert rebuked de Baas for his conduct,[51] but he withdrew, nevertheless, the prohibition to import Irish beef.

A royal ordinance was proclaimed on May 10, 1673, which stated that as the existence of a war had rendered commerce by sea difficult, and traders had ceased to salt

[45] Arch. Nat. Col., C$_8$, I, de Baas to Colbert, November 20, 1672.
[46] Ibid., de Baas to Colbert, December 28, 1672.
[47] Arch. Nat. Col., C$_8$, I, du Clerc to Colbert, January 20, 1675.
[48] Arch. Nat, Col., C$_8$, I, de Baas to Colbert, December 28, 1672.
[49] Arch. Nat. Col., C$_8$, I, de Baas, February 6, 1674.
[50] Arch. Nat. Col., C$_8$, I, du Clerc to Colbert, January 20, 1675.
[51] Ibid., B, 6, fol. 32, Colbert to de Baas, May 15, 1674.

beef and to export it to the islands, and as the planters of the said islands might suffer as a consequence, "His Majesty has permitted and permits to all French traders to export and sell in the said islands beef purchased in foreign countries in the same manner as was the custom to do before the ordinance of November 4, 1671."[52] The ordinance seems to have produced a good effect, for de Baas wrote shortly afterwards: "I believe that I should tell you that the abundance of meat is so great in the islands that this year a barrel of beef sells for 350 pounds of sugar and a barrel of bacon for 450 pounds, whereas the price of the former was formerly 800 pounds and of the latter was 1200 pounds."[53]

Even after the close of the war, Colbert did not return to the fight. The intendant, Patoulet, suggested in 1680 that the planters be forced to raise cattle and that "His Majesty should announce that after a period of three years the importation of Irish beef would not be permitted."[54] The reply made to this suggestion is instructive in showing that Colbert had learned by experience that some things, which he thought desirable from the standpoint of the interests of the state, were, nevertheless, impossible of realization. "His Majesty does not think it wise," he wrote, "to prohibit the importation of Irish beef and Madeira wine into the islands. The suggestion which you make to compel the planters to devote themselves to the raising of cattle, by declaring that the importation of Irish beef will not be permitted after a period of three years, does not seem practicable, for the lands which have been cleared are along the seashore and produce only cane. Thus there would be no land suitable for

[52] Moreau de Saint-Méry, I, 270.

[53] Arch. Nat. Col., C$_8$, I, de Baas to Colbert, June 26, 1675.

[54] Arch. Nat. Col., C$_8$, 2nd series, I, Mémoire par Patoulet, December 20, 1680.

TOWARD THE FRENCH WEST INDIES

the pasturage of cattle."[55] Instructions were sent to de Blénac under the same date to admit Irish beef as had been the custom since 1673.[56]

Patoulet himself placed an order with Allaire, a merchant of La Rochelle, for 500 barrels of Irish beef at twelve livres the barrel.[57]

Irish beef continued to maintain its place of importance in the trade of the islands, for Gastines, the commissioner of the marine at Nantes, stated that the basis of all cargoes sent to the islands from that port was Irish beef.[58] When an import duty of five livres per hundredweight was laid in France on Irish beef by an *arrêt* of June 29, 1688, some merchants at Nantes, interested in the commerce of the islands, met and drew up a memoir of protest, asserting that the duty was excessive, as it represented a duty of 100 per cent ad valorem and that, if maintained, the traders of Nantes and the West India planters would suffer.[59]

It is certain, therefore, that Irish beef continued, throughout the ministry of Colbert, to be a most important article of food for the slaves of the French West Indies. The attempt of Colbert to prevent its importation between November 4, 1671, and May, 1673, proved futile.

[55] Bib. Nat. MSS., fonds français, 11315, Colbert to de Baas, May 4, 1681, and also Arch. Nat. Col., B, 9, fols. 12-23, April 30, 1681.

[56] Arch. Nat. Col., B, 9, fols. 1-12.

[57] Bib. Nat. MSS., fonds français, 11315, fols. 19-22, Anthoine Allaire to Patoulet, October 29, 1679.

[58] Arch. Nat. Mar., B$_3$, 55, fol. 492, Gastines to Seignelay, July 20, 1688.

[59] Arch. Nat. Mar., B$_7$, 495, fol. 198, Mémoire sur le bœuf salé d'Irlande, June 29, 1688.

CHAPTER XV

Colonial Imports—Live Stock, Lumber, Manufactured Goods

THE introduction of the cultivation of sugar-cane in the French West Indies brought with it an increased demand for live stock. De Poincy, the governor of St. Christopher, stated in 1640, that the lack of water power would have to be supplied by the employment of horses or oxen to turn the sugar-cane mills.[1] This was actually done, for de Rochefort asserted in 1658, that five of the six sugar-cane mills operated by that governor were turned by oxen or horses brought from Curaçao.[2] Later, Dutch and French traders maintained pastures in Ireland for raising cattle, some of which were shipped to the West Indies as live stock to turn the sugar-mills.[3] Nacquart, in his plan of 1663 to establish a company to carry on trade with the West Indies, proposed to include in the cargoes of each vessel, "twenty-five or thirty horses of the kind that are ordinarily sent from Amsterdam to the islands and that cost from sixty to eighty *florins* and sell for 2500 to 3500 pounds of sugar, according to quality."[4] He also proposed that "while the company's ships were waiting in the islands for return cargoes, one or two of them be sent to Curaçao and Bonayre for cargoes of asses and horses."[5]

[1] Arch. Col., F₂, 15, Letter, November 15, 1640.
[2] Du Tertre, II, 289-290.
[3] Arch. Nat. Col., C₈, 2nd series, I, Mémoire contenant les avis et sentiment de diff. capit., 1661.
[4] Arch. Nat. Col., C₈, 2nd series, I, Proposition au Roy d'une Nouvelle Compagnie à establir, etc., 1663.
[5] Ibid.

TOWARD THE FRENCH WEST INDIES

Curaçao remained the principal source of supply even after the beginning of Colbert's ministry, for de Baas was instructed by the West India Company in 1668 to admit Dutch ships from Curaçao, bringing slaves and horses, and he admitted them freely until the close of 1669.[6] Furthermore, du Lion, the governor of Guadeloupe, complained in 1669 that Cartier, the general agent of the West India Company, was monopolizing the supply of horses "imported by the Dutch from Curaçao," in order to sell them at the exorbitant price of 2500 to 3000 pounds of sugar for horses and from 3000 to 4000 pounds for mares.[7] Finally, Téméricourt, governor of Marie Galante, informed Colbert that he had sent a small vessel to Curaçao for a cargo of slaves and horses.[8]

But news reached Guadeloupe in 1670 that the Dutch West India Company had forbidden, for two years, the exportation of horses from Curaçao.[9] Du Lion then asked that permission be granted for Jean Vaulit, a Dutch inhabitant of Guadeloupe, to bring from Flushing a cargo of "good Norman horses, lumber and other things of which the colonies are in need." "It would be," he said, "an advantage for the colony, if he brought a cargo of Norman horses, because they are much stronger than those which we have been receiving from Curaçao."[10] We learn from the same governor in a letter of July 25 that the agent of M. Formont at Guadeloupe was expecting a cargo of mares from Ireland and Norway.[11]

Thus the French islands were dependent upon foreign markets for their supply of live stock. But Colbert regarded this fact as an evil and made efforts to remedy it.

[6] Arch. Nat. Col., C$_8$, I, de Baas to Colbert, December 22, 1669.
[7] Arch. Nat. Col., C$_7$, I, du Lion to Colbert, December 1, 1669.
[8] Arch. Nat. Col., C$_7$, I, December 14, 1669.
[9] Arch. Nat. Col., C$_7$, I, du Lion to Colbert, May 5, 1670.
[10] Ibid.
[11] Ibid.

THE COMMERCIAL POLICY OF COLBERT

He instructed de Baas on March 25, 1670, not to admit under any circumstances slaves or horses brought by foreigners or imported from foreign countries.[12] At the same time he instructed the West India Company to devote special attention to the importation of live stock into the islands.[13] He attempted to force the West India trader to find a supply in France. A royal ordinance was proclaimed on December 20, 1670, which required every vessel going to the islands to take two mares or two cows or two she-asses. A promise to do so was made the condition of obtaining a passport.[14]

What definite results these regulations attained, the writer is unable to say, but it is to be noted that du Lion complained in 1672 of the exorbitant price demanded by the West India Company for horses of Poitou. This would seem to imply that the company imported some horses from France. France, however, did not have a supply of good horses, for Vauban noted the fact near the close of the century.[15] It would seem to imply that horses offered for sale were exceedingly scarce. At any rate, we know that by 1680 the French planters were again receiving live stock from the foreigner. Patoulet stated in one of his letters to Colbert that he had succeeded in establishing trade in horses and mules with the Spaniards of Porto Rico,[16] and de Pouançay stated in the following year

[12] Arch. Nat. Col., B, 2, fol. 19 verso.

[13] An account of this will be found in Chapter VII.

[14] Arch. Nat. Col., B, 2, fol. 145. A slight modification in the regulation was made on January 22, following, by which vessels of 100 tons or less were allowed to substitute two servants for each mare, cow or she-ass. Ibid., 3, fol. 8 verso; Moreau de Saint-Méry, I, 207.

[15] Vauban, Oisivétés, I, 92. "Il y a encore une raison en France qui empêche qu'il ne s'y trouve que tres peu de bons chevaux, c'est que les paysans sont trop pauvres pour les pouvoir nourrir et attendre quatre on cinq ans pour s'en défaire; il les vendent ordinairement à dix huit mois ou deux ans ou les font tirer ou porter presqu'aussitôt, ce qui les empêche de croitre et les ruine de forte bonne heure."

[16] Arch. Nat. Col., C₈, III, Patoulet to Colbert, December 26, 1680.

TOWARD THE FRENCH WEST INDIES

that live stock was being imported into St. Domingo from the Spanish colonies.[17]

It seems probable that the efforts of Colbert to find within the empire a supply of live stock for the West India planters proved futile, as they had in the case of salt beef.

A supply of lumber was necessary in the West Indies for building purposes, for repairing ships and in form of staves, hoops and headings for making sugar barrels. Du Tertre remarked during his sojourn at St. Christopher that a supply of lumber was obtained from the Dutch at Saba.[18] He notes also the presence in the islands of woodchoppers and dressers of lumber, and adds the comment that they demanded exorbitant prices for their lumber.[19] But the return for labour was greater on the plantation than in the forest and the islands relied upon the foreigner for a supply of lumber which they needed.

But Colbert was unwilling to let this continue. Thus, in his instructions to de Baas of September 15, 1668, is to be found the following passage: "The thing which is lacking most in the islands and of which there is a very great and pressing need, is lumber for the construction of vessels and the making of sugar-barrels. As Canada is well supplied with timber . . . Sieur de Baas will exert his efforts to persuade the inhabitants to undertake to obtain a supply by trade with Canada."[20] He had previously instructed Talon, the intendant of Canada, to encourage the same trade. The story has been told elsewhere of how these efforts proved unfruitful.[21]

[17] Arch. Nat. Col., C$_9$, I, Mémoire du Sieur de Pouançay concernant la coste de St. Domingue envoyé à M. Colbert, January 30, 1681.

[18] Du Tertre, II, 453.

[19] Ibid., p. 454.

[20] Arch. Aff. Etrang., Mém. et Doc., Amérique, V, 237, September 15, 1668.

[21] See Chapter XIV.

THE COMMERCIAL POLICY OF COLBERT

After 1669 the supply of staves, hoops and headings for barrels, in part at least, seems to have come from the ports of France. The few cases found in the admiralty records of the several ports, where the cargoes of outgoing vessels are given in detail, show that nearly all of them took these articles to the islands.[22] But France was not able to satisfy for a long time the growing demand of her West India islands for these articles, for she was compelled in the eighteenth century to admit their importation from the British North American colonies.

The principal articles of manufacture imported into the islands were cloth, of qualities varying from a coarse grade, used for making shirts, breeches and short skirts for the slaves,[23] to the finest grades, used by the more prosperous planters, clothing, hats, shoes, utensils for the farm and household, caldrons and copper vessels of various sizes, and implements used in the sugar-mills.

After Colbert had excluded the Dutch who had been accustomed to furnish these articles, he removed one by one the restraints which had long discouraged the French traders from exporting them to the islands. In the first place, he granted to the West India Company, by an *arrêt* of May 30, 1664, exemption from half the duties ordinarily levied on exports from France.[24] He removed all such duties both for the company and for private traders by an *arrêt* of June 4, 1671.[25] Exemption from all export

[22] Arch. Dépt., Loire Inf., B, 3, 4, 5, 6, 7, passim. *La Tartane,* 30 tons, sailing from Nantes on March 14, 1674, took staves for 120 barrels, 28 bundles of hoops, 2 barrels nails, etc. *L'Africaine,* 250 tons, sailing on January 18, took staves and headings for 900 barrels, and 36 bundles hoops. *L'Espérance,* 200 tons, sailing January 10, took dressed lumber and staves, hoops and headings.

[23] Peytraud, *op. cit.,* 226. The master was required by the twenty-fifth article of the *Code noir* of 1685 to furnish yearly to each slave *"deux habits de toile ou quatre aunes de toile."*

[24] Moreau de Saint-Méry, I, 114-115.

[25] Arch. Nat. Col., B, 3, fols. 127-128. This was re-enacted on

TOWARD THE FRENCH WEST INDIES

duties on goods sent to the coast of Guinea to be used in the slave trade was granted on September 18 of the same year.[26] Finally, by a royal ordinance of June 9, 1670, duties levied in the islands on goods imported from France were abolished.[27] As an explanation of this last action, Colbert wrote to de Baas as follows:

"The custom which has been followed up to the present of levying duties on incoming and outgoing cargoes was a very good practice for the time when foreigners and only a few Frenchmen carried on this trade, but at present, when the foreigners have been entirely eliminated and only French traders remain, the custom must be abolished."[28]

Colbert thus removed all the barriers which had impeded for two generations the trade between the mother country and her colonies. Henceforward the way was perfectly free. Cargoes of manufactured goods could be exported to the islands free from all duties. The French traders took advantage of this fact and built up a profitable trade with the West Indies.[29]

November 25. Arch. Nat., AD,vii, 3, and Moreau de Saint-Méry, I, 255-256.

[26] Arch. Nat. Col., B, 3, fols. 129-130, and Moreau de Saint-Méry, I, 242.

[27] Moreau de Saint-Méry, I, 194.

[28] Clément, III, 2, p. 478, April 9, 1670.

[29] The following will illustrate the relative amount of manufactured articles in cargoes taken from Nantes: *Le Charles,* 130 tons, Dubois, captain, took "1th. vin Nantais, 1 boite verres ouvragés, 1 bal. couverture et toile, 1 balle papier, 20 caisses couteaux et oustils, 1 ballot selles à cheval, 5 paq. marchandises, 1 caisse chapeaux, 3 bal. toile façon Bilbao, 1 quart toile, 3 ballots droguets, 1 1-4 barrique mercerie et soies, 1 caisse d'espées et toile, 300 barrils en botte, 5 quarts lard, 1 caisse savon, 57 quarts farine, 2 bar. pigalles, 1 caisse fayence, 6 quarts biscuits, 3 quarts bœuf du pays, 6 bar. huile d'olive, 4 quarts huile de poisson, 150 feuillards de cercles, 3 bar. 1 quart 1 ballot souliers et estoffe." Arch. Dépt., Loire Inf., B (Registre de Sorties), 4, December 23, 1675.

CHAPTER XVI

Conclusion

THERE are some obvious, but at the same time fundamental principles which underlay the whole of Colbert's colonial commercial policy. First of all, he considered the chief end of establishing colonies to build up trade. He instituted the practice of subsidizing colonial enterprises with no other purpose than that of creating an over-sea commerce. Colonies should contribute to this end by becoming markets for the manufactures of the mother country and for other articles brought by her traders, and by furnishing raw products which might be used either as a supply to her manufacturing industries or as articles of trade with other nations. In the second place, he considered colonies as the exclusive property of the mother country. Foreigners should not be allowed to profit from them, either by being allowed to import even the articles which the mother country did not produce or which her traders could not or did not supply, or by being permitted to take away even the surplus products for which there was no market in the realm. As a corollary to this was the principle that the growth and expansion of a colony were only desirable when they had been made possible by a strict exclusion of foreigners from all profit therein. Finally, the interests of the colonies should be subjected to those of the mother country. Wherever they came into conflict, the former should always be sacrificed to the latter.

In the application of these principles, as we have had occasion to see in the preceding chapters, Colbert formulated many regulations. Those which he made to keep out the foreign trader, together with the measures which he took to insure their enforcement, caused much suffering to the planters and checked, at least temporarily, the development of the islands. The wisdom of forcing such a sudden change from a *régime* of Dutch to that of French trading may be seriously questioned. The suggestion made by Formont, in his memoir of 1662, to effect this change gradually, by permitting, for a few years, trade with foreigners under a *régime* of preferential treatment to French ships, would undoubtedly have proved less revolutionary and less burdensome to the colonies. It might have saved them from the long state of unrest and rebellion which prevailed from 1665 to 1670, for French traders proved unable to satisfy all the needs of the islands and the Dutch might have been utilized advantageously, for a time at least, in aiding them. This was especially true of a supply of slaves and live stock. The directors of the West India Company clearly recognized the wisdom of this and freely admitted into the islands Dutch ships bringing such a supply. As late as 1668, it will be recalled, they instructed de Baas to admit them. Colbert, however, was not willing to tolerate such an exception to the strict principle of excluding all foreigners. The result was, as we have seen, that the planters were forced not only to discontinue the clearance of new lands, but also were unable to replace slaves that died, and hence were unable to maintain the former level of production.

The desire to exclude all foreigners from profit in the island trade led Colbert to go to extremes. A case in point is to be found in his efforts to exclude Irish beef from the islands. Irish beef not only offered an article for profitable trade between Nantes and Ireland, but also, as an article of export to the islands, yielded a good middleman's profit to French traders. It was, to say the least, somewhat an exaggeration of mercantilist principles to attempt to force its production in France, where the cost was much greater, and to disregard the suffering of the hungry planters and of their starving slaves. It must be added, however, that the short experiment which was made convinced Colbert of the error of his way and that he never tried afterwards to carry out this policy. Another example of extremes to which he went was his refusal to permit the exchange of rum and molasses—two waste products of the sugar industry which could not be marketed in France—for New England food-stuffs and lumber, of which the mother country could not furnish a sufficient supply. Events proved that this exchange was so profitable that the French government was forced to make definite provisions to permit and encourage it.

Colbert's plan to make the islands absolutely independent of all foreign aid and to reserve the profit of their development entirely to the French could have proved permanently successful only by building up what might be termed an ideal colonial empire. Such an empire would have required four essential parts to make it complete, namely, the mother country, temperate zone colonies, West India colonies, and trading-posts on the coasts of Africa. In general, the mother country should furnish a supply of manufactured articles of all descriptions, and a sufficiently large market for the products of the West India colonies, as well as an abundance of vessels and of capital necessary for the development of shipping and commerce; the West India colonies should produce such articles as sugar, tobacco, indigo, cotton, ginger, dye-woods, and other articles for which there was always a profitable market in Europe; the temperate zone colonies should yield a supply of food-stuffs, live stock and lumber, sufficient to satisfy all the needs of the West India colonies and be a good market for the manufactures of the mother country; and finally, the trading-posts of the coast of Africa should be able to supply a sufficient number of slaves to satisfy the needs of the planters in the West Indies.

It was generally true of all West India colonies that their exports to Europe far outweighed their imports. This was so, because the consumption of European manufactures was relatively small and because in most cases European countries did not produce a surplus of lumber, live stock or food-stuffs sufficiently large to satisfy the needs of the planters. The balance of trade with the mother country was therefore always in their favour. It was by this balance that they gained a means of buying in other markets a supply of the articles most essential to their welfare and progress.

Exactly the opposite was true of the temperate zone colonies. They imported much from and exported little to Europe. They produced, in general, articles which were produced in the mother country and for which it offered them no market. They were consequently forced to find a middle market where their commodities could be exchanged, either for letters of credit, or for commodities which could be marketed in the mother country. It was only in this way that they could meet the balance of trade against them. They found this middle market in the West India colonies, which needed an abundance of the very articles they offered, and could give them in exchange the letters of credit against the mother country or commodities which they could use to settle their bills in Europe.

The same thing was true of the trader at the coast of Africa. His cargo of slaves could be readily exchanged in the same way with the West India planter.

An ideal empire, so to speak, would have been one in which all of these four parts were sufficiently productive to supply the needs of the others and sufficiently prosperous to furnish a market for their commodities and in which a balance was maintained between the several parts.

THE COMMERCIAL POLICY OF COLBERT

No such empire ever existed. The British had very productive West India and southern colonies, as well as prosperous northern temperate zone colonies. But the development of the latter was too rapid for the former and the balance was destroyed. The northern colonies were forced to seek, outside of the empire, larger and more profitable markets. The French empire had productive West India colonies, but was very weak in its temperate zone colonies and in trading-posts on the coast of Africa. Colbert's efforts to stimulate the development of trade between Canada and the West Indies, and to build up the slave trade at the coast of Africa indicate that he was awake to the importance of this fact.

We have had occasion to see that his efforts to build up the slave trade bore some fruit, but that they were not sufficiently successful to prevent a serious check to the normal development of the islands. We have seen also that the development of Canada was so slow and its markets so distant and inaccessible, that trade with it proved both unimportant and unprofitable to the West India planter. But in spite of these two very important facts, Colbert persisted in enforcing his policy of excluding all foreigners. The only statistics which have been found for 1669-1683, the period in which the foreigners were excluded so rigourously, rather indicate that as a consequence the development of the islands was retarded. Thus the total population of the French colony of St. Christopher in 1671 was 8120, of which 4468 were slaves, in 1682 it was 7278, of which 4301 were slaves, showing a decrease in both white and slave population.[1] In Guadeloupe the total population in 1671 was 7477, of which 4167 were slaves, and in 1684 it was 8161, of which 4954 were slaves.[2] The increase for thirteen years was thus

[1] Arch. Col., G₁, 471, Recensement de St. Christophe, 1671, 1682.
[2] Ibid., pp. 468, 469, Recensement de la Guadeloupe.

TOWARD THE FRENCH WEST INDIES

very slight. In St. Domingo alone does the development seem to have been rapid. Its population was 1500 in 1669,[3] 6648 (2102 slaves) in 1681.[4] But it was exactly at St. Domingo that Colbert's efforts to exclude the foreigner were not successful. We have had occasion to see that they were trading freely with the Dutch in 1670 and again in 1676. The inference is natural that the other islands suffered from the enforcement of his policy.

Colbert would have replied to this by saying that it was better for the development of a colony to be less rapid and to retain the profit thereof for the mother country, than for it to be more rapid and to let the foreigner share in the profit. He remarked, in fact, in a letter to a colonial administrator that he should not be surprised, if the enforcement of the regulations against the foreigner resulted in *"quelques inconvenients"* to the planters.[5] "I know very well," he wrote to another, "that these innovations [the regulations against foreign traders] will prove at first somewhat irksome, and that people who do not see beyond the present good or ill prove rather difficult to control, when they are forced to make some real sacrifice, but it is precisely at such times that reason, justice and, if necessary, force, should be employed to make them submit."[6]

There are, perhaps, many other features of Colbert's policy which modern economists would be inclined to criticise severely, such as his tendency to pay little heed to the larger economic interests of the colonies by placing the sale of their tobacco in the hands of a monopoly, which destroyed the industry in the Windward Islands and seri-

[3] Charlevoix, II, 82, Mémoire par Ogeron, 1669.

[4] Arch. Nat. Col., C₉, I, Dénombrement gen. de l'isle de la Tortue et Coste de St. Dom. mai, 1681; Arch. Col., G₁, Recensement de St. Domingue.

[5] Clément, III, 2, p. 484, letter to Pélissier, June 21, 1670.

[6] Arch. Nat. Col., B, 2, fol. 135, letter to de Baas, December 21, 1670.

ously hurt it at St. Domingo, or by subjecting colonial sugar to the mercy of French refiners which brought a period of distress from 1670 to 1679, and finally by providing no means to prevent French traders from demanding exorbitant prices for their wares during the period of transition, before there were enough of them for competition to insure fair prices.

But one redeeming feature of Colbert's whole commercial policy, which makes one pardon many a fault, was the fact that it was eminently patriotic. Colbert worked indefatigably for the interests of France and of her people. Personal interests, the interests of commercial companies and of the colonies were all subjected to sacrifices which would insure the realization of his larger plan to increase the wealth of the nation and to lift France to a position of real and abiding power.

It had another, as M. Pigeonneau has pointed out: "Good or bad in theory, in conformity or not with the principles of economy, Colbert's policy had one merit which was more valuable than many: it was successful."[7] Colbert had found the French in 1661, at the beginning of his ministry, in possession of some rich West India colonies, but he saw their whole profit going to enrich the enterprising traders of Holland. Only a few straggling French vessels, three or four in 1662, out of a total of 150, he said, were finding their way to these colonies. At his death in 1683, he had driven the Dutch from the field and more than 200 French vessels were trading annually at Martinique, Guadeloupe and St. Domingo. He had awakened the ports of La Rochelle, Bordeaux and Nantes, especially, to new life, and the West India trade became henceforth a source of much profit to their merchants and

[7] La Politique coloniale de Colbert in *Annales de l'Ecole des Sciences Pol.*, 1886, pp. 487-509.

TOWARD THE FRENCH WEST INDIES

traders and served as a base of their whole commercial development in the eighteenth century.

It is curious to note that in 1664 Colbert viewed with much scepticism the enthusiasm of de Tracy as to the possibilities to be realized in the development of the West India colonies. He wrote in the margin of his letter, dated July 2 of that year: "He (de Tracy) exaggerates the great advantages which the nation may derive from these colonies."[8] In reality their development proved to be the most valuable colonial asset which France possessed and contributed more to her commercial prosperity than any other single branch of trade. And it was in this trade, established after a long and determined fight, that Colbert made his most permanent contribution to the commerce of France.

[8] Arch. Nat. Col., C$_8$, I, Dépêche de M. de Tracy de l'isle de la Martinique, July 2, 1664. In the margin in Colbert's hand, "Il exagère les grands avantages que l'estat peut retirer de ces establis."

BIBLIOGRAPHY

The manuscript material for the history of the French West Indies prior to the ministry of Colbert, treated in Chapter I of the present work, is very meagre. This is to be explained by the fact that these islands were in the hands either of private commercial companies or of proprietors throughout the period. The ministries of Richelieu and of Mazarin were only indirectly connected with their administration. The few documents which remain from the official relations of the government are to be found principally in Paris, at the Foreign Office in vols. IV and V of the section of its archives, *Mémoires et Documents, Amérique*. Their preservation at the Foreign Office is to be explained by the fact that during this period the administration of the colonies fell within the duties of the Secretary of Foreign Affairs. Little has remained to us from the private papers of the Company of St. Christopher (1626-1635) and the Company of the Isles of America (1635-1648). From those of the latter company there does remain a register of the minutes of the meetings of its directors. It is noted below under series F_2 of the Archives Coloniales. The private papers of the several proprietors who held the islands from 1648 to 1664 seem to have completely disappeared. This loss is all the more deplorable because the "Fouquet papers," which undoubtedly contained most valuable material, have also been lost. Attention has been called in Chapters I and II to the important rôle which Nicolas Fouquet played in colonial affairs, and Du Tertre notes the existence of his papers. (See Du Tertre, I, *passim*, and Dampierre, pp. 210-212.) The chances of finding the "Fouquet papers" seem slight and the great gaps in the manuscript material for the

BIBLIOGRAPHY

period will probably remain unclosed. Fortunately, we have some excellent contemporary chronicles, travels and histories which cover the period. A list of them is given below and a critical estimate of their authors and of their value will be found in Dampierre. (See below.) The most important of them all is the general work of Du Tertre, which records the history from the beginning to the year 1667. The more deeply and carefully one studies the period and attempts to analyze Du Tertre's work, the greater grows his admiration for that historian. His history is based upon a careful and impartial study of the best contemporary material, contains an abundance of documents, cited textually, and has an enhanced value from the fact that its author knew the West Indies from travel and residence in them.

For the period from the ascension of Colbert to power, in 1661, to the formation of the West India Company in 1664, which we have preferred to call the period of preparation, our manuscript sources are confined to a few documents at the Foreign Office (noted below under *Mém. et Doc., Amérique*, V) and at the Colonial Office (noted below under series C_{14}, Cayenne), relating to the formation of the Company of Cayenne, and to a few memorials addressed to Colbert during the years 1660-1663, and preserved in the second series of the correspondence of Martinique of which a list is given below.

For the period of the rule of the West India Company (1664-1674), there is a wide gap in our source material occasioned by the disappearance of the company's registers and private papers. Prolonged research has failed to find a trace of them. Their loss is irreparable. For the years 1664-1669, we are forced to rely upon Du Tertre (to the year 1667), upon Moreau de Saint-Méry (*Loix et Constitutions*, see below) and upon a few memorials and letters addressed by the directors of the company to Col-

BIBLIOGRAPHY

bert. A list of the more important of the last named will be found below under the series F_2 of the Archives Coloniales. It will be seen that the list includes also documents for the period 1669-1674. To the knowledge of the writer these papers have never been made use of before. The loss of the company's papers is less serious for the years 1669-1674, because in the former year Colbert came officially in charge of colonial affairs and began at once to direct both the policy of the company and the trend of affairs in the West Indies. He placed all students of the West Indies under lasting obligations to him by commanding the preservation both of his own correspondence and of that of the colonial governors, intendants and other officials.

The material thus preserved by Colbert constitutes our richest collection of source material for the period 1669-1683. It is to be found today at the Archives Nationales, having been deposited there by the Minister of the Colonies in the spring of 1910. Research is long and difficult from the fact that neither a catalogue nor a calendar has ever been made. A very summary inventory in manuscript is the only aid to guide one to the various series and dates of volumes. Pains have been taken, therefore, to give elsewhere in this bibliography enough data about the material to make it easy for a student to find it readily.

To supplement this valuable collection we have yet another in the Archives Coloniales, namely, the *Collection Moreau de Saint-Méry*, consisting of 287 volumes. (A short sketch of Moreau de Saint-Méry will be found in Dampierre, pp. 192-194, and in a paper read by the author of the present work before the American Philosophical Society of Philadelphia and to be found in the proccedings of that society for April, 1912.) The character of the collection is shown by the data given below and is such that it offers to the student of French West India history a mine of information.

BIBLIOGRAPHY

Colbert apparently retained among his own private papers many official documents which are most important for a study dealing with any phase of his ministry. In the Salle de MSS of the Bibliothèque Nationale are to be found two large collections of Colbert's papers, the one known as the *Cinq Cents de Colbert*, and the other, as the *Mélanges de Colbert*. Research in either of these collections is difficult, but is indispensable.

The intimate relations existing between the history of the marine and of the colonies render it obligatory for the investigator to consult the large and rich collection of documents deposited some years ago at the Archives Nationales by the Minister of the Marine. This is especially true, because the administration of the colonies remained in the hands of the Department of the Marine until 1892.

Our researches in the ports of France which carried on trade with the West Indies have been on the whole disappointing. In many cases the admiralty records have completely disappeared. This is especially true for Rouen, Havre and Dieppe. Only unsatisfactory fragments have remained at La Rochelle, while at Bordeaux there are many wide gaps in the material. At Nantes alone was the reward great for many days of patient work. In the case of the last three ports, the material found has been tabulated below and the results utilized in Chapter X above.

This study has been based in large measure upon the manuscript material thus briefly described. Collections of printed documents, such as Moreau de Saint-Méry, *Loix et Constitutions des colonies françaises de l'Amérique sous le Vent* and of printed official correspondence such as the publications of Clément, Depping and Boislisle (see below) have been found convenient for a more careful study of many documents found in manuscript. Dessalles, *Histoire générale des Antilles*, the only general history of the

BIBLIOGRAPHY

French West Indies which we have, may be used as a historical guide. Dessalles' work is based upon the study of some of the material in the Archives Coloniales referred to above, but it was evidently hastily written and its value is much decreased by the failure of the author to cite his sources. Moreover, it treats economic and commercial questions only very superficially, a fact which has considerably reduced its utility for this work. The same criticism holds good for Sidney Daney's *Histoire de la Martinique* and Jules Ballet's *La Guadeloupe.* Of the general works on Colbert, those of Clément and Joubleau are the most valuable. Neither of them treats, however, the question of Colbert's colonial policy except in its broadest outlines. Benoit du Rey has attempted a special study on Colbert's colonial policy, but it is very superficial and inadequate. The author gives no evidence of having ever darkened the door of the Ministry of the Colonies to find material. Peytraud's *L'Esclavage aux Antilles françaises avant 1789,* is the most serious monograph which has been written on any subject connected with the history of the French Antilles. It is to be regretted, however, that M. Peytraud attempted to prove a thesis and was not content to use his valuable data to write a real history of slavery in these islands. M. Chemin-Dupontès in his *Les compagnies de colonisation en Afrique occidentale sous Colbert,* has presented a short, but valuable study of the West India Company and of the two companies of Senegal. In regard to the former company, M. Chemin-Dupontès apparently overlooked the very important documents at the Colonial Office and we have been compelled to disagree with him in some of his conclusions as to the two last named companies. Malvezin's *Histoire du commerce de Bordeaux* is the only work treating the history of any of the several ports engaged in the West India trade that is of much value. It is a work of sound scholarship.

BIBLIOGRAPHY

Of the remaining works included in the bibliography below, there are none of immediate value for our subject, but they have been referred to for their indirect value, which will be readily understood from their titles.

BIBLIOGRAPHIES

There is only one bibliography, properly speaking, for any part of the period covered by this study, namely, Jacques de Dampierre, *Essai sur les sources de l'histoire des Antilles Françaises* (1492-1664), Paris, 1904, being vol. VI of *Mémoires et Documents publiés par la société de l'Ecole des Chartes*.

MANUSCRIPT SOURCES

ARCHIVES COLONIALES

(Deposited at the Archives Nationales. Referred to in notes as Arch. Nat. Col.)

Série A. *Actes du pouvoir souverain, Edits et arrêts,* vol. 24 (1669-1715). A register of regulations of the *conseil d'état,* of the *conseil souverain* of Martinique, incomplete and lacking order in the arrangement of documents.

Série B. *Correspondance générale, Lettres envoyées.* Registers of letters written by the Minister of the Marine to governors, intendants, naval officers, etc., in regard to colonial affairs.

Vol. 1 (1663-1669), vol. 2 (1670), vol. 3 (1671), vol. 4 (1672), vol. 5 (1673), vol. 6 (1674-1675), vol. 7 (1676-1678), vol. 9 (1679-1682), vol. 10 (1683).

Série C. *Correspondance générale, Lettres reçues.* Bound volumes of the original letters and memorials received from colonial governors, intendants, and other officials. The documents are arranged according to their date and locality from which they came.

BIBLIOGRAPHY

C₇ (*Guadeloupe*), vol. 1 (1649-1670), contains only three documents of importance for this study prior to 1669, namely, two letters from du Lion, the governor of Guadeloupe, of April 8 and May 11, 1665, and one of February 17, 1666. The remainder of the volume contains du Lion's correspondence for 1669 and 1670.

Vol. 2 (1671-1673) and vol. 3 (1674-1691) contain du Lion's correspondence and that of his successor, Hinselin, as well as that of de Téméricourt, governor of Marie Galante.

C₈ (*Martinique*), vol. 1 (1663-1676), is of capital importance as it contains the interesting letters of de Baas, governor-general of the islands from 1668 to 1676. The date of the first letter preserved is December 26, 1669. After that date his correspondence seems to have been preserved with but few gaps. The volume contains also two interesting memoirs, one by Gabaret, commander of the three vessels sent in 1670 to drive Dutch traders from the islands, the other, by Pélissier, whose mission to the islands in 1670 is treated in Chapter VI. For the years anterior to December 26, 1669, the volume contains an important memoir of 1663 addressed by d'Estrades to Colbert, an *abrégé* of the letters written by de Tracy from Martinique in 1664, and some extracts of letters written by de Baas in May, 1669, to the West India Company. Vol. 2 (1677-1680) and vol. 3 (1681-1684) are chiefly important for the correspondence of de Blénac, de Baas's successor, and of Patoulet, the active and intelligent intendant-general of the islands.

C₈ (*Martinique*), 2ᵐᵉ Série. A collection of miscellaneous, unbound documents in cartons, classified chronologically and relating to the history of Martinique. Carton 1 (1635-1689) contains a number of documents referred to in Chapters I and II of the present work. Among them the following are the most important: Règlement de M. de Tracy pour le gouvernement, police et commerce de la Martinique, 17 mars 1665; Relation des Isles de l'Amérique Antilles en l'Estat qu'elles estoient l'année 1660; Mémoire contenant les avis et sentiments de différents capitaines de navires voyageurs et

BIBLIOGRAPHY

autres sur les moyens de former des établissements à l'Amérique méridionale, 1661; Mémoire du Sieur Formont pour montrer l'utilité du commerce des Isles et les moyens de le bien établir, 1662; Proposition au Roy d'une nouvelle compagnie à establir pour les Isles françaises de l'Amérique par le Sieur Nacquart, 1663; Relation de ce qui s'est passé aux Isles de l'Amérique, 4 avril 1667; Mémoire du Sieur Bellinzani sur le Commerce des Isles, 12 mars 1672; Mémoire pour M. Bégon par M. Patoulet; and four letters from de Baas bearing dates of March 4, September 21, 1670, January 14, 1671, and August 28, 1674.

C_9 (*St. Domingue*), vol. 1 (1664-1688), contains many interesting letters and memoirs from the hand of Ogeron and of Pouançay, the governors of St. Domingo from 1664 to 1683.

C_9 (*St. Domingue*), 2me Série. Carton 1 (1666-1710) contains a number of memoirs and miscellaneous letters relating to St. Domingo.

C_{10} (*Iles diverses*). A series of twenty-four cartons containing miscellaneous documents, classified chronologically and relating for the most part to the small Windward Islands.

C_{10} (*St. Christophe*). Carton 1 (1627-1689) contains many documents concerning the relations of the English and French at St. Kitts. Of special interest are two memoirs of 1679 entitled: Mémoire particulier présanté à M. le Chevalier de St. Laurent, gouverneur pour le roy de St. Christophe et Isles adjacentes, par Cloche —— directeur du Dom. Royal d'Occident dans les Isles de l'Amérique pour l'interruption du négoce étranger, etc., and Estat où est l'Isle de St. Christophe au sujet de l'interruption du commerce des Etrangers.

C_{10} (*La Grenade*). Carton 1 (1654-1724) contains the passport of the Dutch trader, Drik Jansen, whose case is discussed in Chapter IX.

C_{11} (*Canada*). Vols. 4 and 5 contain some letters and memoirs from the hand of Talon, the intendant of Canada,

BIBLIOGRAPHY

which concern the efforts made to establish trade between Canada and the West Indies.

Série F. *Services divers* (464 registers, 41 cartons).

F_3 (*Collection Moreau de Saint-Méry*, 287 vols.).

Vols. 18-20 (1635-1790). *Historique de la Guadeloupe*. A carefully chosen and arranged set of documents bearing on all phases of Guadeloupe's history. Vol. 18 covers the period 1635-1758.

Vols. 26-38 (1635-1801). *Historique de la Martinique*. Vol. 26 covers the period 1635-1722.

Vol. 39. *Déscription de la Martinique*.

Vols. 52-53 (1627-1784). *Historique de St. Christophe*. Vol. 52 deals with our period.

Vol. 63. *Description de Tabago*.

Vols. 64-65. *Historique de Tabago* (1645-1788).

Vols. 67-72. *Instructions aux Administrateurs* (1665-1788). Vol. 67 deals with period 1665-1701.

Vols. 96-101. *Description de la partie française de St. Domingue*.

Vols. 102-105. *Description de la partie espagnole de St. Domingue*.

Vols. 132-155. *Notes historiques sur St. Domingue par Moreau de Saint-Méry*.

Vol. 157. *Administration des Isles sous le Vent*.

Vols. 161-163. *Culture, manufactures des Colonies*.

Vols. 164-202. *Historique de St. Domingue* (1492-1806). Vol. 164 (1492-1685).

Vols. 221-235. *Code de la Guadeloupe* (1635-1806). Vol. 221 (1635-1699).

Vol. 236. *Recueil des Lois particulières à la Guadeloupe* (1671-1777).

Vol. 237. *Description historique de la Guadeloupe* (1687-1812).

Vols. 247-263. *Code de la Martinique* (1629-1784). Vol. 247 (1629-1672) and vol. 248 (1673-1685).

Vols. 269-281. *Code de St. Domingue* (1492-1789). Vol. 269 (1492-1720).

BIBLIOGRAPHY

(At the Ministère des Colonies, rue Oudinot, Paris. Referred to in notes as Arch. Col.)

Série C$_6$. *Compagnie du Sénégal.* A series of unbound memoirs, letters, accounts, etc., of the first two Companies of Senegal. Carton 1 (1588-1690).

Série C$_{14}$. *Correspondance générale, Lettres reçues, Cayenne.* Vol. 1 contains much interesting material concerning the organization and history of the Company of Cayenne which has been utilized in Chapter II.

Série F$_2$. *Compagnies de Commerce avant 1715.* A series consisting of nineteen cartons and containing some precious fragments which remain from the papers of various commercial companies of the seventeenth and eighteenth centuries. The following are of importance for our study.

Carton 15. *Compagnies des Isles de l'Amérique et Compagnies des Indes Occidentales.* This carton, together with F$_2$, 17, contains the most important documents which remain to us of the West India Company's papers. The most important found in this carton are the following: Mémoire des Directeurs de la Cie. des Indes Occidentales pour rendre raison à Mgr. Colbert de leur conduite et luy faire connoistre l'estat où se trouve ladite Compagnie (1665); Mémoire sur l'estat véritable où se trouve la Cie. des Ind. Occid. (1666); Mémoire Important pour la Cie. des Ind. Occid. pour faire connoistre le besoin quelle a d'estre soutenue (1667); Mémoire sur l'estat des affaires de la Cie. des Ind. Occid. (November, 1667); Estat des vaisseaux qui restent à la Cie. des Ind. Occid. (November, 1667); Mémoire de ce qui a esté fait pour l'établissement et conduite de ladite Compagnie et de ce qu'il reste à faire présentement (by Béchameil, January 15, 1668); Extrait du Mémoire sur l'estat de la Cie. des Ind. Occid. Cie. d'Occident a esté fort avantageuse au Roy et à l'estat, etc.; Procès Verbaux de 1673 et de 1674.

Carton 17. *Compagnies des Indes Occidentales, Edits, ordres du Roy, Mémoires, 1664-1716, 1722.* This carton contains about sixty documents relating to the history of

BIBLIOGRAPHY

the West India Company up to its dissolution in 1674 and many more for the period of its liquidation. Besides manuscript copies of many edicts, *arrêts* and ordinances, the most important of which were published by Moreau de Saint-Méry in his *Constitutions et Loix des Colonies françaises de l'Amérique sous le Vent,* vol. I, the most important documents for our study are the following: Contract d'acquisition de la Martinique vendue par le Sieur Dyel d'Enneval à la Cie. des Ind. Oc. (August 14, 1665); Mémoire de la Cie. des Ind. Oc. sur l'état où elle se trouve et les secours qu'elle attend du Roy (1665); Mémoire des Directeurs de la Cie. des Ind. Occid. à Colbert (1665); Mémoire pour les Isles (1665); Mémoire de ce qui doibt estre payé par les soubstraittans des taxes faicts pour la descharge des recherches de la Chambre de Justice dans les générallitez de ce Royaume à la Cie. des Ind. Oc. (May, 1666); Ordre ou jugement du conseil privé du Roy d'Angleterre sur la requeste de la Cie. des Ind. Oc. de France touchant les navires pris avant la déclaration de la guerre; Estat présent des affaires de la Cie. des Ind. Occid. de France (May, 1666); Mémoire sur les besoins des Isles et Terreferme de l'Amérique et la nécessité de pourvoir à la seureté des vais. de ladite Compagnie, etc. (1665); Mémoire de l'estat présent des Isles et de ce que la Cie. peut faire pour leur conservation (par M. Béchameil, 27 janv. 1667); Mémoire des pièces touchant les navires pris par les Anglais avant la déclaration de Guerre sur la Cie. des Ind. Oc. de France (1667); Sommaire des Matières contenues en ce Mémoire sur lesquelles Mgr. doit prononcer (1667).

Vol. 18. *Histoire abrégée des Compagnies de Commerce qui ont esté établies en France depuis l'année 1626 avec la collection générale de tous les privilèges qui ont esté accordés depuis 1664 tant à ces différentes Compagnies qu'à la Compagnie perpétuelle des Indes, etc., par le Sieur Dernis employé dans les Bureaux de ladite Compagnie,* 1742, pp. 515. (A bound volume in manuscript.)

Vol. 19. *Ordres du Roy et autres Expéditions de la Cie. des Isles de l'Amerique, de 1635 à 1647 avec les Actes*

BIBLIOGRAPHY

d'assemblées tenues par cette compagnie pour ce qui concerne ses affaires particulières depuis 1635 jusqu'en 1648. For full description see Dampierre, p. 219. It is a bound volume in manuscript of 516 pages and has been used in the preparation of Chapter I above.

Série F. *Commerce des Colonies.* Carton 1 (1663-1747) contains one memoir of interest: Mémoire des moyens qu'il faudroit tenir pour empescher aux estrangers le négoce des Isles de l'Amérique et de l'utilité qui en reviendroit à la France (1663).

ARCHIVES DE LA MARINE

(Deposited at the Archives Nationales and referred to in notes Arch. Nat. Mar.)

Didier-Neuville, *Etat Sommaire des Archives de la Marine antérieures à la Revolution,* Paris, 1898.

Inventaire des Archives de la Marine, Sèrie B, Service général, Paris, 1885-1904. The first six volumes have appeared.

Série A_3. Vol. 1 (1182-1671), vol. 2 (1672-1784). A chronological list of edicts, declarations, *arrêts,* ordinances, etc., concerning the marine, commerce and the colonies.

Série B_2. *Correspondance générale: Lettres envoyées, ordres et dépêches.* Vols. 7, 9, 14, 23, 26, 29-31, 34, 36, 38, 40 and 51. This collection is of importance for our subject because it contains many letters addressed to intendants and commissioners of the marine resident in the ports of Havre, Dieppe, St. Malo, Nantes, La Rochelle and Bordeaux and to other officials in regard to colonial affairs.

Série B_3. *Correspondance générale. Lettres reçues* (1628-1789). Vols. 7-10, 13, 15-17, 19, 27, 28, 31, 33, 35, 39, 42. It has been noted elsewhere in this bibliography that the departmental archives are exceedingly meagre in material throwing light upon the commercial relations of the several ports with the West Indies. This fact renders the letters written by the intendants and admiralty officials of those ports all the more valuable. It is these letters which may be consulted in this series.

BIBLIOGRAPHY

Série B₄. *Campagnes 1572 à 1789.* Vols. 5-9 contain material relating to campaigns in the West Indies. Vol. 5 contains some interesting material on the war with Holland (1672-1676).

Série B₇. *Pays étrangers, Commerce et Consulats* (1261 à 1789). The series contains many interesting letters and memoirs to and from consuls and merchants in regard to matters of trade. It is especially rich for the latter half of the reign of Louis XIV for memoirs on the Spanish-American trade. These memoirs almost invariably contain material of interest on the West Indies. Vol. 207, 209, 485-488 have been consulted with profit for the period of Colbert's ministry. Vol. 209 contains a memoir of especial interest entitled, Mémoire sur le commerce d'Espagne aux Indes et voyages des Flottes, by de Bellinzani (January 19, 1679). It was written at the command of Colbert for the instruction of de Seignelay, his son and successor.

ARCHIVES NATIONALES

Série AD. This series contains some material of prime importance to our subject. Divisions vii and xi contain the most complete collections of legislation concerning the colonies which we have found.

Carton AD,vii, 2A. *Colonies en général (1667-1789).* Contains many édits, ordonnances, arrêts, etc., concerning commerce.

Carton AD,vii, 2A, 3. *Canada, St. Domingue, traite des nègres, troupes coloniales (1667-1789).*

Carton AD,vii, 3. *Edits, arrêts, lettres-patentes, police et traite des noirs (1670-1785).*

Carton AD,vii, 5. *Galères et gardes-cotes (1547-1786).*

Carton AD,ix, 384-386. *Compagnies des Indes et du Sénégal (1664-1787).*

Carton AD,xi, 9. *Commerce en général (1617-1688)*;
       37-40, *Grains et farines (1569-1789)*;
       48, *Sucres (1660-1786)*;
       48-51, *Tabac (1629-1789).*

BIBLIOGRAPHY

Série G₇, 1312-1328. *Domaine d'Occident (1673-1714)*. The Domaine d'Occident was a revenue farm created at the dissolution of the West India Company with the right to collect taxes and duties in the islands. Its papers contain the history of the liquidation of the West India Company and contain material which throws light upon the operation of the laws of trade. Cartons 1312-1316 cover the period of our study.

ARCHIVES DU MINISTERE DES AFFAIRES ETRANGERES

Inventaire sommaire des Archives du Départment des Affaires Etrangères, Mémoires et Documents, 2 vols., Paris, 1892-1893.

Mémoires et Documents, Amérique, vols. IV (1592-1660) and V (1661-1690) contain many documents relating to the history of the West Indies during the seventeenth century. The guide, whose title is given above, is easily accessible in all large libraries and makes it unnecessary to give a list of these documents. Attention must be called to the fact, however, that vol. V contains the letters-patent and the list of stockholders of the Company of Cayenne, which have been utilized in Chapter II, as also the instructions of de Tracy of November 19, 1663, and the extremely interesting letter and memoir of Père Plumier on conditions at St. Domingo in 1690.

Mémoires et Documents, France, vols. 1991, 1992, 1993, 2018, all contain memoirs of interest on West India trade. Vol. 2017 contains a table of edicts, *arrêts* and ordinances concerning trade (1619-1759).

BIBLIOTHEQUE NATIONALE, SALLE DE MSS

Charles de la Roncière, *Catalogue de la collection des Cinq Cents de Colbert*, Paris, 1908.

Collection des Cinq Cents de Colbert.
  Vol. 126. Registre contenant diverses expéditions et dépesches dont les minutes sont de la main de Monseigneur,

BIBLIOGRAPHY

1666-1667. This register apparently belongs to the series of registers described above under *Archives Coloniales*, B, and *Archives de la Marine*, B$_2$. Why it was retained in this private collection, we have not been able to find out.

Vol. 199. *Inventaire général et description de tous les vaisseaux appartenans aux sujets du Roy en l'année 1664, en conséquence d'un arrest du Conseil royal des finances donné au rapport de M. Colbert.* The title is self-explanatory. The volume is of capital importance in revealing the condition of the merchant marine at the beginning of Colbert's ministry. Only a relatively small part of the material has ever been utilized.

Vol. 201. *Remarques faictes par le Sieur Arnoul sur la marine d'Hollande et d'Angleterre dans le voyage qu'il en fit en l'année 1670 par ordre de M. Colbert.*

Vol. 203. *Recueil de pièces et mémoires sur la marine, le commerce maritime et les manufactures, 1515-1664.*

Vol. 204. *Registre de dépêches et correspondance de Colbert concernant le commerce extérieur et intérieur* (1669) contains, especially, letters to Colbert de Croissy, French ambassador at London, in regard to the surrender of St. Christopher.

Vol. 207. *Recueil d'arrêts du Conseil d'Etat, du Conseil de Commerce et de privilèges concernant les manufactures, 1661-1669.*

Mélanges de Colbert. A valuable collection of papers and letters addressed to Colbert. The catalogue (in manuscript) for the collection is entirely too summary and is of small aid to research. Another is in preparation and will be published shortly. Letters addressed to Colbert by different directors of the Company of Cayenne and of the West India Company, such as Béchameil, Matharel and Bibaud, and by colonial administrative officers, such as de Chambré and du Lion, and by officials in France, such as Bellinzani and Colbert de Terron, are to be found in vols. 103-114, 116 *bis*, 118 *bis*, 121, 122-124.

Collection Margry relative à l'histoire des colonies et de la Marine française. (Nouvelles acquisitions, 9256-9510.) A large

BIBLIOGRAPHY

collection of miscellaneous documents, some originals, some copies, relating to the history of the French colonies. For a short notice and criticism of Margry and of his plans see Jacques de Dampierre, *Essai sur les sources de l'histoire des Antilles françaises, 1492-1664*, pp. 178 ff. Vols. 9318-9336 relate to the Antilles and to the coast of South America. For the most part we have found only copies of documents of which the originals had already been studied in various other depositories of Paris. Vol. 9325 is an exception, as it contains some biographical data concerning Ogeron, governor of St. Domingo. Vol. 9326 is a copy of Histoire de St. Domingue par de Beauval Segur, a history in manuscript which was probably written shortly after 1750.

Fonds français, vols. 8990-8992. *Mémoires pour l'histoire de l'isle de St. Domingue par le Père J. B. Le Pers, Jesuite*. A most interesting discussion as to the relations and relative merits of this work and of Charlevoix, *L'histoire de l'Isle espagnole* is to be found in H. Lorin, *De prædonibus Insulam S. Dominici celebrantibus* and in J. de Dampierre, *op. cit.*, pp. 158 ff.

Vols. 11315-11318. *Correspondance de Patoulet* (1679-1685). Special attention has been called in Chapter XII to the important work which Patoulet did in the islands as intendant from 1679 to 1681. Letters addressed to him during his sojourn in the islands are of both interest and importance. These volumes contain among others original letters from Seignelay, de Blénac, governor-general of the French West Indies, and Anthoine Allaire, a merchant of La Rochelle. The letters from the last named are of unusual interest in throwing light on some of the practical problems of trade, as Patoulet seems to have carried on regular trade in colonial products with Allaire.

ARCHIVES DEPARTEMENTALES

Archives départementales de la Gironde (at Bordeaux). Of the admiralty records for the port of Bordeaux, the following volumes have been examined:

BIBLIOGRAPHY

Série B. *Registres d'entrées,* vols. 150 (1640-1643), 151 (1643-1645), 153 (1661), 154 (1667), 155 (1669), 156 (1670), 157 (1672), 158 (1682), 159 (1684).

Registres de sorties, vols. 181 (1649), 182 (1651-1653), 183 (1663), 184 (1671), 185 (1672), 186 (1673), 187 (1682), 188 (1683).

Série C. *Chambre de Commerce de Guienne,* vol. 940. Some correspondence concerning armaments for the American colonies.

Carton 1649. Correspondence of the intendants of Guienne . . . in regard to the duty of three per cent on sugar (1649-1772).

Archives départementales de la Charente Inférieure (at La Rochelle). Unfortunately the Admiralty registers for the port of La Rochelle seem to have been lost. Only a fragment of a register bearing the date 1682-1696, classified as B, 235, has been found. A large number of unclassified papers consisting of passports, lists of crews, certificates of inspection of vessels, still remain and contain valuable data, but they are in such wild disorder and were so damaged by dampness before being deposited in their present locality that it is almost impossible to conduct any satisfactory methodical researches. The task proved too gigantic to search at haphazard through all the mass of unclassified papers. Some of them were examined and the results are stated in Chapter X above. Unfortunately the archives of the Chamber of Commerce of La Rochelle do not bear dates anterior to 1719.

Archives départementales de la Loire Inférieure (at Nantes). Léon Maitre, *Inventaire sommaire des Archives départementales antérieures à 1790, Loire Inférieure, Séries C et D,* Nantes, 1898.

The Admiralty records for the port of Nantes offer a rich unexplored field. They are very complete for the second half of Louis XIV's reign. It was apparently planned to keep four sets of registers: one for vessels coming (1) from other ports of Brittany ("province"), (2) from ports of France outside of Brittany ("hors province"), (3) from

BIBLIOGRAPHY

foreign ports ("étranger"), and (4) from colonial markets ("long cours"). Records of sailings were to be kept after the same classification. Registers were also kept of declarations made by captains or proprietors of vessels for the purpose of obtaining passports. In actual practice this classification was not followed for it is not very unusual to find the sailing or arrival of a vessel engaged in colonial commerce ("long cours") entered in a register bearing the title "hors province" or "étranger."

Unfortunately for the present study the registers of sailings have not been preserved for the period anterior to 1673, nor the registers of arrivals anterior to 1694.

Série B, 1. *Registre d'enregistrement des passe-ports pour province, hors province et étranger* (January-May, 1673).

Ibid., 2. *Idem* (May 10, 1673—5 March, 1674).

Ibid., 3. *Déclaration de Sorties, étranger (1674-1675)*, including registration of passports for ports of France, foreign European ports and colonial ports.

Ibid., 4 (1675-1677), 5 (1677-1679), 6 (1679-1685). *Idem*.

ARCHIVES DE LA CHAMBRE DE COMMERCE DE NANTES

(Léon Maitre's *Inventaire sommaire* referred to in the preceding section includes under series C an admirable catalogue of these archives.)

Série C, 722, 1652-1791. *Cies. des Indes Occidentales et de St. Domingue.*

Ibid., 724, 1671-1789. *Edits, ordonnances . . . portant règlements pour l'entrée et la sortie des Marchandises venant des Isles françaises de l'Amérique et du Canada . . . listes d'arrêts concernant les isles d'Amérique de 1665 à 1714,* etc.

Ibid., 730, 1670-1789. *Industrie et commerce des sucres raffinés.*

Ibid., 733 and 734, 1671-1790. Contain many documents concerning the production, refining and commerce of sugar.

Ibid., 735, 1670-1789. *Commerce extérieur avec les isles.*

BIBLIOGRAPHY

PRINTED SOURCES

COLLECTIONS OF LAWS, LETTERS, MEMOIRS AND OTHER CONTEMPORARY DOCUMENTS

Petit de Viévigne (Jacques), *Code de la Martinique,* St. Pierre (Martinique), 1767.

Moreau de Saint-Méry, *Loix et Constitutions des Colonies Françaises de l'Amérique sous le Vent,* Paris, 1784-1790, 6 vols. Vol. I.

Clément (Pierre), *Lettres, Instructions et Mémoires de Colbert,* Paris, 1861-1882, 10 vols. Vol. III, part 2.

Depping (G. B.), *Correspondance Administrative sous le règne de Louis XIV,* Paris, 1850-1851, 4 vols.

Boislisle (A. M. de), *Correspondance des contrôleurs généraux des finances avec les intendants des provinces,* Paris, 1874-1897, 3 vols.

Bréard (Charles et Paul), *Documents relatifs à la marine Normande et à ses Arméments aux XVIe et XVIIe siècles pour le Canada, l'Afrique, les Antilles, le Brésil et les Indes,* Rouen, 1899.

CONTEMPORARY CHRONICLES, HISTORIES, ETC.

Bouton (Le Père Jacques), *Relation de l'etablissement des Français depuis l'an 1635 en l'isle de la Martinique l'une des Antilles de l'Amérique,* Paris, 1640.

Coppier (Guillaume), *Histoire et Voyage des Indes Occidentales,* Lyon, 1645.

Pacifique de Provins (Le Père), *Relation du Voyage des Isles de l'Amérique,* Paris, 1646.

Du Tertre (Le R. P. Jean-Baptiste), *Histoire générale des isles de St. Christophe, de la Guadeloupe, de la Martinique et autres dans l'Amérique,* Paris, 1654.

Idem., *Histoire générale des Antilles habitées par les François,* Paris, 1667-1671, 4 vols. in three. It is to this edition that all references are made in the notes.

BIBLIOGRAPHY

Pelleprat (Pierre), *Relation des PP. de la Compagnie de Jésus dans les Isles et dans la Terre Ferme de l'Amérique Méridionale*, Paris, 1655.

St. Michel (Maurile de), *Voyage des Isles Camercanes en l'Amérique qui font partie des Indes Occidentales*, Mans, 1652.

Rochefort (César de), *Histoire naturelle et morale des Antilles de l'Amérique*, Rotterdam, 1658. Second edition, 1665. It is to the latter that references are made.

Biët (Antoine), *Voyage de la France Equinoxiale en l'isle de Cayenne entrepris par les Français en l'année MDCLII*, Paris, 1664.

Recueil des Gazettes: nouvelles ordinaires et extraordinaires, Paris. Files consulted for years 1664-1675.

La Barre (Lefebvre de), *Description de la France équinoctiale cy-devant appellée Guyanne*, Paris, 1666.

Ibid., *Relation de ce qui s'est passé dans les Isles et Terre Ferme de l'Amérique*, Paris, 1671, 2 vols.

Delbée (le Sieur), *Journal du Voyage du Sieur Delbée, commissaire général de la Marine aux Isles, dans la coste de Guinée pour l'etablissement du commerce en ces pays en l'année 1669*, in vol. II, 347-494, of preceding.

Savary (Jacques), *Le parfait négociant*, Paris, 1675.

SPECIAL WORKS ON COLBERT

Joubleau (Félix), *Etude sur Colbert, ou Exposition du Système d'Economie Politique suivi en France de 1661 à 1683*, Paris, 1856, 2 vols.

Clément (Pierre), *Histoire de Colbert et son administration*, Paris, 1874, 2 vols.

Neymarck (Alfred), *Colbert et son temps*, Paris, 1877, 2 vols.

Pigeonneau (H.), *La Politique Coloniale de Colbert* in *Annales de l'École des Sciences Politiques*, 1886.

Bénoit du Rey (E.), *Recherches sur la politique coloniale de Colbert*, Paris, 1902.

Chemin-Dupontès (Paul), *Les Compagnies de colonisations en Afrique occidentale sous Colbert*, Paris, 1903. A reprint

BIBLIOGRAPHY

with revision and many additions of the article which appeared in the *Questions Diplomatiques et Coloniales* of October 15, 1899, under the title of *L'Afrique Occidentale sous Colbert.*

SPECIAL WORKS ON THE ANTILLES

Charlevoix (Pierre-François-Xavier), *Histoire de l'Isle Espagnole ou de St. Domingue,* Paris, 1730-1731, 2 vols.
Labat (Le R. P.), *Nouveau Voyage aux Isles de l'Amérique,* Paris, 1722, 6 vols.
Ducœurjoly (S. J.), *Manuel des Habitants de St. Domingue,* Paris, 2 vols.
Renouard (Félix), *Statistique de la Martinique,* Paris, 1822, 2 vols.
Malo (Charles), *Histoire d'Haiti depuis sa découverte jusqu'en 1824,* Paris, 1824.
Placide (Justin), *Histoire politique et statistique de l'ile d'Haiti,* Paris, 1806.
Boyer-Peyreleau (E. E.), *Les Antilles Françaises particulièrement la Guadeloupe, depuis leur découverte jusqu'au 1er janv. 1823,* Paris, 1823.
Daney (Sidney), *Histoire de la Martinique depuis la colonisation jusqu'en 1815,* Fort Royal (Martinique), 1846, 6 vols.
Dessalles (Adrien), *Histoire Générale des Antilles,* Paris, 1847, 5 vols.
Margry (Pierre), *Belain d'Esnambuc et les Normands aux Antilles,* Paris, 1863.
Idem., *Origines Françaises des Pays d'outre-mer, Les Seigneurs de la Martinique,* three articles in *Revue Maritime et Coloniale,* vol. 58, pp. 28-50, 276-305, 540-547.
Ballet (Jules), *La Guadeloupe, Renseignements sur l'histoire, la flore, la faune, la géologie, la mineralogie, l'agriculture, le commerce, l'industrie, etc.,* Basse Terre (Guadeloupe), 1890-1902. Five volumes have appeared. It is to be complete in twelve.
Guët (Isidore), *Le colonel François de Collart et la Martinique de son Temps,* Vannes, 1893.

BIBLIOGRAPHY

Idem., *Origines des Petits Antilles* . . . 1609-1674, a series of articles which appeared in the *Revue Historique de l'Ouest*, 1897-1899.

Lorin (Henri), *De Prædonibus insulam Sancti Dominici celebrantibus sæculo septimo decimo*, Paris, 1895.

Peytraud (L.), *L'Esclavage aux Antilles Françaises avant 1789*, Paris, 1897.

Saint-Yves (G.), *Les Campagnes de Jean d'Estrées dans la mer des Antilles, 1676-1678*, Paris, 1900. (Reprint from the *Bulletin de géographie historique et descriptive*, no. 2, 1899.)

Idem., *Les Antilles Françaises et la Correspondance de l'Intendant Patoulet*, Paris, 1902. A short pamphlet (Bib. Nat. Lk. 12, 1516), giving an account of the correspondence in Bib. Nat. MSS., Fonds français, 11315, referred to above.

Vaissièrre (Pierre de), *Saint-Domingue (1629-1789), La Société et la vie Créoles sous l'Ancien Régime*, Paris, 1909.

SPECIAL WORKS ON THE SEVERAL PORTS ENGAGED IN THE WEST INDIA TRADE

Malvezin (Théophile), *Histoire du Commerce de Bordeaux depuis les Origines jusqu'à nos jours*, Bordeaux, 1892, 4 vols. Vol. II.

Garnault (Emile), *Le Commerce Rochelais au XVIIIe Siècle*, La Rochelle, 1887-1891, 3 vols. Vol. II.

Le Beuf (E. B.), *Du Commerce de Nantes, Son Passé, Son Avenir*, Nantes, 1857.

Parfouru (Paul), *Les Irlandais en Bretagne aux XVIIe et XVIIIe Siècles*, article in *Annales de Bretagne*, vol. IX, 524-533.

Maître (Léon), *Situation de la Marine marchande du Comté de Nantes d'après l'enquête de 1664*, in *Annales de Bretagne*, vol. XVII, 326-343.

Gabory (Emile), *La Marine et le Commerce de Nantes au XVIIe Siècle et au Commencement du XVIIIe*, 1661-1715. (Reprint from *Annales de Bretagne*, XVII, 1-44, 235-290, 341-398.)

BIBLIOGRAPHY

Augeard (Eugène), *Etude sur la Traite des Noirs avant 1790 au point de vue du Commerce Nantais,* Nantes, 1901.
Borely (A. E.), *Histoire de la Ville du Havre,* Havre, 1880-1881, 3 vols.

SPECIAL WORKS ON ARTICLES OF COMMERCE

Boizard (E.) et Tardieu (H.), *Histoire de la Législation des Sucres,* 1664-1891, Paris, 1891.
Sabatier (Antoine), *La Ferme du Tabac,* Lille, 1905. (Reprint from the *Bulletin de la Société archéologique, historique et artistique,* November, 1905.)

GENERAL WORKS

Savary (Jacques), *Dictionnaire Universel de Commerce,* Paris, 1732, 4 vols.
Véron de Forbonnais (F.), *Recherches et Considérations sur les Finances de France depuis l'Année 1595 jusqu'à l'année 1721,* Basle, 1758, 2 vols.
Gouraud (Charles), *Histoire de la Politique commerciale de la France et de son Influence sur le Progrès de la Richesse publique depuis le Moyen Age jusqu'à nos Jours,* Paris, 1854, 2 vols.
Duval (Jules), *Les Colonies et la Politique coloniale de la France,* Paris, 1864.
Ségur-Dupeyron (P. de), *Histoire des Négotiations commerciales et Maritimes aux XVIIe et XVIIIe Siècles,* Paris, 1872-1873, 3 vols.
Berlioux (Etienne-Félix), *Andre Brüe ou l'Origine de la Colonie Française du Sénégal,* Paris, 1874.
Marcel (Gabriel), *Le Surintendant Fouquet, Vice-Roi de l'Amérique.* (Reprint from the *Revue de Géographie,* 1885.)
Norman (C. B.), *Colonial France,* London, 1886.
Pigeonneau (H.), *Histoire du Commerce de la France,* Paris, 1887-1889, 2 vols.
Deschamps (Léon), *Histoire de la Question Coloniale en France,* Paris, 1891.
Vignon (Louis), *L'Expansion de la France,* Paris, 1891.

BIBLIOGRAPHY

Leroy-Beaulieu (Paul), *De la Colonisation chez les peuples modernes,* Paris, fifth edition, 1902. (A sixth edition appeared in 1908.)

Bonnassieux (Pierre), *Les grandes Compagnies de Commerce,* Paris, 1892.

Chailley-Bert (J.), *Les Compagnies de Commerce sous l'Ancien Régime,* Paris, 1898.

Martin (Germain), *La grande Industrie sous le Règne de Louis XIV,* Paris, 1899.

Gaffarel (Paul), *Les Colonies Françaises,* Paris, 1899.

INDEX

Acadia, sugar refiners of Guadeloupe and Martinique propose establishment of trade with 220
Africa, Dutch on western coast of, 288; French West India Company's possessions on, 288; ceded to private company, 288; du Casse appointed governor at western coast of, 289; monopoly of Company of Senegal in, 293. *See also* Company of Senegal, Company of Guinea, Slaves, Slave trade, etc.
Alou, Sieur de l', sent to St. Christopher in command of troops, 136.
André, Jean, Baron de Woltrogue, associated with Carolof in Slave trade 118
Antigua, attacked by French, 139; capture of, 139; trade of Sieur Cartier with, 157; trade with Dutch, 207.
Ardres, W. I. Co. sends vessels to trade with king of, 167; king grants privileges of slave trade, 167.
Arguin, captured by du Casse 289

Baas, de, succeeds de Clodoré at Martinique, 152; governor-general of the French West Indies, 155; accused of favouring trade with Dutch, 158; complains of W. I. Co.'s price of slaves, 162; letter to Colbert regarding supply of salt beef, 175; receives instructions from W. I. Co. concerning trade with foreigners (1668), 184, 188-189; commanded by Colbert to enforce strictly regulations against foreign traders, 186; receives letters from Colbert concerning same, 187, 187-188, 190, 191; warns Colbert exclusion of foreigners will bring suffering to planters, 189; writes Colbert of case of trade with foreigners, 190-191; complains of de Gabaret's severity toward Dutch traders, 197, 198; writes sarcastic letter to Colbert concerning same, 198-199; promises to be severe with Dutch, 199; comments upon effect of de Gabaret's sojourn in W. I., 200; appealed to by Ogeron for aid at St. Domingo, 202; receives letter of encouragement from Colbert, 207; instructed to maintain patrol against foreign traders, 208; permits provisions to be brought from Martinique and rebuked by Colbert, 210; correspondence concerning trade with foreigners discussed, 210-215; trades with Dutch at Curaçao, 211-212; accusation against discussed, 212-215; character, 215; dis-

INDEX

likes private traders and favours W. I. Co.'s monopoly, 227; receives letters from Colbert concerning same, 228-229; complains of high prices demanded by French traders, 228; receives instructions regarding freedom of trade, 232; complains of varying policy, 232; writes of overproduction and depreciation of sugar, 267; writes concerning establishment of refineries, 272; receives instructions regarding same, 273; writes in regard to slave trade, 287; comments upon importance of salt beef, 312; instructed to encourage trade with Canada, 317; opposes Colbert's policy of excluding Irish beef, 321-323; permits trade with English, 323.

Barbadoes, trade of French with, 191; provisions imported into Martinique from, 209; indentured servants at, 282; trade with permitted by de Baas, 323.

Bayonne, duties imposed upon sugar at 267
Béchameil, a stockholder of Company of Cayenne and of W. I. Co., 80; becomes director of latter and specially charged by Colbert with management, 83; reports plans of company, 83-84; receives news concerning Dutch and West India trade, 84; suggests plan to send supplies to West Indies, 85; writes of urgency in sending vessels, 102; plans to send 200 soldiers to Martinique, 109; appeals to Colbert for aid, 111; asks for convoys, 113; suggests closing subscriptions, 152; favours private traders, 153-154; explains company's failures and advocates reforms, 156.

Bégon, intendant, writes joint memoir with St. Laurent concerning trade with foreigners 223
Beinchk, Jacob, in command of Dutch squadron, attacks Marie Galante, 246; attempts to win over colony at St. Domingo, 246 and note 72; destroys French vessels at Petit Goave, 246.

Bellefond, Villant de, makes treaty for W. I. Co. on coast of Guinea 285
Bellinzani, writes memoir concerning W. I. trade, 244; letter concerning monopoly of tobacco, 254; sketch of official career, connection with W. I. Co. and trade, dishonesty, indictment of Jacques Savary against, death in Bastille, etc., 298-299.

Berruyer, a director of Company of the Isles of America 23
Berthelot, a director of Company of Cayenne and of W. I. Co., 68, 75, 80, 83.

Blénac, de, governor-general, receives instructions regarding trade with foreigners at St. Christopher, 192, 218; arrives at Martinique, 218; proposes treaty with English at St. Christopher regarding trade, 218; ordered to exclude foreign traders, 219; issues ordinance in regard to same, 219-220; writes Colbert concerning, 223; at St. Domingo, 255; estimates num-

INDEX

ber of slaves imported, 300; encourages trade with Canada, 317-318; instructed to admit Irish salt beef, 325.

Bibaud, a director in Company of Cayenne and W. I. Co., 66, 77, 83; writes Colbert in regard to state of latter company, 77-78.

Boisseret, de, instructed by Houel to purchase Guadeloupe 42

Bonaire, proposal to establish trade in live stock with 56

Bouchardeau, Sir, assists in organization of Company of Cayenne..64

Bordeaux, development of trade with West Indies, 1650-1683, 236-238; exports to West Indies, imports from, 238; admiralty records of, 236-237 and bibliography; tonnage and log of vessels engaging in W. I. trade, 237-238; sugar refineries at, 239; trade with West Indies interrupted by Dutch war, 244-245; duties imposed upon sugar at, 267; importance of W. I. trade in eighteenth century, 238-239.

Boston, a ketch from trades at Martinique, 210; trade with proposed by colonial refiners, 221; character of settlers according to French, 222.

Bouchet, a director of W. I. Co................................83

Boutet, Claude, granted monopoly of tobacco in France 225

Bounties, offered on French salt beef, 209, 320; on slaves, 286.

Bourg, du, sent to coast of Guinea by W. I. Co...............165-168

Brandy, article of export from Bordeaux, 238; from La Rochelle, 240; Nantes, 241; made from sugar-cane and exported from West Indies to Canada, 318.

Brazil, cassonades imported into Provence from, 263; duties on, 266.

Breda, treaty of 142

Brunet, a director of W. I. Co., correspondence with Colbert, 173, 174, 175; buys salt beef and live stock for W. I. trade, 175, 319-320.

Buc, du, clerk of W. I. Co., encounters rebellion at Martinique....92

Buccaneers, on northern coast of St. Domingo 202

Butter, Irish, article of export from Nantes 241

Cacao, cultivation of at St. Domingo instead of tobacco 258

Cadiz, vessel from Nantes calls at on way to Martinique 219

Cuhuzac, in command of a fleet to protect French at St. Christopher, 18; forces English to respect treaty, but leaves colony at mercy of Spaniards, 19.

Calle, de la, chief agent of W. I. Co. at Martinique 133, 157

Canada, occupied by W. I. Co., 118; trade of company with, 112, 116; assets of company in, 146; efforts to establish trade between West Indies and, 220, 221; cultivation of tobacco forbidden in, 252; Colbert attempts to find supply of lumber in, 329; explanation of failure of trade, 318, 319.

INDEX

Canonville, district of Martinique, scene of rebellion 106
Cape Verde Islands, trade of W. I. Co. with 86, 116, 131, 146, 148
Caribs, Colbert urges incitement of against the Dutch, 198; slave trade with, 303.
Carolof, makes contract with W. I. Co. for slave trade, 117, 285; terms of contract and privileges, 118; sent to Guinea by W. I. Co., 165; establishes trade relations with king of Ardres, 167; arrives at Guadeloupe with cargo of slaves, 172.
Cartier, Sieur, general agent of W. I. Co. in islands, 156; proves corrupt, 157; accepts bribes from Dutch traders, 157, 212, 285, 327.
Casepilote, district of Martinique, scene of rebellion 104
Cassonades, *see* Sugar.
Cassava, planted at Cayenne, 65; cultivation of abandoned at Martinique, 261; bread made from as food, 310, 311, 312.
Casse, du, appointed governor of Senegal, captures Arguin from Dutch, occupies Gorée, quells rebellion on coast, 289; services to Company of Senegal, 292; in charge of company's affairs at Martinique, 303.
Cayenne, French settlement at, 2; population of in 1660 and 1664, 65, 67; first expedition of Company of Cayenne to, 77; trade of W. I. Co. with, 86, 112, 131, 147, 148, 177; captured by English, 142; governor ordered to enforce regulations against foreign traders, 185; trade with Bordeaux, 237; recaptured by French, 247; slave trade at, 304.
Cérillac, de, proprietor of Grenada, 44; cedes it to W. I. Co., 73, 74, note 8.
Champigny, cedes possessions to W. I. Co......................73
Chambré, de, general agent of W. I. Co., writes of first fleet, 85-86; sails for West Indies, 86; at Martinique, 89; Guadeloupe, 90; St. Christopher, 91; writes of scarcity of provisions at Guadeloupe, 99; opinion regarding rebellions at Martinique, 107; superintends removal of English from St. Christopher, 127; assists in regulating trade at Martinique, 138; recalled, 156.
Chemin-Dupontès, statements regarding W. I. Co. refuted, 75, 119; quoted, 292; estimates number of slaves imported by Company of Senegal, 296; same discussed, 297-298.
Clodoré, de, governor of Martinique, sails for West Indies, 86; inauguration, 87; puts down rebellion, 92-93; character, 93; commended by Colbert and company, 94; pacifies spirit of rebellion, 101-102; grows alarmed, 102; crushes rebellion at Martinique, 104-106; prepares for war with English, 124; quells another rebellion in Martinique, 132-135; aids in regulating trade, 138; fights at Antigua, 139; dispute with de

INDEX

La Barre, 140; commands at St. Pierre, 141; returns to France, 152.

Colbert, on condition of French commerce, 2; plans inquest of 1664, 2; estimates number of vessels in merchant marine of France and other countries, 2-3; official career and activity sketched, 7-8; decides to organize East and West India Companies, 9; attitude toward same, 10; authorizes many commercial companies, 12; attitude toward, 12-13; problem in West Indies, 50-51; alarmed over affairs at Martinique, 58; sends de Tracy to reclaim West Indies for crown, 58-59; commends de Tracy for conduct, 61; approves plan to organize Company of Cayenne, 62, 66; plans W. I. Co., 68; letter to German princes concerning company, 71, note 5; appealed to by W. I. Co., 78; forces subscriptions to both companies, 79; appeals to king to support both, 79; subscribes personally to W. I. Co., 81; task assigned company, 83; frames legislation to exclude Dutch traders, 83; provides small source for company, 98; authorizes company to borrow, 98; opens royal treasury, 102-103; partially successful in excluding Dutch, 108; subscribes liberally to W. I. Co., 109-110; receives memoir concerning company, 116-117; plan of uniting East and West India Companies, 122; neglects W. I. Co. during war, 144-145; makes partial provision of funds, 145; subscribes funds, 147; opposes continuance of Dutch trade in islands, 150; also restoration of proprietary rule, 150; attitude toward W. I. Co. at close of English war defined and discussed, 151-154; has company declare first dividend, 156; instructions to de Baas, 156; correspondence with Pélissier, 159; instructions to same defining duty of W. I. Co., 159-161; policy of complete freedom of trade to all French traders, 160; advises encouragement of early marriages, 160; urges reduction of amount of sugar produced in islands, 161; instructs Pélissier to favour private traders, and exclude foreign traders, 161; correspondence with Pélissier, 161; urges colonies to engage in commerce, 162; orders census made, protects private traders, considers means of perfecting manufacture of tobacco and sugar, orders price of slaves lowered, 162; appreciates private traders, restricts W. I. Co.'s commerce, reasons for same, 163; decides to abandon company, 164, 175, 176; plans slave trade with Spaniards, 171; attempts to exclude Irish salt beef from W. I. trade and correspondence with Brunet, 173-175; orders de Tracy to exclude Dutch traders, 182; refuses to compromise, 184; forbids W. I. Co. to grant passports to foreigners, 183; reserves right of granting passports, 184; commands all governors to enforce regulations against

INDEX

foreign traders, 185-186; correspondence with de Baas on same, 186, 188, 189, 191-192, 197-198, 214-215; commands W. I. Co. to supply slaves and live stock, 190; plans trade with Spanish Main at Grenada, 192; exceptions regarding foreign trade, 192-193; meaning of system of excluding foreigners, 193; explains why trade with Spaniards should be prohibited, 193; decides to maintain patrol in islands, 195; urges drastic measures against Dutch and explains, 198; replies to objections of English, 199-200; protests against conduct of Dutch traders at St. Domingo, 203; orders de Gabaret to quell rebellion and destroy Dutch vessels at St. Domingo, 203; commends Ogeron, 205; successful in fight against Dutch, 206-207; refuses special privileges to colonial ships, 208; fails in attempts to exclude Irish beef from islands, 208-210; rebukes de Baas for trade with English, 210; rebukes du Lion for insubordination and conduct, 213-214; censures de Baas, 214; unable to prevent trade with English at St. Christopher, 218; refuses to honour claims of Dutch and rebukes Patoulet for failure to enforce regulations, 219; rejects proposal of trade with New England, 222; results of fight against foreign traders, 223-224; policy regarding freedom of trade defined and discussed, 225-236; forces reduction of taxes levied on private traders, 225-226; grants passports to private traders, 226; protects their freedom and removes restrictions of trade, 228; writes de Baas concerning same, 228-229; attitude toward monopolies defined and discussed, 229 ff.; key to understanding colonial policy, 233-236; rise of private trader, 236; results of work at Bordeaux, La Rochelle and Nantes, 239 ff.; tariff of 1664, 251; legislation regarding tobacco, results, 251 ff.; builds up sugar refining industry in France, 262-263; aids enterprise personally, 262; high duties on foreign refined sugar, 263-266; writes concerning same, 266; offers drawback on French refined sugar, 262; wishes destruction of Dutch refiners, 269; attitude toward limiting production of sugar defined, 268-269; toward re-exportation of raw sugar, 269-271; policy toward colonial refiners, 273 ff.; results of, 279-280; encourages importation of indentured servants, 282; plans for slave trade, 286; creates monopoly for same, 288; protects Company of Senegal, 295; attitude toward reorganization of company, recruits stockholders, 301; results of policy regarding slave-trade, 308-309; efforts to build up trade between Canada and West Indies, 315-317; failure explained, 319; fight against Irish salt beef, 319-320; failure and refusal to renew fight, 323-325; efforts to supply live stock and lumber from Canada futile, 329; removes restraints

INDEX

on trade, 330; principles underlying colonial policy, 332; criticism of, 332-339; general results, 338-339.

Colbert de Terron, intendant at Brouage, and Company of the North, 12; becomes stockholder in Company of Cayenne and W. I. Co., 80; warns Colbert of de La Barre's character, 129; receives letter from Colbert, 226.

Commerce, state of in France, 1-6; Colbert's policy regarding, 7 ff.; attempts to establish with West Indies, 36-40; state of, 46-50; further plans to establish with West Indies, 53, 55; state of, 110-111, 113, 142, 148, 156, 157; W. I. Co. attempts to establish with Guinea, 165-173; regulations governing, 185; with West Indies traced statistically, 236 ff.; state of, 244-247; between Canada and West Indies encouraged, 318.

Companies, Commercial, Colbert's attitude toward, 12 ff., 233. *See also* Company of Cayenne, Company of the Isles of America, Company of the Levant, Company of the North, Company of the Pyrenees, Company of Senegal, West India Company.

Company of Cayenne, plan of organization approved by Colbert, 62; chief object, 63; stockholders, 66; letters-patent and first expedition to Cayenne, 66; makes treaty with Dutch, 67; serves as basis for W. I. Co., 75-77, 83.

Company of Guinea, organization and privileges 308

Company of the Isles of America, organization, letters-patent and work, 23-24; promotes cultivation of sugar-cane, 31-35; attempts to build up trade and results, 36-40; failure and causes, 40-43; sells islands to proprietors, 42.

Company of the Levant, organization 12-13

Company of the North, established by Colbert, 12; authorized to charter vessels from W. I. Co., 176.

Company of the Pyrenees, organized by Colbert 12-13

Company of St. Christopher, organized, 15; letters-patent, 16; sends vessels to St. Christopher, 16-17; appeals to Richelieu for protection against Dutch traders, 22; failure, 23.

Company of Senegal, buys W. I. Co.'s possessions in Senegal, 178; equips vessels at Dieppe, 243-244; urged to establish sugar refinery at Martinique, 275; history, 288-298; trade in Africa, 289; appoints du Casse governor, 289; makes conquests, 290; contracts to furnish slaves to West Indies, 291; character, personnel and capital, 292; enlarged, 292; terms of contract, 293; activity, 293-294; losses and misfortunes, 294-295; unsuccessful efforts to prevent bankruptcy, 295; supposed bounties paid to, 296; number of slaves carried to West Indies, 296-301; reorganization, 301; capital and privileges, 302; establishes agents, 303; number of slaves imported into West Indies, 304-308; failure to satisfy contract and

INDEX

reasons, 304-305, 307; debts owed to, 305; monopoly partly revoked, 308-309.

Contraband trade, *see* Foreign trade.

Cotton, cultivation ordered in islands, 30; cultivated at Cayenne, 65; imported at Bordeaux from West Indies, also at Nantes, 238, 242; cultivated instead of tobacco, 258; proves less profitable than sugar-cane, 261; cultivation encouraged by Colbert, 269.

Curaçao, proposal to establish trade in live stock with, 56; sends oxen and horses to West Indies, 189, 326, 327; slave trade with Spanish Main, 192-193; with French, 285-286; exportation of live stock forbidden, 327.

Currency, tobacco serves as 250

Cussy, de, succeeds de Pouançay, as governor of St. Domingo ...257

Dalibert, a director in W. I. Co. 83

Darriet, a merchant of Bordeaux, engaged in W. I. trade 238-239

Dartiagne, convicted of illicit trade 190

Delbée, Sieur, records expedition to Guinea and facts concerning slave trade 165, 169

Desirade, becomes a proprietary, 43; ceded to W. I. Co., 73.

Dieppe, trade with West Indies, 236, 242-243; Company of Senegal equips vessels at, 243-244; trade in indentured servants, 281.

Domaine d'Occident, revenue farm, 178; attempts to exclude foreign traders, 215-216; plan to unite with Company of Senegal, 301.

Drawbacks, on sugar refined in France 264-265

Dunkerque, trade with West Indies 157

Dupas, Sieur, judge at St. Christopher, orders confiscation of foreign merchandise 216

Dutch, as carriers and traders in France, 3; success in trade with East Indies, Baltic, West Indies, etc., 9; begin trade at St. Christopher, 20-22; service as traders, 21; trade with French colonies becomes regular, 22-23, 29; importance, 39-40; settle St. Martin conjointly with French, 43; control trade with French islands, 45-50; explanation of superiority as traders, 48-50; yield Cayenne to French, 67; barred from French islands by Colbert, 83; attempt to embarrass W. I. Co., 84-85; furnish capital for sugar mills at Guadeloupe, 91-92; sell vessels to W. I. Co., 94; cry of *Vive les Hollandais!* raised at Martinique, 101; suspend trade with French colonies, 108; trade with W. I. Co., 113; aid Guadeloupe, 125; permitted to trade in West Indies, 138, 150; aid French in war, 140; opposed by Colbert, 150, 153; bribe officials in order to trade,

INDEX

157; sell slaves to French, 162, 172; trade in Guinea, 166-168; attempt to prevent W. I. Co. from trading with king of Ardres, 168; slave trade with Spaniards, 171; Colbert renews fight against, 182 ff.; carry on illicit trade, 184; St. Eustatius specially watched by Colbert, 186-187; continue to import slaves and live stock, 188; prohibited from doing so, 189-190; contraband trade at St. Eustatius, 191; trade with Spanish Main, 192-193; Colbert's long fight against, 195-224; instructions to de Gabaret, 196; captured by French patrol, 196-197; Colbert plans to drive from West Indies, 198, 199-200; stir up rebellion at St. Domingo, 201 ff.; affected by de Gabaret's sojourn in West Indies, 206-207; de Baas trades with Curaçao, 211-212; trade with French islands, 212-215, 217, 218-219; driven out, 223; obtain raw sugar at St. Malo and Nantes, 240; prey upon French commerce, 244; war, 244-248, 288; attack French West Indies, 246-247; emigrate from Brazil to Guadeloupe and cultivate sugar-cane, 260; import slaves into French islands, 283-286; surrender Gorée and Arguin to French, 288-289.

East India Company, organized, 8; importance, 9-11; subscriptions, 79; enjoys monopoly, 231.

Embargo, laid in ports of France 245

English, manufacturers of woollens, 1; driven from Tortuga by French, 29; trade with French at St. Christopher, 91; capture vessels of W. I. Co., 108, 110-111; war declared, 124; defeated at St. Christopher, 126-127; blockade St. Christopher, 139; fleet arrives in West Indies, 139; attacked by French at Antigua, 139; attacked by de La Barre's fleet, 140; attack St. Pierre, 140-142; obtain control of sea and capture Cayenne, 142; contraband trade, 157; on coast of Guinea, 166, 168; smuggling at Nevis, 191; protest against French regulations, 199; permitted to sell cargoes at Guadeloupe and Martinique, 209; trade with, 215, 217, 218; reject treaty offered by French at St. Christopher, 218.

Eon, Jean, quoted 1, 3, 5-7

Esnambuc, Pierre d', sets sail for West Indies, 14; decides to found colony at St. Christopher, 15; returns to France and obtains permission, 16; founds colony, 17; seeks aid in France, 18; fights valiantly against Spaniards, 19-20; flees, but returns, 20; decides to abandon colony, but aided by Dutch and remains, 21; makes settlement at Martinique, 27; death, 40.

Estrades, Count d', writes Colbert of state of Martinique 56-57

Estrées, Count d', vice-admiral in command of squadron in West Indies, 195, 220, 247; recaptures Cayenne and takes Tobago,

INDEX

247; plans to attack Curaçao, but shipwrecked, 247; captures Gorée, 288, 292.

Fermiers généraux des aides, subscribe to W. I. Co., 81; make loan to same, 99, 145.

Filibusters, on northern coast of St. Domingo 202

Flour, article of export from French ports to West Indies, 238, 240, 242, 311-312.

Food-stuffs, scarcity in West Indies, 45; efforts to provide supply, 116; increasing demands for, 224; scarcity at Martinique, 261; food of planters, 310; supply at first obtained in islands, 310; legislation concerning, 310-325; cargo sent from Canada, 315; efforts to obtain regular supply in Canada, 318-319.

Foreign Commerce, prohibited at St. Christopher without passport, 22-23; forbidden by Company of Isles of America, 37; prevalent in French West Indies, 38-40; under proprietary rule, 46; at St. Christopher, 91; ordered stopped by Colbert, 162; regulations, 182-194; *arrêt* of June 12, 1669, 184-185; instructions to governors, 185-186; royal ordinance, June 10, 1670, 187-189; Colbert insists on enforcement, 188-190; de Baas protests, 189; case at Martinique, 190; permitted in two cases, 192-193; with Porto Rico forbidden, 193; patrol maintained in French islands, 195; Dutch vessels seized, 196-197; English protest against regulations and receive explanations from Colbert, 199-200; de Gabaret's mission and results, 195-200, 206; rebellion at St. Domingo, 205-206; not eliminated, 207; patrol maintained, 208; ordinance of July, 1671, governing colonial ships, 208; with English, 209-210; in poultry and live stock, 211; de Baas' correspondence, 210-215; cases, 211-214; French traders complain of competition, 214; corruption of officials, 212-215; regulations of 1677, 215-216; difficulties of enforcement at St. Christopher, 216-218; Colbert's instructions, 219; ordinance of October 11, 1680, against, 219-220; squadron on patrol duty, 220; Colbert refuses to permit trade with New England, 221-222; results, 223-224; Dutch furnish slaves to French, 283-286; Colbert interferes, 286-287; cases, 323, 326.

Formont, de, discusses W. I. trade, 83; and W. I. Co., 176; trades in West Indies, 243.

Fouquet, Nicolas, and colonial affairs 23, 52

François, François, director Company of Senegal ..288, 291, 296, 297

Freedom of trade, Colbert's policy, 225-236; defined, 229; results attained, 248; Colbert's definition, 277.

French, and manufacture of woollens, 1; and shipping, 2; fail to meet Dutch competition, 49; fight English at Martinique,

INDEX

140-142; and slave trade, 168; relations with English at St. Christopher, 217-218, 284.

Gabaret, de, in command of three vessels on patrol in West Indies, 195; importance of mission, 196; Colbert's instructions, 196; captures Dutch vessels, 196-198, 200; effect of work, 200; sent to quell rebellion at St. Domingo, 202-205; explains causes of rebellion, 205-206; results attained, 206.

Gazette, as source of information ....95, note 28

Ginger, cultivated in West Indies, 211; imported at Bordeaux and Nantes, 238, 242; cultivated at Martinique, 261; Colbert encourages cultivation, 269.

Gorée, captured from Dutch by French, 288; occupied by du Casse, 289.

Grenada, possession of du Parquet, 43; sold to de Cérillac, 44; ceded to W. I. Co., 74, 90; Colbert plans contraband trade with Spanish Main, 192; trade with Dutch, 196, 197.

Guadeloupe, settled by French, 25; early history, 25-27; cultivation of sugar-cane, 34-35; revenue from, 42; estimated value of production, 42; becomes proprietary, 43; partially ceded to W. I. Co., 73; W. I. Co. inaugurated, 90; state of in 1665, 99; arrival of cargo of slaves, 172; trade with foreigners, 190, 209; scarcity of meat, 209, 323; trade, 237-238; tobacco staple product, 250; establishment of sugar refineries, 272-274; slaves imported by Dutch, 284, 286; W. I. Co. sends cargo of slaves, 287; debts owed Company of Senegal, 306; supply of live stock, 327; population, 336.

Guinea, trade with, 112, 116, 117-118, 148, 164, 231, 285; W. I. Co. attempts to organize slave trade, 286; description of trade, 286 ff.; trade freed from restraints, 293.

Harman, Sir John, commands English fleet in attack upon Martinique 140-141

Havre, trade with West Indies, 236, 242-243; trade in indentured servants, 281.

Hides, imported at Bordeaux from St. Domingo 238

Holland, *see* Dutch, Foreign trade, etc.

Honfleur, trade in indentured servants, 29; trade with West Indies, 242-243.

Houel, Charles, takes charge of plans to cultivate sugar-cane at Guadeloupe, 33-34; governor of Guadeloupe, 34; raises sugar-cane, 36; selfish administration, 42; becomes joint proprietor of Guadeloupe, 43; sent to France to answer for conduct, 62; refuses to cede possessions to W. I. Co., 73-74.

INDEX

Ile de Ré, entrepôt for trade in Irish beef 174, 320
Indentured servants, numbers sent from Normandy and Brittany, 29, 281; early importance, 45-46; form of contract, 281; prices, 281; devices to seduce, 281; Colbert attempts to arrest decrease, 282-283; reasons for failure, 283.
Indigo, cultivation encouraged, 31; cultivated at Cayenne, 65; rate of transportation, 103-104; cultivation forced by low price of sugar, 211; imported at Bordeaux and Nantes, 238, 242; slight importance as colonial commodity, 249; cultivated instead of tobacco at St. Domingo, 258; Colbert encourages production, 261.
Ireland, supplies salt beef to French West Indies, 173, 208, 241, 313; supplies live stock, 189; Colbert attempts to interrupt trade with, 209-210, 319-320; French and Dutch traders maintain pastures in, 313; trade with Nantes and La Rochelle, 313-314, 325; suffering in West Indies from interruption of trade with, 322; Colbert restores trade with, 323; Colbert refuses Patoulet's suggestion to prohibit trade with, 324.

Jacquier, director of W. I. Co. 83
Jamaica, smuggling trade with 206
Janon, consul at Middleburg, employed by W. I. Co. 94, 113
Jansen, Drik, arrested at Grenada for illicit trade, 196; released, 197.
Jews, at Cayenne 65

Knights of Malta, proprietors at St. Christopher 43

La Barre, de, *see* Le Febure.
Labot, quoted and refuted 305-306
Lagny, de, relation to Company of North 12
La Rochelle, trade with West Indies, 38, 236, 239-241; Colbert favours traders of, 240; tonnage of vessels engaged in West India trade, 240; merchants complain of tobacco monopoly, 256; trade in indentured servants, 281; entrepôt for Irish beef, 313.
La Sablière, de, stockholder in Company of Cayenne and W. I. Co. 80
Laubière, de, lieutenant-governor of Martinique 93, 105, 136
Le Febure de La Barre, and colony at Cayenne, 60-64; plans commercial conquest of French West Indies, 64; statement regarding capital of Company of Cayenne, 76-77; explains employment of inexperienced clerks, 87-88; advises de Clodoré concerning rebellions, 107; urges W. I. Co. to send strong fleet to islands, 129; put in command, 129; character

INDEX

and conduct, 129-130; arrives at Martinique, 137; aids in regulating commerce, 138; attacks Antigua, 139; captures Montserrat, 139; withdraws to St. Christopher, 140; accuses de Clodoré of disobedience, 140; accused of cowardice, 140; returns to Martinique and fights with English, 140.

Léogane, rebellion at 202

Levasseur, leads colony to settle Tortuga and becomes governor, 29; character of administration, 41.

Lion, du, placed in command of Guadeloupe, 62; made governor by W. I. Co., 90; complains of scarcity of supplies and vessels, 99-100; fights English at Antigua, 139; charges corruption in trade, 157; complains of high prices charged by Pélissier, 162; accuses de Baas of corruption, 212-213; character, 213-214; plans establishment of sugar refinery at Guadeloupe, 273; asks permission for cargo of live stock to be brought from Holland to Guadeloupe, 327.

Live stock, furnished by Dutch, 157; price at Martinique, 162; trade of W. I. Co., 164, 175; supplied by foreign traders, 184, 188; ordinance of December 20, 1670, 190-328; raised in French islands, 211; Colbert rejects proposal to obtain supply at Boston, 221-222; increasing demand, 224, 326; raised at St. Domingo, 258; regulations, 326-329; imported from Curaçao, 326, 327; price, 326; exportation forbidden at Curaçao, 327; imported from Porto Rico, 328; inadequate supply in France, 328; price, 328.

Lumber, need of supply in West Indies, 329; partially obtained in France, 330.

Madeira Islands, trade with 130, 146

Manufactures, principal articles of, imported into West Indies, 330; regulations governing exportation to islands, 330-331.

Marie Galante, becomes proprietary, 43-44; ceded to W. I. Co., 73, 90; attacked by Dutch, 246; slaves imported from Curaçao, 286, 327.

Marseilles, establishment of sugar refinery at 262

Martinique, settled by French, 27; early history, 27-28; planters ordered to raise cotton, 30; cultivation of sugar-cane, 31-33, 35; becomes a proprietary colony, 43; importation of slaves, 45; corrupt administration, 57; arrival of W. I. Co.'s fleet, 86-87; discontent with the company, 88; official inauguration of W. I. Co., 89-90; rebellion, 99-106; causes and significance, 105-108; another rebellion, 132-135; supplies arrive, 135, 136; petition of planters regarding trade, 137-138; attacked by English, 140-141; de Baas becomes governor, 152; price of slaves, 162; arrival of cargoes of slaves, 170-171; cases of

377

INDEX

smuggling, 190; de Gabaret maintains patrol, 196; provisions imported from English, 209, 210; scarcity of salt beef, 210; trade with Bordeaux, 237-238; attacked by Reuyter, 245; low price of sugar, 245; tobacco first staple product, 250; cultivation of sugar-cane becomes chief industry, 260; sugar refineries established, 272-275; number of slaves imported, 1654, 284; Dutch import slaves, 286; lack of slaves, 300, 306; scarcity of salt beef, 322-323.

Matharel, stockholder in Company of Cayenne and W. I. Co., 80, 83, 85.

Menjot, stockholder in Company of Cayenne and W. I. Co., ..80, 176

Molasses, exportation to France unprofitable, 220; estimated value, 220; price, 221; proposal to market in New England, 222.

Monopoly, granted to W. I. Co., 70; Colbert's attitude toward principal of monopoly, 229 ff.; of sale of tobacco farmed out, 252, 255; granted to Company of Senegal, 288, 293; probably granted to Oudiette, 290; granted for slave trade, 302; of slave trade granted conjointly to Company of Senegal and Company of Guinea, 308.

Montserrat, captured by La Barre, 139; Dutch trade with, 207.

Muscovado, *see* Sugar.

Nacquart, Sir, proposes to establish company for trade with West Indies 55

Nantes, trade with West Indies, 38, 219, 236, 241-242; exports to West Indies, 241; imports from West Indies, 241; development of trade, 243; export colonial raw sugar to Holland, which angers Colbert, 240-241; privileges of trade withdrawn and restored, 241; import duties upon colonial sugar, 313; trade with Ireland, 313; ships salt beef to West Indies, 321 and notes 42 and 43, 325.

Nevis, fight with French, 139-140; smuggling trade with French, 191; trade with Dutch, 207; trade with St. Christopher, 217.

New England, trade with, 191, 210; proposal to trade with, 224.

Nymwegen, treaty of 219, 248, 289

Ogeron, governor of St. Domingo, vainly tries to assert W. I. Co.'s authority, 91; encounters revolt, 201-205; explains causes of rebellion and suggests remedies, 205-206; appeals to Colbert for aid, 245; proposes establishment of colony in Florida, 203; leads freebooters to cultivate soil, 251.

Olive, de l', makes settlement at Guadeloupe 25-27

Olive oil, exported from Nantes to West Indies 241

INDEX

Orange, Guillaume d', sent to explore Guadeloupe, Martinique and Dominica 25
Otterinck, governor of Curaçao, corresponds with de Baas 212
Oudiette, Jean, farmer of *Domaine d'Occident* 290, 291

Parquet, du, shows courage in fighting Spaniards, 19; in command at Martinique, 27; character and administration, 28, 41; becomes proprietor of Martinique, St. Lucia and Grenada, 43.
Passports, W. I. Co. forbidden to issue to foreign traders, *arrêt* September 10, 1668, 183; king reserves right to issue, 184-185; regulations concerning, 185, 226, 228, 328.
Patoulet, intendant, receives special instructions to prohibit foreign trade, 219; rebuked by Colbert for violating instructions, 219; approves plan to establish trade with New England, 221-222; writes concerning tobacco industry, 254; explains low price of sugar, 272; plays important rôle in building up sugar refineries, 274; personally interested in refinery, 275; trades with merchant of La Rochelle, 275, 325; states advantages of refining industry in West Indies, 277; protests against favouritism for home refiners, 279; estimates number of slaves needed at Martinique, 306; suggests raising of live stock in islands, 324.
Pélissier, director of W. I. Co. sent to West Indies, 152; charged with duties of intendant, 158-159; receives full instructions, 159-161; spends two years in islands, 161; correspondence with Colbert, 161-162; writes memoir concerning West India trade, 163; arouses complaints, 172, 175; receives further instructions from Colbert, 189-190, 192; plan for trade with Canada, 317.
Plessis, du, settles Guadeloupe conjointly with de l'Olive 25-26
Pièce d'Inde, defined, 297 and note 70.
Poincy, de, governor-general sends expedition to take Tortuga, 28-29; makes agreement with English to limit production of tobacco and issues ordinance, 30, 250; cultivates sugar-cane, 36, 260; trades with Dutch and attempts to monopolize trade, 39; character, 40; refuses to obey company and heads rebellion, 41; victorious, 41; sends colony to St. Martin, 43; orders attack on Spaniards and occupation of St. Croix, 43-44; large slave owner, 45, 284.
Population, *see* Martinique, Guadeloupe, St. Christopher, etc., etc.
Porto Rico, trade with 193, 328
Pouançay, de, governor of St. Domingo, writes regarding tobacco industry, 254, 257, 258; complains of lack of slaves, 300; succeeded by de Cussy, 257.

INDEX

Private traders, permitted to trade by Company of Isles of America with conditions, 39-40; number in West Indies in 1668, 153; Colbert's attitude toward, 153; passports granted freely to, 154; attitude of W. I. Co. toward, 154; Colbert issues instructions for protection of, 160-163; share monopoly of slave trade, 172, 287; increase, 175, 176, 180; favoured by Colbert, 225-226; entire W. I. trade entrusted to, 225; insolent according to de Baas, 226-227; defended by Colbert, 227; regulations favouring, 228-229; Colbert defines policy toward, 229; rapid rise of, 236; distribution in several ports of France, 236 ff.; little interest in slave trade, 287, 288; excluded from trade with Africa, 293.

Rambouillet, de, stockholder in Company of Cayenne and W. I. Co. 75
Refineries, sugar, number increases in France, 207; established at Bordeaux, 239; at Rouen, 243; Colbert urges increase of, 262-263; Colbert furnishes part of capital, 262; number in France in 1683, 263, note 11; proportion of raw sugar required, 264; enjoy monopoly of colonial sugar, 271; Colbert encourages establishment in West Indies, 272-275; first established, 272; rôle played by Patoulet, 274-275; results, 276; advantages of refining sugar in West Indies shown, 278; in West Indies subjected to increased import duty, 278; new establishments forbidden in West Indies, 278-279; in France favoured, 279; export refined sugar, 280.
Reuyter, attacks Martinique 245
Richelieu, aids organization of Company of St. Christopher, 15; sends protection to colony, 18; subscribes to Company of Isles of America, 23.
Roissey, Urbain de, sets forth with d'Esnambuc to found colony, 14-16; joint command at St. Christopher, 17; joins de Razilly for expedition in Irish Sea, 18; cowardice and imprisonment in Bastille, 19.
Roucou, cultivation encouraged, 30; at Cayenne, 65; cultivated at Martinique before 1660, 261; imported at Bordeaux, 238; never important, 249.
Rouen, trade with West Indies, 236, 242-243; two refineries, 262; special tax on sugar, 265, 267; special drawback on refined sugar, 265.
Rum, no market in France, 220; proposals to market in New England, 221-222.

St. Bartholomew, settled by French, 43; becomes possession of W. I. Co., 90.

INDEX

St. Christopher, settled by French, 14; early history, 18-22; cultivation of tobacco, 30; cultivation of sugar-cane begun, 35-36; becomes possession of Knights of Malta, 43; slaves, 45; trade with Dutch, 48; ceded to W. I. Co., 90; opposition to company, 91; French defeat English and gain whole island, 126-127; state, 132; blockaded by English, 139; harvest damaged by storm, 143; illicit trade, 185, 196; trade with English permitted under conditions, 192; Dutch vessels captured, 197; attempts to prevent enforcement of regulations, 215-216; regulations, 217-218; trade with Bordeaux, 237-238; quality of tobacco, 250; excellent sugar, 260; slaves imported by Dutch, 283; price of slaves, 284; debts owed Company of Senegal, 306; population, 1671, 1682, 336.

St. Croix, Spaniards driven from and occupied by French, 44; ceded to W. I. Co., 90; scarcity of food-stuffs, 323.

St. Domingo, early French settlement, 29; granted to W. I. Co., 90; opposition of colony, 91; trade with foreigners, 185; revolt against W. I. Co., 201-205; causes, 205-206; de Gabaret attempts to quell rebellion, 203-205; trade with Bordeaux, 237-238; Dutch attempt to win colony, 247; tobacco staple product, 250-251; memorial of planters regarding monopoly of tobacco, 255; conditions at, 257; average production of tobacco, 1683-1688, 258; regulations concerning indentured servants, 282; slave trade, 300, 304, 306; trade with Spaniards, 329; population, 337.

St. Eustatius, trade with French 186-187, 191, 196, 207, 217

St. Laurent, fights against English at St. Christopher, 126-127; chosen to succeed de Sales as governor, 128; prevents revolt, 132; tries to prevent foreign trade, 217; writes memoir on foreign trade, 223.

St. Lucia, settled by French and becomes possession of du Parquet 43-44

St. Malo, trade with West Indies, 236, 240, 242-243; import duties on sugar, 267; trade in indentured servants, 281.

St. Marthe, governor of Martinique, convicted of illicit trade 215

St. Martin, settled conjointly with Dutch, 43; ceded to W. I. Co. ..90

St. Thomas, import duties laid on sugar from 266

Saints, the, settled by colony from Guadeloupe 43-44

Sales, de, governor of St. Christopher 123, 126

Salt beef, lack of supply in French West Indies (1665), 99; attempt to provide, 116; trade of W. I. Co., 173-175; supply ordinarily obtained in Ireland, 173, 313; Colbert decides to exclude Irish, 174, 208, 319; *arrêt* of August 17, 1671 and royal ordinance of November 4, 1671, 320; price of French beef, 174; bounties offered by Colbert, 320; results, 175, 209-

381

INDEX

210, 321; suffering in islands, 210; price, 217, 322-324, 325; importance as food, 312-313; proposal to obtain supply at Boston, 221-222; trade between Ireland and Nantes, 313; attempt to obtain supply in Canada, 318; Colbert restores privilege of exporting Irish, 323; results, 324; protests against import duty of 1688, 325.

Salt pork, forbidden to be imported from foreign countries, 219-220; exported from La Rochelle, 240; from Nantes, 241; as food, 310; price, 324.

Senegal, W. I. Co.'s trade with, 112, 116, 117, 146. *See also* Company of Senegal.

Shipping, state of in France, 49-50. *See also* Commerce.

Slaves, at St. Christopher in 1625, 283; imported by Dutch in 1635, 283; imported into Guadeloupe for cultivation of sugar-cane, 33-34, 284; cheaper than indentured servants, 283; price in 1643, 1646, 1654, 284; number in French West Indies in 1655, 44, 284; growth of trade, 45; profit in trade estimated by de Tracy, 284; number in Dutch settlement at Cayenne, 65; W. I. Co. makes contract for supply, 117-118; price in sugar, 162; Dutch supply Spaniards, 171; supplied to French by Dutch, 184, 188, 196, 285-286; increasing demand, 224; W. I. Co. ordered to supply, 164; company's efforts, 165-173, 285 ff.; expedition to Guinea and description of trade, 165 ff.; contract with king of Ardres, 169; W. I. Co. sends two cargoes to West Indies, 169-170, 171, 286, 287; trade encouraged by Colbert, 172; trade opened to private traders, 226; private traders show little interest, 287; import duty removed, 286; bounties offered, 286; log of a vessel engaged in slave trade, 171; loss in transportation, 171; Colbert plans to supply Spaniards, 286; price, 172, 286; arrival of cargoes at Guadeloupe, 172; numbers regulated at St. Domingo, 282; fed on salt beef, 208; history of trade, 283-309; scarcity in 1675, 287, 290; monopoly created, 231, 288; Oudiette's contract, 290; Company of Senegal makes contract, 291-293; bounties and price, 293; number imported by company, 296-301; supposed bounties paid, 296; sold at Guadeloupe for Bellinzani, 299; *pièce d'Inde* defined, 297, note 70; numbers imported, 300; imported from foreigners, 303; second Company of Senegal makes contract, 304-308; numbers imported by company, 304-305; numbers required, 306; failure of company to satisfy contract, 307; monopoly shared by Company of Guinea and Company of Senegal, 308; results of Colbert's efforts, 308-309; condition of slave labour at Martinique, 322-323; population, 1671, 1684, 336.

Smuggling, *see* Foreign commerce.

INDEX

Spaniards, attempt to destroy French colony at St. Christopher, 18-19; driven from St. Croix, 44; trade with Dutch, 171; Colbert plans to sell slaves to, 171; trade with Spanish Main planned, 192-193; trade with Porto Rico forbidden, 193; furnish live stock to French, 328, 329.

Sugar, history of production in French West Indies and legislation concerning, 260-280; plans to cultivate sugar-cane in 1640, 31-32; successful, 33-36; causes for slow progress, 36; becomes chief product in Windward Islands, 250, 258; influence upon planters, 44; Colbert estimates quantity produced, 45; of French West Indies refined in Holland, 54; import duty in France, 54; drawback on refined, 70; rate of transportation to France, 103-104; as currency, 162, 172, 175, 250; exported from several islands, 260, 261; profit, 261; imported from Holland and Brazil into Provence, 263; import duty on foreign refined, 239, 263; drawback, 265; special duties and drawbacks at Rouen, 265; duties, 266; price in 1665, 118; trade with Dutch, 157; overproduction and depreciation, 267; Colbert's instructions to Pélissier concerning same, 161, 268; price in France (1670), 267; perfecting manufacture, 269; exported from France, 207; price at Martinique, 211, 245; freed from export duty in West Indies (ordinance of June 9, 1670), 228; imported at Bordeaux, 237-239; exported from Nantes and St. Malo to Holland, 240, 242; imported at Rouen, 243; Colbert's attitude toward re-exportation of raw sugar, 269-271; re-exportation forbidden by *arrêt* of 1684, 271; low price in France (1679) and causes, 271; refined at Guadeloupe, 272; growth of colonial refineries, 272-275; duties on refined in colonies, 273-274; rise in price (1679), 276; benefits of refining, 276-278; *arrêt* of April 18, 1682, 278; results, 279-280; increase of production, 280; freed from import duty in Canada, 318. *See also* Refineries.

Talon, intendant in Canada, tries to build up trade with West Indies, 315-317; sustains losses, 318.
Téméricourt, governor of Marie Galante 327
Thoisy, de, appointed governor-general, but defeated by de Poincy 41
Tobacco, history of cultivation and trade, 249-259; early production at St. Christopher, 30; excellent quality, 250; staple, 36, 250; depreciation and agreement with English to limit production, 30, 250; as currency, 250; exported to Holland, 54; import duties in France, 54, 251, 252; cultivation at Cayenne, 65; rate of transportation to France, 103-104; cargo arrives at Dunkerque, 109; imported into France, 157, 162,

INDEX

171, 183, 238; cultivation becomes secondary in Windward Islands, 250; remains staple in St. Domingo, 251; cultivation in France restricted, 252; forbidden in Canada, 252; monopoly of sale in France, 252-253; results, 253-255; monopoly renewed, 255; re-exportation permitted, 256; estimated production (1674), 258; results at St. Domingo, 258; freed from import duties in Canada, 318.

Tortuga, English expelled and French settlement made, 28-29; rebels against W. I. Co., 91; trade with, 146, 177; Dutch trade with, 201.

Tobago, captured by French 247

Tracy, Alexander Prouville de, mission to America, 59; character and duties, 59; administration, 60; commended by Colbert, 61; restores order, 62; inaugurates W. I. Co., 88-90; correspondence, 261; estimates profit of slave trade, 285.

Trade, see Commerce, Foreign commerce.

Treillebois, Sieur de La Rabesnières, de, commands squadron in West Indies 151, 195

Trezel, makes contract to cultivate sugar-cane in West Indies, 31-33, 35, 39.

Warner, Sir Thomas, governor of English at St. Christopher ...17-18

West India Company, preparation for organization, 68; establishment, 68 ff.; letters-patent analyzed, 70; administration, 71; resources according to Colbert, 71-72 and note; opposition by proprietors, 73-74; contracts with proprietors, 74 and note 8; analysis of subscriptions, 75 ff.; stockholders and directors, 75 ff.; relation to Company of Cayenne, 75-77; real character, 82; history, 1664-1665, 83-122; preparation for trade, 83; delay, 84; description of first fleet, 85-86 and note 9; inexperience of clerks and explanation, 87-88; inauguration in West Indies, 89-90; agents and correspondents in France and Holland, 94; builds and buys vessels, 94; sends vessels to West Indies, 95, 99; discontent among planters, 90-92; revolt at Martinique, 98-99; state of finances, 1665, 96; borrows, 98-99; fails to supply needs, 99-100; complaints against, 101; receives aid from king, 102-103; sends vessels, 103; revolt at Martinique, 103-106; suits against at Dieppe and Rouen, 104; authority sustained by de Clodoré, 106; de La Barre admits lack of success, 107; failure to meet conditions in West Indies, 108; sends out vessels, 108; receives cargoes, 109; financial condition November, 1665, 109; receives aid from king, 109-110; commerce embarrassed, 110; authorized to seize English goods, 110; awarded claims by British, 111; distribution of trade, 111-112; contracts for ships, 116; makes

INDEX

contract for slave trade, 117; sends vessels to Canada, 118; state of trade, May, 1666, 114-115; summary of activity, 1664-1665, 115-121; directors suggest union with East India Company, 121; history, 1666-1667, 123-149; financial condition at outbreak of war with England, 128; in control of St. Christopher, 128; sends fleet, 128-131, 135; sends more vessels, 136; permits Dutch to trade, 139; vessels in attack upon Antigua, 139; losses from English attack at Martinique, 140-142; disastrous effects of war, 142-144; financial embarrassment, 144; statement November, 1667, 145-147; distribution of assets and value, 147; receives aid, 147; number of vessels, 147-148; prepares vessels for Cayenne, Cape Verde and Guinea, 148; history, 1668-1670, 150-164; attitude of Colbert after war, 150-154, 235; shares trade with private traders, 153, 227; forbidden to grant passports to Dutch, 153, 189-190; reforms in administration, 155; confined to wholesale trade, 156; first dividend, 156; commerce declines, 156-157; sends new agent to West Indies, 158; Colbert's instructions, 159 ff.; commerce limited to certain articles, 163, 190; declines, 164; history, 1670-1674, 165-181; sends vessels to Guinea and opens slave trade, 165-173; treaty with king of Ardres, 169, 285; trade in salt beef, 173-175; trade in live stock, 175, 189; dissolved by Colbert, 175, 176, 179; liquidation, 176-178; financial condition, 177-178; reasons for failure, 179; service rendered, 179-181; revolt at St. Domingo, 201-205; sends refiners to West Indies, 273.

West Indies, establishment of French, 14 ff.; population, 1642, 30; become proprietaries, 43; population in 1665, 44; condition in 1664, 50-51; absorb attention of W. I. Co., 112; governor-general placed in command, 155; Colbert encourages increase in population, 160; trade with France, 236 ff.; decrease of trade with Normandy and Brittany, 243-244; cultivation of tobacco, 250; storms, 295; trade by Company of Senegal, 296-301; trade with Canada, 315-316; causes for failure, 318-319; nature of trade, 335. *See also* Martinique, Guadeloupe, St. Domingo, etc., etc.

Wine, article of export to West Indies at Bordeaux, La Rochelle, Nantes 238, 240, 241

THE LIBRARY
ST. MARY'S COLLEGE OF MARYLAND
ST. MARY'S CITY, MARYLAND 20686

087010